D0742196

BLACKS IN THE NEW WORLD

August Meier, Series Editor

BOOKS IN THE SERIES:

Before the Ghetto: Black Detroit in the Nineteenth Century   *David M. Katzman*

Black Business in the New South: A Social History of the North Carolina Mutual Life Insurance Company   *Walter B. Weare*

The Search for a Black Nationality: Black Colonization and Emigration, 1787–1863   *Floyd J. Miller*

Black Americans and the White Man's Burden, 1898–1903
Willard B. Gatewood, Jr.

Slavery and the Numbers Game: A Critique of *Time on the Cross*
Herbert G. Gutman

A Ghetto Takes Shape: Black Cleveland, 1870–1930   *Kenneth L. Kusmer*

Freedmen, Philanthropy, and Fraud: A History of the Freedman's Savings Bank
Carl R. Osthaus

The Democratic Party and the Negro: Northern and National Politics, 1868–92
Lawrence Grossman

Black Ohio and the Color Line, 1860–1915   *David A. Gerber*

Along the Color Line: Explorations in the Black Experience   *August Meier and Elliott Rudwick*

Black over White: Negro Political Leadership in South Carolina during Reconstruction   *Thomas Holt*

Keeping the Faith: A. Philip Randolph, Milton P. Webster, and the Brotherhood of Sleeping Car Porters, 1925–37   *William H. Harris*

Abolitionism: The Brazilian Antislavery Struggle   *Joaquim Nabuco, translated and edited by Robert Conrad*

Black Georgia in the Progressive Era, 1900–1920   *John Dittmer*

Medicine and Slavery: Health Care of Blacks in Antebellum Virginia   *Todd L. Savitt*

King: A Biography   *David Levering Lewis*

The Death and Life of Malcolm X   *Peter Goldman*

Race Relations in the Urban South, 1865–1890   *Howard N. Rabinowitz*

Alley Life in Washington: Family, Community, Religion, and Folklife in the City, 1850–1970   *James Borchert*

ALLEY LIFE IN WASHINGTON

"O'Brien's Court," by H. Armstrong. Alley Dwelling Authority,
National Capital Housing Authority Collection.

Alley Life in Washington: Family, Community, Religion, and Folklife in the City, 1850-1970

James Borchert

University of Illinois Press

Urbana | Chicago | London

©1980 by the Board of Trustees of
the University of Illinois
Manufactured in the United States of America

LIBRARY OF CONGRESS CATALOGING IN PUBLICATION DATA

Borchert, James, 1941–
   Alley life in Washington.

   (Blacks in the New World)
   Bibliography: p.
   Includes index.
   1. Afro-Americans—Washington, D. C.—Social condi-
tions.   2. Afro-American families—Washington, D. C.
3. Washington, D. C. Social conditions.   4. Rural-
urban migration—Washington, D. C.   I. Title.
II. Series.
E185.93.D6B63   305.8'96073'0753   80-12375
ISBN 0-252-00689-5

TO:

Mom and Dad

Frank and Kitty

Mae Owen, Grace Barnum, Mack Rolkosky

The Bakers, Elsons, and Hinsdales

And the rest of my extended-augmented family

226242

Preface

Thus there are two kinds of community. One is the community established through the practice of benevolent despotism. It is predicated upon power for the few and acquiescence by the many. . . . For their passivity about power, therefore, the many are rewarded with an opportunity, restricted though it is, to create a limited community of their own based on participation and love. The resulting culture of the many under benevolent despotisms has often been vital and warm. . . .—William Appleman Williams, THE CONTOURS OF AMERICAN HISTORY

In his controversial Labor Department report, *The Negro Family: The Case for National Action*, Daniel Patrick Moynihan summarized social scientific and historical thought on the impact of urbanization on rural migrants. "Country life and city life are profoundly different," he pointed out. "The gradual shift of American society from a rural to an urban basis over the past century and a half has caused abundant strains, many of which are still much in evidence." The impact of urbanization, moreover, was indiscriminate. The "wild Irish slums of the nineteenth century" which were marked by "drunkenness, crime, corruption, discrimination, family disorganization, and juvenile delinquency" represented the same process that black migrants faced in the twentieth century.[1]

Moynihan was not alone in viewing the city as responsible for much, if not all, of the disruption faced by the United States and other countries in the nineteenth and twentieth centuries. From such early European sociologists as Simmel, Durkheim, Tonnies, and Weber through the Chicago School of Sociology, and from Oswald Spengler to Oscar Handlin, scholars universally reported the breakdown of the primary groups and the destruction of folk society as a result of urban migration.[2] Not only has the "urban mode

1. U.S. Department of Labor, *The Negro Family: The Case for National Action* (Washington, 1965), p. 17.

2. For a complete discussion of this literature and its impact, see James Borchert, "Social Scientists and the City: The Impact and Implications of the 'Urban Impact' School," paper delivered at the Social Science History Association meeting, Ann Arbor, Mich., Oct. 21–23, 1977.

of life" caused the "substitution of secondary for primary contacts, the weakening bonds of kinship, and the declining social significance of the family, the disappearance of the neighborhood, and the undermining of the traditional basis of social solidarity," but it also has been "largely responsible for the increase of vice and crime in great cities."[3]

In recent years this interpretation has come under attack by sociologists and some historians. Sociologists, however, have focused largely on the period since 1930 and have concerned themselves mainly with migrants from Europe and Russia; historians have also concentrated on European migrants, although over a longer period. Students of black folk migrants have tended to emphasize the first part of the twentieth century, with the "Great Migration" and the rise of massive ghettoes. Those studies that have considered the last half of the nineteenth century, and ghetto development in the twentieth, have generally adopted the breakdown thesis. However, because the main thrust of these studies is directed toward explication of race relations and the resulting residential and social patterns, their adoption of the breakdown thesis has been largely passive, rather than the result of substantive research.

The object of this study, then, is to analyze the impact of the urban environment on folk migrants—especially to examine the experience of black migrants in order to determine whether the primary groups of folklife weakened or remained strong, and to assess the extent to which the migrants' lives were marked by either order or disorder. Because this is a massive and complicated task, involving the reconstruction of the social life and patterns of organization of people who left little or no written record, one must use the "case study" approach. There are obvious limitations to such an effort, but, as Whitney Cross noted in his own microcosmic study of *The Burned-Over District*, "In the small theater of investigation, integrated treatment of cultural, social, economic, political, and ideological causations may be more satisfactory than in larger ones." One seeks through "the microcosmic approach to produce a reliable and broadly meaningful bit of general American history."[4]

The site for this study is Washington, D.C. Since shortly after the Civil War the nation's capital has been a major center of black popula-

3. Louis Wirth, *On Cities and Social Life*, ed. Albert Reiss, Jr. (Chicago, 1964), pp. 61, 79–80; Robert Park, "The City: Suggestions for the Investigations of Human Behavior in the Urban Environment," in Robert Park, Ernest Burgess, and Roderick McKenzie, *The City* (Chicago, 1967), p. 25.

4. Whitney R. Cross, *The Burned-Over District* (New York, 1965), pp. ix–x.

tion, both in absolute numbers and in terms of their proportion of the city's total population. This provides a long time period for analysis, and the additional fact that Washington experienced a number of waves of migration beginning with the Civil War makes it all the more useful.

My choice of the alley population may initially seem more obscure, but the reasons for that choice are many and substantive. In the first place, there is an extensive body of literature about alley dwellings and dwellers that does not exist for residents of other housing, or for folk migrants in general. Second, alley residents were often migrants from the countryside; everyone considered them not only as a "separate class," but as one at the bottom of society. Alley dwellers were most likely to suffer from the disorientations of urban life, and the literature about alley dwellers universally concludes that they did. In addition, alley housing was a common form of residence for folk migrants to other American, British, and European cities through the nineteenth and into the twentieth centuries; thus the alley experience has some relevance and applicability to other cities and other folk migrants. Finally, black residents continued to occupy Washington's alleys in fairly large numbers until recent years. The case, then, seems to be a fair one for testing the city's impact on the primary groups, on social organization, and on the folkways of migrants from the countryside.

My method of organization follows the community studies model. The first chapter provides an overview and context by considering the evolution of black residence patterns in Washington, as well as outlining the specific origins, growth, and decline of alley housing. The next two chapters consider the primary groups of family and neighborhood in order to determine the extent of social order and control, the persistence of traditional forms, and adaptations to the new environment. Chapter 4 considers childhood in the alleys in order to determine how external institutions and forces disrupted the socialization process, and thus restricted or limited the transmittal of traditional ways of life to later generations. The fifth chapter describes the occupational structure and work experience of alley residents. By considering those conditions that more recent studies have pointed to as the causes of breakdown—low income, unemployment, disease, and exploitation by store owners—as well as the alley dwellers' response to these conditions, the extent of social order and positive adjustment can be determined. In the final chapter, the roles played by other traditional activities, such as religion and folklife, as well as newer forms of social organization, are considered in light of the theory of cultural breakdown. In addition, since this is a case study, the issue of applicability to migrant groups in other cities is taken up briefly in the conclusion.

Because this study differs in approach, organization, methods, sources, and analyses from most historical studies, a number of issues need further discussion. The appendices attempt to explicate the nature, validity, and representativeness of my sources, and the methods used to tie them together, as well as to discuss the methods used in the photoanalysis and the analysis of census data. Finally, I have included a partial list of sources on alley housing in other American and British cities.

This study contends that, in contrast to the "conventional" social scientific and historical theory that folk migrants undergo a period of disorder as a result of their exposure to urban life, migrants actually used their primary groups and folk experiences to create strategies which enabled them to survive the often harsh and difficult urban experience.[5] Moreover, the migrants demonstrated considerable ingenuity in modifying and adapting their rural folk culture to the new environment without, for the most part, either rejecting or dismissing those traditional patterns of behavior. Folk migrants also "remade" their urban environment, both physically and cognitively, to fit their needs. While change did occur, it happened slowly and was a matter of degree, not a change in kind.

A note of warning is in order, however. The nature of the sources and the newness of several of the methods employed here, as well as the lack of sources deriving directly from alley residents themselves, make this a tentative study. Moreover, I am not concerned with the evolution of race relations in Washington; rather, I wish to focus on the patterns of social order and control. These qualifications entail omission of at least part of the story; this omission is not critical, because that aspect of the black experience in Washington has already been written about by a number of fine scholars.[6] Nevertheless, the persistent racism and very difficult experience faced by all black residents of the city, especially those who lived in the alleys, should not be forgotten. As John Dos Passos once observed of World War I, "it might have beauty if he were far enough away to

5. The harshness and difficulty are not necessarily related to the city; in fact, many folk migrants have a "better" life there. These factors are, rather, the products of hostility, prejudice, and a maldistribution of wealth and power.

6. E.g., Constance Green, *The Secret City* (Princeton, 1967); Thomas R. Johnson, "The City on the Hill: Race Relations in Washington, 1865–1885" (Ph.D. dissertation, University of Maryland, 1975).

clear his nostrils of the stench of pain."[7] The task here is to unearth that "beauty" without forgetting that the stench of pain is never far away.

I am deeply indebted to a large number of people who contributed greatly to this study. While it is impossible to acknowledge everyone individually, I do wish to thank especially the staffs of the Columbia Historical Society; the Franklin D. Roosevelt Library; the George Eastman House; the Prints and Photographs and Geography and Map Divisions of the Library of Congress; the Washingtoniana Room of the Martin Luther King, Jr., Memorial Library; the National Archives; the National Capital Housing Authority; and the Washington *Star* Photo-Archives.

This study began at the suggestion of Harold Skramstad, who provided much-needed help and guidance throughout, while the late Otho Beall encouraged, spurred, and guided the original work through to completion as a dissertation. At different points in the research a number of people were especially helpful in providing insights, methods, or sources; these included Paul Groves, Ted Muller, E. Richard Sorenson, Gladys Fry, Esther Birdsall, Dorothy Provine, Dana White, Clark Everling, John King, Mike Franch, Lonnie Waits, Claude Holloway, Michael Katz, Ted Hershberg, Laurence Glasco, David Katzman, Barbara Fant, Bill Barnes, and Tom Johnson. I am also deeply thankful to Francis Coleman Rosenberger, Rod French, and the late Letitia Brown for the opportunity to present, orally and in written form, parts of this study.

Many others provided valuable technical assistance which greatly aided the study. Joan Hodgson tracked down my obscure references and produced copies faster than I could use them, while Judy Rood transformed my confused data and maps into sharp and comprehensible illustrations. Paul Groves kindly made available a copy of his map of residential patterns (Map 1), while Denis Le Cam devised a computer program to permit the analysis of family form from the manuscript census. Virginia Moore, Peggy Merrell, and Sheri Quistini patiently tolerated my continual changes while typing the final manuscript, as did Dorothy Hollinger, Ellen Borger, Cheryl Van Unen, and Evelyn Day on earlier drafts.

Financial aid from a variety of sources proved invaluable to the completion. Both the University of Maryland and the University of California, Santa Cruz, granted computer time, while further funds from UCSC made possible a new computer program, maps, and

---

7. John Dos Passos, *One Man's Initiation: 1917* (Ithaca, N.Y., 1969), p. 71.

some of the photographs used here. An honorary grant from the Mabelle McLeod Lewis Memorial Fund gave moral support, and a Smithsonian Fellowship made possible a full year of uninterrupted research and writing, as well as funding for photographs.

My interest in interdisciplinary study was sparked many years ago by Fred Cottrell and encouraged by students and colleagues at Alabama A. and M. College and UCSC, especially the Community Studies Board at UCSC. Similarly, University of Illinois Press Director Richard L. Wentworth has been supportive throughout, while Ann Lowry Weir made my prose more readable.

Most important, a number of fine scholars have gone out of their way to provide assistance and direction. At one point or another in the writing, Wilcomb Washburn, James Flack, Ted Muller, Myron Lounsbury, Bill Friedland, Maurice Beresford, David Allmendinger, and Jay Martin read the entire manuscript and made extensive and extremely valuable comments that were central to the revised manuscript. Moreover, I have been very fortunate to have had August Meier as series editor. His knowledge, insights, sharp criticism, and kind support throughout the rewriting have greatly strengthened the study, as any reading of earlier drafts will reveal. Finally, I am greatly indebted to Sally Rogers, who supported much of the research, did part of it, and supplied many of the insights.

The problems, errors, and inaccuracies that remain in the text are there despite the best efforts of those mentioned above, and as a result are clearly my responsibility.

—J.B.

Contents

Maps

Drawings

Photographs

Tables

*In more than one province I know of folksongs, songs in
dialect, peasant songs which, as regards vivacity, and
rhythm, simplicity and strength of language, would
certainly concede nothing to many of those collected by other
nationalities. But who would collect them? Who would
trouble himself about the songs of the people on the streets,
in alleys and fish markets, in the simple roundelay of the
peasant rhymes? . . . We would rather read, even though
only for pastime, our modern beautifully printed poets.*
　　　　　　　　　　　　—Johann Gottfried von Herder

Chapter 1
The Rise
and Fall of
Washington's
Inhabited Alleys

*Every grantee becomes his own free holder and his plot of
land was under his own absolute control, with this result:
that Bedfordbury commenced its career by everyman doing
what was right in his own eyes in the way of building. A
number of alleys came into existence and instead of a single
house being put upon a single plot . . . a man would put
two or three or four on it, maybe half-a-dozen houses, or
cottages, or anything he pleased upon it, and that went on
in perpetuity. . . . It was a perfect by-word and a
proverb for everything that was disorderly and disgraceful.*
—Select Committee on Town Holdings (London, 1887)

In 1909 Charles Weller, executive officer (1901–8)
of the Associated Charities of Washington, D.C., exposed the evils
and dangers that existed in the "hidden" alley communities of the
nation's capital.[1] His book, *Neglected Neighbors*, was written at a time
when alley dwellings housed a substantial number of the city's
working-class black population; through it Weller hoped to draw attention to what he considered a problem "with few if any parallels
in other American cities."[2] Unlike many of the newly developing

1. This chapter is a revision of an earlier article, "The Rise and Fall of Washington's Inhabited Alleys, 1852–1972," *Columbia Historical Society Records* 48 (1971–
72): 267–88. Francis Coleman Rosenberger, editor of the *Records*, has kindly given
me permission to use parts of that article here.

2. Charles F. Weller, *Neglected Neighbors* (Philadelphia, 1909), p. 9.

ghettoes in northern cities, where black residents grew increasingly concentrated in a single section, Washington's "mini-ghettoes" were spread throughout the city, often in close proximity to the most expensive and elegant houses. Behind imposing homes that lined the streets, Weller warned, were hidden communities marked by immorality, crime, and disease. (See Drawing 1 for a similar description.) Moreover, because these hidden dwellings could be reached only by unobtrusive, narrow alleys that cut through the blocks, "resourceful people live for years in attractive residences on the avenues without knowing or affecting in the slightest degree the life of the alley hovels just behind them."[3]

Weller's claim for the uniqueness of Washington's alley communities was incorrect.[4] And while in the last quarter of the nineteenth century Washington led major American cities in both the percentage and the numerical size of its black population, the nation's capital was not especially unique in these statistics either. In southern and border cities, especially Washington, many black migrants first experienced urbanization.[5] The white response to that migration, and the resulting residential patterns, set the context in which alley housing flourished.

Before considering the specific conditions and events that led to Washington's residential patterns, it is useful to note that most studies of the development of the twentieth-century northern black ghetto report the existence of black enclaves prior to the Great Migration. No city, however, had a single concentration that encompassed most of the city's blacks. In many cases blacks were fairly widely dispersed, and there was often little or no overt pressure to segregate. With the migration of working-class blacks from the South, however,

3. *Ibid.*

4. E.g., Oscar Handlin, *Boston's Immigrants: 1790–1865* (New York, 1971), pp. 107–8; Richard Wade, *The Urban Frontier* (Chicago, 1959), pp. 120, 122, 125, 221; Sam Bass Warner, Jr., *The Private City* (Philadelphia, 1968), pp. 15–16; David Katzman, *Before the Ghetto* (Urbana, Ill., 1973), pp. 74–75. Nor were American cities the only ones to experience this phenomenon. For alley dwelling in English cities, see Maurice W. Beresford, "The Making of a Townscape: Richard Paley in the East End of Leeds, 1771–1803," in *Rural Change and Urban Growth: 1500–1800*, ed. C. W. Chalklin and M. A. Havinden (London, 1974) pp. 281–320; Iain C. Taylor, "The Court and Cellar Dwelling: The Eighteenth Century Origin of the Liverpool Slum," *Transactions of the Historical Society of Lancashire and Cheshire*, 122 (1970): 67–90; Walter L. Creese, *The Search for Environment* (New Haven, 1966); Donald J. Olsen, *Town Planning in London* (New Haven, 1964). For a more complete discussion, see the Conclusion and Appendix D.

5. For a more complete discussion, see Paul A. Groves and Edward K. Muller, "The Evolution of Black Residential Areas in Late Nineteenth-Century Cities," *Journal of Historical Geography*, 1 (Apr., 1975): 169–91.

THE
BLIND ALLEY <u>OF</u> WASHINGTON, D.C.
SECLUSION BREEDING CRIME AND DISEASE
to kill the alley inmates and infect the street residents.

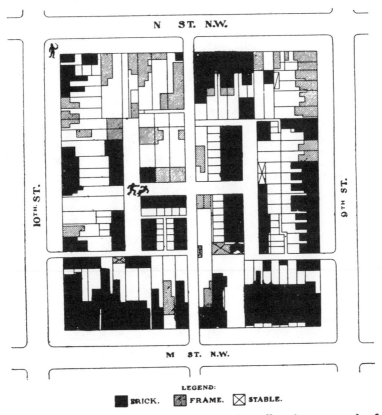

LEGEND:
■ BRICK.   ▨ FRAME.   ⊠ STABLE.

Conversion into minor streets is the effective remedy for the larger alleys.

Complete elimination of dwelling houses is the cure for the smaller alleys.

DRAWING 1.
"The Blind Alley of Washington, D.C. Seclusion Breeding Crime and Disease . . ." From the Monday Evening Club, Directory of Inhabited Alleys of Washington, D.C. *(Washington, 1912), p. 1.*

clear patterns of residential segregation and ghettoization began to appear. While racism is clearly a major factor in this development, implicit in the studies of northern ghetto formation is the notion of the "tipping point," a condition that exists "once the portion of non-whites exceeds the limits of the neighborhood's tolerance for interracial living." Once this point is reached, the white population moves out.[6] Thus, as the numbers of black migrants to northern cities increased dramatically, so did white hostility. While some whites fled "invaded" neighborhoods, others sought to exclude black residents. In many northern cities the more informal and benign forms of social control earlier utilized by whites were no longer effective in the changed circumstances. Whites then sought through a variety of forms, of which segregation and ghettoization were most central, to maintain their dominance and control over the black newcomers.

While black ghettoes did not exist in the nineteenth century, at least not on the scale to which we have been accustomed in the twentieth, nevertheless many cities, especially in border and southern cities, did experience substantial black migrations. These migrations were imposed on a city form that had constraints different from those of the more "spatially liberated" twentieth-century city. While we should not expect to find massive ghettoes in the nineteenth century, we may see this form of segregation and social control being worked out in cities that, as yet, lacked the resources to permit full implementation.[7]

Perhaps the most striking fact about the black experience in Washington is that the city experienced not one large migration, but several.[8] Moreover, as one student of the antebellum period noted of the substantial increases in the free black population between 1820 and 1850, this early migration was greeted by an "increased hostility on the part of whites toward free Negroes."[9] Efforts to assess the meaning of this increased hostility in terms of residential location are problematic at best, if only because it is difficult to es-

6. Morton Grodzins, *The Metropolitan Area as a Racial Problem* (Pittsburgh, 1958), p. 6. See also Karl E. and Alma F. Taeuber, *Negroes in Cities* (New York, 1969), p. 100. For a review of the literature on "tipping," see John M. Goering, "Neighborhood Tipping and Racial Transition: A Review of Social Science Evidence," *Journal of the American Institute of Planners*, 44 (Jan., 1978): 68–78.

7. Implied here, in part, is that the technology was inadequate to permit white dispersal to the suburbs and black concentration near the city core on the scale that develops in the twentieth century. Nevertheless, the origins of that latter development can be seen in the nineteenth century.

8. This is true for many cities as well.

9. Dorothy Sproles Provine, "The Free Negro in the District of Columbia, 1800–1860" (M.A. thesis, Louisiana State University, 1963), pp. 9, 13.

tablish a frame of reference against which such hostility may be judged. Letitia Brown found that "no clear pattern of separatism in housing had yet emerged" by 1860.[10] In contrast, Thomas Johnson noted that segregation "was highest in 1862, dropped markedly by 1870, and was on the rise again in 1880."[11] Nevertheless, Johnson concluded that, as late as 1880, "Washington's Negro community still lived fairly well intermixed with whites."[12] Finally, Melvin Williams found "evidence that some residential segregation existed in 1860," but added that "there is also evidence that some residential mixing occurred."[13]

The problems one confronts in attempting to determine residence patterns in Washington in 1860 result, in part, from inadequate sources, imprecise definitions of residential segregation, and the complexities of the nineteenth-century city. Nevertheless, we can make some tentative observations about residence patterns for the last half of the century. On the eve of the Civil War, Washington City was still relatively small, with only about 60,000 inhabitants.[14] Whites tended to live in the urban core, while black residences ringed that core. To the north, K Street "proved to be such a formidable dividing line that one might speak of a 'K Street rule' which dictated that, with few exceptions, blacks lived to the north of the street, whites to the south."[15] South and west of the white core, blacks dominated part of the low-lying lands of Tiber Island (Southwest, between the Mall and the Potomac), and Foggy Bottom (west of the Mall).[16] In spite of this core-periphery tendency, many

10. Letitia W. Brown, "Residence Patterns of Negroes in the District of Columbia, 1800–1860," Columbia Historical Society *Records*, 47 (1969–70): 77.

11. Thomas R. Johnson, "The City on the Hill: Race Relations in Washington, 1865–1885" (Ph.D. dissertation, University of Maryland, 1975), p. 173.

12. *Ibid.*, p. 299.

13. Melvin R. Williams, "A Blueprint for Change: The Black Community in Washington, D.C., 1860–1870," Columbia Historical Society *Records*, 48 (1971–72): 362.

14. Washington City is exclusive of Georgetown and the County. All three of these entities make up the District of Columbia. The Federal City refers to the area laid out by L'Enfant, bordered on the north by Florida Avenue.

15. Johnson, "City on the Hill," p. 150. While Johnson's study is a fine one, his method for determining residential patterns, which involves mapping random samples from the city directory and generalizing patterns from these maps, is questionable. Nevertheless, it at least suggests what the patterns might be. Howard Rabinowitz's recent study of five smaller southern cities for the same time period also reports that black residences tended to form circular belts around those cities. (*Race Relations in the Urban South, 1865–1890* [New York, 1978], p. 99).

16. Johnson, "City on the Hill," p. 175. Part of the concentration in Southwest dated back to 1824, when blacks began to purchase land in this area. Brown, "Residence Patterns of Negroes," p. 76.

free blacks owned or rented homes throughout the city, although these may well have been in clusters, with several black families surrounded by whites.[17] "For example, one census taker in 1860 visited fourteen families in succession—thirteen black and one white—and got information about seventy-two blacks and eight whites. . . . Similarly, another census-enumerator visited seven successive houses and nine families—all white—and recorded information about thirty-nine whites and one black female servant."[18] Over a hundred black families also lived in the hidden alleyways, effectively separated from whites of the city. Thus, while blacks were found in virtually every part of the city, they tended to cluster in small groups in the core and to form enclaves outside it. Many blacks who lived on the streets in integrated areas were probably middle or upper class; most often the working class was effectively segregated from whites, because their residences were in the alleys of the core or in enclaves on the periphery. Live-in servants, who often maintained separate residences for their families, both confuse and confirm these tendencies.

The second great migration of blacks to Washington accompanied the Civil War and its aftermath, and witnessed an increase in hostility. As Constance Green has noted, the "predominant white attitude toward all colored people became increasingly hostile from mid-1862 onward."[19] Nevertheless, Johnson found that segregation had decreased by 1870. While this change may have been the result of Radical Reconstruction, the short tenure and very limited successes of that effort suggest a need to search for other explanations.[20] More likely the residential distribution was, in part, a continuation of pre–Civil War patterns; it probably also resulted from the rapid imposition of an incredible number of new residents, both black and white. The population of Washington City leaped from just over 60,000 in 1860 to nearly 110,000 a decade later. The resultant housing shortage undoubtedly helped minimize racism as a factor in housing choice. But even the alleys, where racial separation was most marked, tended to be more mixed than in later years. When Private Alfred Bellard inspected the off-limits Tin Cup Alley in Tiber Island (Southwest) late in 1863 as part of a patrol squad, he found the alley "occupied by white and black, all mixed up to-

17. Letitia W. Brown and Elsie M. Lewis, *Washington from Banneker to Douglass, 1791–1870* (Washington, Nov., 1971), pp. 20–21.

18. Williams, "Blueprint for Change," p. 361.

19. Constance Green, *The Secret City* (Princeton, 1967), p. 66.

20. Johnson, "City on the Hill," p. 150.

gether, on the principal that you pays your money and takes your choice."[21]

Too much should not be made of this apparent increase in integration, for as soon as the city had a chance to begin reordering itself, segregation became more marked. The postbellum real estate and housing boom provides some evidence of white Washingtonians' interests and concerns. As city historian Wilhelmus Bryan noted, "an entirely new residence section . . . [was] developing in the locality between M and S Streets and 7th and 14th Streets, [Northwest] where a number of citizens who up to that time had their homes near the business centre built homes for their own use."[22]

This northward movement of whites out of the core had, by 1850, "swept aside black residential areas, forcing Negroes either into enclaves within the advancing white areas, or into their own segregated residential areas."[23] The peripheral settlement north of K Street was literally pushed aside and to the north by this influx of affluent white residents. By 1897 black and white residents shared a strip six blocks wide west of North Capitol Street, beginning north of New York Avenue and extending up to Florida Avenue, then following Florida Avenue west.[24] (See Map 1.) While "many of the most prestigious Negro families . . . still maintained their homes" despite white in-migration, it became increasingly difficult for black families to move into the newer sections.[25] Moreover, fragmentary and incomplete evidence does seem to indicate that a variety of groups, ranging from white property-owners and neighborhood associations to real estate agents and bankers, conspired to limit certain neighborhoods to white residents in the last twenty years of the nineteenth century.[26]

21. Private Alfred Bellard, *Gone for a Soldier*, ed. David H. Donald (Boston, 1975), p. 256.

22. Wilhelmus Bryan, *A History of the National Capital* (New York, 1916), II, 587–88. Similarly, Constance Green reported that "the purchase of city lots or suburban tracts became a fetish among people of small means as well as large," but concluded that most of the houses constructed were "contractor-built pseudo Queen Anne red brick rows" (*Washington* [Princeton, 1963], II, 11–12).

23. Johnson, "City on the Hill," pp. 306–7.

24. Groves and Muller, "Evolution of Black Residential Areas," p. 180; Green, *Secret City*, p. 127.

25. Johnson, "City on the Hill," p. 303; Green, *Secret City*, p. 127.

26. I am greatly indebted to Thomas Johnson and Constance Green for uncovering this information; Johnson, "City on the Hill," pp. 299–300; Green, *Secret City*, p. 127; Edward T. Devine and Associates, "Citizens' Associations of a

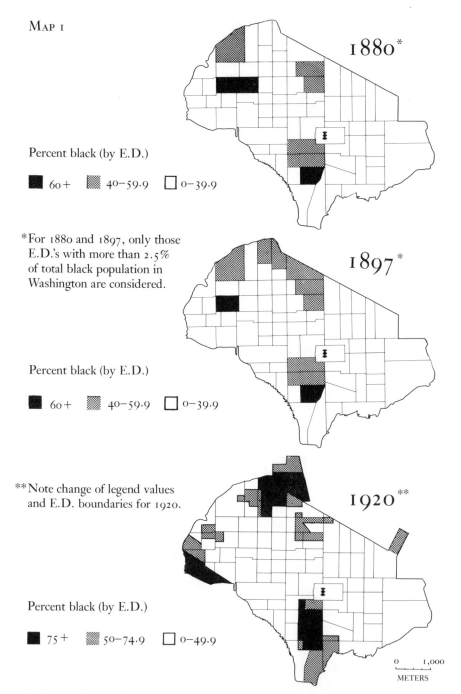

Map 1

Percent black (by E.D.)

■ 60+   ▨ 40–59.9   ☐ 0–39.9

1880*

*For 1880 and 1897, only those
E.D.'s with more than 2.5%
of total black population in
Washington are considered.

1897*

Percent black (by E.D.)

■ 60+   ▨ 40–59.9   ☐ 0–39.9

**Note change of legend values
and E.D. boundaries for 1920.

1920**

Percent black (by E.D.)

■ 75+   ▨ 50–74.9   ☐ 0–49.9

0   1,000
METERS

Washington: Blacks as a Percentage of Enumeration District Population, 1880–1920. Reprinted with
the kind help and permission of Paul A. Groves and Edward K. Muller, "The Evolution of Black
Residential Areas in Late Nineteenth-Century Cities," *Journal of Historical Geography*, 1 (1975): 180.
Copyright by Academic Press (London), Ltd.

Those black families who did continue to live on the streets in predominantly white neighborhoods also continued to cluster in small groups. Based on the manuscript census returns of 1880, in a twelve-block sample area in Northwest Washington the typical black family lived next to at least one other black family and/or shared the house with another black family. Exceptions included two shopkeepers who did not actually live behind or above their stores (7th Street and 9th Street), and Senator Blanche K. Bruce and his family, who lived on M Street between 9th and 10th Streets. (See Map 2.) Many of the clusters in this area were considerably larger than two families. Finally, the occupations of many of these black residents indicated that they were either middle or upper class, since nearly half of the heads of household were employed as skilled, white-collar, proprietorial or professional workers. A nearly equal number were employed in menial service or unskilled occupations. Some doubled and tripled up in houses with similarly employed workers; on the other hand, in a number of households headed by laborers, teachers and skilled workers were also part of the family. There is little question that occupations of black residents of houses facing the streets of the sample area were considerably more varied than those of the white street population, and that even within a family one could expect to find a considerable range of occupations.[27]

Without conducting an extensive research project, it is difficult to know just what these street clusters of black families meant in terms of everyday life, social patterns, and interactions with neighbors,

---

Unique Community," *Sociology and Social Research*, 13 (1928–29): 140–55; Edward Ingle, *The Negro in the District of Columbia* (Baltimore, 1893), p. 90. The *People's Advocate* in 1881 noted "instances of the discrimination against colored householders by owners of property or their agents. The exceptions to the rule are apparent rather than real." Two years later the *Advocate* warned that "this opposition to renting houses to colored people is more marked than ten years ago" (June 25, 1881, p. 2; Sept. 8, 1883, p. 2). As Mary Church Terrell recalled, "When I started in quest of a house for the second time and asked several real estate firms to show me what they had on their list, I discovered . . . that, as a colored woman, I would be unable even to SEE the kind of house I desired" (*A Colored Woman in a White World* [Washington, 1940], p. 115). Rabinowitz also found that "When Negroes succeeded in moving into a white neighborhood, it was often in the face of concerted opposition" (*Race Relations in the Urban South*, p. 103).

27. This suggests that solely occupational criteria for determining class are not especially useful in the black community. Moreover, it seems reasonable to assume that the black community has its own hierarchy of occupations based on past experience. Federal Population Census Schedules, 1880, vol. 2, pt. 2, Record Group 29, National Archives.

MAP 2

Physical and Demographic Map of the

BUILDINGS

▨ Stable

▭ Other Building

▣ Store or
Artisan's Shop

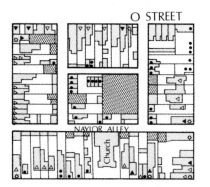
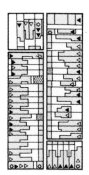

O STREET

NAYLOR ALLEY

Church

N STREET

10TH STREET

BLAGDEN ALLEY

9TH STREET

8TH STREET

M STREET

SHEPHERD ALLEY

L STREET

Physical and Demographic Map of the Sample Area between 6th
and 10th, L and O Streets Northwest, 1880–88. Based on
Sanborn Map Publishing Company, *Insurance Maps of Washington,*

Sample Area, 1880–88

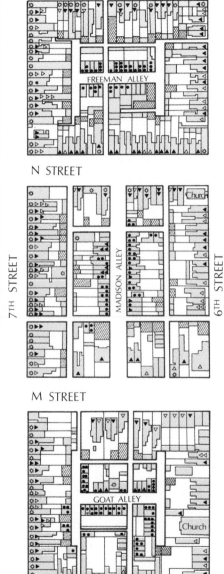

HEADS OF
HOUSEHOLD

△ Native-born
whites

▲ Foreign-born
whites (born
outside North
America or
parent[s] born
outside North
America)

• Blacks
₅• number (when
more than 3)

D.C. (New York, 1888); and Federal Population Census
Schedules, 1880, Washington, D.C., vol. 2, part 2, RG 29, NA.

black and white. It would be dangerous to jump to conclusions concerning these "apparent patterns," if only because to do so would be to adapt a dubious residential determinism which is no more justified here, unaccompanied by evidence, than when applied to larger settlement patterns. Whatever the meaning and context of these patterns, however, they do not appear to display random distribution.[28]

Black residents made up only 9 percent of the street population of this sample area; yet of the 5,000 residents of this neighborhood, two-thirds were white and one-third were black—the exact racial breakdown for the city as a whole.[29] Nearly a quarter of the area's population faced onto one of the alley complexes that honeycombed the six largest blocks. In sharp contrast to the white domination of the street, blacks accounted for 93 percent of the alley dwellers. Put another way, 97 percent of whites lived on the streets of this "integrated" neighborhood, while almost 78 percent of the black population resided in the alleys. Moreover, if most of the street households were headed by people employed in skilled, white-collar, proprietorial, or managerial occupations, with a few professionals also represented, alley dwellers were employed largely (82 percent) in unskilled or service occupations. Finally, regardless of the time period and the racial composition of the street population surrounding them, alley dwellers differed significantly in a wide variety of factors, ranging from occupation, literacy, family size, and age, to the ratio of females to males.[30]

28. One of the clusters, located on the west side of 9th Street between N and O streets in 1880, must have been part of a peripheral black settlement that disappeared with the white influx into the neighborhood. No houses are shown for those addresses on the 1888 insurance maps which form the basis for Map 2.

29. One of the problems of utilizing census tracts, wards, grid squares, or even blocks as units of measurement is that such units can throw together populations that are obviously different and that do not interact, as in the case of the street-front and alley dwellers. Furthermore, use of such measures assumes a certain level of residential determinism that may vary considerably from house to house, block to block, and section to section. For a methodological discussion of units of aggregation and their problems, see John P. Radford, "Patterns of White-Nonwhite Residential Segregation in Washington, D.C. in the Late Nineteenth Century" (M.A. thesis, University of Maryland, 1967), Ch. 2; Oliver Zunz, William A. Ericson, and Daniel J. Fox, "Sampling for a Study of the Population and Land Use of Detroit in 1880–1885," *Social Science History*, 1 (Spring, 1977): 307–32.

30. Daniel D. Swinney, "Alley Dwelling and Housing Reform in the District of Columbia" (M.A. thesis, University of Chicago, 1938), pp. 94–105, 124–34; Radford, "Patterns of White-Nonwhite Residential Segregation"; Paul A. Groves, "The Development of a Black Residential Community in Southwest Washington: 1860–1897," *Columbia Historical Society Records*, 49 (1973–74): 272; Leonise Ruth Aubry, "Ambitions of Youth in a Poor Economic Status" (M.A. thesis, Catholic University

If some middle-class and working-class black families tended to cluster in predominantly white areas in the core, and working-class blacks congregated in much larger numbers in alley communities on blocks in that core, many other blacks from both middle and working classes found themselves living in enclaves that were increasingly black. As early as 1865 the *National Intelligencer* reported on a small enclave "on Eleventh Street East," where "two or three families are crowded into the same apartment" of tiny one-story "cabins." Residents of this section "found employment in washing for Lincoln and Emory Hospitals" and "in cutting wood for the Quarter Master's Department."[31] Even more striking was the enclave on Tiber Island (Southwest), which was "studded with the same sort of cabins." And close to the Mall area "all sorts and sizes of them may be found, wedged in every conceivable shape into vacant spaces and yards and alleys"; in this enclave were "shops, and streets, and little gardens," with many two-story houses. Moreover, "at the church on Sunday there was a goodly display of broadcloth and crinoline," which constituted a "sort of aristocracy of color."[32] This enclave, which was restricted to the area in Southwest east of Four-and-a-Half Street, grew rapidly after the Civil War. By 1880 blacks made up 78 percent of this enclave's population, or nearly 10 percent of the city's blacks. In 1897 blacks accounted for 83 percent of this population, although it was still largely restricted to the area east of Four-and-a-Half Street.[33] A substantial part of that population, however, lived in its alley communities.

The enclave along North Capitol and Florida Avenue was not as concentrated as the one in Southwest, but it remained important. There was yet a third enclave in Northwest, which was predominantly black in both 1880 and 1897, although it had moved and grown smaller by the latter date. By 1920 the three enclaves within or contiguous to the Federal City were all at least three-quarters black and were close to the locations of earlier concentrations: Southwest, along Florida Avenue in Northwest, and near Foggy Bottom.[34]

of America, 1938); James Borchert, "Race and Place: A Historical Community Study" (unpublished manuscript, 1972).

31. *Daily National Intelligencer*, July 25, 1865, p. 3.

32. *Ibid*.

33. Groves, "Development of a Black Residential Community," p. 273.

34. Groves and Muller, "Evolution of Black Residential Areas," p. 180. It is important to note that Rabinowitz reported similar patterns of clustering and enclaves in five smaller southern cities: "There were usually one or more main concentrations of Negroes and numerous other smaller clusters" (*Race Relations in the Urban South*, pp. 98, 105, 112). See also John Kellogg, "Negro Urban Clusters in the Postbellum South," *Geographical Review*, 67 (July, 1977): 310–21.

It is extremely difficult to determine the precise connection between the alley communities, the black enclaves, and the eventual
emergence of large-scale ghettoes in Washington. While alley spillover onto the street may have led to the enclaves, and then to the
ghetto, spillover alone cannot account for such development, since
some alleys continued to exist in areas of all-white street residence.
More likely a combination of alley communities and street clusters
eventually led to enclaves.[35] Certainly other factors must have played
a part as well; for example, much of the land in Southwest and Foggy Bottom was low-lying, and hence considered unhealthy, making
it unlikely to be developed for middle- or high-income housing.
Because of the close proximity to major employment centers for unskilled laborers, these areas were also attractive locations for working-
class housing. These latter factors seem less important for the formation of the North Capitol–Florida Avenue enclave.

Of course, a constant in this process was white Washingtonians'
racism. Each wave of black migration to the city was greeted by increased white hostility. While these influxes did not immediately lead
to the massive ghettoes of the twentieth century, segregation did take
place, within the technological, spatial, and mental constraints of the
nineteenth. Many middle-class black families found that they might
live on predominantly white streets only when at least one other
black family lived next door. For working-class blacks, alley communities within the blocks of predominantly white (or black) neighborhoods and black enclaves were the most common experience, and it
was one of nearly complete segregation.[36] These segregated residen-

35. Rabinowitz noted, although with little evidence or discussion, that "Once a
block became more than 20 percent black, it was on its way to the predominant pattern of segregation" (*ibid.*, p. 106). In seeking to explain the development of slums
(and, by implication, the ghetto) in Washington, James Ring, executive director of
the National Capital Housing Authority, provided the following scenario: "From the
squares wherein were located the most populous alleys, the occupants of the street
houses moved away, as soon as they could—selling or renting their old homes—moving into newer residence districts where no alley houses were to be found." As a
result, "the old street houses then had less chance to survive than before; for they not
only continued subject to the malign influence of the alleys," but also experienced
encroachments by business, industry, and heavy traffic, as well as overcrowding and
absentee ownership and management. See "The Development of Slums in the District of Columbia," *Report of the National Capital Housing Authority for the Ten-Year
Period, 1934–44* (Washington, 1944), p. 139. While the explanation for Washington
patterns may be more complicated, these elements are, nevertheless, suggestive.

36. This is not to suggest that middle-class blacks did not live in the enclaves.
From the beginning black landowners had been important in the Southwest enclave,
and many of the key institutions of middle-class life had located there well before
1880. Groves, "Development of a Black Residential Community," pp. 267–71.

tial patterns may help explain the almost universal late nineteenth century descriptions of the black community as a "secret city." As the Washington *Star* put it in 1883, "the colored race lives as separate and as exclusive a life as in the days of slavery."[37] Finally, while the enclaves were the immediate forerunners of the massive ghettoes of the twentieth century, the alley "mini-ghettoes" are perhaps more representative of the nineteenth century and are closer to the origins of the ghetto itself.

In spite of considerable individual variations between and within cities, the forces and conditions that led to the development of alley housing were remarkably similar. The most crucial of these factors were capitalism and the lack of adequate transportation systems in the growing pedestrian city.[38] Cultural values, intense pressures for more housing, and existing patterns of landholding also influenced the forms of housing that developed.

Capitalism clearly provided the decision-making context that led to alley house construction. As Sam Bass Warner observed, "cities . . . depend for their wages, employment and general prosperity upon the aggregate successes and failures of thousands of individual enterprises, not upon community action. . . . the physical forms of American cities, their lots, houses, factories, and streets have been the outcome of a real estate market of profit-seeking builders, land speculators, and large investors."[39]

While the capitalist ethic set the stage for alley housing, the lack of a transportation system that could permit dispersal of the population led to increased pressures on land close to the city's center. As cities expanded to house the growing population, the pedestrian journey from home to workplace grew. Eventually most cities reached the point where spatial expansion was no longer possible, because only the very rich and those employed at peripheral manufacturing locations were willing or able to travel from the periphery, where open land was available, to places of work in the city's center.

This condition led to intensive land use both in the built-up parts of the city and in areas being developed on the periphery. Intensifica-

37. Washington *Star*, Dec. 19, 1883.
38. "Capitalism" here is used in its broadest sense, including values and motivations. Sam Bass Warner chose to use the word "privatism" instead, but his definition provides the best sense of what I mean here: "Its essence lay in its concentration upon the individual and the individual's search for wealth. Psychologically, privatism meant that the individual should seek happiness in personal independence and in the search for wealth. . . ." See Warner, *Private City*, p. 3; and Bruce M. Stave, "A Conversation with Sam Bass Warner, Jr.," *Journal of Urban History*, 1 (Nov., 1974): 93–94.
39. Warner, *Private City*, p. 4.

MAP 3

Washington
City
1857

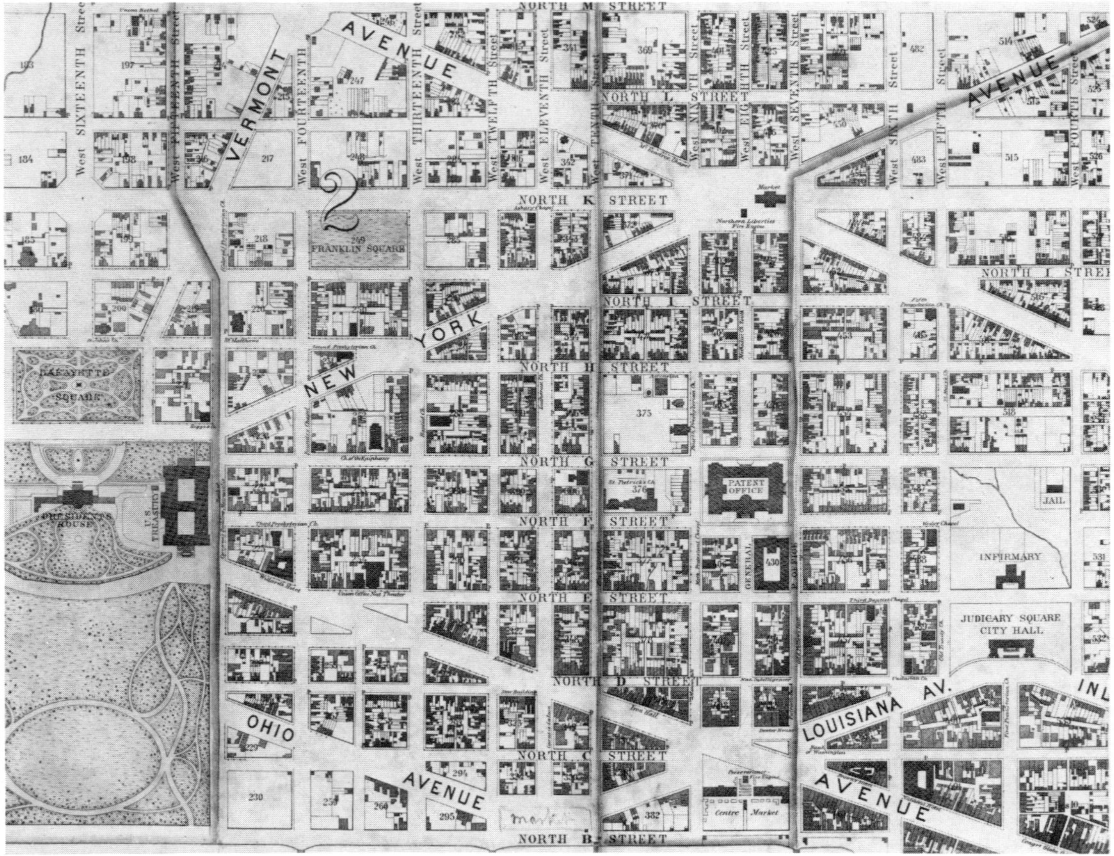

A. Boschke, "Map of Washington City," 1857. Geography and Map Division, Library of Congress. Selected portion from M Street NW (North) to B Street NW (South) to 3rd Street NW (East) to 17th Street NW (West).

tion of land use could take many forms. In Paris, for example, one response was to stack people on top of one another, with the poor living in the upper stories and the more well-to-do below them. In Leeds, where land was held in long, rather narrow parcels, and where it was difficult to acquire contiguous pieces of land, developers constructed rows of back-to-back houses "crowded so closely that there was less than a street's width between facing rows, and made up into so short a cul-de-sac that there was no through ventilation."[40]

By 1774, such density of housing and such methods of land division in Philadelphia had led to the "practice of subdividing blocks with alleys and jamming tiny houses on vacant rear yards." This practice continued unabated for nearly ninety years, and "by 1860 the density of population in Philadelphia's inner wards reached its all-time peak."[41] In other American cities speculators and developers also subdivided the backs of large lots and built tiny houses facing on alleys for the working classes. By 1860, however, major cities were experiencing such population growth that the rear and alley houses were gradually replaced by more land-efficient tenements, covering nearly an entire lot.

Because Washington's development was slow and rather late, the capital was only beginning to approach its size constraints in the last half of the nineteenth century. Utilizing the large blocks that were distributed throughout the Federal City, developers responded to population growth by building on both a street and its alley nearly simultaneously. Their implicit assumption seemed to be that the middle classes would live on the streets, while working-class people would reside in the alleys.

In 1850 Washington was a pedestrian city of about 40,000 inhabitants. As the 1857 Boschke map of building indicates, several building clusters stand out; each is clearly oriented toward specific work places. The major cluster was between Third and Fifteenth Streets, Northwest, with others forming around the White House, Capitol Building, the Navy Yard in Southeast, and just south of the Mall in Southwest. These clusters reflected the pedestrian nature of the city.

During the 1850s Washington's population increased by 50 percent, and the impact of the pedestrian city's spatial constraints becomes visible in various sources.[42] The 1852 plat book shows how

40. Maurice W. Beresford, "The Back-to-Back House in Leeds, 1787–1937," in *The History of Working Class Housing*, ed. S. D. Chapman (London, 1971), pp. 105, 109.

41. Warner, *Private City*, p. 16.

42. While it is entirely possible that alley dwellings existed earlier, either as sheds or shacks or as houses, the first substantial evidence for their existence on a large scale comes in the 1850s.

landowners subdivided five blocks into street-front and alley-front lots, with the latter facing twenty- to thirty-foot-wide alleys that bisected the block. All five subdivided blocks were located in the most built-up parts of the city.[43] The 1856 plat book shows a continuation of this trend, with four more squares having such subdivisions.[44] While two of these blocks were laid out like those of 1852, two others had further subdivisions on interior alleys that were connected to the outside of the block only by another alley. This "blind" or "hidden" alley was later to become the most common. Unlike the former alleys that were easily accessible and visible from the streets, blind alleys were virtually hidden—a feature that disturbed reformers and police alike, as Drawing 2 suggests.[45] Photograph 1, of Logan Court in 1935, provides a good visual example of this hidden world.

From the available sources one cannot determine whether dwellings were built on these subdivisions as early as 1852, or even ear-

43. *Maps of the District of Columbia and City of Washington and Plats of the Squares and Lots of the City* (Washington, 1852), pp. 61, 71, 86, 94. Squares 386 and 465 in Southwest and 568, 569, and 624 in Northwest.

44. William Forsyth, *Plats of Subdivisions of the City of Washington, D.C.* (Washington, 1856), pp. 15, 17, 21, 60. Squares 367, 378, 448, and Reservation 10 in Northwest.

45. A typical blind alley was thirty feet wide and "H" shaped. Its only connection to the street was through the ten- to fifteen-foot alley that bisected the block. The block maps of Blagden Alley (Maps 12 and 13) demonstrate this. However, other alley layouts were more problematic. Many "alleys" were really minor streets; they were usually forty-five feet wide and ran straight through the block. Some were referred to as alleys at one time and as streets at others: Organ Alley of 1858 became Madison Street in 1871 (see Map 2), although no physical change occurred. Police census takers, housing reformers, and federal census enumerators often included some of these "minor streets" in their alley enumeration, while many others were never so included. As a result, the definition of an inhabited alley includes social as well as physical dimensions. William Henry Jones noted "that the short streets which are inhabited by Negroes usually deteriorate—at least in external appearance—much more rapidly than do the long streets. Negroes who are particularly concerned about their social positions in the city tend to avoid the short streets as residential habitats, because they are not sufficiently well known to give the desired dignity and status, and because of fear—on account of the small amount of traffic—of being unnoticed. . . . A number of persons stated that they would not live on short streets, either because they have to be apologized for, or are likely to be confused—in the minds of persons who are not acquainted with the alleys" (*The Housing of Negroes in Washington, D.C.: A Study in Human Ecology* [Washington, 1929], p. 46). Ulf Hannerz's recent participant-observer study of a Washington neighborhood, "Winston Street," involved such a minor street. Although he was not especially concerned with the spatial and physical dimensions, Hannerz notes that they did play an important role in determining "friend," "neighborhood," and "community" (*Soulside: Inquiries into Ghetto Culture and Community* [New York, 1969]).

lier. However, it seems safe to assume that, even if construction had not yet begun, the "developers" of these areas had certainly conceived of building dwellings that would face onto narrow alleys. The size of the lots virtually precluded their use for nonresidential purposes.

The 1854 *Report of the Board of Health* does suggest that some alleys were inhabited by that year. Seeking to account for the higher death rate for persons under fifteen, the Health Officer observed that "much the larger proportion of these deaths are from among the children of negro, of foreign, and of destitute native parents, who usually reside in alleys, and in the suburbs."[46]

The 1857 Boschke map gives a clue to the locations of inhabited alleys. Although in many squares it is difficult to determine whether the buildings are sheds, stables, or houses, in at least thirteen blocks in Northwest and six in Southwest distinguishable row houses with small but demarcated back yards front onto the alleys. (See Map 3.) These inhabited alleys all fall within the most densely settled part of the city—between First and Fifteenth Streets West, F Street South, and N Street North.[47]

The most concrete evidence of the existence and extent of pre–Civil War alley housing comes from the 1858 city directory, which sought to list the name, address, occupation and race of each head of household. It contains at least 348 names with alley addresses, from which we can locate 49 inhabited alleys.[48] (See Map 4.) Since census and city directory enumerators are notorious for missing many people (especially those in "hidden" alleys), and because only the household head was reported, the names in the city directory probably represent only the tip of the population iceberg.[49] By

46. *Report of the Board of Health of the City of Washington—1854* (Washington, 1954), p. 1.

47. See especially Square 378 between 9th and 10th, D and E Streets, Northwest.

48. William Boyd, comp., *Boyd's Washington and Georgetown Directory 1858* (Washington, 1858). Unfortunately, many of the addresses listed in the directory are impossible to locate: e.g., "Alley between G and H." Addresses which list three streets do provide an approximate location, but it is impossible to pinpoint many such alley locations. Thus alleys indicated on Maps 4 and 5 are, in many cases, located approximately. It should be noted that Georgetown alley inhabitants appear in city directories before their Washington counterparts, although they are not mapped here.

49. Knights's research into city directories of antebellum Boston suggests that they report about 75 percent of the heads of household listed in the census, but that strong variations occur with regard to race and class. Not surprisingly, blacks and the poor tend to be underreported. See Peter Knights, "City Directories as Aids to Ante-Bellum Urban Studies: A Research Note," *Historical Methods Newsletter*, 2 (Sept., 1969): 1–10.

<small>PHOTOGRAPH I.</small>
"Alley Dwellings in Logan Court, Northwest," November, 1935. Photograph by Carl Mydans. Farm Security Administration Collection, Library of Congress.

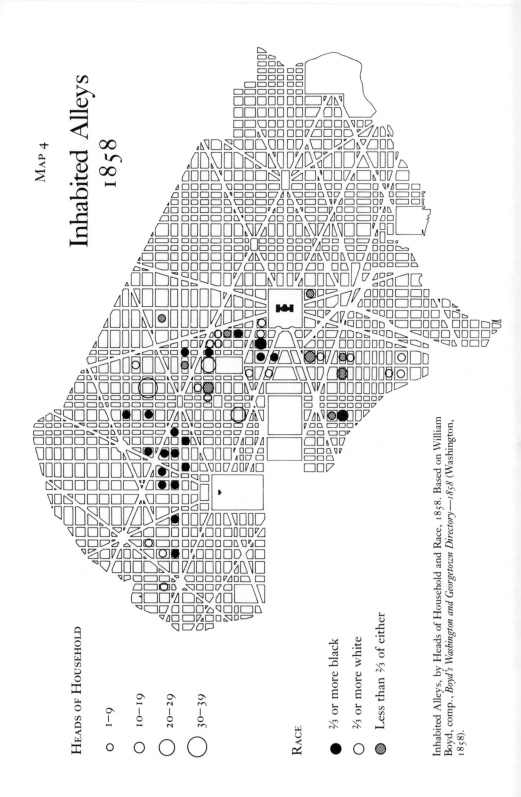

MAP 4

Inhabited Alleys
1858

HEADS OF HOUSEHOLD

○ 1–9

○ 10–19

○ 20–29

○ 30–39

RACE

● ⅔ or more black

○ ⅔ or more white

◑ Less than ⅔ of either

Inhabited Alleys, by Heads of Household and Race, 1858. Based on William Boyd, comp., *Boyd's Washington and Georgetown Directory—1858* (Washington, 1858).

1860, the Commissioner of Health warned that "of late years alleys are being closely built up with tenements in which many people are crowded together." These alleys were "narrow and a large proportion of them" had "only a single outlet."[50]

Although alley dwellings were a fairly well established institution prior to the Civil War, the substantial growth of the city's population—especially the black population—spurred on the building of alley houses. In the 1860s more than half of the city's 48,000 new migrants were black. Washington possessed neither sufficient buildings to house the newcomers, nor an efficient means of moving them daily from one part of the city to another. For those with enough money and leisure time, horse-drawn cars did offer the rudiments of a transportation system. Nevertheless, because most people's journeys about the city remained pedestrian ones, there was a substantial impetus for the continuing and expanding alley dwelling construction.

The result is strongly reflected in the city directory of 1871: nearly 1,500 heads of households have addresses distributed among 118 alleys. As in 1858, the alleys were concentrated in the older sections of the city, between First and Fifteenth Streets West, with the beginnings of a new focal point in Foggy Bottom.[51] (See Map 5.) These 1871 figures are undoubtedly very conservative, for only two years later the Board of Health reported 500 inhabited alleys.[52] Nevertheless, the directory figures reflect substantial growth in the number of inhabited alleys and in the population of each. By 1871 six alleys had forty or more household heads listed, and five others had at least thirty.

While alley housing was largely a response to the constraints of the pedestrian city, it was also the result of many individual decisions by landowners, builders, and others to an apparently inexhaustable demand for low-cost housing. This potential for profit, and the efforts to realize it, profoundly affected the nature and character of the alley communities that developed.

Having said this, I must point out that the early history of alley house construction remains largely unknown.[53] There are several

50. *Report of the Commissioner of Health—1860* (Washington, 1860), p. 4.

51. William Boyd, comp., *Boyd's Directory of Washington, Georgetown and Alexandria 1871* (Washington, 1871).

52. Board of Health, *Second Annual Report* (Washington, 1873), p. 105.

53. This is largely due to the nature of the sources. Building permits were not required until 1877, and while it might be possible (and rewarding) to track down the owner-builders through multiple sources, it would surely be an arduous task.

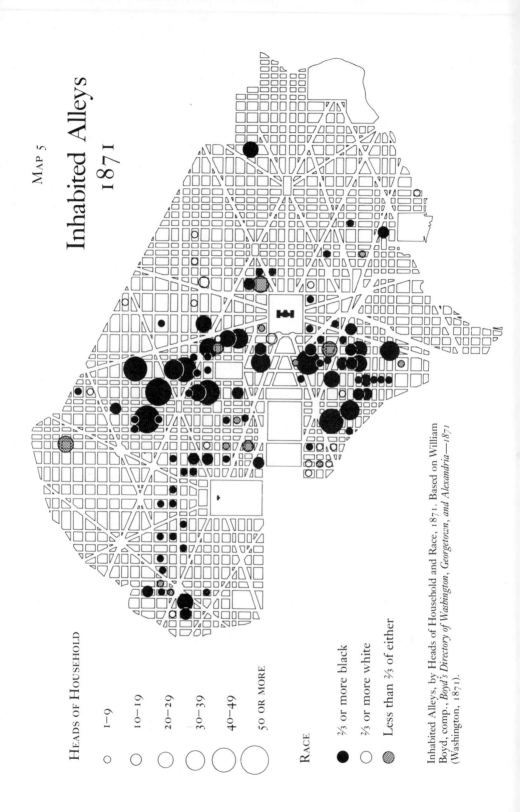

MAP 5

Inhabited Alleys
1871

HEADS OF HOUSEHOLD

1–9
10–19
20–29
30–39
40–49
50 OR MORE

RACE

⅔ or more black
⅔ or more white
Less than ⅔ of either

Inhabited Alleys, by Heads of Household and Race, 1871. Based on William Boyd, comp., *Boyd's Directory of Washington, Georgetown, and Alexandria—1871* (Washington, 1871).

theories as to who built alley houses prior to the Civil War; one suggests that the "space in the back of the houses was used for slave quarters, thus they became a gathering place for slaves."[54] Letitia Brown found, however, that

> Slaves . . . whether they worked in domestic establishments or on one of the public works, were by law and custom expected to live on the premises of their owners or the persons to whom they were hired. Generally, the household slaves were accommodated in apartments back of the main house, often separated from it by the back court yard. The whole complex was usually enclosed and was referred to as "the area." Within this space the slave was considered off the street and thus free from the nightly pick up after curfew.[55]

Alley houses, on the other hand, faced directly onto the alley and were separated from the block's outward-facing houses by a narrow alley, fences, and sheds.[56] A more plausible explanation of construction was offered by a long-time resident of Foggy Bottom who remembered that C. A. Snow, publisher of *The National Intelligencer*, had owned property in Square 28 (Snow's Court between Twenty-fourth and Twenty-fifth Streets, New Hampshire and K Streets Northwest). Prior to the Civil War, Snow "constructed a greenhouse and four frame houses in the interior of the block, and it was called Snow's Alley. The four houses were occupied by Irishmen,

54. Marion M. Ratigan, *A Sociological Survey of Disease in Four Alleys in the National Capital* (Washington, 1946), p. 177.

55. Brown, "Residence Patterns of Negroes," p. 72. Richard Wade has noted similar conditions in other southern and border cities (*Slavery in the Cities* [New York, 1964], pp. 59–60). What appears to be a visual example of this phenomenon can be found in Harold K. Skramstad, "The Engineer as Architect in Washington: The Contribution of Montgomery Meigs," Columbia Historical Society *Records*, 47 (1969–70): 273, "Watercolor View by Montgomery Meigs looking northwest from 'Franklin Row' on K Street, between 12th and 13th, N.W.," July 11, 1850.

56. In an earlier study, Wade notes that "the urban colored population was split up into small units, with a few Negroes living behind the master's house in a cabin facing on an alley lined with the shacks of other slaves" (*Urban Frontier*, pp. 125, 221). While both explanations are probably partly correct, the practice of hiring out slaves, and the constraints of housing slaves in the city, probably led to a practice found in other border and Deep South cities: such slaves sought out their own housing, often in alleys along with free blacks and working-class whites. While this undoubtedly happened in Washington, alley housing probably did not originate as slave quarters facing on the alley, since most antebellum alley residents listed in the city directory were white. The subdividing of alley land from street-front property prior to the war also suggests that such housing was for residents who had little or no connection with the street-front inhabitants.

one of whom Mr. Snow employed in the greenhouse."[57] Boschke's map tends to confirm this story, although Snow's Alley is not listed in the city directory for 1858. During the Civil War, however, the government used the houses as barracks for disabled soldiers.[58]

Other inhabited alleys must have started in a similar fashion. Probably one or several landowners in a block subdivided the property at the rear of their houses, constructing tiny wooden row houses and then renting them to unskilled workers who could not afford the new dwellings being constructed on the urban fringe. A number of sources support this theory. Since most alleys had the names of fewer than ten people listed as living in them, this initial development was compatible with local owners developing their own property on a small scale. Furthermore, 12 percent of the alley residents in 1858 were employed in service occupations that might have involved domestic work in their landlord's houses.

While it is difficult to determine just how common this practice was, its implications for the social relationships between owner and alley tenant are clear and important. The proximity of owner and tenant would make social control of the latter from outside the alley more likely. With economic ties, as in the case of the Irish alley tenant who was employed in Snow's greenhouse, the extent of outside social control would be considerable.

Little is known about the early builders and owners of alley houses, but somewhat more is known about their tenants. The city directory shows that the great majority of alley dwellers were of the laboring classes, with over 70 percent employed as unskilled or service workers. As in Snow's Alley, most alley dwellers were white, including 65 percent of the household heads in 1858.[59] Despite the sizable minority of black alley residents, the alleys were highly segregated. Of the forty-nine alleys, twenty-one were all white, seventeen all black, and only nine had less than a two-thirds majority of one race.

The question of who was responsible for alley house construction from the end of the Civil War until building permits were required in 1877 is as problematic as for the antebellum period. Some freedmen who came during and after the war were housed in barracks "in and around Washington." Many others set up living quarters in shanty-towns like "Murders Bay," a "vile place, both physically and

57. Swinney, "Alley Dwellings and Housing Reform," pp. 70–71.
58. *Ibid.*
59. Most studies, however, contend that "Negroes were the original inhabitants of alleys and are destined to be the final occupants of the dwellings" (Jones, *Housing of Negroes in Washington*, p. 31).

morally," on the site of today's Federal Triangle.[60] Some freedmen must have erected their own houses on alley property, obtaining much of the material "from abandoned army camps and hospitals."[61] In contrast, an elderly woman stated that "the first alley dwellings, exclusive of servants and slave quarters, were constructed prior to the Emancipation Proclamation by philanthropic individuals who were interested in providing shelter for the runaway slaves from the South." The informant was the daughter of a former member of the Society of Friends, which "during and after the Civil War . . . built a number of alley dwellings for philanthropic and not economic reasons."[62] The 1871 directory does carry a listing for "Quaker's Buildings" in Square 276, but with no names at that address. Later alley censuses do, however, indicate residents of "Quaker Alley."[63]

While some builders, such as the Quakers, may have worked from philanthropic motives, fragmentary evidence suggests that profit was a more typical motivation. The increased postwar demand for inexpensive housing appears not to have been satisfied,

60. Commissioner of the United States Bureau of Refugees, Freedmen and Abandoned Lands, *Report* (Washington, Nov. 1, 1866), 1; Bryan, *History of the National Capital*, II, 523.

61. Ratigan, *Sociological Survey of Disease*, p. 76; George M. Kober, *The History and Development of the Housing Movement in the City of Washington, D.C.* (Washington, 1907), p. 5.

62. Swinney, "Alley Dwellings and Housing Reform," pp. 16–17. Virtually all sources, including those which considered slave houses as the forerunners of alley dwellings, agreed essentially that "The first of the ill-fated alleys, as present-day Washington knows them were laid out in 1867" (Federal Writers' Project, *Washington: City and Capital* [Washington, 1937], p. 75). Only Constance Green and Dorothy Provine have demonstrated that alley dwellings were well established prior to the war (Green, *Washington* [Princeton, 1962], I, 211; Provine, "Free Negro in the District of Columbia," pp. 108–10). The tremendous increase in alley housing following the war, as well as the changes in racial composition of alley populations, undoubtedly led many observers to conclude that alley dwellings were the product of that period without looking for earlier evidence. Swinney, who suggests antebellum origins for Snow's Court, concluded that "The philanthropic motives of a few individuals and the Friends' Society probably started the movement to inhabit the alleys" ("Alley Dwellings and Housing Reform," p. 18). Similarly, James Ring argued that the initial builders of alley dwellings constructed them for philanthropic reasons, and that speculators followed them into the market.

63. Alleys often had uncommon names, and name changes were frequent. Some alleys were named by "the Directory men while canvassing, generally from some local cause" (Boyd, *Boyd's Directory 1871*). M. Goat, Pig, and Willow Tree Alleys undoubtedly got their names from some local circumstance, although several writers report finding no willow tree in the latter alley. Others took their names from a large landowner or developer of the block, while still others were clearly named by or after alley residents (e.g., Limerick Alley and Ambush Court).

making it possible for alley-house owners to charge higher rents. Increased rents resulted in severe overcrowding in many alleys; it also effected the conversion into "dwellings" of many alley buildings originally intended for other uses. *The Intelligencer* reported in 1865 that these alley houses were "generally made of the cheapest lumber, covered with felt and tar, and divided into apartments, some 12 by 14 feet in dimensions."[64] The actual cost of the rooms for the builder "was from $40 to $100 each, (rarely exceeding the latter sum) and the rents already paid have, in many instances, exceeded the entire outlay in erecting them."[65] Eight years later, health officials found that many alleys were "lined on both sides with miserable dilapidated shanties, patched and filthy," while many frame dwellings had "leaky roofs, broken and filthy ceilings, dilapidated floors." They were "unfit for human habitation," but most owners were "mean enough to charge rent for them."[66] In fact, virtually any building fronting on an alley could be converted for dwelling purposes; for example, in 1877 William Walker converted two brick stables in Carlin's Alley, Southwest, into "dwelling houses."[67] Occasionally street houses were moved to alley property as well.

Fortunately, much new building in the late 1870s and 1880s was of more substantial frame and, increasingly, brick construction. Normally these buildings were two-story row houses of four or more units, as illustrated in the photographs throughout this study. Although houses varied, an average dwelling was about twelve feet wide and twenty-four to thirty feet deep, with one or two rooms on each floor. A small backyard contained a water hydrant, privy, and shed.[68]

Various sources suggest that, from 1865 until 1877, blocks were often subdivided into street-facing and alley-fronting land prior to development. Moreover, both the Boschke map of 1857 and the *Real Estate Directory of the City of Washington for 1874* confirm that alley construction could occur before street development, with street development, or as fill-in later.[69] A study of land ownership, subdivision, and alley construction in one alley sheds considerable light on

64. *National Intelligencer*, July 25, 1865, p. 3.
65. *Ibid.*
66. Board of Health, *Second Annual Report*, p. 105; *Third Annual Report* (Washington, 1874), p. 186; and *Annual Report, 1877* (Washington, 1878), p. 46.
67. Washington *Post*, Dec. 27, 1877, p. 3.
68. Edith Elmer Wood, "Four Washington Alleys," *Survey*, 31 (December 6, 1913): 250.
69. Ernest Faehtz and Frederick Pratt, *Real Estate Directory of the City of Washington*, *D.C.* (Washington, 1874).

the development process for the later years. Fenton Place (Square 621, between North Capitol, First, K, and L Streets, Northwest) and the surrounding street property remained largely untouched until the 1880s, when street and alley development began simultaneously. Little subdivision had even taken place until the 1880s, when small "house" lots, both alley and street, were carved out of the larger tracts into which the block had been divided. For the most part, the subdivision was almost immediately followed by the sale of street-front and alley land to different buyers.[70] Moreover, some "tracts" of subdivided alley land passed rapidly through the hands of a number of different owners before houses were actually built on them. In other cases the houses were built and sold off immediately, and also had a number of owners in a short period of time. Either way, many tracts were broken up into smaller holdings. What is striking about this development is both the rapid turnover of property (especially in light of the stability and continuity of ownership over the preceding eighty years), and the speed with which the entire block was built up.[71]

Both of these conditions suggest considerable speculation both in property (probably including street as well as alley land) and in housing construction and sale. Moreover, several factors—the high turnover in alley property; the subdivision, construction, and sale of single-family houses on the street to individual families; and the separate ownership of alley land and street-front land—meant that most owners of street-front land in Square 621 were not likely to own any land facing the alley.

The institution of building and repair permits in 1877 dispelled much of the mystery concerning these builders' identities and their

70. There is some evidence that street land and alley land were sold to different buyers in the earlier years as well. For example, an advertisement for an auction for two lots in Square 513, one fronting on a street and the other on a "minor street" alley, indicates that the two would presumably be bought and developed by different people (*National Intelligencer*, Sept. 25, 1865, p. 3). On the other hand, in the same year many properties were sold which had a two-story house on the street and a two-story brick building in back, although the function of these "back buildings" is never indicated. Others, of course, include a "carriage house with servant's room above" (*ibid.*, Sept. 23, 1865, p. 3).

71. The earliest subdivision of land into residential lots did not occur until 1860, and there were only two taxable buildings in 1874. Much of the subdivision into house-sized lots, whether on the street or on the alley, did not occur until about 1885. From then until 1892 there was a boom in subdivision, sales, and construction. This discussion is largely based on the work of Rev. Fr. Daniel O'Connell, "The Inhabited Alleys of Washington and the Early Social History of One Alley," (M.A. thesis, Catholic University of America, 1953), pp. 84–108, and Plates 1–9.

TABLE 1.
Alley House Construction by Year, 1877–92*

		1877	1878	1879	1880	1881	1882	1883	188
Number of houses per permit	1	1	5	9	2	4	3	2	9
	2	4	6	2	4	1	5	5	*
	3			2	1		1		
	4	2	1			2	2	2	
	5		1	2	1	1	2		
	6–10	1				1	1		
	11–15								
	16–20								
	21–25								
	26–30								
TOTAL		25	26	29	18	29	42	20	102
Average number of houses per permit		3.1	2.0	1.9	2.2	3.2	3.0	2.2	4.4

*Based on projected construction from Building and Repair Permits of the District of Columbia, 1877–1949, RG 351 NA.
** Represents six months only.

relation to their property. Perhaps the most striking fact about these builders is that they were so numerous. The independent decisions of a large number of individuals, rather than a few large-scale "developers," brought about alley house construction. From 1877 through 1883 the average number of houses built with a single construction permit was only 2.5, suggesting that development was still occurring on a relatively small scale.[72] (See Table 1.)

Despite the similarities with earlier alley building, it is clear that these later owners were not developing land at the back of their own

72. Building records used here indicate only the *intention* to build, not actual construction. There are other problems with these records as well. In one case, Carl Auerbach took out two different permits for the same Fenton Place buildings, while permits for some buildings, like those of George Mueller (Fenton Place), do not currently appear in the records. Nevertheless, these records do give the best indication of the owners' identities, and as a result perhaps provide the closest approximate glimpse of reality without a complete and exhaustive study of all records relating to building and ownership. Building and Repair Permits of the District of Columbia, 1877–1949, RG 351, NA.

Table 1—*continued*

1885	1886	1887	1888	1889	1890	1891	1892**	Total	%
13	20	19	19	18	16	13	21	174	7
13	17	17	25	13	17	14	33	366	14
8	6	11	16	5	18	13	14	285	11
3	6	11		7	8	10	14	276	11
5	5	2	4	4	6	4	7	220	8
11	10	12	6	6	14	12	15	705	28
		1	3	2		1	9	224	9
1	2	1	1	2			3	203	8
			2					44	2
	1			1				52	2
205	265	258	241	252	301	246	490	2,549	100
3.8	4.0	3.5	3.3	4.3	3.8	3.7	4.2	3.7	

yards. Map 6 demonstrates the considerable distance between the owners' residential locations and their alley houses. Although at least one owner (T. W. Bartley) constructed "my coachman's dwelling" at the back of his lot, and several others lived on their alley property, they prove to be the exceptions.[73] Moreover, these own-

73. Map 6 was constructed by gathering selected repair permits and all building permits issued from 1877 to 1884, and searching for the owners' names in the city directories for the appropriate years. Of the 103 permits, 42 owners were not identifiable, either because no such name appeared in the directory or because inadequate information made it impossible to link the owner to a given name. Although the name and address of the owner were requested on the permit form, often the builder (usually different from the owner) put down his address, or the address was left blank. It was possible to tentatively link to city directory addresses 62 owners who took out 76 permits; from these data, the spatial relationship between the owner's residence and his alley houses was mapped. The 42 unlocated owners had 85 houses, or an average of 2 per permit. Not surprisingly, those who were traceable in the city directory represented more substantial owners; their 231 houses averaged out to 3.8 per each owner. While this is certainly a biased sample, the overwhelming separation of the owner's residence from his alley property suggests that even smaller holders

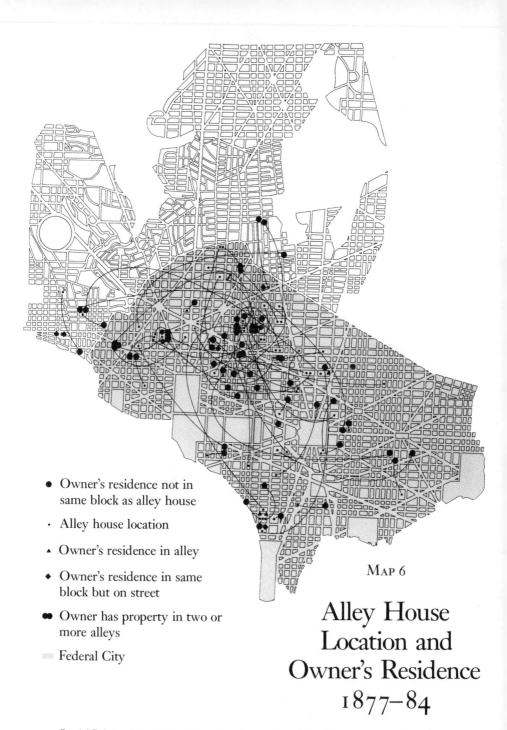

- Owner's residence not in same block as alley house
- · Alley house location
- ▲ Owner's residence in alley
- ◆ Owner's residence in same block but on street
- ●● Owner has property in two or more alleys
- ▦ Federal City

MAP 6

Alley House Location and Owner's Residence 1877–84

Spatial Relationship of Alley House Location to Owner's Residence, 1877–84. Based on Building and Repair Permits of the District of Columbia, 1877–1949, RG 351, NA. (See footnote 73.) Due to the number of owners and the map size, locations are approximate.

TABLE 2.
Occupations of Alley House Owners, 1877–84*

Occupation	Number of owners	Houses owned	Average holding of each	Occupation's Holding as % of total
Professional and executive	11	78	7.1	33.8
Proprietor (includes real estate and contractors)	27	93	3.4	40.3
Managerial and white collar	7	14	2.0	6.1
Skilled worker	2	6	3.0	2.6
Semi- and un-skilled worker	9	13	1.4	5.6
No occupation given	6	27	4.5	11.6
TOTAL	62	231	3.7	100

*Table 2 was constructed by gathering selected repair permits and all building permits issued from 1877 to 1884, and searching for the owners' names in the city directory for the appropriate year. Of the 103 permits, 42 owners were not identifiable, either,because no such name appeared in the directory or because inadequate information made it impossible to link the owner to a given name. It was possible to tentatively link 62 owners who took out 76 permits. Building and Repair Permits of the District of Columbia, 1877–1949, RG 351, NA; William Boyd, *Directory for the City of Washington, D.C.* (Washington, 1877–84).

ers' occupations suggest that most alley property was developed by the well-to-do, rather than by the small property owner. As Table 2 indicates, professionals, executives, and proprietors owned 74 percent of the alley houses. Those who lived close to or in their alley houses were most likely to be skilled, semi-skilled, or unskilled workers—those who owned the fewest houses.

In contrast to the relatively small amount of alley construction from 1877 to 1884, building permits reflect a boom from 1884 until

probably exhibited the same tendency, albeit perhaps to a lesser extent. See Building and Repair Permits of the District of Columbia, 1877–1949, RG 351, NA. O'Connell also reported that most owners of Fenton Place "did not live in nor own other property in the block; when they purchased, they bought only alley lots" ("Inhabited Alleys of Washington," p. 89).

TABLE 3.
Building Permits, 1877–92 and 1913*

	Building permits 1877–92	1913 Ownership
Total number of houses	2,549	2,528
Average number of houses (per permit)/(average holding)	3.8	2.9
Total number of permits/owners	671	881

*Based on Building and Repair Permits of the District of Columbia, 1877–1949, RG 351 NA; and 63rd Congress, 1st session, Senate, Committee on the District of Columbia, *Persons Owning or Renting Houses in the So-Called "Inhabited Alleys" in the District of Columbia* (Washington, 1913).

TABLE 4.
Large Holdings, 1877–92 and 1913*
(5 or more houses)

	Building permits 1877–92	1913 Ownership
Number of owners	137	154
Number of houses owned	1,588	1,294
Average holding	11.6	8.4
% of total alley houses (for 1877–92 existing houses are excluded, since it is impossible to determine their number)	62.3	51.2

*SOURCE: same as Table 3.

1892, when Congress approved legislation that effectively stopped further building. (See Table 1.) During the later years many more permits were issued, and the average number of houses per permit increased from 2.5 in 1877–84 to nearly 4 in 1884–92. This increase reflects the growing role of "larger" developers in the alley housing market. We can identify at least 137 such "large developers" (those who planned to build at least five houses), although others who constructed such houses one, two, or three at a time in different blocks may have been missed. These 137 builders planned to construct 1,588 houses, an average of 11.6 per developer, or over 62 percent of all houses planned. While these owner-developers included such well-known architects and builders as Montgomery Meigs and Charles Gessford, many were directly involved in real estate, banking, and construction, and their role here seems to have been clearly speculative. When housing reformers finally succeeded, in 1913, in getting Congress to investigate the "alley-slum-landlord," the ensuing study turned up 881 different owners who controlled 2,528 houses. As Table 3 indicates, the average holding per owner in 1913 was 2.9 houses, while the average number of houses planned per building permit issued from 1877 to 1892 was 3.8. Multiple ownership, of course, makes this latter figure very conservative.[74] Similarly, the "large holders" controlled more houses (11.6 vs. 8.4) and owned a larger proportion of the total alley dwelling market in the earlier years (62% vs 51%). (See Table 4.) Moreover, large developers' holdings diminished considerably over the ensuing years. While depression, death, and dispersal to relatives explain some of the diminution, as does decline of business, it seems reasonable to assume that many "developers" built with the intention of selling the houses as soon as possible, both for profit and for reinvestment in the construction of more dwellings. Certainly some owner-developers appear on building permits both as owners and as builders for other owners. The active involvement in alley construction by real estate, construction, and banking interests further supports this contention.

Given the wider dispersal of alley property in 1913, it is not surprising that the distance between the owner's residence and his/her alley property had widened, as Map 7 demonstrates.[75] Not only had ownership become more dispersed, both numerically and spatially, by 1913; it had also become more equitably distributed among the various occupations. As Table 5 indicates, professional, executive, and proprietorial control had slipped from 74 percent to less than 40 percent, while the size of the average holding had also declined. While proprietors who owned alley property in the early years also owned substantial businesses, their counterparts in 1913 often ran marginal ones. White-collar workers and managers, many

74. Alley houses constructed prior to 1877 are not considered here. If figures for such construction were available, they would undoubtedly make the two average ownership rates much closer.

75. Of course, this expansion of lines connecting owners' residences and their alley properties also reflects the city's spatial growth. Map 7 is based on a random sample of 113 names drawn from a list of owners; their total alley property ownership is compiled from 63rd Congress, 1st session, Senate, Committee on the District of Columbia, *Persons Owning or Renting Houses or Rooms in the So-Called "Inhabited Alleys" in the District of Columbia* (Washington, 1913). These 113 names were sought in the 1913 city directory; 97 either already had addresses or were located in that directory.

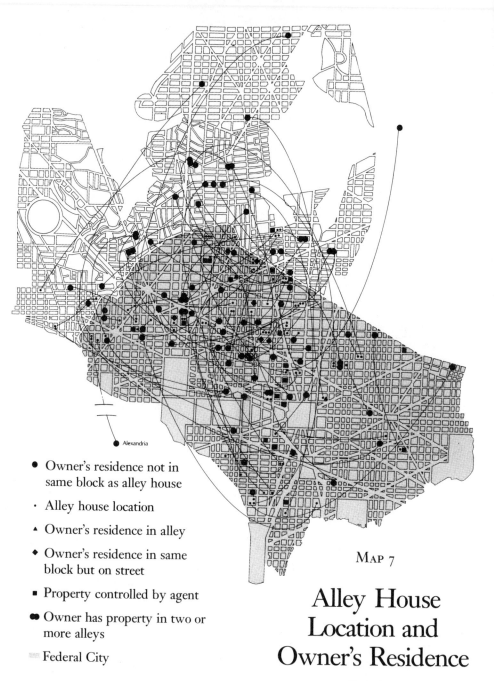

Alexandria

- Owner's residence not in same block as alley house
- Alley house location
- Owner's residence in alley
- Owner's residence in same block but on street
- Property controlled by agent
- Owner has property in two or more alleys
- Federal City

MAP 7

Alley House Location and Owner's Residence
1913

Spatial Relationship of Alley House Location to Owner's Residence, 1913. Based on 63rd Congress, 1st session, Senate, Committee on the District of Columbia, *Persons Owning or Renting Houses or Rooms in the So-Called "Inhabited Alleys" in the District of Columbia* (Washington, 1913). (See footnote 75.) Due to the number of owners and the map size, the locations are approximate.

TABLE 5.
Occupations of Alley House Owners, 1913*

Occupation	Number of owners	Houses owned	Average holding	Occupation's holding as % of total
Professional and executive	10	39	3.9	14.9
Proprietor	30	65	2.2	24.8
Managerial and white collar	14	45	3.2	17.2
Skilled worker	2	13	6.5	5.0
Semi- and un- skilled worker	10	18	1.8	6.9
No occupation given or not listed in city directory	15	39	2.6	14.9
Held in trust, managed by real estate, etc.	16	43	2.7	16.3
TOTALS	97	262	2.7	100.0

*Based on random sample of 113 names drawn from listing in 63rd Congress, 1st session, Senate, Committee on the District of Columbia, *Persons Owning or Renting Houses or Rooms in the So-Called "Inhabited Alleys" in the District of Columbia* (Washington, 1913). Only 97 names could be traced in the city directories.

of whom were clerks, substantially increased their holdings of alley property, perhaps as a way of gaining social mobility. While skilled and other workers increased their holdings only slightly, another influence—the management and control of alley property by trustees, real estate agents, or others who were not owners—added to the physical and social distance between tenant and owner. The extent of this separation was suggested in a 1948 study of Dingman Place. There Mrs. Mattie Coleman rented her home from an agent, who in turn rented the building from the owner, Mrs. Mary Slattery. Mrs. Slattery reported that she "had not visited the property since before prohibition." Mrs. Emma Cobbs, who rented a house nearby, had an even more tortuous connection to its owner. James Gilbert, from whom she rented, in turn rented the property from the owner, who lived in Philadelphia, through the latter's property manager in Washington. The manager had not seen the property for "a long time."[76] Finally, at least some of those without occupations were widows and retired persons who used income from alley property as a means of support in their declining years.[77]

As ownership slipped down the occupational hierarchy, the implications for alley residents can be speculated upon, if not confirmed.[78] Since only fifteen alley families owned their homes in 1913, these conditions affected virtually every resident.[79] While concern for maintenance and tenant comfort might vary more due to personal attitudes than to class or occupational standing, those owners with the least resources would, despite their intentions, be unable to provide repairs, improvements, or reasonable rents. Moreover, as marginal businessmen and clerks acquired more alley property as a means to social and economic mobility, the alley tenant was more directly exposed to variations in the business cycle from yet another angle. These marginal owners, especially businessmen, were themselves caught up in a vicious cycle not of their own making. Regardless of their sales, they had to meet their payments for merchandise purchased, and most likely pay the alley property mortgage as well. Small businessmen and clerks who owned alley property were probably forced to pass on increased expenses, or to make up for business losses by drawing more profit from their ally investments. Those who refused to pass on the greater costs were undoubtedly forced to sell their property. The motivations and good intentions of owners probably mattered little,

76. Washington *Post*, Dec. 19, 1948.

77. The 97 names were also sought in *Sherman's Directory and Ready Reference of the Colored Population in the District of Columbia 1913* (Washington, 1913) to determine each owner's race and occupation. Five owners were listed in the directory: one man (a produce dealer) and four women (two domestics, one laundress, and one cook).

78. In her study of property owners in four alleys in 1913, Edith Wood reported that, "of the twenty-two" out of forty-seven "whose occupations could be ascertained, five are real estate men (a striking witness to the profitable character of this type of property), two are lawyers, two are proprietors of clothing stores, and two . . . are clerks. There are, besides, an architect, a druggist, an engineer, a dentist, a manufacturer, the president of a corporation, a maker of relief maps, a dealer in tombstones, a manager, a saloon-keeper, and a seamstress. One rather extensive owner is the Washington City Orphan Asylum" ("Four Washington Alleys," p. 251). Nevertheless, the larger random sample used here seems to allow better evaluation of alley property owners; my analysis revealed slightly greater ownership by those in lower occupational levels, such as white-collar employees, petty proprietors, and skilled workers.

79. The difficulty in purchasing an alley house is suggested by Mrs. Lloyd's effort to buy her Dingman Place house in 1948. Unlike many alley residents, she was able to obtain a $2,800 bank loan; but to make the $30 monthly payments while supporting "her household of eight persons, six of them children," she had to work "sixteen hours a day" (Washington *Post*, Dec. 19, 1948).

for they were caught up in a system with which they had to cooperate fully in order to survive.

Many alley landlords, regardless of wealth or occupation, ignored their tenants' complaints.[80] When repairs were made, "All added expenses for construction or repairs appear to be speedily expressed in higher rentals."[81] The practice of subletting further complicated the process; a tenant who reported a leaking hydrant was told by the owner that "she, the tenant, was out of order in making the report! The report should have come from the person who rented the house, who was safely out of the city."[82] Finally, almost every alley survey reported that owners made substantial profits on their investments. Clare de Graffenried found that "One conclusion at least is evident: that rents in these alleys are dear, considering the accommodations and environment." Marion Ratigan noted that "The landlord who exploits the tenants is the most formidable peril in alley housing," although "This is not true of all owners."[83] Nearly every survey reported that return on investment for alley property was at least twice that for street property.[84]

The dispersal of alley property to more owners can be interpreted in other ways as well. By 1913 only three alleys were owned by one person. Although alley sizes varied considerably, the average number of owners per alley was slightly over 9 by 1913, suggesting a wide variation of tenant-landlord relations and obligations within a given alley. The dispersal of owners throughout the city also made it unlikely that owners of property within the same alley would know each other, thus adding to the separation and isolation of tenant and owner.

This rather lengthy discussion of alley ownership is intended to

80. Clare de Graffenried, "Typical Alley Houses in Washington, D.C.," *Woman's Anthropological Society Bulletin*, 7 (Washington, 1897): 8; Leonor Enrequez Pablo, "The Housing Needs and Social Problems of Residents in a Deteriorated Area" (M.S.W. thesis, Catholic University of America, 1953), pp. 49–50; Ratigan, *A Sociological Survey of Disease*, p. 84.

81. Weller, *Neglected Neighbors*, p. 83.

82. Ratigan, *Sociological Survey of Disease*, p. 84.

83. de Graffenried, "Typical Alley Houses," p. 11; Ratigan, *Sociological Survey of Disease*, p. 81.

84. See also Jones, *Housing of Negroes in Washington*, p. 32; Wood, "Four Washington Alleys," pp. 250–51; Swinney, "Alley Dwellings and Housing Reform," p. 147; Washington *Post*, Dec. 19, 1948; Ratigan, *Sociological Survey of Disease*, p. 81. Pablo notes that the occupants of Temperance Court "could have paid for their own dwelling structures in one year" if all their rent payments had gone toward the principal. "Considering further that if the valuation was equal to the selling price, they could have bought the place five times over" ("Housing Needs and Social Problems," p. 30).

TABLE 6.
Occupations of Alley Dwellers by Race, 1858–71

	1858					
	Black		White		Total	
Occupation	N	%	N	%	N	
Unskilled and menial service	68	56	137	61	205	5
Semi-skilled and service	30	25	12	5	42	1
Petty proprietor, Manager and Official	1	1	6	3	7	
Skilled	8	7	41	18	49	1
Clerical and Sales	0		1		1	
Semi-Professional	0		2	1	2	
Proprietor, Manager and Official	0		0		0	
Professional	0		1		1	
Miscellaneous	14	11	27	12	41	1
TOTAL (N)	121		227		348	

SOURCE: William Boyd., comp., *Boyd's Washington and Georgetown Directory—1858*. William Boyd, comp., *Boyd's Directory of Washington, Georgetown and Alexandria—1871*. Occupational categories based on those used in Peter Knights, *The Plain People of Boston: 1830–1860* (New York, 1971), pp. 148–52.

demonstrate that for many years, beginning at least in the 1870s if not earlier, the immediate proximity of the owner's residence to his alley property diminished. The spatial relationship suggested by the antebellum story of Snow's Court became less and less common as the nineteenth century advanced. Moreover, that later construction was largely for speculative purposes is suggested by the actions of alley property owners in the first half of 1892, just before Congress restricted further alley house construction. During this six-month period owners took out nearly twice as many building permits as any preceding full year, indicating the lucrative nature of alley investments. The 1892 legislation prohibited further housing construction on alleys less than thirty feet wide and not provided with sewers, water mains, and lights.[85]

85. It is not entirely clear why these restrictions were such deterrents to potential builders. It appears from the building permits that, for several years prior to adoption of the legislation, builders had to seek special exemptions if their proposed houses were on an alley less than thirty feet wide, and one that had no connection to sewers or water mains. The added expense of these "luxuries" was apparently enough to stop further building, for the inspector of buildings reported that "certain restrictions and conditions on dwellings to be erected in alleys . . . have practically prevented the construction of this class of building, for since the passage of the law no applicant has been able to comply with all the conditions imposed" ("Report of the Inspector of

`able 6—*continued*

			1871			
Black		*White*		*Total*		
N	%	N	%	N	%	
646	54	130	45	776	52	
318	26	29	10	347	23	
39	3	22	8	61	4	
85	7	50	17	135	9	
8	1	5	2	13	1	
6	1	3	1	9	1	
0		3	1	3		
1		0		1		
101	8	49	16	150	10	
,204		291		1,495		

In view of the wide dispersal of ownership and the speculative nature of alley property, it seems reasonable to conclude that most alley residents were left to their own devices. The actual contacts between landlord and tenant or sublessor and sublessee seem to have been extremely limited and tenuous. Landlords, then, were not able to maintain social control over their tenants, resulting in situations which will be discussed more fully in Chapter 3.

Not only had the spatial relationships of owner and tenant changed since the Civil War, but so, too, had the racial makeup of the alley population. The large influx of freedmen during and after the Civil War reversed the white majority of 1858. By 1871, 81 percent of the heads of household reported in the city directory were black. While white heads of alley households had increased by only 64 in the thirteen years since 1858, Negro heads of households had increased by 1,083. (See Map 5.) Nevertheless, the occupational structure remained basically the same, with the vast majority of alley residents falling into the unskilled and menial service categories.

Buildings," in the *Report of the Commissioners of the District of Columbia* [Washington, 1893], p. 269). The flood of applications also represents the concern of owners whose alley property was as yet undeveloped, and who probably feared that the new restrictions would make their land financially unproductive.

As Table 6 indicates, however, white alley residents appear to have gained some occupational mobility, moving to higher occupational levels. Their black counterparts, excluded by racial antagonism from many economic activities, maintained the same occupational distribution in 1871 as in 1858.

The level of segregation in alleys had increased by 1871. Only 12 percent of the alleys (as opposed to 18 percent in 1858) had less than a two-thirds majority of any one race, and only three of these had twenty or more household heads listed. By 1880 this trend was even more marked. (See Map 8.) Although the 1880 manuscript census was conservative, it does provide the first rough estimate of the total alley population. In the entire District of Columbia, 10,614 people were listed as having addresses in 210 alleys. Blacks continued to increase their dominance over whites in the alley population, representing 87 percent of that total. Moreover, by 1880 only 7 percent of the alleys had less than a two-thirds majority of either race, and the population of those alleys was less than 5 percent of the total. In contrast, 123 alleys, with slightly less than half of the total population, were completely segregated.[86]

By 1897 black dominance was even more complete. The Police Department's special census of the alleys reported a population of 18,978. The Federal City alone contained 17,244 alley dwellers (11 percent of that area's population), of whom 16,046 were black and 1,198 white. Blacks now made up 93 percent of alley residents, and black alley dwellers accounted for nearly one-fourth of the city's nonwhite population.[87] (See Map 9.) Of the 237 inhabited alleys in the Federal City, nearly 70 percent were totally segregated.

While the 1897 census was taken at about the height of alley dwelling, it, too, was undoubtedly conservative. Many police were

86. Federal Population Census Schedules, 1880, RG 29, NA. (Since the microfilm copies of the census that are available from the National Archives had, in at least one instance, two pages omitted in the filming process, I was very fortunate to be able to use the manuscript volumes at the Columbia Historical Society.) The exact breakdown of the 1880 alley population by race was 9,250 black (87 percent) and 1,364 white (13 percent). Finally, while just over 45 percent of the population was totally segregated, nearly 55 percent did share the alley with someone of another race. Nevertheless, the relatively small white alley population meant that the general experience was one of isolation from, rather than contact with, the other race. My use of two-thirds as a cut-off point is, of course, arbitrary; yet more than 67 percent of one race in an alley would tend to give that race dominance. Moreover, the population of the city in 1880 was roughly two-thirds white and one-third black, which provides a useful basis for comparison.

87. Commissioners of the District of Columbia, *Annual Report 1897* (Washington, 1897), pp. 195–202.

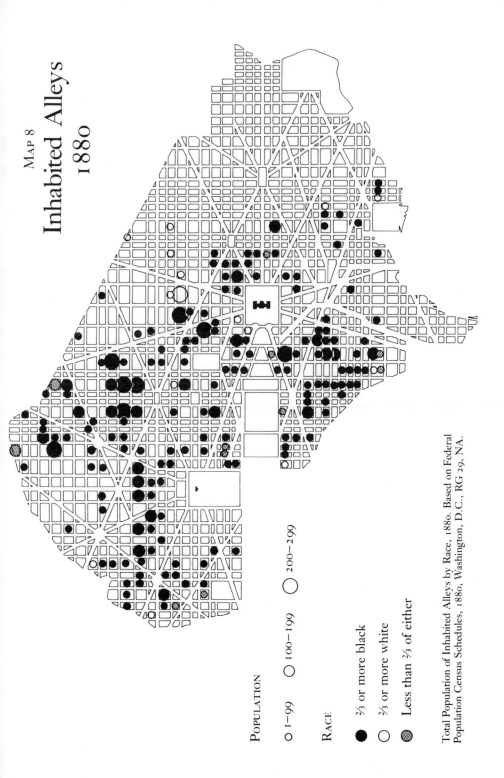

MAP 8

Inhabited Alleys
1880

POPULATION

○ 1–99   ○ 100–199   ◯ 200–299

RACE

● ⅔ or more black

○ ⅔ or more white

◉ Less than ⅔ of either

Total Population of Inhabited Alleys by Race, 1880. Based on Federal
Population Census Schedules, 1880, Washington, D.C., RG 29, NA.

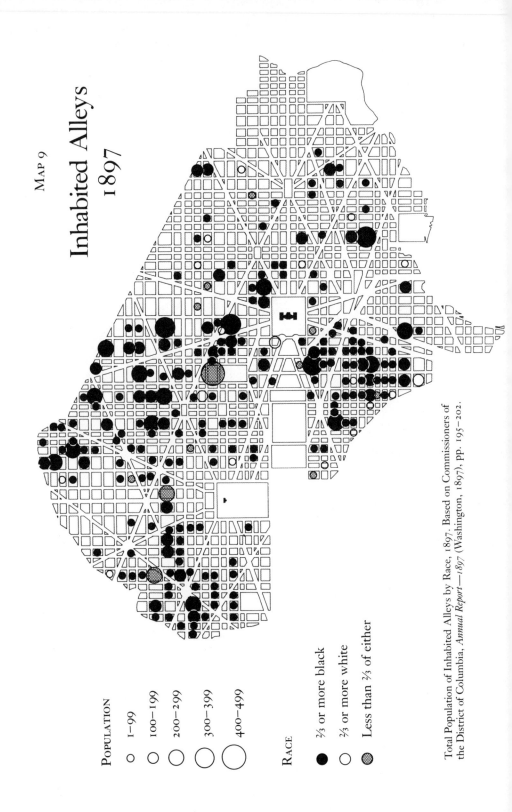

MAP 9

Inhabited Alleys
1897

POPULATION

○ 1–99

○ 100–199

○ 200–299

○ 300–399

○ 400–499

RACE

● ⅔ or more black

○ ⅔ or more white

◉ Less than ⅔ of either

Total Population of Inhabited Alleys by Race, 1897. Based on Commissioners of
the District of Columbia, *Annual Report—1897* (Washington, 1897), pp. 195–202.

allegedly afraid to enter the alleys alone, and even when accompanied by reinforcements they generally kept their "pistols at the ready."[88] Since many alley dwellers had little love for the police, or for any stranger in their alley, gaining accurate information could not have been very easy. In 1896 a special agent for the Department of Labor concluded an intensive study of thirteen alleys by observing, "I have no doubt that lodgers are harbored in these alleys whose presence . . . is always concealed."[89]

Another approach to alley enumeration was made by the Monday Evening Club, which in 1912 compiled a "Directory of Alleys" in an effort to publicize the "hidden" communities "menacing the city." Club members found 240 blocks with inhabited alleys in the Federal City, and 3,201 alley houses.[90] Since dwelling construction had virtually ceased by 1892, there had been little change in the general spatial patterns of the alleys. (See Map 10.) There were, however, three more alleys reported in 1912 than in 1897, and some changes in location among smaller alleys.[91] Nevertheless, the Monday Evening Club estimated the total alley population to be about 16,000, or 3,000 fewer than in 1897.

A number of forces were responsible for this slow erosion of the alley population. The most obvious force was governmental officials and housing reformers who sought to remove alley housing. The conditions in alleys had not gone unnoticed by health officials; from 1873 until its abolition in 1877, the Board of Health condemned 985 alley shanties, of which nearly 300 were demolished.[92] But governmental reorganization in 1878 and 1879 failed to give the health officer the power of condemnation earlier held by the Board, and without such power little could be done about unsound and unsanitary alley houses.

The 1892 congressional restrictions on construction were followed, beginning in 1894, by the organization of reform-minded citizens' groups that began agitating for the abolition of all alley housing, either by demolition or by the opening up of blind alleys. Reformers argued that alleys were dangerous not only for health reasons, but because they were "hidden communities" which bred

88. Jones, *Housing of Negroes*, p. 46.
89. de Graffenried, "Typical Alley Houses," p. 12.
90. The entire District of Columbia had 270 alleys with 3,337 houses. Monday Evening Club, *Directory of Inhabited Alleys of Washington, D.C.* (Washington, 1912).
91. This movement reflects one of the continuous problems involved in alley enumeration: the tendency for alleys with smaller populations to appear or disappear as the result of a move by one or two families.
92. Board of Health, *Annual Report 1877*, p. 47.

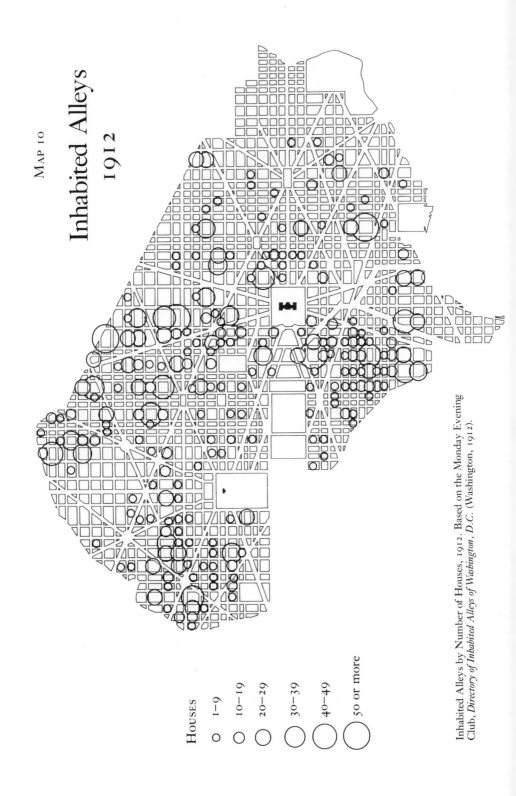

MAP 10

Inhabited Alleys
1912

HOUSES

○ 1–9

○ 10–19

◯ 20–29

◯ 30–39

◯ 40–49

◯ 50 or more

Inhabited Alleys by Number of Houses, 1912. Based on the Monday Evening
Club, *Directory of Inhabited Alleys of Washington, D.C.* (Washington, 1912).

conditions of vice, crime, and immorality. In 1904 reformers brought Jacob Riis to Washington to visit the alleys and report his findings to Congress. Riis's report, coupled with a major publicity campaign, convinced President Theodore Roosevelt. Roosevelt urged Congress to conduct a systematic study of the alleys, emphasizing that the "hidden residential alleys are breeding grounds of vice and disease and should be opened into minor streets."[93]

Few alleys were converted, but the reformers' agitation resulted in two rewards: the restoration of condemnation powers, and the appointment of the President's Homes Commission. With these successes, the reform movement temporarily dissipated, and even the publication of the Commission's reports in 1908 and Charles Weller's *Neglected Neighbors* in 1909 failed to revive any interest. The Board for Condemnation of Insanitary Buildings did, however, have an impact on the alleys. From its creation in 1906 until 1911, the Board reported 375 houses destroyed and 315 repaired.[94]

By 1911 the housing reform movement was again active, with publicity campaigns that surpassed even those of 1900 to 1906. This time reformers were able to gain conversion of one major alley. Congress appropriated $78,000 to clear and reclaim Willow Tree Alley, Southwest (Square 534), one of the city's largest and most "notorious," and the one visited by Private Bellard fifty years earlier. (It was converted into an interior playground.) By 1914 the movement reached its peak, having enlisted the cream of Washington society to make a "grand tour" of the alleys. The First Lady, Ellen Wilson, led some of these tours and actively sought passage of legislation to end alley dwelling. Her deathbed request was largely responsible for the passage of such legislation, which was to go into effect on July 1, 1918.[95] However, World War I and the accompanying housing shortage led to postponement of the provision. After the War, Congress passed further extensions of the deadline, and the legislation was finally emasculated in 1927 by an adverse court ruling.

93. Jacob Riis, "The Housing Problem Facing Congress," *Charities*, 12 (Feb. 6, 1904): 161–66; Theodore Roosevelt, *State Papers as Governor and President* (New York, 1926), p. 229.

94. Thomas Jesse Jones, "Alley Homes of Washington," *Survey*, 28 (Oct. 19, 1912): 68. Nevertheless, in surveying the building and repair permits, I discovered that numerous repair permits for alley houses must have been taken out as a result of tenants' complaints or at the owner's own volition, even after the condemnation powers had been taken away.

95. "Mrs. Wilson's Death and Washington's Alleys," *Survey*, 32 (August 15, 1914): 515; Mrs. Ernest P. Bicknell, "The Home-Maker of the White House," *Survey*, 33 (Oct. 3, 1914): 22.

Thus, despite more than twenty years of vigorous reform efforts, little change had been brought about. Although police census statistics showed a one-third decline in the alley population between 1897 and 1913, few viewed this as accurate reporting.[96] In spite of the reform movement's relative ineffectiveness, a 1927 survey of alleys in the Northwest and Southwest sections did show a substantial decrease in the number of buildings used for residential purposes. (See Map 11.) While 26 new houses had been added in the fifteen years, 868 others were no longer used as dwellings. Nearly 40 percent of the houses, then, had been removed from the housing market, largely due to forces unrelated to the reform movement.[97]

One such force was challenging alley houses long before 1912. A sample study of changing land use in six Northwest alleys from 1888 to 1904 suggests that alley housing was barely holding its own against other land uses. While the number of houses increased 7 percent, stables increased by 16 percent and warehouses, shops, and businesses by 314 percent.[98] Business demands on alley property varied greatly, depending on an alley's proximity and accessibility to business needs.

A comparison of land use for nine sample alley blocks between 1904 and 1928 confirms this increasing intrusion of business uses. It also reveals another even more important incursion: by 1928 automobile garages had become a major factor in the alleys. While dwellings in the nine sample blocks decreased by half, and stables all but disappeared, garages increased in number from 0 to 244. A substantial number of former residences were converted into garages. In Blagden Alley, for example, business use took over 15 houses, and garages 27. Only 15 of the 57 dwellings inhabited in 1904 were used for housing in 1928.[99] (See Maps 12 and 13.)

Where the progressive housing reformers largely failed, business, and especially Henry Ford's inexpensive automobiles, inadvertently succeeded in removing many alley houses. But other factors, less obtrusive and more difficult to document, helped sound retreat for the inhabited alleys. While Congress was imposing restrictions on alley house construction in 1892, city trolley construction was al-

96. Commissioners of the District of Columbia, *Annual Report 1913* (Washington, 1913), III, 8.

97.. Jones, *Housing of Negroes*, pp. 161–65.

98. Borchert, "Race and Place," pp. 19–20.

99. Five of the sample blocks were from Northwest, two from Southwest, and one each from Northeast and Southeast. Sanborn Map Publishing Company, *Insurance Maps of Washington, D.C.* (New York, 1904), I, II; and *Insurance Maps of Washington, D.C.* (Pelham, N.Y., 1928), I, II, IV.

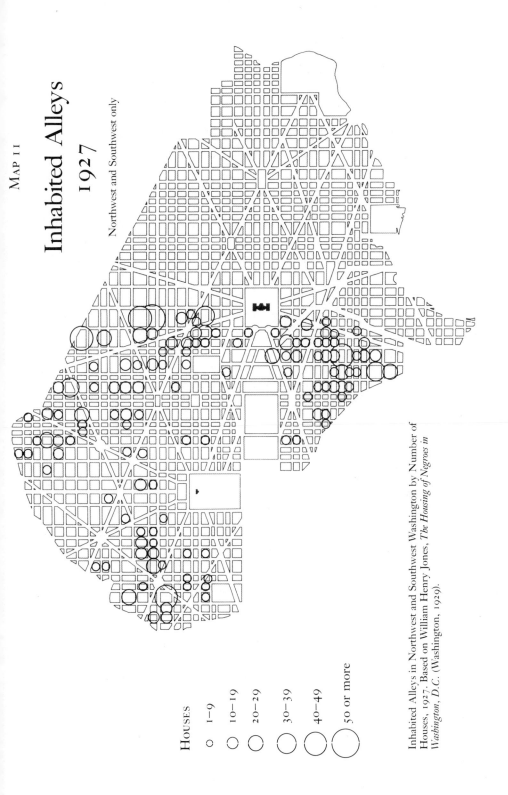

MAP 11

Inhabited Alleys

1927

Northwest and Southwest only

HOUSES

○ 1–9

○ 10–19

○ 20–29

○ 30–39

○ 40–49

○ 50 or more

Inhabited Alleys in Northwest and Southwest Washington by Number of Houses, 1927. Based on William Henry Jones, *The Housing of Negroes in Washington, D.C.* (Washington, 1929).

MAP 12

Blagden Alley, 1904

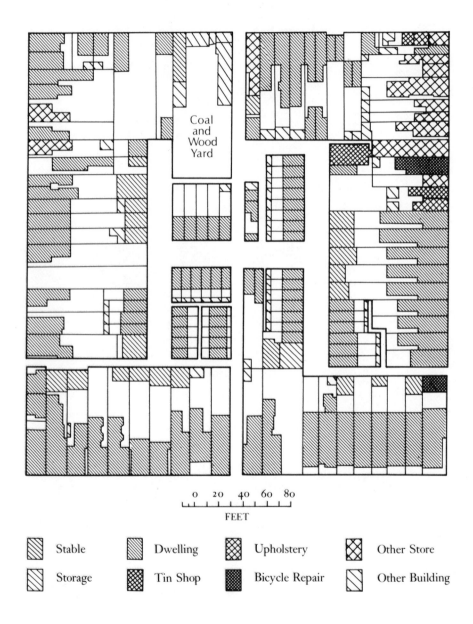

Coal
and
Wood
Yard

0   20   40   60   80
FEET

| | Stable | | Dwelling | | Upholstery | | Other Store |
| | Storage | | Tin Shop | | Bicycle Repair | | Other Building |

Blagden Alley, Northwest, 1904. Based on Sanborn Map Publishing Company, *Insurance Maps of Washington, D.C.* (New York, 1904).

MAP 13

Blagden Alley, 1928

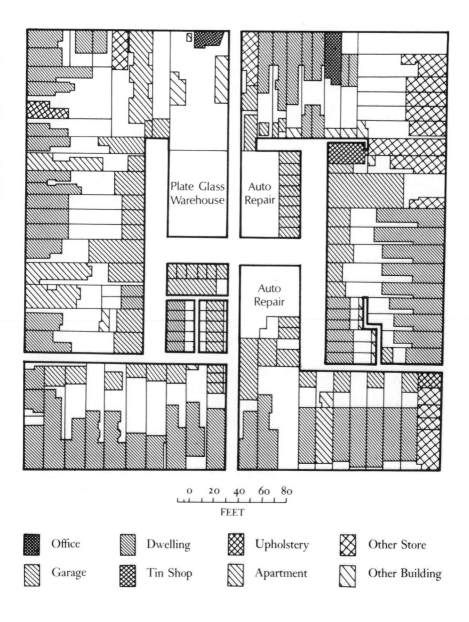

Plate Glass
Warehouse

Auto
Repair

Auto
Repair

0   20   40   60   80
FEET

▨ Office	▨ Dwelling	▨ Upholstery	▨ Other Store
▨ Garage	▨ Tin Shop	▨ Apartment	▨ Other Building

Blagden Alley, Northwest, 1928. Based on Sanborn Map Publishing Company, *Insurance Maps of Washington, D.C.* (Pelham, N.Y., 1928).

ready underway. Offering an inexpensive and efficient means of transportation, the trolley would ultimately help release the concentrated population of the pedestrian city.[100] As the trolley began to permit population dispersal, the pressure that had helped to create alley housing diminished. At the same time, housing became available on the street, as former street residents moved to homes in the suburbs.[101] The automobile came into wider use in the 1920s, bringing the potential for an even greater exodus. Thus the alley dwelling, a product of the pedestrian city, became an anachronism in the twentieth-century city. It was an anachronism for other reasons as well: while the compact city of the nineteenth century tolerated "alley ghettoes" within its blocks, the twentieth century "city beautiful" thrived on order and segregation of functions and people. The alley, as a threat to that new social consciousness, had to be removed.[102] Anachronisms, however, do not always disappear simply because they are anachronistic. Although the number of houses had decreased by nearly 40 percent by 1927, 1,346 alley dwellings remained occupied in Northwest and Southwest alone.[103]

During the Depression, New Deal reform leaders, including Eleanor Roosevelt, again sought the removal of the alley housing. In 1934 Congress created the Alley Dwelling Authority "to provide for the discontinuance of the use as dwellings of the buildings situated in alleys in the District of Columbia."[104] No alley houses were to be inhabited after July 1, 1944. Despite legal entanglements and limited funds, the A.D.A. did make considerable progress in opening alleys and rejuvenating the old dwellings.[105] But, as with the earlier

100. Green, *Washington*, II, 50.
101. This exodus and the resultant empty houses probably drew many former alley residents to the streets. That situation made empty alley houses availiable for conversion to garages, rather than the other way around—although at this point only the result, and not the process, is known.
102. See Appendix A for a more complete discussion. See also James Borchert, "Progressive Housing Reform in the District of Columbia: It's a Nice Place to Visit, But We Don't Want You to Live There" (unpublished manuscript, 1972); for the New Deal reformers, Barbara Fant, "The Alley Dwelling Authority: Public Housing and the Urban Environment in Washington, D.C."; Robert M. Preston, "Desegregating and Resegregating Public Housing in the Nation's Capital," papers delivered at the second annual conference on Washington, D.C., Historical Studies, Jan. 10, 1975; William Barnes, "The Origins of Urban Renewal: The Public Housing Controversy and the Emergence of a Redevelopment Program in the District of Columbia, 1942–49" (Ph.D dissertation, Syracuse University, 1977).
103. Jones, *Housing of Negroes*, pp. 161–65.
104. *U.S. Statutes at Large*, 48, part I (June 12, 1934), p. 930.
105. The role of another First Lady, Mrs. Eleanor Roosevelt, was crucial in the establishment and maintenance of the A.D.A.

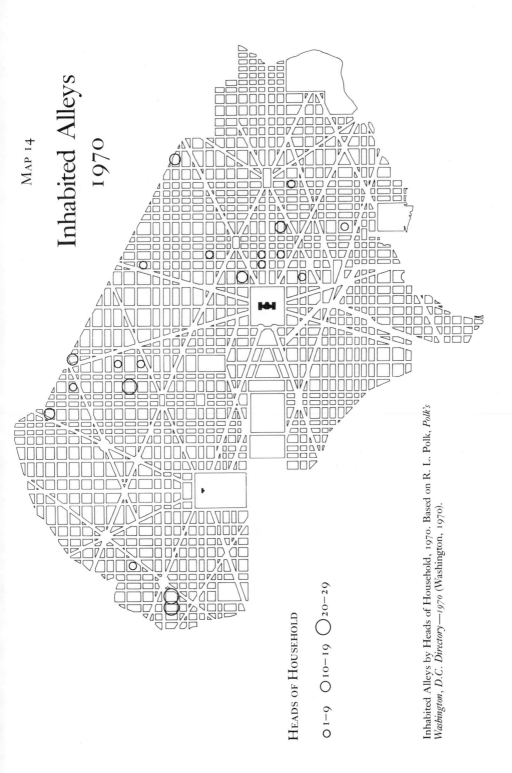

MAP 14

Inhabited Alleys
1970

HEADS OF HOUSEHOLD

○ 1–9 ◯ 10–19 ◯ 20–29

Inhabited Alleys by Heads of Household, 1970. Based on R. L. Polk, *Polk's Washington, D.C. Directory—1970* (Washington, 1970).

PHOTOGRAPH 2.
"Unrestored Alley Dwellings" in Groff Court, N.E., 1970. Photograph by author.

reform movement, a World War and the resulting housing shortage postponed enforcement of the ban—this time until 1955.

Paradoxically, the changes in transportation that made alley dwellings anachronistic also insured their survival, albeit on a small scale. As suburban tracts spread out farther and farther from the city during the late 1940s and early 1950s, a countermovement, small but distinguishable, began. The movement to restore George-town started in the 1930s, and by the late 1940s and 1950s small-scale urban restoration had begun on Capitol Hill and Foggy Bottom. In 1954 citizens' groups involved in the restoration movement successfully engineered repeal of the ban on alley dwellings that was to go into effect the following year. The former "slum" houses saved by this maneuver were then mistakenly renamed "coach-houses."[106]

By 1970 at least 20 inhabited alleys remained with 192 heads of household reported in the city directory. Forty-two houses were

106. Suzanne Berry Sherwood, *Foggy Bottom, 1800–1975: A Study in the Uses of an Urban Neighborhood* (Washington, 1978), p. 29.

PHOTOGRAPH 3.
"Restored Alley Dwellings" in Brown's Court, S.E., 1970. Photograph by author.

listed as vacant. (See Map 14.) While virtually every dwelling was improved in the 1950s to include electricity and indoor plumbing, there were sharp contrasts between alleys. Although some alleys in the Northwest and Northeast had retained their earlier socio-economic status, others in Foggy Bottom and on Capitol Hill had changed considerably. Unskilled workers, who once accounted for the vast majority of employed alley dwellers, made up only 7 percent of the total in 1970, while professionals constituted 9 percent.[107]

Thus, alley dwellings that began as housing for working-class whites, and which became "mini-ghettoes" for black residents following the Civil War, have recently become expensive and highly sought-after residences for affluent Washingtonians. This is an ironic culmination to the efforts of two First Ladies and countless reformers. Perhaps the greatest irony is that, in 1970, two senators and three congressmen resided in the same alleys which Jacob Riis had warned Congress about in 1904: "There is nothing good in that

107. R. L. Polk, *Polk's Washington, D.C., City Directory 1970* (Washington, 1970).

kind of alley. The people who live in there are as far off from the life that goes on outside as though they did not belong to you. . . . What ever standard you set up to live by and to live up to, they do not have. They can do almost as they please in there."[108]

The rest of this study concerns life inside the alley, a life that so upset Riis and his fellow reformers.

108. Jacob Riis, "Housing Problem Facing Congress," p. 163.

Chapter 2
Alley Families

Let the poor family, consisting of a man, his wife, and five children, two or three of whom are adolescent, be imagined occupying one of these chambers, in a cul-de-sac *. . . shut up in a chamber not containing more than* 1000 *feet for the whole . . . we found brothers and sisters, and lodgers of both sexes, sharing the parents' sleeping room, whence arise consequences at the contemplation of which human feeling shudders.*—REPORT OF THE CONDITION OF THE LABORING CLASSES IN THE TOWN OF LEEDS

According to the conventional wisdom, urban life causes the migrant folk family to disintegrate, degenerate, and then lose much of its role in maintaining social control and socialization. The first step in this process involves a change from an extended to a nuclear family, isolating parents and children from the more traditional views of grandparents.[1] The next step involves the separation of parents, with an increasing number of families being headed by one adult—in the black community, most often a woman. Moreover, members of the second generation (the first to be born or raised in the city) are thought to be socialized into the urban environment much more rapidly than their parents, resulting in an unbridgeable generation gap. Of course, this intergenerational distance reflects the decline of the family's influence, as well as suggesting reasons for the rise of juvenile delinquency and crime in areas of high folk concentration.[2] The tendency for folk migrants to take in boarders represents yet another factor contributing to the decline of the family. Further evidence of the family's declining ability to maintain itself can be found in the migrants' heavy reliance on charity and welfare, rather than on finding resources from

1. This development is reported to result largely from migratory patterns that tend to attract the young, as well as from the limited space available in urban housing and the decreased "need" for older people in the urban economy.

2. Increased juvenile delinquency and adult crime resulting from urbanization are considered in chapters 4 and 5, respectively.

within. The folk family's need to find housing in quarters that do not provide adequate privacy, and especially the failure to separate sexes and/or children in sleeping arrangements, allegedly led to sexual immorality and deviance, often at an early age. Finally, the clutter, filth, and physical disorder in and around the urban folk house supposedly resulted from the disintegration of the folk family itself, as well as being symptomatic of the city's destructive impact. Nucleation, separation and divorce, the generation gap, boarders, reliance on welfare, sexual immorality and juvenile delinquency, and physical disorder all testify to the destruction of the folk family and the development of a pathological way of life.

These assertions will be tested in light of the alley experience, beginning with consideration of the nuclear, two-parent family. Because this family form has become the key subject for recent "revisionist" studies by historians, we will expend considerable effort on suggesting the limits of that endeavor, while also proposing more reasonable and promising areas of research. Sex roles that vary considerably from those of "mainstream" America will be considered, as well as attitudes toward marriage within the context of order and tradition stemming from the slave experience. We will analyze the nature, function, and importance of the extended and the augmented family, as well as the hypothesis that kinship networks continued to be important for many alley families. Dependence, overcrowding, filth, and disorder will also be considered within a cultural and historical context.

Perhaps the most striking aspect of recent findings on family form is that the nuclear family is not the result of recent urbanization; rather, it has been the dominant form since the late sixteenth century.[3] Recent studies of the form of rural black families also suggest that the nuclear form is the most common.[4] It is not surprising, therefore, that studies of the urban black family also report that the nuclear form occurs most often. Moreover, virtually all these studies report the presence of two parents in most families.

Rather than demonstrating the "family breakdown" reported by earlier scholars, these recent studies suggest considerable stability

3. Peter Laslett and Richard Wall, eds., *Household and Family in Past Time* (Cambridge, Mass., 1972), pp. 1–89. See also Virginia Yans-McLaughlin, *Family and Community: Italian Immigrants in Buffalo, 1880–1930* (Ithaca, N.Y., 1977), pp. 63–64.

4. For example, see Herbert G. Gutman, "Persistent Myths about the Afro-American Family," *Journal of Interdisciplinary History*, 6 (Autumn, 1975): 196; Gutman, *The Black Family in Slavery and Freedom* (New York, 1976), pp. 443–44; and Crandall A. Shifflett, "The Household Composition of Rural Black Families: Louisa County, Virginia, 1880," *Journal of Interdisciplinary History*, 6 (Autumn, 1975): 239.

of the black urban family form. Elizabeth Pleck found that 82 percent of the black families in Boston in 1880 had two parents present, and that 87 percent of the households were headed by males.[5] The black family of the nineteenth-century Ohio River valley cities showed similar "signs of being structurally patriarchal, with two-parent nuclear households the rule not the exception."[6] Moreover, Herbert Gutman and Laurence Glasco found that "Although the percentage of two-parent families varied between New York City, Brooklyn, and Mobile, it never fell below 67 percent and rose to 86 percent" for the period from 1855 to 1875.[7] Finally, although he reports a growing number of extended and augmented families among New York City blacks in 1905, and a relative decline in the number of nuclear families (to 49 percent), Gutman does note that 83 percent of families were headed by two parents.[8]

Analysis of the family structure of Washington's entire 1880 alley population also reveals the dominance of the two-parent form. Of the 2,604 alley households reported in the census, 297 (11 percent) consisted of either one adult living alone or several unrelated persons living together, while 2,307 were family units. Nearly three-fourths of the latter were two-parent households, although there was some variation by race: 79 percent for whites and 74 percent for blacks, respectively. Since the remaining one-quarter of alley household units were headed by widowed adults, only a fairly small proportion of family units can properly be considered "broken." Of these, only 0.3 percent reported divorce.[9] (See Table 33 in Appen-

5. Elizabeth K. Pleck, "The Two-Parent Household: Black Family Structure in Late Nineteenth Century Boston," *Journal of Social History*, 6 (Fall, 1972): 3–31.

6. Paul J. Lammermeier, "The Urban Black Family of the Nineteenth Century: A Study of Black Family Structure in the Ohio Valley, 1850–1880," *Journal of Marriage and the Family*, 35 (Aug., 1973): 455.

7. Herbert G. Gutman and Laurence A. Glasco, "The Buffalo, New York, Negro, 1855–1875: A Study of the Family Structure of Free Negroes and Some of Its Implications," (unpublished paper, 1966), pp. 20–21. See also Frank F. Furstenberg, Jr., Theodore Hershberg, and John Modell, "Family Structure and Ethnicity: A Historical and Comparative Analysis of the Black Family," paper delivered at the American Sociological Association meeting, New York, 1973, Table I.

8. Gutman, *Black Family in Slavery and Freedom*, pp. 452, 530. In Richmond, however, he notes that between 1880 and 1900 the extended family "increased even more rapidly"; by the latter year only 40 percent of households were nuclear. *Ibid.*, p. 448.

9. Since heads of household encompass all units, as opposed to just family units, it should be clear that single-parent household heads are not necessarily widowed. Nevertheless, unsanitary living conditions, crowding, and inadequate income and diets, as well as the dangerous and difficult work alley dwellers were permitted to do, affected health and mortality, as Chapter 5 suggests. Many families undoubtedly had to face the premature death of one or both parents.

PHOTOGRAPH 4.
"Family and Their Home in an Alley Dwelling Area." July, 1941.
Photograph by Ed Rosskam. Farm Security Administration Collection,
Library of Congress.

TABLE 7.
Alley Families, 1880: One- and Two-Parent Families

| | Two-Parent | | |
| | Black | | White |
Generations	N	%	N
One	348	15	42
Two	945	41	168
Three (but only two present)	17	1	1
Three	166	7	18
Subtotals	1,476	64	229
TOTAL		1,705	75%

*This figure does not include one-generation "other related" family units (8), and four generation families (14), which accounts for the difference in the number of families that appear here (2,285) and the total number of families (2,307). See Appendix C, Table 33.

dix C.) Alley families also tended to be nuclear, with 85 percent of white and 78 percent of black families assuming that form.[10]

There is also evidence that the two-parent family form persisted in the alleys well into the twentieth century. Daniel Swinney's study of two Washington alleys in 1938 reported that two-thirds of the 106 households were male-headed. However, Swinney warned that "the data on marital status can only be used as an indication of the situation that really exists, for the concepts of morality in the alley are apparently based on a philosophy that is different from that commonly accepted." He cited "Many couples . . . living together and rearing children" without being legally married. While "some of these liaisons can be considered common-law marriages . . . many are continued for too brief a period to be considered anything other than an illicit relationship." In interview after interview, he was told that "the head of household was married, and then told that the purported spouse was a 'roomer,' or 'housekeeper.'" Moreover, the "records of social agencies with which the inhabitants have been identified reveal many complicated marital situations."[11]

10. Federal Population Census Schedules, 1880, Washington, D.C., RG 29, NA. Computer time was made available through grants from the University of Maryland and the University of California, Santa Cruz.
11. Swinney, "Alley Dwellings and Housing Reform," p. 85. While most qualitative information on alley families comes from the late 1890s through the 1930s, sug-

Table 7—*continued*

	One-Parent			Total	
Black		White			
N	%	N	%	N	%
—	—	—	—	390	17
18	18	54	2	1,585	69
8	1	1	—	27	1
93	4	6	—	283	12
19	23	61	3	2,285*	100
	580	25%			

Swinney's findings reflected those of other alley studies. William Henry Jones found that "an abnormal proportion of alley families are without male breadwinners. Hence, a large number of unmarried mothers may be found in the alleys."[12]

The issue raised by Jones—what is "an abnormal proportion?"—has been with us now for years. It was the basis on which E. Franklin Frazier and Daniel Patrick Moynihan warned the nation about the crisis of the black family; likewise, it is the concern of many historians and other social scientists who have sought to challenge that view. Both sides, of course, have based their arguments on statistical analyses of one census or another, demonstrating either the increase in one-parent families, or the relative persistence of two-parent families until recent years. Unfortunately, both are trying to infer family structure, function, and relations on the basis of data accumulated once every ten years, from a questionnaire that requires conventional responses in terms of household head and relationship. The whole argument revolves around certain ethnocentric assumptions as to the definition of a family, and about what family form is best. Neither the critics nor the defenders in this historical

---

gesting that the migrant family may have broken down from 1880 to 1900, the survey form initially used by Swinney continued to produce substantial "evidence" that two-parent families persisted.

12. Jones, *Housing of Negroes in Washington*, p. 46.

TABLE 8.
Alley Families, 1880: One- and Two-Parent Families, by Race

	Two-Parent		One-Parent		Total	
	N	%	N	%	N	%
Black	1,476	74	519	26	1,995	100
White	229	79	61	21	290	100
TOTAL	1,705	75	580	25	2,285*	100

*For explanation of this total, see Table 7, note.

numbers game have transcended the moralistic boundaries established by the reformers.[13]

Unfortunately, the statistical controversy over the black family's historical development fails to raise the crucial questions of function within a cultural context; it also fails to deal with the various family forms, and how these relate to each other in specific contexts. Determining which side is correct in the controversy is less important than understanding how the family or families function.[14] Moreover, one must consider not just the "form" of one family or another, but how "ideal types" are actually related to one another. Certainly all studies suggest that a substantial minority of families were headed by single parents, and in the alleys two-parent and one-parent families often lived next to each other. Since cliometricians consider one form

13. Several historians considered here are aware of the limitations of these data, and of the value judgments involved. Gutman and Glasco have sought to "describe the formal structure of the free Negro family between 1855 and 1875, but do not discuss its functions or comment on the related roles of family members" because of the danger of inferring "too much about family relations from just the formal structure of individual households" ("Buffalo, New York, Negro," p. 21). Nevertheless, in seeking to destroy the "old" model of the black family, they mistakenly chose the opponent's framework, and are locked into the moralistic, ethnocentric assumptions on which it was based. As a number of scholars have recently pointed out, "the relative frequency of family types, both black and white, may not tell us much about family structure" (Shifflett, "Household Composition of Rural Black Families," p. 243). Several recent studies by social scientists and historians have begun to utilize both ethnographic information and quantitative data with more promising results, while more sophisticated use of each has also helped raise new questions and provide new insights on family function. See Shifflett's article; Gutman, *Black Family in Slavery and Freedom*; and Virginia Heyer Young, "Family and Childhood in a Southern Negro Community," *American Anthropologist*, 72 (Apr., 1970): 269–88.

14. Young, "Family and Childhood," pp. 269–88.

organized and the other disorganized, what does it mean when they are found in close proximity?

It is also dangerous to study family patterns via census reports because census figures are based on assumptions and definitions that may not be shared by the people being surveyed. A recent study has demonstrated that some black (as well as many white) people use terms such as mother, father, brother, sister, aunt, or uncle to refer to people with whom they have no actual blood ties. While non-blood "relatives" often do function in these roles, the census inclusion of them under "conventional" definitions obscures far more than it reveals.[15] On the other hand, some repondents have been known to give "conventional" answers that reflect what they thought the interviewer wanted to hear. This kind of response only furthers the potential for distortion.[16]

Another recent study suggests a more useful and workable typology for low-income black families. Ulf Hannerz's participant-observer study of a black community on a "minor street" in Washington finds three general categories: mainstream, swinger, and street family. "Mainstreamers are those who conform most closely to mainstream American assumptions about the 'normal' life." These "relatively stable working-class people" are usually "married and live in nuclear families with a quite stable composition." The street families "are childbearing households. This means that there is practically always an adult woman in the household who is the mother of all, most, or at least some of the children there"; her age is "between the upper twenties and the fifties." The composition of street families "is quite variable, both between households and in a single household over time," and these families tend "to maintain relatively open household membership boundaries." In contrast, the swingers represent a point in the life cycle as well as a lifestyle, encompassing those who are "somewhere between the late teens and the middle thirties in age." Swingers include the offspring of both mainstream and street families. Moreover, Hannerz found a fluidity between these three groups, with the child of a street family becoming a swinger in his twenties, and then developing into a mainstream parent in later years; of course, the opposite was also possible. The close proximity of all three family patterns provided knowledge of and experience

15. Theodore Kennedy, "You Gotta Deal with It: The Relations in the Black Domestic Unit" (Ph.D. dissertation, Princeton University, 1974).

16. As an enumerator for the 1970 census in a racially mixed, blue-collar area of Washington, I developed firsthand awareness of the limitations as well as the strengths of such data.

TABLE 9.
Alley Families, 1880: Nuclear, Extended, and Augmented Families, by Race

	Nuclear				Extended*			
No.	Black		White		Black		White	
Generations	N	%	N	%	N	%	N	%
1	272	12	36	2	23	1	5	—
2	1,044	45	193	8	141	6	13	
3	—		—		246	11	26	
4	—		—		14	1	—	
Subtotal	1,316	57	229	10	424	18	44	
TOTAL		1,545	67%			468	20%	

with the various alternatives. Moreover, there was a visual component to this ordering and structure. While Hannerz notes that "the small row houses in the neighborhood all look rather much alike," it "is usually not very hard to detect from the outside which houses . . . are the homes of mainstreamers. The new metal and screen doors, the venetian blinds, and the flower pots in the windows are usually absent from other people's houses." When entering a mainstreamer's home, one finds that behind "the drab exterior there is often a home which looks quite out of place in a predominantly low-income neighborhood."[17]

Daniel Swinney made similar observations about the two alleys he studied: "Although most of the houses are in the same physical state of disrepair, it is interesting to note that the inhabitants have made several of the dwellings quite habitable." Moreover, "The habits of the different tenants can be noted by glancing back and forth down the long row of houses. One will be found in a clean sanitary condition; others will be found without a visible symbol of cleanliness. . . . Only the more resourceful have sufficient courage and persistence to try to make their homes more habitable."[18] Swinney was not the only student of alley life to make such observations. Earlier, Clare de Graffenried found in one home "intelligence and cleanliness that would be a credit to any one," while Charles Weller reported on an

17. Hannerz, *Soulside*, pp. 38–39, 46, 50, 42, 39.
18. Swinney, "Alley Dwellings and Housing Reform," p. 147.

Table 9—*continued*

Augmented**				Total	
Black		White			
N	%	N	%	N	%
61	3	1	—	398	17
78	8	16	1	1,585	69
38	1	—		310	13
—		—		14	1
77	12	17	1	2,307	100
	294	13%		2,307	100

"impressively well kept" home of "a colored minister and his wife."[19] In his description of O Street Alley, Weller vividly depicted the dirtiest home and the cleanest one; the residents of the latter "even had the brass valve polished in the toilet," while "The floors upstairs were clean enough to serve literally as tables for an attractive meal."[20] Marion Ratigan concluded a survey by noting that, "With all the notoriety, the alleys remain fundamentally unchanged; some of the homes are comfortable, some are fair and some are, to use an over-used adjective, 'deplorable.' The people who live there represent many different grades of culture; some are coarse migrants, some suspicious and bitter, and others gracious and poised."[21]

Substantial evidence, then, supports the thesis that within a given alley there was considerable variation among families in terms of outlook, aspirations, and values. In referring to this variation, Ratigan

19. de Graffenried, "Typical Alley Houses," p. 11; Weller, *Neglected Neighbors*, p. 97.

20. Weller, *Neglected Neighbors*, p. 109.

21. Ratigan, *Sociological Survey of Disease*, p. 21. In Ernest H. Culbertson's play, *Goat Alley*, the two major male characters reflected these differences. Sam Reed "allas a wuk steady," while Jeff Bisbee "nevah wukked 'less he had ter. He's—he a hard niggah—allas drunk, an' fightin', and shootin' crap ... boas' how many cops he cut" (*Goat Alley: A Tragedy of Negro Life* [Cincinnati, 1922], p. 21). Equally interesting are the similar descriptions of two working-class homes in Robert and Helen Lynd's classic study of Muncie, Indiana (*Middletown* [New York, 1956], pp. 99–100). Unfortunately, the Lynds chose not to use these descriptions as unobtrusive guides to different attitudes, values, and aspirations in the working class.

TABLE 10.
Black Alley Families, 1880: Nuclear, Extended, and Augmented
(87% of All Alley Families)

	Nuclear		Extended*		Augmented**		Total	
	N	%	N	%	N	%	N	%
Families	1,316	65	424	21	277	14	2,017	100

TABLE 11.
White Alley Families, 1880: Nuclear, Extended, and Augmented
(13% of All Alley Families)

	Nuclear		Extended*		Augmented**		Total	
	N	%	N	%	N	%	N	%
Families	229	79	44	15	17	6	290	100

*Includes all extended-augmented families.
**Does not include any extended-augmented families.

noted that the "stable, home-loving people . . . have nothing to do with people 'like that' but isolate themselves and pay little attention to their puerile and frivolous neighbors."[22] While this undoubtedly happened in many cases, the interaction between those with different aspirations is more likely, and important. Swinney asked an elderly man who had "indicated that he was religiously inclined" what he thought about the "'bad folk in the alley.' He replied that they didn't bother him except that he occasionally lost a little sleep when one of them got drunk and frequently he had to be 'God's servant' and help them out of trouble."[23]

22. Ratigan, *Sociological Survey of Disease*, p. 118.

23. Swinney, "Alley Dwellings and Housing Reform," p. 137. Ethel Waters, who grew up in several Philadelphia alleys, remembered that "Mom had the curious idea that she could keep me out of mischief by continually sending me on errands or by telling me to take a walk in the park. Hating the neighborhood as violently as she did, she always pulled the shades down low and wouldn't look out on the alley even if she heard an explosion out there." Nevertheless, Waters noted, "This permitted me to play in peace with children she disapproved of, right in front of my own door" (Ethel Waters with Charles Samuels, *His Eye Is on the Sparrow: An Autobiography* [Garden City, N.Y., 1951], p. 22). "Mom," who was really her grandmother, was a mainstreamer, while her own mother and aunts were swingers, suggesting again the diversity not only between families, but within a given family as well (*Ibid.*, p. 9).

Because of this tendency, because the similarities between those with different aspirations are greater than their differences, and because of the implicit danger of dividing families into value-laden groups, my effort here is directed toward explicating the central tendencies of alley family life. Nevertheless, the fact that considerable variation exists is critical in its own right, and has important implications for potential changes in the forms of alley life. The alley family had several alternatives, and the family's realization that choices were possible—and made—suggests considerable order.

Isolating the central tendencies of alley family life is not easy. Given the nature of available sources and records, we can only determine some of the parameters of the alley family. The subtleties are difficult to discern, and even some of the more central tendencies are obscure. Nevertheless, much can be learned about the order and form of alley families. We can consider, for instance, Aunt Jane, whose family was one of several that provided the focus for three different studies in the late 1930s and early 1940s.

> Auntie Jane is about forty years old, she is heavy-set and strong. . . . She dresses in men's shoes, wears a man's hat and sweater, and a heavy dark dress. She gets up early and takes excellent care of her children, they are always neat and attractively dressed and have gentle, pleasant manners.

> The four-room house is crowded and disorderly but comfortable. It has all necessary furniture. The sitting room is heated with an oil stove and in the kitchen is a large stove in which wood gathered from the streets or wrecked buildings is used.

> Auntie Jane is the mother of two grown daughters, Gladys and another girl whose name I do not know and whom we have seldom seen, though she is said to live in the Court. Auntie Jane was the common-law wife of the father of these girls. Lonnie, Gus and Joe are said to be the children of her second or third common-law husband, although they do not bear his name . . . this man is the older brother of Bill Hutchins [head of another household in this court]. Through the Juvenile Court he pays for the support of his children. He is very domestic and will sit for hours in the doorway with Joe in his lap. He is a steady worker and is respected by everyone in the court.

> Aunt Jane has lived in the Court for many years, everyone turns to her when they are in trouble. She is energetic herself

and, though she believes that others should help themselves, she never refuses to give to others.

Auntie Jane does not attend any church although she went to elder Mischeaux's [*sic*] services in the Ball Park.

Whenever she meets us on the street she offers to help in carrying bundles. I would turn to her for help and protection at any time, sure that she, not only is fond of me and will-ing to help but that she knows how to meet all the dangers of life in Central Court.

I always think of her as I saw her one cold, dark, wintry day when I came suddenly around the corner of the alley. The two small houses in which Mrs. Merrill had lived were being torn down. Auntie Jane in her men's clothing, led a group of women and children in collecting and storing the wooden planks as they were torn off the beams. . . . Auntie Jane was full of vigor, joyous as a hunter or fisher securing food—she had secured *warmth* for the Court. The children stayed home from school, Gladys was there, the workmen obligingly slid the freed planks to the women.

Gladys is Auntie Jane's daughter. She is the mother of Her-man, age seven. We know relatively little about Gladys but she is a power in the court. . . . She is a handsome woman of perhaps twenty-five, well built, and full of vitality, [a night club hostess], and she is utterly fearless. Herman is an il-legitimate child.

Gladys has a long record of giving help when needed and knowing what to do "standing up for herself and the Court" in dealing with the world outside Center Court.

Gladys' child, Herman, has quiet, charming manners . . . to be Gladys' boy gives prestige in the Court. He is always neat and clean when he leaves home. His mother loves him dearly. His eleven-year-old aunt and two uncles, seven and three years of age treat him as a brother.

Auntie Jane's youngest girl, Lonnie, is a model child, eleven years of age, she is well-built and healthy.

Her mother had twenty-six dresses washed and ironed for Lonnie when she began school; wearing one a day she care-fully rotates through the supply. They are never torn or faded, yet, she always has a "new dress" at Christmas or for her birthday.

Auntie Jane's next to the youngest child is seven years old. Gus . . . is always neat and clean when he comes in the morning but by noon!

Auntie Jane's "baby" is a well-built boy of three, he is always out playing with Gus and Herman. . . . He has much more initiative than Lonnie or Gus and is affectionately known as "Joe Louis" and always called a "bad boy."

Aunt Jane's mother lives next door to her and takes a very active interest in the children. She is the only one in the court who takes the children to Church.[24]

One of the most striking aspects of this case record and many others was in its portrayal of the woman's role in the alley family. According to three observers, Aunt Jane was the central figure in her family. While it was easy for these students to see this as a matriarchy, an example of disorder, it was in fact continuing patterns developed in the slave family, which "rested on a much greater equality between men and women than had the white family." Slavery "had bred strong women. The strength of the women did not necessarily undermine the men; often, it supported them."[25] Weller noted this tendency when he observed that "Alley folks speak usually of the 'lady who has the room upstairs,' ignoring her male companion. They refer to Alice Weaver's house instead of Harry Weaver's."[26] Similarly, in her 1953 study Pablo observed that "the woman holds more prominence than the man in Temperance Court."[27]

24. Compiled from the "case records" presented in Gladys Sellew, *A Deviant Social Situation: A Court* (Washington, 1938), pp. 58–70; Aubry, "Ambitions of Youth," pp. 15–16; and Dora Bessie Somerville, "A Study of a Group of Negro Children Living in an Alley Culture" (unpublished M.A. thesis, Catholic University of America, 1941), pp. 25–26.

25. Eugene D. Genovese, *Roll, Jordan, Roll: The World the Slaves Made* (New York, 1974), p. 501. In a discussion of his concentric zone theory, the noted urban and family sociologist Ernest W. Burgess referred to the commuter's zone as an area where "the mother . . . become[s] the center of the family life," because the male household heads were gone for such a large part of the day and so many of the local activities were run by women. See his "Urban Areas," in *Chicago: An Experiment in Social Research*, ed. T. V. Smith and L. D. White (Chicago, 1929), p. 123.

26. Weller, *Neglected Neighbors*, p. 28.

27. Pablo, "Housing Needs and Social Problems," p. 48. Young notes that this is because "In many families the mother is thus the permanent figure. Her children may have a series of fathers as she first has children out of wedlock and then may

The more active role of women is partly due to the labor market. "Seemingly, the life of the alley family depends almost entirely upon the female supporter," Jones's interviewers concluded. "In most instances, the woman was found to be the financial manager, and the productive wage earner of the family."[28] Most sources, however, place at least part of the blame for this situation on the male. The Washington *Star* noted that it is "a fact of alley life that most of the burden of providing for the household falls upon the women, who are busy all day in service or taking in laundry work. The men perhaps earn a larger wage per day, but they are often idle on account of sprees or sickness."[29] Similarly, Weller observed that "in the Ashton family the woman keeps steadily at work in service; the man, a plumber's helper, earns more per day than she but he is idle a great deal on account of drunken sprees or spells of sickness."[30] Nevertheless, Weller does concede that "the limitations and difficulties by which colored men are handicapped in finding employment" afford a partial explanation for the greater reliance on female support. (This subject will be considered more fully in Chapter Five.)

It is useful and important to note that while these observers found men to be significantly active in the alley family, they failed to make use of those findings. Jones mentions a man who is "kept" by a woman, in return for which he maintains "a reasonable amount of order about the house."[31] In another case, a man belonged to a gang involved in bootlegging and thievery. "This type of work enabled him to be home a great deal, where his work was that of looking after a six-year-old child that is being brought up as a juvenile member of his gang. The mother of this child is a regular worker. Daily she goes to her job in order to meet the demands of her home."[32] The case record of Aunt Jane also depicted her husband caring for their son.

---

have one or more marriages" (Young, "Family and Children in a Southern Community," p. 274). Finally, women dominated the alley population 54 percent (5,730) to 46 percent (4,884), a condition that encouraged a central role.

28. Jones, *Housing of Negroes in Washington*, p. 48; see also Weller, *Neglected Neighbors*, p. 28. Jones often quotes from an unpublished manuscript which consisted of the personal notes (undated) of two female investigators. The similarities of wording between Weller's quotes from one of his fieldworkers, Janet E. Kemp, and Jones's later study suggest that Jones or his investigators relied heavily on Kemp's findings, or that they are both working from the same notes.

29. Washington *Star*, July 30, 1911.

30. *Neglected Neighbors*, p. 28.

31. Quoted in Jones, *Housing of Negroes in Washington*, p. 49.

32. Quoted *ibid.*, p. 48.

Photograph 5 suggests the results of a life of hard manual labor on alley men, as well as illustrating this "domestic role." It is impossible to determine the prevalence of this role, yet at least some men obviously took care of the children on days when they could not find work. Jones reports that "In three out of every five homes visited, [the investigators] were greeted at the door by men." The fact that men were so frequently at home, and possibly active in child care, certainly calls into question studies which assert that young black males lacked role models.

Attitudes toward marriage also differed considerably from those alleged to be mainstream; yet within the alley community they reflected a common experience, as well as a moral order. Aubry reports that Louise, a common-law wife for two years, had a typical (if not universally held) attitude toward marriage: she did "not want to be tied to one man all her life."[33] Since she already had one illegitimate child, Aubry noted that Louise's "tendency toward promiscuity" might lead one "to believe that she will continue to abide by the laws of the Court."[34] Most observers noted the comparatively high rate of illegitimacy in the alleys.[35] As one woman stated in an interview, "'this my son, but he has no father'. . . when asked if she had ever been married, she exclaimed emphatically, 'No,' and stated that she had no idea of doing so soon."[36] Although recent studies have demonstrated that premarital sexual relations and pregnancy were common, from the slave era to the present, this reflects not "licentiousness," but culturally defined and acceptable prenuptial intercourse.[37] The occurrence of an "early pregnancy" created few problems for either the woman or her family. Jones quoted his interviewers as concluding that "Being an unmarried mother seems to be nothing of which these young women are ashamed. Rather, it is something of which they boast."[38]

33. Aubry, "Ambitions of Youth," p. 46.
34. *Ibid.*
35. The city's health officer reported that, in 1914, half of the children born to alley women were illegitimate. See Jones, *Housing of Negroes in Washington*, p. 46.
36. Quoted *ibid.*, pp. 47–48.
37. Gutman, *Black Family in Slavery and Freedom*, pp. 45–100.
38. Quoted in Jones, *Housing of Negroes in Washington*, p. 46. See also Swinney, "Alley Dwellings and Housing Reform," p. 85. Nor did it seem to be a problem for many people. Gutman quotes a British physician who in 1833 reported that "sexual intercourse was almost universal prior to marriage in the [English] agricultural districts," while Genovese notes that diaries of "the ladies of the planter class" described "their own quota of premarital and extramarital adventures." Finally, "by any reasonable standard there was a great deal of illicit sex activity in the Puritan small town of New England and the Middle West . . . the general tolerance with which they

PHOTOGRAPH 5.
"Schoots [sic] Court with Senate Office Building in the background. Four very small rooms rent for fifteen and eighteen dollars a month with water and privy in backyard. It used to rent for six and eight dollars. Frank

Coles and his friend are sitting on the bench. He was a cement plasterer but has been on relief for the past year. He has frequent heart attacks and swollen feet and ankles." September, 1941. Photograph by Marion Post Wolcott. Farm Security Administration Collection, Library of Congress.

We cannot know how many alley families resulted from short- and long-term liaisons. For many women, premarital affairs and pregnancy were probably fairly common. But, as with English peasants, once a mate was decided upon, the couple's union lasted until one of them died. For others (probably a substantial minority) a sequence of unions and marriages was the pattern. Either kind of case had clear guidelines to follow. A recent study of black family patterns in a small Georgia town may give some indication of these, although the limited data on alley families only suggest (rather than prove) that these were the operating principles.

> In Georgiatown, the Negro family is functional and sys-
> tematic. The potential for social dysfunction in the high il-
> legitimacy rate and frequent marital dissolutions is compen-
> sated for by other parts of the system, so that as a whole the
> patterns of family organization are functional. Indeed, il-
> legitimacy and separation are necessary concomitants of the
> emotional underpinning of the system. Illegitimate births are
> especially common before the first marriage. Of forty-four
> women who gave life histories, at least twenty-one had one or
> more children before marriage. The unwed mother almost
> never forms a separate household, but remains with her own
> childhood family, sometimes working and relying on her fam-
> ily for help in child care. . . . The child probably does not
> suffer from its illegitimacy. Its mother shows the immense
> pride in her baby that is typical of all births in this com-
> munity. . . . The first child is the most fondled and most
> stimulated and often becomes the most self-confident and ca-
> pable of all the children in a family, whether or not he is
> illegitimate as many first children are.[39]

Because young unmarried mothers often stayed in their parents' homes, it is not surprising that a substantial minority of extended

---

were regarded was an encouragement to potential sinners." (Quotations from Gutman, *Black Families in Slavery and Freedom*, p. 64; Genovese, *Roll, Jordan, Roll*, p. 465;
and Page Smith, *As a City Upon a Hill* [Cambridge, Mass., 1966], p. 63.)

39. Young, "Family and Children in a Southern Community," p. 273. See also
Demitri B. Shimkin, Gloria J. Louie, and Dennis A. Frate, "The Extended Black
Family: A Basic Rural Institution and a Mechanism of Urban Adaptation," paper
delivered at the International Congress of Anthropological and Ethnographical Sci-
ences, Chicago, 1974 (for a summary of that paper, see Hamilton Bims, "The Black
Family: A Proud Reappraisal," *Ebony*, 29 [Mar., 1974]: 118–27; Raymond T. Smith,
"The Nuclear Family in Afro-American Kinship," *Journal of Comparative History*, 1
(Autumn, 1970): 56. See Waters, *His Eye Is on the Sparrow*, pp. 3–11, for an example
of this process.

PHOTOGRAPH 6.
"Youngsters in the Doorway of an Alley Dwelling." November, 1935.
Photograph by Carl Mydans. Farm Security Administration Collection,
Library of Congress.

families continued to exist. Extended families constituted over one-
fifth of all alley families in 1880. Not only did this system provide
added support for young daughters beginning motherhood, but it
also established a significant link to the past.

Maternal grandmothers, and occasionally paternal ones as well,
played central family roles. "Mae's mother," for example, "lives
with her and is considered by the children to take the place of a
mother, the children call both their father and mother by their first
names and their grandmother is called 'mother.'"[40] Moreover, she
appears to fulfill much of that role. Two-parent families also could
be expected to perform the same function, as in the case of a mid-
dle-aged couple in Dixon's Court who had "four children. Two of
the children belonged to the residents' daughter and were born out

40. Sellew, *Deviant Social Situation*, p. 96. Similarly, Ethel Waters: "Mom (when I
say that I mean my grandmother; when I was very small I called my mother Louise
and later on Momweeze)" (*His Eye Is on the Sparrow*, p. 3).

of wedlock. The mother, a young girl, apparently just gave these children to this woman who very kindly took them in and is taking care of them. She is not receiving financial aid from any agency at this time."[41] Finally, in cases of tragedy or trouble, maternal grandmothers often took on family responsibilities. One "old grandmother of eight children" took up "the burden of providing for the children's welfare" after her daughter died and her son-in-law was unable to care for them.[42] The case records of the Board of Children's Guardians describe a similar situation, in which the grandmother assumed responsibility for a child when the father died and the mother had to work to support her family.[43]

The alley family had considerable fluidity and flexibility in its membership. Certainly the most common variation was for a nuclear family to take in other relatives, making an extended family. In Aunt Jane's family Gladys' son, Herman, was taken in, while Snow Kelley of Bell Court had assumed responsibility for several of his brother's children.[44] The Brown family, who lived near Aunt Jane, had taken in Stanton, Mrs. Brown's nephew, when the boy's mother died and his father became ill. Since Mrs. Brown's sister also lived in the same alley, Stanton was able to stay there with his other aunt on occasion.[45] In another case a family was broken when the mother died and the father was hospitalized. "The youngest was taken by Mrs. X. . . . [the father's sister] when the mother died.

41. Washington *Afro-American*, Dec. 26, 1953. This is the same process reported by Young and others. "The Negro family maintains strong ties over three or four generations. It is not organized as a multigenerational household, but the grandparental tie on either side is easily and often invoked in a variety of arrangements. These multigenerational ties lend stability to the system by protecting unmarried mothers and children born outside of marriage" (Young, "Family and Children in a Southern Community," p. 274).

42. Washington *Star*, July 30, 1911.

43. Records of the District of Columbia, RG 351, NA. Board of Children's Guardians, *Children's History*, III, 1095. See also I, 452–54; II, 571, 631, 833; III, 1111, 1129, 1174, 1243, 1266, 1284, 1392, 1455; and IV, 1519. Cases where both grandparents were called on to raise the children due to problems or death: II, 599; III, 1098. Cases where grandfathers were called on: III, 1124. The case records do not include every child taken in for parental neglect, parental inability to care for, incorrigibility, or crime; nevertheless, they do represent a considerable proportion of such cases. I searched each case record for an address. If the parents, the supporting parent, or in some cases the child had an alley address, I took extensive notes on the record. This source proved especially valuable for insights into family structure and function, location and extent of contact with relatives, residential persistence and mobility, spatial relationship between residence and place of work, as well as sex roles and juvenile delinquency.

44. Washington *Star*, Feb. 24, 1950.

45. Sellew, *Deviant Social Situation*, pp. 83, 119.

She will bring it up as her own. The other child is with an aunt in Bowie, Md."[46] A substantial number of cases indicate that parental inability to support the family, or incorrigibility of a child, could lead to placement with other relatives.[47]

Swinney's report on another such instance demonstrates the dangers that arise when an interviewer is not persistent. When he asked how many people slept in the interviewee's house, the response was four. However, earlier in the interview "an aunt had been mentioned, so the interviewer asked about her. The reply was, 'Yes sur, she has been sleeping here, but she is just visiting.'" Further questions revealed that the aunt had three children, and that they had all been "visiting" for six months.[48]

This incorporation of kin into the nuclear family clearly demonstrates the persistence of familial obligations and affective ties. Gutman has described this practice between "slave and former slave adult siblings and between slave aunts and uncles and their nieces and nephews."[49] Moreover, because the alley dwellers' difficult living conditions made reliance on kin necessary, and because large numbers of very young mothers continued to live with their parents, many families were probably extended at one point or another, even though only a substantial minority of extended families were ever reported at a given time. Death, disease, injury, or the dissolution of brothers' and sisters' families extended the family unit, as kin sought to help and protect one another. Thus extended and nuclear families were both universal; each reflected a given family's stage in the life cycle, rather than a continuous experience.[50]

The family's expansion by other than procreative means was not limited to the inclusion of additional relatives. Motherless children, or offspring of mothers who could not care for them, would be given to others who were more able or willing. "'No, Sadie isn't

---

46. Board of Children's Guardians, *Children's History*, II, 725.

47. *Ibid.*, I, 78–79, 445; II, 734, 874, 929; III, 1129, 1162, 1179, 1275, 1341, 1394–95, 1425, 1454, 1469.

48. Swinney, "Alley Dwellings and Housing Reform," p. 83.

49. Gutman, *Black Family in Slavery and Freedom*, p. 201.

50. Shifflett has argued that black families in rural Virginia go through stages, and that, based on need, they tend to be nuclear at one point and extended at another. Shifflett, "Household Composition of Rural Black Families," pp. 235–60. Similarly, Young has noted that "Although many families achieve stability well after childrearing is underway, the grandparental families usually serve as secure social units for children until their mothers make a stable marriage. Childbearing usually begins in the middle or late teens, and most women have achieved a relatively stable marriage by their midtwenties" (Young, "Family and Children in a Southern Community," p. 274).

mine,'" a Blagden Alley resident reported, "'her mother just left her here an' there was no one else to bring her up.'"[51] Similarly, "Mrs. Colvin kept and reared a motherless girl who afterward went wrong and became . . . 'nothing but a runabout.' Yet when this runabout brought back her sickly, syphilitic infant to Mrs. Colvin, she accepted the burden and is raising the unattractive child tenderly, regardless of the fact that she has no responsibility whatever for it and that its mother proved unsatisfactory and ungrateful."[52]

Even more interesting is the role played by those who are generally referred to as lodgers or boarders. While most studies stress the dangers of lodgers to a stable family, such people "cannot literally be characterized as lodgers since the majority of them are living there as part of the families and not as roomers or boarders even though they are not a member of the immediate family."[53] In Snow's Court, Swinney reported forty such "boarders," who "are in many instances an economic asset to the families with whom they are residing. Some of them pay $1.50 to $2.50 per room per week, and are given the use of the kitchen to prepare their meals if they so desire. Others, particularly in the case of relatives, share equally in the expenses of the household." Nevertheless, an "unknown percentage of the lodgers are . . . liabilities rather than assets from an economic viewpoint. They live and often eat with the family and seldom are able to contribute to the income." Swinney was impressed by the generosity of the alley inhabitants, noting that "if they like someone their homes are open to him. Sleeping quarters are arranged and available food is portioned out. If these extra persons are unable to contribute to household expenses nothing is said, and they are seldom evicted unless they become quarrelsome in an obnoxious manner."[54] In a case cited earlier, where the gang-member father stayed home to take care of the child while his wife worked, "When both the father and mother are out, a young male boarder and member of this same underworld gang is kind enough to take care of this little child."[55] Finally, in her study of Temperance Court, Pablo also found that "three households had independent roomers or friends who shared the household expenses; including the monthly rent."[56]

To Weller and others, the above activities represented "discord,

51. Weller, *Neglected Neighbors*, p. 33.

52. *Ibid*. Gutman notes a similar practice among slaves; see *Black Family in Slavery and Freedom*, pp. 224–26.

53. Swinney, "Alley Dwellers and Housing Reform," pp. 79–81.

54. *Ibid*., pp. 90–91.

55. Quoted in Jones, *Housing of Negroes in Washington*, p. 48.

56. Pablo, "Housing Needs and Social Problems," p. 48.

disorder, and a constant seething 'mixup' of the population."[57] In fact, the family's network was merely expanding to include more and more members. Certainly one factor influencing this development was the existence of resources so limited that they could not, in times of sickness, unemployment, or death, avert total destruction of the family. One way to combat this ever-present possibility was to expand the family's network so that more people could be drawn on for help in times of trouble. Taking a boarder meant incorporating another person into the family; it also meant that aid and support were reciprocal. If such persons were ill or unable to find work, the family would assist them, as it would any member, with the expectation that they would help in return when they could.[58] This practice is also clearly a continuation from the slave experience, when "slaves often took orphans, old people, or single friends in to live with them rather than leave them to a barracks-like existence."[59] This is meant to suggest not that boarders were never disruptive influences on family life, but that for many alley dwellers the practice was well known, and had established guidelines which helped to mitigate these disrupting influences.

Yet another way of tracing the parameters of the alley family is by examining the family forms more closely. It has already been noted that most alley families in the 1880s were nuclear, consisting only of parent(s) and their children. Studies of the black family elsewhere report similar majorities. Unfortunately, these findings seriously distort reality: in 1880 over one-third of all family units were either extended, augmented, or both. Moreover, a careful ex-

57. Weller, *Neglected Neighbors*, p. 69. Although only slightly over 13 percent of all family units had boarders living with them in 1880, this low figure is somewhat deceptive. Alley dwellers were always secretive about the numbers of people living in a household. Moreover, taking in boarders probably reflected family need (or the need of friends), and as a result was often related to a family's point in the life cycle. Many families undoubtedly had boarders at one point or another.

58. Smith has noted that "Lower-class Afro-American households in particular, have highly elastic boundaries. There is a constant coming and going of people, and it is frequently difficult to determine just which household a given individual belongs to at any particular moment" ("Nuclear Family in Afro-American Kinship," p. 68). Nevertheless, this clearly patterned behavior permits survival in difficult circumstances. For a complete discussion of this process, see Carol B. Stack, *All Our Kin: Strategies for Survival in a Black Community* (New York, 1974); Jacquelin S. Mithun, "Cooperation and Solidarity as Survival Necessities in a Black Urban Community," *Urban Anthropology*, 2 (Spring, 1973): 25–34; Shifflett, "Household Composition of Rural Black Families," p. 250. Yans-McLaughlin has reported the same practice among Italian immigrants in Buffalo; see *Family and Community*, p. 56.

59. Genovese, *Roll, Jordan, Roll*, p. 524. See also Gutman, *Black Family in Slavery and Freedom*, pp. 197, 220, 228.

amination of the manuscript census revealed some interesting results. By comparing names, ages, birthplaces, and parental birthplaces of alley residents, it was possible to find nearly seventy household units that appeared related to other individual units in the same alley, while on four occasions the relationship involved three different units in an alley. At least four families were also found to have relatives in nearby alleys. The most striking example of this extended kinship network was visible in Donohue's Alley in Southwest, where three different houses held one extended kinship network of sixteen people. In other cases, people who were obviously relatives were listed as boarders.[60] Because my method involved accidental and haphazard discovery, rather than any "scientific linkage system," these figures mean very little. Moreover, my linkages were facilitated by a similar last name; since married relatives would often have different names, it is quite likely that many more families had blood relatives living nearby, not to mention "adopted relatives."[61]

Qualitative sources support these assertions. As noted earlier, Aunt Jane's mother lived next door, while her husband's brother was head of another household and her two eldest daughters also lived in the same alley. Mrs. Brown, who took in her brother's child, Stanton, also had a sister living in the same alley. Pablo reported that the "residents of six of the twenty-six households" in Temperance Court "are interrelated to one another by blood or affinity."[62] Similarly, Swinney, in explaining why some people chose to live in alleys, found one woman who stated "that her mother and two married sisters lived in separate dwellings in the alley. This fact

60. Federal Population Census Schedules, 1880, RG 29, NA. One of the few benefits of doing one's own coding is that the boredom resulting from the task frees one's mind to consider just what use, value, and significance (if any) the census or related material has. I slowly developed the opinion that the census was of little immediate value, at least for answering qualitative questions concerning people's lives. However, it does spark ideas and questions that might not otherwise be considered. In this case, the census led me to formulate the hypothesis that extended families existed on a greater scale than a "straight" analysis of family would normally reveal, and that the extended family went beyond individual household units to include those relatives living under the same roof but in a separate household, as well as relatives living nearby. Researchers began to discover this phenomenon among the alleged nuclear families of suburbia in the 1950s (Scott Greer, "Individual Participation in Mass Society," in *Approaches to the Study of Politics*, ed. Roland Young [Evanston, Ill., 1958], pp. 329–42). This was a very small "gem" of insight for my six months' work.

61. Since the mother-daughter tie is so important in the Afro-American kinship network, it is likely that many more relatives lived near one another but could not be readily discovered because of name changes.

62. Pablo, "Housing Needs and Social Problems," p. 41.

was verified by subsequent interviews with them."[63] Weller found thirteen people in Odd Fellow's Alley who made up "three separate but related families" and were "housed in the six rooms of this two-story frame" house, while in a "white alley" there was a recently married woman who lived next door to her parents.[64] The case records of the Board of Children's Guardians are also occasionally complete enough to confirm that related families lived in the same or nearby alleys.[65]

This was not necessarily a new practice. Genovese notes that "Many plantations had cabins of two rooms separated by a 'dog trot,' or open hall." While some reformers complained about such layouts because of the greater possibilities of quarreling and trouble, "They may, however, have been to the slaves' taste, for they enabled them to live closely as an extended family and to take better care of their children and old folks."[66] Gutman's massive study similarly reveals that plantation slaves developed kinship networks so extensive that every slave on a given plantation might be related to every other.[67]

These extended kinship networks functioned in times of trouble. Stanton was taken in by his father's sister, Mrs. Brown. "For a few hours on Saturdays" Elizabeth Brown, Mrs. Brown's fourteen-year-old daughter, "works . . . scrubbing and cleaning and helping with the babies" of her aunt, who also lives in the alley.[68] Aunt Jane's mother had "a very active interest in the children" and took them to church. Three other families were aided by neighboring relatives when they were evicted from their houses.[69] The case rec-

63. Swinney, "Alley Dwellings and Housing Reform," p. 138.

64. Weller, *Neglected Neighbors*, pp. 80, 45.

65. Board of Children's Guardians, *Children's History*, III, 824. For brother living next door, see III, 1162; for sister and aunt living in the same alley, III, 1320–21; for cousin and godmother living in same alley, III, 1365; for mother and aunt living nearby, III, 1418.

66. Genovese, *Roll, Jordan, Roll*, p. 524.

67. Gutman, *Black Family in Slavery and Freedom*, esp. pp. 96–97, 181. Nor are these the only sources reporting the widespread existence of kinship networks. Shifflett found extended kinship networks in rural Virginia in 1880, while Smith and Stack noted their existence and importance in the 1970s. (Shifflett, "Household Composition of Rural Black Families," p. 259; Smith, "Nuclear Family in Afro-American Kinship," pp. 68, 90–107.) Finally, the alley's extended kinship network conforms closely to the requirements for an "extended family network" described by Elmer P. and Joanne Mitchell Martin, *The Black Extended Family* (Chicago, 1978), pp. 5–16.

68. Sellew, *Deviant Social Situation*, p. 72.

69. Aubry, "Ambitions of Youth," p. 16; Washington *Daily News*, Aug. 29, 1941; Pablo, "Housing Needs and Social Problems," p. 50.

ords of the Board of Children's Guardians also indicate a number of cases where relatives were relied on to adopt children that the immediate family could not support or control.[70]

Finally, these extended kinship networks were cemented by funeral and birth rituals. Relatives from the country visited their alley kin, while the latter made return visits, suggesting that considerable distance did not break the familial ties. Sellew describes one reunion in the Hutchins family: "When the baby was a few weeks old Aline's relatives came down from the country to see the infant. . . . Four generations were in the room. . . . Aline's mother . . . held her infant grandchild and her great-grandchild in her lap and rocked back and forth as she sang. Aunts and uncles and cousins filled the room. The only light came from a small oil lamp. . . . They had been singing for an hour or more in the half-darkness."[71]

Perhaps one of the most enlightening aspects of alley family life concerns the extent to which residents turned to public and private agencies for help and support. Just before Temperance Court's demise in 1953, Pablo reported that "Four families are active cases with the Public Assistance Division," while six families had been cases earlier. Two of these active cases involved aid to dependent children; the others involved a sixty-eight-year-old woman who received old-age assistance, and a fifty-five-year-old deaf man on general public assistance. The latter "whenever possible . . . accepts odd and end jobs in the court."[72] These four active cases represent about 15 percent of the alley's family units. Swinney's study reports considerably more reliance on both public and private agencies in 1938, admittedly a Depression year. Nevertheless, Swinney asserts that "the inhabitants of the alley have not been chronically dependent. The greater majority of them have been known to agencies only since the year 1932 and their contacts with relief agencies have been of short duration. The records reveal that the majority of cases needed relief only as a stop-gap for relatively short periods of unemployment." Moreover, "alley dwellers do not reveal attitudes that chronically dependent families are thought to possess. They accept-

70. Other studies have reported similarly; e.g., Bims, "Black Family," p. 121; Smith, "Nuclear Family in Afro-American Kinship," p. 69.

71. Sellew, *Deviant Social Situation*, p. 113. See also the extensive description of the Brown family attending the funeral of a rural relative in Somerville, "A Study of a Group of Children," pp. 52–55. The case records of the Board of Children's Guardians also indicate visits by children and parents "back home." These visits took alley dwellers to such places as Orange and Madison Run in Orange County, Virginia; Liberty Town, Frederick County, Maryland; and Chester County, Pennsylvania. Board of Children's Guardians, *Children's History*, III, 1162; IV, 1518; III, 1392, 1129.

72. Pablo, "Housing Needs and Social Problems," pp. 55, 56.

ed relief as a stop-gap measure, and if it were denied or discontinued for some reason they assumed that they would be 'able to manage.' Many of them expressed this attitude during interviews with the writer."[73] Ratigan also found "Categorical assistance . . . conspicuously rare among the five hundred and thirty-nine persons studied"; more striking to her were the number of people who could have received aid, but did not.[74]

Alley families, then, found a number of ways to manage. One of the most common strategies involved expanding the numbers of people on whom the family could draw for help; yet, because these networks were reciprocal, and because all of those included in them were confronting the same daily problem of trying to get by, alley families had to find other ways to reduce their expenses. One involved living in fewer rooms, and thus paying less rent. This, of course, led to overcrowding, which was severe in some cases. The map of the sample area in Northwest in 1880 (Map 2) indicates the number of family units living in each alley house. In Shepherd Alley as many as six different families reportedly lived in the same small house; generally, however, crowding was not that severe. These six alleys had an average of 1.6 households per dwelling, while the mean household size for all alleys in 1880 was four.[75] Nevertheless, the alley literature universally expressed horror at the numbers of people sharing common rooms, especially when children and parents slept in the same room. For example, in 1905 an investigator in O Street Alley "found a separate family living in each room [of a four-room brick dwelling]. One room measuring fifteen by fourteen feet by eight feet high with only one small window, contained a father with his grown daughter, the latter's three illegitimate children and another woman who said she was the man's cousin."[76] Weller found "a family of eight people" who lived in two rooms in a brick house in Snow's Court; he noted that both rooms were "filthy. Their small back room, where they all appear to sleep, is particularly dirty."[77]

Such situations are an anathema to the twentieth-century urban

73. Swinney, "Alley Dwellings and Housing Reform," p. 91.

74. Ratigan, *Sociological Survey of Disease*, p. 73. She also pointed out that "Negroes everywhere seem to fare less well than the white recipients of categorical assistance. Proportionately more white people . . . receive benefits" (*ibid.*, p. 72).

75. Borchert, "Race and Place," Table 7. Undoubtedly, many of those houses that reported 4–6 households were in fact extended or augmented to incorporate those "separate" units.

76. Weller, *Neglected Neighbors*, p. 107.

77. *Ibid.*, p. 95. Most alley families were able to separate their children's sleeping areas by sex, and they were often apart from parents.

middle class, who seem to need a different room for every human function. Yet throughout history few save the rich and powerful have been able to afford such luxuries as separate rooms or indoor plumbing. Since most alley families, or at least the heads of household (77 percent in 1880), were born in Virginia or Maryland, they undoubtedly came from rural and slave experiences. As a result, they were used to small and crude living quarters with outdoor plumbing. Genovese reports that the "model" slave quarters, in a design recommended by reformers and seldom realized in practice, were to consist of log cabins "sixteen by eighteen (or twenty) feet, located as many as seventy-five yards apart, raised two or three feet off the ground, and equipped with large fireplaces and chimneys, plank floors, and large if unglazed windows."[78] But few slave houses met these standards, even by 1860. Many had no windows or floors. Josiah Henson described his slave house in Maryland at the end of the 1700s as a log hut without floors: "In a single room were huddled, like cattle, ten or a dozen persons, men, women and children. . . . There were neither bedsteads, nor furniture of any description. Our beds were collections of straw and old rags, thrown down in the corner and boxed in with boards; a single blanket the only covering."[79] Ulrich Bonnell Phillips likewise noted that slave "housing was in huts of one or two rooms per family, commonly crude but weather tight."[80]

In many cases, then, the well-built alley houses were a considerable improvement over the old, poorly constructed one-room slave or sharecropper houses that many alley residents had lived in before migrating to the city.[81] Many people now had the opportunity to rent two separate rooms, one for food preparation, eating, laundry, and entertaining, and another for sleeping; some could even afford to rent an entire four-room alley house and keep at least two rooms for sleeping only. Either arrangement must have been a vast improvement for

78. Genovese, *Roll, Jordan, Roll*, p. 524.

79. Josiah Henson, *Father Henson's Story of His Own Life*, quoted in Genovese, *Roll, Jordan, Roll*, p. 529.

80. Ulrich Bonnell Phillips, *Life and Labor in the Old South* (Boston, 1963), p. 197. Gutman also provides some excellent descriptions of slave houses, and of the slaves' efforts to overcome the limitations of the one or two rooms provided. Gutman, *Black Family in Slavery and Freedom*, pp. 83, 301.

81. Ratigan noted that alley houses, "in keeping with nearly all construction of the last century, are well built" (*A Sociological Survey of Disease*, p. 77). Moreover, while reformers complained about the monotony of the rows of alley houses, these houses (like much of Washington's vernacular residential architecture) have much to commend them aesthetically, if one is willing to look closely enough. Consider, for example, the interesting and decorative brickwork.

those who remembered the one-room slave houses. The important factor here, then, is the continuity with past experience. Overcrowding might have been an affront to middle-class sensibilities, and was undoubtedly detested by those who had to live in those circumstances; however, it does not necessarily imply social disorganization.[82] In some cases such conditions did lead to disorder, but (as in the case of taking in boarders) the experience was not new, and there were clear precedents for handling such conditions.[83] And most alley residents attempted to get their own houses as soon as it became financially possible.

The problems of filth and bad housekeeping are another issue. Many houses were described as "dirty and unkempt," "very dirty and untidy," with yards "full of ashes and trash."[84] The observers who made such statements also saw contradictory evidence, even if they did not act on it. Consider, for example, Aubry's description of Aunt Jane's home, which was preceded by the statement, "The children are kept very clean."[85] Sellew described the same house as "crowded and disorderly, but comfortable."[86] The dirty and unkempt house of the Hutchins family was due to Mrs. Hutchins's illness following the birth of her child; when she recovered, her house was described as "neat and clean."[87] And while a Snow's

82. Ethel Waters commented, "In crowded slum homes one's sex education begins very early indeed. Mine began when I was about three and sleeping in the same room, often in the same bed, with my aunts and my transient 'uncles.' I wasn't fully aware of what was going on but resented it" (*His Eye Is on the Sparrow*, p. 19).

83. Recent research seems to suggest that the "spatial imperative" of Afro-Americans (and at least some West Africans), as expressed in the average size of rooms in folk housing, is a twelve-foot square, approximately the room size of alley houses. John M. Vlach, "Shotgun Houses," *Natural History*, 86 (Feb., 1977): 51–57; Vlach, "The Shotgun House: An African Architectural Legacy," *Pioneer America*, 8 (Jan., 1976): 47–56; (July, 1976), 57–70; and James Deetz, *In Small Things Forgotten: The Archeology of Early American Life* (Garden City, N.Y., 1977), pp. 149–54. Similar research on Anglo and Anglo-American folk housing suggests a different spatial imperative, based on a sixteen-foot square. Henry Glassie, *Folk Housing in Middle Virginia: A Structural Analysis of Historical Artifacts* (Knoxville, 1975), p. 118; Deetz, *In Small Things Forgotten*, pp. 149–54. Given this difference, it is easy to understand why Anglo housing reformers, used to much larger rooms, were so concerned and disturbed by what appeared to be severe crowding. For Afro-Americans, whose cultural experience included many years of living in and construction of rooms of that size, crowding takes on a quite different meaning.

84. Aubry, "Ambitions of Youth," p. 15; Sellew, *Deviant Social Situation*, p. 109; Wilbur Vincent Mallalieu, "A Washington Alley," *Survey*, 29 (Oct. 19, 1912): 70.

85. Aubry, "Ambitions of Youth," p. 15.

86. Sellew, *Deviant Social Situation*, p. 58.

87. *Ibid.*, p. 113.

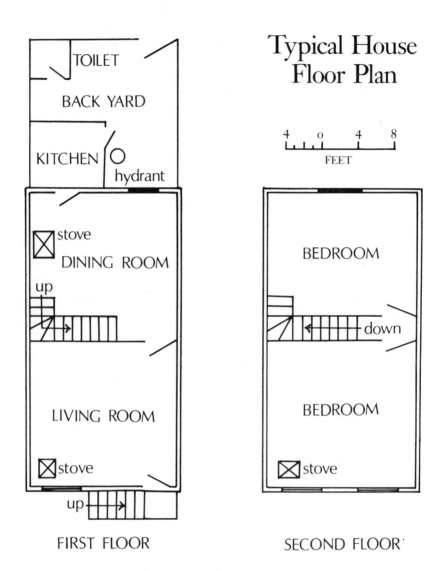

Typical House Floor Plan

TOILET

BACK YARD

KITCHEN ◯ hydrant

stove
DINING ROOM

up

LIVING ROOM

stove

up

FIRST FLOOR

4   0   4   8
FEET

BEDROOM

down

BEDROOM

stove

SECOND FLOOR

DRAWING 2.
Floor Plan of a Typical House. From Leonor Enriquez Pablo, "The Housing Needs and Social Problems of Residents in a Deteriorated Area" (M.S.W. thesis, Catholic University of America, 1953), p. 22. This house is somewhat wider than most alley houses.

Court house had a backyard "full of ashes and trash," the "linens laundered here are beautifully white and well done."[88]

Drawing 2 is a floor plan of a typical alley house. The layout includes two rooms on the first floor, "a living room and a dining-kitchenette room, and a small porch. . . . [See Photographs 7 and 8.] The second floor is reached by a narrow, rickity, dark stairway and has two rooms, also. If the dwelling structure is used as a one-family unit the second floor is the bedrooms." If, however, "the family is big, the living room is converted into a bedroom and oftentimes the dining-kitchenette room too." When a dwelling is "converted into two-family dwelling units, one room is kitchen-dining room while the other is used as bedroom."[89] Some houses were also converted into four one-room apartments. (See Photograph 9.)

Despite the resultant overcrowding, alley dwellers adjusted well to limited space. Ratigan reports that a one-room apartment occupied by five people "was well-kept. We called at 10:00 A.M. and everything was in perfect order. This calls for incomparable skill as a housekeeper."[90] Photograph 9, while perhaps reflecting less than "perfect order," nevertheless is far from unkempt. While there is no doubt that the interiors of some alley houses were shambles, and contained little or no furniture, the vast majority were "generally orderly and clean in spite of old furnishings."[91] Photographs of alley interiors reveal that most houses were simply furnished and organized on the basis of function and utility. During the height of alley housing, reformers and social scientists considered these pho-

88. Mallalieu, "Washington Alley," p. 70. Gutman provides an interesting parallel to the outsider's view of disorder. He quoted Charles Nordhoff's visit in 1863 to rural slave cabins in the South Carolina Sea Islands: "To us, who have been long accustomed to a certain air of comfort and tidiness, it seems extraordinary that these people should live contentedly in the way they do, one moment longer than is absolutely necessary. In our minds this squalor is linked with drunkenness and vicious improvidence; and we unconsciously dislike those who live in this condition. These were my emotions, I confess, when I first entered the cabins of the people here. Those astounding agglomerations of rags, this which seemed to me the most dreary discomfort . . . all this made my heart sink, at first, and I said to myself: Oh! dear! Oh! dear! what can be done with all this. But I found the rags were clean . . . and that the whole affair is not nearly so bad as it looks" (Charles Nordhoff, "Freedmen of South Carolina," in Frank Moore, ed., *Papers of the Day*, no. 1 [1863]: 18–19; quoted in Gutman, *Black Family in Slavery and Freedom*, p. 302).

89. Pablo, "Housing Needs and Social Problems," p. 21. This drawing shows a "summer kitchen" attached to the back of the house. Pablo reported that many of these were too deteriorated to use. Most alley houses did not have such an addition, however.

90. Ratigan, *Sociological Survey of Disease*, p. 5.

91. Somerville, "Study of a Group of Children," p. 23.

PHOTOGRAPH 7.
"Alley House Interior—First Floor Front: Logan Court." Alley Dwelling Authority, National Capital Housing Authority Collection.

PHOTOGRAPH 8.
"Alley House Interior—First Floor Rear: Logan Court." Alley Dwelling Authority, National Capital Housing Authority Collection.

PHOTOGRAPH 9.
One-Room Apartment. "Down in the slums . . . This was a combination bedroom–dining room–kitchen in one of the old houses demolished by the N.C.H.A. on the site of the Carrollsburg Dwellings. Note the oil lamps and the stove. The picture recalls the sentence from the devastating indictment of the Washington slums by the District's Territorial Board of Health in 1877. . . . 'So domiciled are families with all the dignity of tenants having rent to pay.'" National Capital Housing Authority Collection.

tographs as exemplary not only of "slum" conditions, but also of the disorganization that resulted from alley life. Certainly these conditions varied from the middle-class experience, but, given the limited space (and high rents), alley dwellers appear to have adapted in positive and realistic ways. Lacking a cultural or architectural perspective that provides movable walls to make up for limited space (as in Japan), most alley dwellers adapted their rooms, making beds into couches during the day (see Photographs 7 and 9), or folding them up against the wall. Although most furniture was probably secondhand, it was tastefully covered and practically arranged. Interesting adaptations were sometimes engineered—for instance, a trunk might serve as the bottom of a bed, thus combining storage space and sleeping facilities (see Photograph 10), or an icebox which

PHOTOGRAPH 10.
*Trunkbed. "This old stove, which used to heat the former dwelling of an
A.D.A. tenant, is characteristic of many found in older sections of Wash-
ington. Note the ash container below the stove and the soot-blackened
wall." December 4, 1941. National Capital Housing Authority
Collection.*

served both its original purpose and as a table (Photographs 11 and
12). If there was little private space, there were places where one
could go to "escape," as well as communal-family places. A mother
could work in the kitchen and instruct her children in her arts, or at
least be in the same room where children could amuse themselves
near the warmth of the stove. The entire family might also gather
there for meals. (See Photographs 11 and 12.) Windows had curtains, tables had tablecloths, and floors were often covered with car-
pets. Frequently, framed pictures or calendars hung on the walls,
while window boxes occasionally adorned the exterior windows.[92]
Other observers have noted the alley residents' ingenuity in arranging and developing furniture for their specific needs. In 1911 the
Washington *Star* reported that alley residents "often show ingenuity

92. See Appendix B.

<small>P H O T O G R A P H 1 1.</small>
Kitchen. "Woman and Baby in a Slum Area." October, 1937. Photograph by Arthur Rothstein. Farm Security Administration Collection, Library of Congress.

in . . . arranging things for their comfort and health." In one alley home, the "four boys slept in the kitchen downstairs and the girls in a room overhead. Both rooms were unbearable in summer weather," so their mother "set about to find a way to make the children more comfortable." She stretched "an old awning that a patron had given her across the fence and let the children sleep in the back-yard. . . . She found, however, that this scheme didn't admit suffi-cient air, so she nailed several poles at each corner of the fence and raised the awning several feet. This proved a success and the chil-dren were no longer confined to their stuffy room."[93]

Marion Ratigan, who paid the greatest attention to interior deco-ration, arrangement, and furnishings, drew a similar conclusion.[94]

93. Washington *Star*, July 30, 1911.
94. She went to the extent of giving the mean number of furnishings per house-hold: stoves, 1.6 per household (4.3 per house); beds, 2.2 per household; iceboxes, 0.97; tables, 1.6; dressers, 1.3; chairs, 5.1; sets of overstuffed furniture (2 or 3 pieces each), 0.2; pictures, 2.9; radios, 0.14; victrolas, 0.1; pianos, 0.01; and telephones, 0.01. Ratigan, *Sociological Survey of Disease*, pp. 86–94.

PHOTOGRAPH 12.
Kitchen. "Woman and Baby in a Slum Area." October, 1937. Photograph by Arthur Rothstein. Farm Security Administration Collection, Library of Congress. (Photographs 11 and 12 suggest a three-generation family.)

PHOTOGRAPH 13.
Bedroom. "O'Brien's Court." September 14, 1935. Alley Dwelling Authority, National Capital Housing Authority Collection.

In contrast to "general surmise, there is no stereotyped alley home. Many present the commercial artists' delineation of the home of tomorrow; they have a four-piece living room suite, with coffee table of plastic or glass or bedroom suites of flamboyant futuristic or impressionistic designs." One home was even "reminiscent of a sketch from *Godey's Lady's Book*. There were Biedermeier and Hepplewhite chairs, a pier-glass table and a Governor Winthrop desk filled with such treasures as a Cappi della Monte plate, a Meissen group, odd pieces of Wedgewood and Sèvres China, hobnail and milk glass and innumerable figurines and dolls." While not quite as luxurious as the home just described, a bedroom in O'Brien's Court (Photograph 13) does suggest that some homes were comfortable and well furnished. Nevertheless, others were "poor, some very poor with the scantiest furnishing. One had only a mattress on the floor, a kerosene burner and a small pan; there was no table, no dishes, not even a cup from which to drink."[95] Despite these extremes, most houses were orderly and clean, albeit perhaps with old furnishings.

95. *Ibid.*, pp. 80–81. Most interiors and furnishings showed a marked improvement over the "standard" furnishings of a slave cabin, which consisted of "several

Even if the interiors failed to demonstrate the disorganization of alley life, observers were certainly correct about the conditions of alley yards, which were universally described as "filled with uncollected garbage, rubbish and filth."[96] Photographic analysis confirms this condition. Of course, this phenomenon could involve a continuation of medieval folkways. Describing the cramped slave cabins, Genovese noted that "with the physical demands of daily labor so pressing, with insects impossible to control, and with poultry and small animals virtually part of the household, clean, neat, well-ordered cabins required herculean effort and an improbable degree of concern. . . . The slaves, like so many traditional agriculturists, did not draw a sharp line between house and yard and did not highly value household regularity and order."[97] While this explains much of the exterior disorder, an even more interesting and important explanation was offered by Washington *Post* reporter Benjamin Bradlee. Discussing a family in Dingman Place, Bradlee noted that "The backyard is littered with rusted scrap metal to be sold in hours of special need. Broken orange crates are saved for fuel."[98] Certainly Sellew's story of Aunt Jane collecting wood from an alley house's destruction confirms this. "Junking" was a full-time occupation for some alley men, while for others it must have supplemented primary jobs. For young boys it was an important chore.[99] "Junking" involves "collecting of glass bottles and breaking them to be sold as broken glass by the hundreds of pounds; selling of old rags, paper, iron and tin, and any article of value which may be found among trash cans, or on the dumps."[100] Photograph 14 shows a cart that might have been used for this activity. Thus the disorder in the backyard was often the alley family's savings account and insurance policy.

It is important to note that alley residents' efforts to keep their homes and yards clean and orderly were often defeated by the general conditions of alley life. As many of the photographs suggest (es-

---

chairs and a bed, an iron kettle and a brass kettle, an iron pot, and a pair of potracks, a pothook, a frying pan, and a beer barrel" (Genovese, *Roll, Jordan, Roll*, p. 530).

96. Washington Housing Association, "Report on Temperance Court," (Washington, 1952), p. 3.

97. Genovese, *Roll, Jordan, Roll*, p. 528.

98. Washington *Post*, Dec. 19, 1948. Nor was this a new "adaptation," for, as Genovese reports, slaves also "collected jars, bottles, and stoneware, converted the skins of cattle into rawhide for chairs, obtained pots and pans suitable for proper cooking, and built odd pieces of furniture to suit their taste" (*Roll, Jordan, Roll*, p. 531). .

99. Sellew, *Deviant Social Situation*, p. 47.

100. *Ibid.*, p. 61.

PHOTOGRAPH 14.
"Cartman." Washingtoniana Collection, Martin Luther King Memorial Library, Washington, D.C.

pecially Photographs 11 and 12), cracked and broken plaster was common in alley houses, while the city's continual neglect of trash and garbage only helped increase the insect and rodent population. Clearly the most determined housekeeper could be easily discouraged by these conditions.

Nevertheless, the alley family was not the "broken," disordered, and irrelevant institution that most studies have found. Its order, form, and values often differed from those of the mainstream, although certainly many alley residents approached mainstream values to varying extents.[101] The alley family was more flexible than the "ideal" mainstream family, if only because its available re-

101. Whether they meant the same thing is another question. Based on his research on the black family, Theodore Kennedy has suggested that, rather than rejecting the old values and accepting the new (mainstream) ones, the process is additive. Mainstream values "work" in some areas, while in others (most often the black community) different values seem more relevant and useful. As Lawrence W. Levine found, "Emancipation brought educational, occupational, and spatial mobility and mobility that enhanced acculturation. But underlying all the changes there persisted crucial residues of traditional culture which helped shape expression in every sphere of black life" (*Black Culture and Black Consciousness* [New York, 1977], p. 154). See also Gutman, *Black Family in Slavery and Freedom*, p. 261.

sources were so scarce; to survive, alley families had to expand the numbers of people, both related and unrelated, who could help in times of need. Certainly similarities between the slave and alley families suggest that this continues a practice developed much earlier. Simple analysis of family form based on census data therefore provides little insight into the real functions of the alley family. Moreover, the existence of related family units in the same or nearby alleys must certainly alter the description of the family as only or largely nuclear—especially since these family units, while living apart, acted as extended kinship networks, sharing in housework and providing rooms or other necessary assistance. Even country relatives were not isolated from their alley kin, because births, deaths, and family problems brought them together.

Although roles played by alley men and women, as well as their attitudes toward "illegitimacy" and marriage, differed considerably from the "mainstream model," that variance reflects a *different* order, rather than mere disorder. Some studies report that ghetto residents share the mainstream value system, but that, because they are unable to successfully live up to those values, they lead disorganized and hopeless lives. On the other hand, most alley residents rejected (or were unaware of) the mainstream value system. As one study reported, "Being an unmarried mother seems to be nothing of which these young women are ashamed. Rather, it is something of which they boast." And although Aunt Jane "subscribes" to the notion of responsibility for one's self only, she clearly acts out of another value system.[102]

Alley residents were not generally wards of the state. Rather than being indolent "welfare cheaters," they took responsibility for their own lives, demonstrating pride, independence, and strength.

Certainly, few alley houses were finely furnished. If many appeared "disorderly" and "dirty" to observers, it was likely due to the large number of people sharing such a small space. Alley residents demonstrated considerable ingenuity in confronting their space limitations, just as they did in confronting other problems of limited resources.

Not all residents survived the hard alley life without severe problems; certainly some of those households headed by adults living alone or with unrelated adults must have suffered especially. One can see the fragility and tenuousness of alley life by considering

102. This suggests that, in fact, values are additive, but that the alley values prevail because "they work." For an example of the "defeated poor," see Elliot Liebow, *Tally's Corner* (Boston, 1967).

how one small problem, such as an illness, could result in disaster. The lengths to which alley families went to develop strategies for survival indicates the order present in alley life, and serves as an unobtrusive guide to the difficulties and marginality of that life. Alley residents sought to limit the difficulties, reduce the marginality, and exert control over their own lives and environment by constructing neighborhood communities.

Chapter 3
The Alley
Community

*Behind the main street . . . narrow unpaved streets and
alleys harbor prematurely aged, badly deteriorated, urban
housing. . . . In these sections, interior streets and alley
ways are seldom used for wheeled traffic, leaving un-
disturbed the rural functions of the streets as pathway,
meeting place, playground and tethering area for animals.*

*It is this immediate neighborhood, however, which con-
stitutes, after the family, the most important informal social institution for migrants in the city. The cohesiveness of
the neighborhood is strengthened by the tendency of persons from the same village to settle together. Similar to the
situation elsewhere, it is the women, children, and very
old persons who are the most active participants in the
neighborhood-centered social life.—Janet Abu-Lughod,
"Migrant Adjustment to City Life: The Egyptian Case"*

Study of the alley community is difficult. While
there is relatively abundant information on family form and even
function in the manuscript censuses, social surveys, and social welfare agency records, information on the alley itself is often hard to
find and less substantial. One must piece the structure together
from a large number of obscure and tangential sources. Moreover, if
many studies of the family suffer from too narrow a definition and
frame of reference, the definitions of "community" are so diverse
and varied that the word has lost much of its meaning. Twenty-five
years ago one sociologist who sought to come to terms with the various uses of the word found ninety-four different definitions. Despite the obvious variations, the study reported a considerable area
of agreement, with most sociologists holding that community took
place within a geographical area that permitted social interaction.

The specific elements that community required were self-sufficiency; common life; consciousness of kind (homogeneity); common ends, means, and norms; collection of institutions; locality group (proximity); and individuality.[1] More recent efforts to define the elements of community have not varied substantially.[2] Perhaps the most useful one was offered by Robert Nisbet: "By community I mean . . . all forms of relationships which are characterized by a high degree of personal intimacy, emotional depth, moral commitment, social cohesion, and continuity in time." It "is a fusion of feeling and thought, of tradition and commitment, of membership and volition . . . fundamental to the strength of the bond of community is the real or imagined antithesis in the same social setting by the non-communal relations of competition or conflict, utility or contractual assent."[3]

If the task of applying these criteria to existing groups of people seems difficult, it is infinitely harder for the social historian to study people who left little or no written record. One can only sift through the records kept by others, none of which were intended to demonstrate the extent or nature of community. Despite these considerable problems, one can find and describe the form and pattern of the alley community. A number of sociological requirements for the existence of neighborhood and community can be easily established: isolation, proximity, homogeneity, and the need for mutual assistance. The existence and form of community is more difficult to determine, but it can be glimpsed through the alley as a commons and community center, through residential persistence over time, and in residential satisfaction. One can also approach the issue of community by considering the degree of physical and psychic

1. George A. Hillery, Jr., "Definitions of Community: Areas of Agreement," *Rural Sociology*, 20 (June, 1955): 111–23.

2. E.g., Roland Warren identified five major functions that a community must perform: production-distribution-consumption; socialization; social control; social participation; and mutual support. Paul Meadows found six requirements: population, territory, interdependence of specialized parts, integrating culture and social system, consciousness of belonging, and ability to act in a corporate fashion. Warren, *The Community in America* (Chicago, 1972), pp. 9—14; Meadows, "The Idea of Community in the City," in *Perspectives on Urban America*, ed. Melvin I. Urofsky (Garden City, N.Y., 1973), p. 3.

3. Robert A. Nisbet, *The Sociological Tradition* (New York, 1966), pp. 47–48. What is important is not so much the extent to which the evidence presented here approaches the elements of these abstract definitions; no real community fully realizes all aspects implied by the ideal type. Rather, the crucial factor is the extent to which the evidence compiled on the various aspects of alley life adds up to a sum greater than the individual parts, and possesses a form and coherence of its own.

control that alley residents were able to exert over their "turf." The effectiveness of internal social order and control, as well as the existence of a decision-making "body" are vital for the persistence of community. Finally, the community activities, programs, and functions provide evidence for the viability and the form of that community. As with alley families, alley communities varied considerably. While some of these variations will be considered here, the central tendencies of the alley community are the focus of this chapter.

Not every element that makes up the alley "community" is considered in this chapter. Factors such as the extended kinship network, socialization, and worldview are considered, at least in part, in other chapters. However, the extent to which community is inextricably intertwined with all elements of alley life, from family and childhood to work, religion, and folklife, suggests its presence and importance.

As part of the research for his study of Washington alleys, Charles Weller lived as a participant-observer in "Average Alley" (Blagden Alley). His description of his initial entrance into that alley provides considerable information on the alley community:

> It is with some misgivings that one leaves the well lighted outer streets with their impressive residences and turns into a narrow passageway where he must walk by faith, not sight. Noises which faintly recall those of the Midway Plaisance at the world's fair, grow louder as the explorer approaches the wider inside alleys. Night with its dark shadows accentuates the strangeness of the scene. Near a gas light on one of the inner corners a group of people are seen playing together roughly. A cheap phonograph near by rasps out a merry ditty. The shrill cries of children pierce the air as the ragged, dirty youngsters dart about among their elders. Two lads with notably large feet and broken shoes dance skillfully while a slovenly, fat woman picks at her guitar. From the little mission in an alley parlor comes occasionally a wail of primitive, weird chanting. An uncouth black man lounges up to a buxom young woman and hugs her. On a doorstep nearby a young man is heard arguing with his mistress and begging her to "le' me ha' fi' cen'ts."
>
> Older folks, crowded around their doorways, are complaining of the sultry, oppressive August air and some are arranging ironing boards and rocking chairs on which they will sleep all night outside the houses. They call back and

forth to each other across the alley street and speak with notable civility to the policemen who pass, in pairs, at intervals, with their clubs kept close in hand. There is a burst of profane quarrelling occasionally and some fighting, but most of the prevailing noises are merry and careless. Pandemonium reigns. One sees no immediate cause for fear, but feels intuitively a suggestion of evil possibilities and latent danger.[4]

One key element of Weller's description is the sense of isolation from the surrounding streets. Much of this atmosphere results from the alley's physical layout. While street houses faced outward, alley houses faced inward, as Photograph 15 demonstrates. Because fences and sheds were often located at the rear of both the alley and the street houses, neither residents were likely to see or interact with their backyard neighbors. And the street entrance to the interior alley was often unobtrusive at best, ranging from three to fifteen feet in width. (See Photograph 16, and Maps 12 and 13.) The vast majority of houses were built not on this narrow alley that bisected the block, but on the blind thirty-foot H-shaped alley in the block's interior. This alley and the houses on it were not visible from the street. These factors, as well as the distance between owners' residences and their alley properties, resulted in what Weller and others called "hidden communities."[5]

The physical layout of the alley block not only limited interaction between street residents and alley dwellers; it also encouraged social interaction among alley residents. As Leon Festinger noted in his study of student housing at M.I.T.,

> The closer together a number of people live, and the greater the extent to which functional proximity factors cause contacts among these people, the greater the probability of friendships forming and the greater the probability of group formation. If a number of houses are clustered together and also face each other, it is more likely that an informal group will develop than if the houses are more widely spaced and stretch out in a straight line or face away from each other.[6]

Alley houses faced each other across an alley no more than thirty feet wide, and were connected to other houses to form two or more

4. Weller, *Neglected Neighbors*, p. 17.
5. *Ibid.*, pp. 9–11.
6. Leon Festinger, Stanley Schacter, and Kurt Back, *Social Pressures in Informal Groups: A Study of Human Factors in Housing* (Stanford, 1950), p. 161. See also William H. Whyte, Jr., *The Organization Man* (Garden City, N.Y., 1957), Ch. 25.

PHOTOGRAPH 15.
"Aerial View: Logan Court." October 6, 1939. Alley Dwelling Authority, National Capital Housing Authority Collection.

PHOTOGRAPH 16.
"Entrance to Willow Tree Alley." August 3, 1915. Photograph by Roy E. Haynes. John Ihlder Collection, Franklin D. Roosevelt Library.

rows. (See Photograph 15.) The single common entrance to the alley furthered opportunities for face-to-face contact. Since the alleys lacked both vehicle and nonresident pedestrian traffic, the opportunities for knowing one's alley neighbors were even greater.

If the physical layout and ownership patterns tended to severely limit interaction between street and alley residents in a given block, all the other sharp differences between these two groups only increased their social distance. As the 1880 study of the sample area suggested, alley and street dwellers could be clearly different in terms of race, occupation, literacy, family size, and age.[7] On the other hand, alley residents themselves were strikingly alike: in 1880 the population of the six alleys was 93 percent black, with three all black. By 1897 nearly 70 percent of all inhabited alleys were totally segregated. Moreover, alley residents worked almost entirely in unskilled and menial service occupations; 70 percent of employed males in the 1880 alley population, and 95 percent of the employed women, were so occupied. Alley residents also tended to come from the same locales. Half of the heads of household in 1880 were born

7. See Ch. 1, note 30, and Table 22.

in Virginia, while 28 and 10 percent respectively were born in Maryland and Washington. The parents of these household heads were from the same areas (53 percent born in Virginia, and 29 percent and 5 percent in Maryland and the District of Columbia). This homogeneity helped the alleys to achieve a second sociological criterion for the existence of social interaction.[8]

Another factor that probably made neighboring and community easier was the relatively small size of each alley. While alley sizes varied greatly in any given year, the average alley populations for 1880 and 1897 were fifty and seventy-three, respectively. In 1880 half of the alley population lived in alleys of fewer than one hundred, while seventeen years later more than half lived in alleys housing fewer than 150 residents. (See Tables 30 and 32.)

Sociologists have further identified "a strong or continued need for mutual assistance or contact, such as that among newly arrived homeowners (particularly those with children) lacking time to seek out friendships elsewhere."[9] Certainly in the early years alley dwellers were often surrounded by the homes of the white middle class, and in later years by a similarly unfriendly (though most assuredly less threatening) black middle class. The need for mutual assistance was already suggested in the previous chapter, and it requires little imagination for one to understand the possible extent of that need. Since most alley families were young child-rearing units, with very few resources save friends and relatives, it seems reasonable to expect high levels of neighborly interaction.

Although the alleys fit the theoretical requirements for development of neighboring and community, this does not confirm that such communities did, in fact, exist.[10] We must consider a wide va-

8. Herbert Gans, *The Levittowners* (New York, 1967). In contrast to the distribution of birthplaces for heads of households and their parents, most alley residents in 1880 were born in Washington (42 percent), while 32 and 19 percent respectively were born in Virginia and Maryland.

9. William Michelson, *Man and his Urban Environment* (Reading, Mass., 1970), p. 196.

10. Information flow theory also suggests that neighboring and community should exist at high rates. Torsten Hagerstrand and others have demonstrated that "On the average, the density of contacts included in a single person's private-information field must decrease very rapidly with increasing distance." (*Innovations forloppet ur Korologisk Synpunkt* [Lund, Sweden, 1953], p. 237). See also Hagerstrand's *Innovation Diffusions as a Spatial Process*, trans. Allan Pred (Chicago, 1967); Stuart Carter Dodd, "Testing Message Diffusion in Controlled Experiments: Charting the Distance and Time Factors in the Interactance Hypothesis," *American Sociological Review*, 18 (Aug., 1953): 410–16; Dodd, "Diffusion Is Predictable: Testing Probability Models for Laws of Interaction," *American Sociological Review*, 20 (Aug., 1955): 392–406; George

riety of sources to determine whether there was an alley community, and, if so, what that community was like. As with the alley family, only the rough outlines of the alley community are now visible;
yet we can sketch its parameters on a number of levels.

The physical focal point of the alley community was the alley itself, the meeting place and social center. In the early years, residents of Southwest alleys had "no conveniences for cooking or
washing" in their houses; as a result, they often shared "an old broken stove placed outside on the commons."[11] Laundry was done
"on the common," making social interaction both likely and
necessary.[12]

Considerably more information exists on the later use of the alley
as commons. One method that can be used to gain insights on the
extent of neighboring and community is photoanalysis. Numerous
photographs show chairs and benches in front of the alley houses;
evidence of their use, as well as of stoops, stairs, and boxes, is
strong. (See Photographs 4, 5, 6, 14, 17, 18, 19, 20, 21, 22, 23, 24,
25, 26.) Certainly this use was largely due to the small alley houses
and hot, humid summers. Nevertheless, use of these chairs and
benches greatly facilitated neighborly interaction. With front doors
only ten feet apart (and considerably less in some designs), and with
facing houses only thirty feet away, one who stepped outdoors was
instantly immersed in the alley world. Unlike suburban houses,
where private yards and porches protect the privacy of the occu-
pant, and where steps and railings serve a gate-like function, the alley was communal property. Space could not be defined by any
physical barrier; it belonged to everyone. One could only retreat to
the house or backyard. If the photographs upon which this analysis
is based are representative, alley dwellers chose not to retreat to
those more private places. They were found in the alley despite the
weather. Few of these photographs were intended to show people;
rather, the photographer's chief interest was in documenting the
physical alley. When Charles Weller referred to "the usual midday
loafers" in the caption to a photograph of Ball's Alley, he did so not
to demonstrate neighborly interaction, but for clearly moralistic
reasons.[13] The inclusion of "usual" in the caption strengthens the

Kingsley Zipf, "Some Determinants of the Circulation of Information," *American
Journal of Psychology*, 59 (July, 1946): 401–21; and Gunnar Boalt and Carl-Gunnar
Janson, "Distance and Social Relations," *Acta Sociologia*, 2 (1957): 73–97.

11. *National Intelligencer*, July 25, 1865, p. 3.
12. *Ibid.*
13. Weller, *Neglected Neighbors*, p. 82.

PHOTOGRAPH 17.
*"Negroes in Front of Their Homes in the Alley Dwelling Area." July,
1941. Photograph by Ed Rosskam. Farm Security Administration Collection, Library of Congress.*

PHOTOGRAPH 18.
*"Willow Tree Alley." August 3, 1915. Photograph by Roy E. Haynes.
John Ihlder Collection, Franklin D. Roosevelt Library.*

PHOTOGRAPH 19.
"Alley Neighborhood." Washingtoniana Collection, Martin Luther King Memorial Library, Washington, D.C.

PHOTOGRAPH 20.
"Alley Neighborhood." Washingtoniana Collection, Martin Luther King Memorial Library, Washington, D.C. (E. B. Thompson Purchase, June 7, 1945.)

PHOTOGRAPH 21.
"Logan Place." September 26, 1935. Alley Dwelling Authority, National Capital Housing Authority Collection.

PHOTOGRAPH 22.
"Alley Neighborhood." Washingtoniana Collection, Martin Luther King Memorial Library, Washington, D.C.

PHOTOGRAPH 23.
"Alley Neighborhood." Washingtoniana Collection, Martin Luther King Memorial Library, Washington, D.C.

PHOTOGRAPH 24.
"Fenton Place: 1930s." Alley Dwelling Authority, National Capital Housing Authority Collection.

view that the alley was the community center where alley neighbors met to exchange gossip, information on jobs, and stories.[14]

Of course, we cannot know who these people were or where they were from (save in a few instances where the caption provides such information), but, given the isolation of the alley, it seems likely that most resided there.[15] These photographs also suggest that males were more likely to congregate in the alley, at least during the daylight hours. Unfortunately, few if any photographs appear to have been taken during the evening, when such interaction might be expected to be greatest. Certainly, Weller's description of Blagden Alley during the evening confirms this contention. Alley men, who had to rely on the unstable day-labor market (as suggested by Elliot Liebow's study of such men for a later period), might often spend nonworking days with their fellows in the alley.[16] Women, whose more stable employment involved domestic work and washing, were undoubtedly employed during these hours. Of course, children, whose play area was the alley, appear in photographs even more frequently than adults. While there are instances of male-female interaction, the most common pattern seems to involve sex

14. Fried and Gleicher came to similar conclusions in their study of the "slum" in Boston's West End: "Certainly, most middle-class observers are overwhelmed at the degree to which the residents of any working-class district, and, most particularly, the residents of slums are 'at home' in the street. But it is not only the frequency of using the street and treating the street outside the house as a place, and not simply as a path, which points up the high degree of permeability of the boundary between the dwelling unit and the immediate environing area. It is also the use of all channels between dwelling unit and environment as a bridge between inside and outside: open windows, closed windows, hallways, even walls and floors serve this purpose. Frequently, even the sense of adjacent human beings carried by noises and smells provides a sense of comfort. . . . We would like to call this way of structuring the physical space around the actual residential unit a *territorial* space, in contrast to the selective space of the middle class" (Marc Fried and Peggy Gleicher, "Some Sources of Residential Satisfaction in an Urban Slum," in *Urban Renewal: People, Politics and Planning*, ed. Jewell Bellush and Murray Hausknecht [Garden City, N.Y., 1967], pp. 130–31). Similarly, the planner Chester Hartman has suggested that "We tend to think of this other space as anonymous and public (in the sense of belonging to everyone, i.e., no one) when it does not specifically belong to us. The lower-class person is not clearly so alienated from what he does not own." (Hartman quoted *ibid.*, p. 130*n*). See also Richard Hoggart, *The Uses of Literacy* (Boston, 1961), pp. 51–61; the author suggests that "Home may be private, but the front door opens out of the living-room onto the street, and when you go down the one step or use it as a seat on a warm evening you become part of the life of the neighborhood" (p. 51).

15. Swinney noted that groups of men in their late teens and twenties met in Snow's Court almost all the time, but "most of the group lived in neighborhoods adjacent to the court" ("Alley Dwellings and Housing Reform," p. 142). Other studies, however, found fewer intrusions.

16. Liebow, *Tally's Corner*, pp. 29–71.

PHOTOGRAPH 25.
"Purdy's Court, near the Capitol, 1908." Photograph by Lewis Wickes Hine. Lewis Wickes Hine Collection, George Eastman House, Rochester, N.Y.

segregation among the adults, at least during the day, although there is considerable interaction between adults and children. Finally, the casual and relaxed postures of the adult males suggest that those with whom they were interacting were not just acquaintances or mere strangers passing by.

One photograph (25) of Purdy's Court, a predominantly white alley, deserves special consideration. Here the alley's role as a gathering place for play, rest, and relaxation, as well as for social intercourse, is most strongly confirmed. This tranquil setting, which to reformers "proved" the disorganization and degradation of alley life, appears in fact to be one where children could play far from the dangers of the street, and where adults could communicate without interruptions from traffic noise.

While this photograph and several others suggest that some alleys were integrated, black-white interaction occurred infrequently, as the overwhelming majority of photographs indicates. How much this reflects actual practice is hard to say, since it is extremely difficult to determine race from photographs.[17]

Descriptive accounts verify the findings of the photoanalysis. Weller's account of Blagden Alley supports the view of the alley as commons; similarly, Police Officer Maghan reported that, in Dixon's Court, "'There's an intersection of two alleys right in the center of the court. That intersection has always been more or less of a congregating spot for the area.'"[18] While virtually all accounts identify the alley itself as the focal point of neighboring, one study of Snow's Court reported that "the backyards are often veritable beer gardens with beds, tables and chairs," while in Center Court (Sellew's name for Union Court) the Brown family's "home . . . is used for a gathering place. In the evenings, especially on Saturday evenings, people from the Court gather to gamble, buck dance, and talk." This latter case describes the winter months, during which Somerville did her field study, for Sellew noted that the alley is the "common meeting ground for everyone who lives in the court."[19] A reporter for the Washington *Times* who visited Willow Tree Alley (one of the most "notorious" alleys) in 1904 gave a description very much like Weller's:

> On a quiet night the aspect of the alley is peaceful in appearance, and it is hard to believe that the tales told of the

17. This is taken from Appendix B.
18. Washington *Daily News*, Apr. 15, 1954.
19. Mallalieu, "Washington Alley," p. 71; Somerville, "Study of a Group of Negro Children," p. 20; Sellew, *Deviant Social Situation*, p. 17.

inhabitants can be true. Little groups sit about the doorsteps laughing and talking. Here and there is a group of the "boys" playing selections of popular and "coon" songs on stringed instruments.

At one end you will frequently find a capable quartet singing genuine melody. This quartet is made up of Robert Barnes, Charlie Harvey, "Parse" Blackburn and George Edwards. Their fame extends beyond the alley. Crap games flourish at all times.[20]

Another newspaper account described "The mainstreet of Navy Place" as "picturesquely squalid—two rows of tiny brick houses separated by a narrow paved street—with an unusual number of loafers before the doors. One day last week there was an exciting craps game in progress among a half-dozen colored men on one doorstep, while a few feet farther on two were engaged in a peaceful game of checkers."[21]

The alley, then, became the community's focal point, and levels of social interaction there were high. This face-to-face contact was critical for the maintenance of the informal social world that alley dwellers constructed to order and control their environment. In doing this, residents created a behavioral landscape that permitted and supported their ways of life. (Appendix B contains a more complete discussion of this "behavioral landscape.")

The parameters of the alley community can be seen in other ways as well, and from these various angles the meaning and content of that community becomes more apparent. One can, for example, study the rates and nature of residential mobility and persistence. While alley dwellers persisted at about the same rate as black residents in other cities from 1875 to 1900, the important issue here concerns the extent to which they remained in the same alley.[22] As

20. Washington *Times*, Sept. 11, 1904.

21. Washington *Star*, June 6, 1930. See Swinney, "Alley Dwellings and Housing Reform," pp. 141–42, for a similar description of Snow's Court. It is useful to note the continuity of this alley community experience with that of the slave community. As a number of recent studies have shown, slave "Community life centered in the praise-houses and bush-arbors," hidden from view of the owner, overseer, and patrols. Quotation from Genovese, *Roll, Jordan, Roll*, p. 528; see also George Rawick, *Sundown to Sunup: The Making of the Black Community* (Westport, Conn., 1972); John Blassingame, *The Slave Community* (New York, 1972).

22. Nearly 60 percent of the sample area's black alley residents located in the 1880 city directory continued to live in Washington five years later. By 1890 40 percent still remained in the city, although this percentage dropped to 23 in 1895. These figures compare favorably with those for unskilled black males in Birmingham from

TABLE 12.

Persistence and Mobility of Alley Populations, 1880–85

	Black		White		Total	
	Number	%	Number	%	Number	%
Left city before 1885	83	39	11	50	94	40
Moved to another alley by 1885	29	14	1	5	30	13
Moved to street address by 1885	30	14	6	27	36	16
Total alley migrants	142	67	18	82	160	69
Total residents who persisted in same alley, 1880–85	69	33	4	18	73	31
TOTAL SAMPLE POPULATION (traceable in city directories)	211	100	22	100	233	100

Table 12 was constructed by compiling the names of all heads of household and employed persons from the 1880 manuscript census for the six alleys of the sample area: Naylor, Blagden, Shepherd, Freeman, Madison, and Goat Alleys, Northwest. Since city directories claim to list the names of all household heads and employed persons, these 579 names (546 black, 33 white) were sought in the 1879, 1880, 1881, and 1885 city directories. It was possible to locate 233 (about 40 percent; 211 black, 22 white) in the directories. These names were then sought in the 1884, 1885, and 1886 city directories, to determine whether they remained in the city and, if so, where. Federal Population Census Schedules, 1880, Washington, D.C., vol. 2, pt. 2, RG 29 NA; and William Boyd, *Directory for Washington, D.C.* (Washington, 1879, 1880, 1881, 1884, 1885, 1886).

Table 12 suggests, 40 percent of the city directory sample left Washington between 1880 and 1885; 13 percent chose to move to another alley, and 16 percent to a different street address. The remaining 31 percent continued to live in the same alley throughout the five-year period. Since city directories miss many poor and black residents (fully 60 percent of household heads and employed persons in the 1880 census did not appear in any directory), this persistence figure is probably very conservative.[23]

These numbers do indicate a fairly high turnover rate for the alley community hypothesized here. Nevertheless, a presumption

---

1880 to 1895: Paul Worthman, "Working Class Mobility in Birmingham, Alabama, 1880–1914," in *Anonymous Americans*, ed. Tamara Hareven (Englewood Cliffs, N.J., 1971), pp. 172–213. See Appendix C, Table 31, for general persistence rates and a methodological discussion of mobility and persistence studies.

23. Most white alley residents who remained in the city after leaving their original alley chose to live in street-front houses; blacks who moved chose equally between street and alley addresses. When these "migrants" to other alleys are considered, there is a more substantial base for persistence of alley culture and community.

that high turnover is to be equated with a lack of community, while low turnover implies community, is questionable at best. Rather, as Michelson notes, new communities or new residents often demonstrate both the need for and the practice of social interaction. Newcomers must rely on their neighbors to find out where to shop, as well as where to look for work, entertainment, health care, and schools. In contrast, the long-term resident has less need to rely on neighbors for this kind of information.[24]

On the other hand, almost one-third of the alley residents in the sample area did remain residentially stable—a fairly high "retention rate" for non-property-owners. That statistic also suggests some continuity in the alley community upon which social organization could be based. When the factors of high homogeneity of the alley population and the siting of the alley houses are added to the rate of residential persistence, the foundation is laid for forms of organization and social control to develop within the framework of the residents' experience and worldview. Persistence of a substantial minority of residents, then, could provide a basis for the socialization of newcomers into the alley way of life.[25]

Other studies report considerable variation in residential persistence among alleys. Clare de Graffenried, drawing a sample of fifty families from the thirteen alleys she studied in 1896, reported that only 26 percent had lived in the same house for more than five years.[26] (See Table 13.) These figures are misleading, however, be-

24. Michaelson, *Man and His Urban Environment*, p. 186. As will be noted at the end of the chapter, Ratigan observed that the high turnover in a particular alley resulted in only the more stable residents having any meaningful connections (*Sociological Survey of Disease*, pp. 118–19). Although too much turnover might limit the involvement of at least some alley residents, it is important to note that Ratigan still recognizes the presence of community in that alley—it just was not universally shared by all residents.

25. This analysis is based on Borchert, "Race and Place," pp. 13–16, Tables 11, 12. In contrast, Stuart M. Blumin has concluded that since "on the average, only one out of ever four or five adult male inhabitants (and probably their families) remained in a given neighborhood as long as ten years," the "creation of a meaningful community, consisting of informal as well as formal interaction networks," which "depends in large part upon a substantial continuity of personnel," could not have taken place in Philadelphia's neighborhoods "except for a very small proportion of the city's population" ("Residential Mobility within the Nineteenth-Century City," in *The Peoples of Philadelphia*, ed. Allen F. Davis and Mark H. Haller [Philadelphia, 1973], p. 49). Unfortunately, like many who manipulate statistics, Blumin has selected an arbitrary time period (as I have), without considering the full context of the neighborhood experience. When the length of moves, extent of extended families living nearby in separate households, and the full pattern of social relations are considered in a neighborhood context, then these figures may have more meaning.

26. de Graffenried, "Typical Alley Houses," p. 13.

TABLE 13.
Persistence of Alley Families in the Same House,
1896*

Years of residence in same house	N
< 1	14
1	6
2	8
3	4
4	5
5	1
6	2
8	1
12	4
14	1
16	1
18	2
28	1
TOTAL	50
Average length of residence	4.56 years

*Based on a sample of 50 families selected from inhabitants of 13 alleys. SOURCE: de Graffenried, "Typical Alley Houses," p. 13.

cause they refer only to residence in the same house. Swinney reported that one head of household had lived in four different houses in Fenton Place, while four had had three different addresses and twelve reported having had two.[27] Thus it seems fair to assume that considerably more than the quarter of the families had lived in the same alley for five years or more. Swinney found strong variations in the persistence rates for Fenton Place and Snow's Court in 1938. (See Tables 14 and 15.) The former alley had had considerably more transients: 61 percent of the household heads had lived there less than five years, while more than half of their counterparts in the latter alley had lived there at least that long.[28] Nevertheless, substantial numbers of families remained residentially stable in both cases. Finally, a 1953 study of Temperance Court reported extremely high persistence levels, with 73 percent of the household heads

27. Swinney, "Alley Dwellings and Housing Reform," p. 118.
28. *Ibid.*, pp. 119, 86.

TABLE 14.
Persistence of Head of Household in Fenton Place, 1938*

Years of Residence	Washington	Fenton Place	Present dwelling
< 5	3	41	49
5–9	9	8	7
10–14	4	2	1
15–19	5	4	1
20+	43	9	6
Not reported	3	3	3
TOTAL REPORTED	64	64	64
Total household heads	67	67	67

*SOURCE: Swinney, "Alley Dwellings and Housing Reform," p. 119.

TABLE 15.
Persistence of Head of Household in Snow's Court, 1938*

Years of residence	Washington	Snow's Court	Present dwelling
< 5	0	14	23
5–9	0	3	8
10–14	3	9	3
15–19	1	3	0
20+	30	5	0
Not reported	5	5	5
TOTAL REPORTED	34	34	34
Total household heads	39	39	39

*SOURCE: Swinney, "Alley Dwellings and Housing Reform," p. 86.

having lived there for twelve years or more.[29] (See Table 16.) While it is dangerous to speculate on these figures, it does appear that the

29. Pablo, "Housing Needs and Social Problems," p. 44. Other studies confirm the high persistence for this alley; the year before Pablo's study, the Washington Housing Association found that "the period of tenancy ranges from one to forty years, the average being 11 years" (Washington Housing Association, "Report on Temperance Court," p. 3). Similarly, the Washington *Post* reported in 1946 that "the families who live in Snow's Court have been there for periods ranging from 2 to 15 years" (January 13, 1946).

TABLE 16.
*Persistence of Head of Household in Temperance Court, 1953**

Years	N	% Households
2–6	3	12
8–12	4	15
12–20	8	31
20–25	4	15
25–30	1	4
30–35	4	15
35–40	1	4
40–45	1	4
TOTAL	26	100

*SOURCE: Pablo, "Housing Needs and Social Problems," p. 44.

alleys became more residentially stable, although variations between alleys are perhaps more significant.

Many of those who left one alley moved into a neighboring one. Thirteen percent of the 1880 city directory sample moved into another alley. Similarly, Swinney noted that, of those who had lived in two different houses in Fenton Place, three families had earlier lived in neighboring alleys, while of those families who had only one Fenton Place address, five had previously lived in other alleys.[30] He reported a similar situation for Snow's Court, where seven families had previously lived in neighboring alleys.[31] Moreover, Mallalieu noted that Snow's Court "is almost immediately connected with Highes Court, another interior alley. The two form one underworld community."[32]

Unfortunately, these sources do not give the reasons for such moves, or explain the contexts in which they took place. By studying individual families' moves over time, we can get a better sense of this context. Map 15 shows the moves of four selected families over a seventeen- to nineteen-year period.[33] While the experiences of

30. Swinney "Alley Dwellings and Housing Reform," pp. 118–19.
31. *Ibid.*, p. 86.
32. Mallalieu, "Washington Alley," p. 70.
33. This map and Table 17 are based on "selected case records from the Board of Children's Guardians." Because most case records are too incomplete to allow effective tracing of addresses, or because they are of too short duration, I had to rely on

TABLE 17.
*Family Relocation**

Family	Length of known residence	Longest period in one alley	No. alley addresses	No. street addresses	No. moves	No. years in alleys	No. years on streets
A (1893–1911)	18	7	8	2	9	15	3
B (1900–1919)	19	3	2	8	9	6	13
C (1894–1911)	17	9	1	—	2	9	8
D (1893–1910)	17	8	2	2	3	8	9

*Based on Board of Children's Guardians, *Children's History*, RG 351 NA. (See note 33.)

these four families vary from extreme mobility (Families A and B each move nine times) to relative stability (Families C and D make two and three moves, respectively), they display several important similarities. All four families had spent much of their "recorded" lives in alleys, and nearly 40 percent of these parts of their lives had been spent in one alley.

This map strikingly indicates the extent to which alley families tended to remain in the same general neighborhood, assuming they remained in the city. Other sources suggest that many former alley residents continued to maintain ties with the old alley, and in some cases (as with Family A) actually returned to live there. This map and table also indicate that all four families eventually left the alleys "permanently" to live on the streets.[34] Perhaps alley dwelling tended to be involved with a phase in the life cycle for many residents; if so, this would help account for the young families who tended to dominate the alley population. Furthermore, as Table 18 indicates, many alley dwellers were relative newcomers to the city, having migrated during the previous fifteen years.[35] It is quite possible, then,

---

those few cases that did provide good coverage over a substantial period of time. The completeness and persistence of the families in the case record undoubtedly indicates that these are special cases; they certainly are not a "representative" sample in any sense of the word. Nevertheless, they do raise a number of interesting observations.

34. Only Family B returned to an alley after living on the street for five years, and they later returned "permanently" to street addresses three years later.

35. Although this is based on the 1880 census, there are some indications that this remained true until recently; nevertheless, the numbers of new migrants represented a smaller share of the alley population in later years. The youth of the alley population is suggested by the mean age of the total population in 1880: 24 years. The mean age for household heads was 41, however.

TABLE 18.
Date of Urban Migration, *1880**

Born in D.C.		Moved before 1860		1860–64		1865–69		1870–74		1875–79	
N	%	N	%	N	%	N	%	N	%	N	%
260	10	74	3	140	5	364	14	363	14	343	13

*Based on Federal Population Census Schedules, 1880, Washington, D.C., RG 29 NA. These figures were compiled by analyzing each household unit. It was possible to determine the approximate time of migration in cases where one child had been born outside the city and the following children in the city. For many households this information was not available. Some mothers may have returned home to have their children; as a result, these figures are only suggestive. Other evidence does indicate that it is generally correct, however.

that alley dwellings attracted young families who faced extremely limited housing choices. Many were eventually able to move out of the alleys, presumably to better and more expensive street housing; others remained in the alley because of relatives and friends, or because they could not afford to leave. Yet the persisting residents' community role may have been far more significant than their numbers would indicate. As each new wave of rural migrants settled in the alleys, the older residents not only provided important information on jobs, shopping, and other necessities, but also helped the newcomers adjust to the urban environment with minimal disruption.

Turnover or persistence alone, however, provides little real indication of the extent or meaning of community. More useful is a discussion of the extent to which alley residents were satisfied or unhappy with their living conditions. Alley dwellers were not universal in either their condemnation or their approval of the alley; certainly part of the assessment depended on one's aspirations. A white family whom the Wellers had helped to move out of the alley had to return after a month, for financial reasons; yet they pointed out that their new alley house was "'on the entrance alley now, you might say, only just inside the alley edge.'"[36] Weller also reported on a washerwoman who asked "for charitable aid to supplement her earnings and enable her to live upon an outside street. . . . 'My children,' she said, 'are my whole future. If they grow up right they will take care of me when I can't work any longer. But if I take them

36. Weller, *Neglected Neighbors*, pp. 40–41.

able 18—*continued*

	1880		Not ascertainable		Total household units	
	N	%	N	%	N	%
	2	2	1,018	39	2,604	100

to live in an alley they will see all sorts of bad things all the time; they can't get away from the badness. I might as well see them dead today as to take them to live in an alley.'"[37] Dorothy Fax, who was the social worker responsible for relocating the residents of Temperance Court in 1953, reported that one woman who had lived in that alley for six years had never made "the break because she had felt that it was impossible to do so. . . . She was offered a house on Marion Court. She flatly refused it, saying that neither she nor her children would welcome any house in another alley."[38] Although the Washington Housing Association study of Temperance Court reported that "Twenty-six out of the twenty-seven were interviewed and asked whether they wished to move or would be willing to move. All would like to move to better but low-cost houses,"[39] this statement is a bit misleading. By the 1950s Temperance Court houses had deteriorated considerably, and this accounts, in large part, for the respondents' desire to move. Besides, anyone would prefer to move to "better, low-cost houses"; the real question is, who determines what is "better"? As Pablo reported:

at the outset, the heads of the families in Temperance Court were unanimous in their desire to move out of that area de-

37. *Ibid.*, p. 30.
38. Dorothy Fax, "Final Report of Social Worker," in Washington Housing Association, "Report on Temperance Court," p. 4.
39. Washington Housing Association, "Report on Temperance Court," p. 3. We must assume that many of these answers represent "conventional responses" by alley dwellers to middle-class social workers; certainly an old survival technique from slavery was to tell someone in a position of power what that person wanted to hear.

spite some sentimental feelings for the court and the higher
house rents outside. Some of the reasons given for wanting to
move out were "not enough room," "not sanitary," "not con-
venient especially during winter," "rent too high for the poor
housing facilities provided," "not a decent place to raise children," "to get better accommodations," "agents will do no repair work," and "we heard from various sources that the
house will be condemned."[40]

Only one of these reasons, "not a decent place to raise children,"
may relate to the neighbors and community. Given the overwhelming concern for poor physical conditions in the alley, it seems likely
that this is the real issue. Moreover, at least two of the relocated
Temperance Court families moved to the same new location, while
"some of them said they felt lonely in their new surroundings."[41]

Others expressed more positive reasons for living in the alleys,
despite the fact that they might also have been concerned with poor
maintenance by the landlord. One elderly gentleman stated,
"'Wawl, I'll tell you mister, of course I lives here because of cheap
rent but if I had lots of money I wouldn't want to move. I knows
where I'm at here in the alley. All the folks is colored and I don't
have to watch stepping on a white man's toes. Most of us is poor and
live in bad houses but we has a good time.'"[42] Similarly, a forty-
eight-year-old woman with three children who lived in Dixon
Court did not "want to move. . . . 'If they'd spend some money and
fill in the cracks we could still live here,'" she said. A male resident
of that same alley observed, "'It will ruin me when I have to move.
I want to stay home. . . . The only thing wrong with this place is

40. Pablo, "Housing Needs and Social Problems," p. 65. Conditions were certainly bad in Temperance Court. One report described "toadstools growing out of
the wall up near the ceiling in the middle room. They are pulled off, but spring up
again overnight. Continually damp plaster provides good growing conditions for
fungus. The kitchen adjoining that room has a floor so rotted it feels soft underfoot.
Huge chunks of plaster are off the ceiling—two of them fell a couple of weeks ago,
knocking one of the little girls senseless—there are nine children in the house. When
it rains, great streams of water gush down through the roof. . . . The mother says,
'I've begged and begged the landlord to fix the roof over the kitchen. I pay $30.40 a
month for this.'. . . The house is clean" (Hilda Cloud, "Personal Observations on
Temperance Court," in Washington Housing Association, "Report on Temperance
Court," p. 6).

41. Pablo, "Housing Needs and Social Problems," p. 49; Fax, "Final Report of
Social Worker," p. 6.

42. Swinney, "Alley Dwelling and Housing Reform," p. 137. The similarity between this quote and that of Peter, the nine-year-old Boston alley dweller at the beginning of Chapter 4, is striking and important.

that the roof leaks and the door is broken.'"[43] Not surprisingly, Ratigan noted that "The Negroes, whom we studied, lived in continual dread of the demolition of their homes, and often spoke of others who had been forced to move and had no place to go."[44] These views are very similar to those expressed by residents of Boston's West End as described by Herbert Gans in *The Urban Villagers*, and by Marc Fried and Peggy Gleicher in their study of "Some Sources of Residential Satisfaction in an Urban 'Slum.'"[45] Because of these and other sources, it is difficult to take at face value the reports of the social workers who were involved in the relocation of Temperance Court. While the alley residents were unhappy about their poor housing conditions, they wanted to keep their community intact. Swinney found a woman who had "lived at six different addresses" in Snow's Court, as well as "at one in another alley, and at two street addresses within a period of twenty years. Each time she moved out of Snow's Court she became lonely for her friends in the alley, visited them, drank with them, and ultimately returned to live with them." After the last return "a social agency discontinued her relief because of her decision to move back into the alley . . . she maintains that the alley is her home, and that she could receive relief if she would agree to move out of the alley."[46] George Mackey, who was evicted in 1941 from Holly Court so that his house could be torn down for a playground, pleaded, "'This is my homes . . . I been here 10 years. All my friends here. When I get mail, I get it here. Why I got to move?'" Edward Cole, a resident of Temperance Court for forty years, contradicted social workers' claims that everyone wanted to move out of the alley by asserting that "the tenants would have to fight any move to oust them."[47] Moreover, an earlier study reported that alley residents, "when asked if they would rather live on T Street or Florida Avenue," replied unhesitatingly, "'No, I am satisfied.'"[48] Swinney found "the

43. Washington *Star*, Jan. 17, 1954.

44. Ratigan, *Sociological Survey of Disease*, p. 19.

45. Fried and Gleicher, "Some Sources of Residential Satisfaction," pp. 120–36.

46. Swinney, "Alley Dwellings and Housing Reform," p. 88.

47. Washington *Daily News*, Aug. 29, 1941; Washington *Star*, Sept. 26, 1952.

48. Jones, *Housing of Negroes*, p. 47. Jones also reports a story: "Some years ago, Mrs. Pinchot promised to pay the entire moving expenses of an old woman who had lived in the same alley house for twenty-six years, but the Housing Committee of the National Civic Federation could not prevail upon her to move out." He further noted that "some 'old-timers' . . . can boast of having lived in the same house for more than fifty years. It is almost impossible to persuade these older alley inhabitants to move onto the streets. Those who have lived in the same houses for forty or fifty years would be tremendously frustrated if they had to transfer their living quarters to some other locality" (*ibid.*, p. 51).

same emotional attachments to the alley" in both Snow's Court and Fenton Place.[49]

Certainly low rent was one attraction of alley houses. Swinney reported another: "In Fenton Place approximately 30 percent of the families stated that they moved into the alley in order to obtain a house to themselves.[50] They had previously lived in apartment or rooming houses and they wanted the privacy of an individual dwelling."[51]

Despite the low rent and the opportunity to have a house of one's own, even if it was not detached, many alley dwellers expressed satisfaction with their place of residence, if not with the condition of the building, primarily because their friends and family lived there. These people provided a social setting in which alley residents could be secure and comfortable, away from the hostile and threatening white world. This factor of freedom to be oneself is another crucial aspect of the alley community.

Alley residents' interest in their neighborhood was more than a merely passive residential satisfaction. Through a variety of means they sought to establish and control their own community. One of the most important tactics involved using the physical environment to establish "defensible space."[52] The physical and visual isolation of the alley have already been established, as has the social distance between the alley and the street populations. Nowhere is this distance clearer than in the drawing of "The Blind Alley" (Drawing 1). The policeman on the beat could neither see nor hear what was going on in the alley. Moreover, because of the relatively few alley

49. Swinney, "Alley Dwellings and Housing Reform," p. 110.

50. Ethel Waters, who grew up in a number of Philadelphia alleys, fondly remembered "one childhood home," a "three-room shanty in an alley just off Clifton Street. . . . I remember that little alley home as the heaven on earth of my childhood. For once we were all together in a whole house—Vi, Ching, Charlie, me, mom on her days off. After a while Louise also came to live with us. . . . That was the only time I could feel that I had a family that wasn't continually disrupting and belonged in one neighborhood" (*His Eye Is on the Sparrow*, p. 15).

51. *Ibid.*, p. 138. There is considerable irony in this, because one of the chief complaints of housing reformers was that the alley houses had no privacy. These reformers, in providing philanthropic housing, constructed two-story row apartment buildings, with a family per floor, as their solution. While the reformers' writings stressed "privacy" for each family, it is clear the alley houses provided more than that—and a chance for community away from "the man" as well. See Borchert, "Progressive Housing Reform," and Appendix A, for a discussion of these reformers and their plans.

52. Oscar Newman, *Defensible Space: Crime Prevention through Urban Design* (New York, 1973).

residents, the propinquity of their houses, and the common alley property, all alley residents probably knew each other quite well. Since most, if not all, of the alley network was visible to one or more families, visual surveillance by residents was quite easy, making the presence of outsiders as well as the activities of neighbors common knowledge. Alley residents used this information to maintain control over their "turf."

Several students of alley life provided excellent descriptions of the techniques used to maintain this control over the alley, as well as to suggest the intricate and effective intelligence and communication system that it required. Swinney observed:

> With the exception of friends of the inhabitants and persons who have specific missions to perform, the alley communities are rarely visited by outsiders. As soon as an outsider enters the alley the news spreads quickly. People conversing in the middle of the alley streets disappear in the dwellings; those who are in the dwellings come to the door or stick their heads out of windows. If the outsider enters one of the dwellings he will often find when he leaves the dwelling that numerous persons have been trying to eavesdrop through the doors and perhaps his conversation within the dwelling will have been interrupted several times by neighbors dropping in for a few minutes. Before the inhabitants became familiar with the writer he was often stopped and asked, "What you all want?" or "Are you insurance man," or "Are you relief worker?" The writer would tell them that he was interested in finding out about the condition of their houses. As evidence of the rapidity with which word traveled, someone would invariably ask him as he was leaving the opposite end of the alley either to look at the hole in their floor or tell him without being asked, "Don't come to my place cause you ain't going to do no good." Even after they became familiar with the writer the majority of the inhabitants would not reveal the whereabouts of any of their neighbors or any general information about them. In two instances the sought-after neighbors revealed that the person who had disclaimed knowing them was a close relative.

Thus alleys are not only hidden communities because of their physical characteristics but the people living in alleys are definitely a group within themselves. Although they may fight and quarrel among themselves, when an outsider enters they are united. Throughout the interviews made in Fenton Place and in Snow's Court observation and hearsay indicated that the inhabitants of each alley were bound together by many ties and that all that happened within was common property.[53]

Pablo reported of Temperance Court

that when outsiders came into the area the residents showed hostility and resentment toward them. They indicated that they did not want anyone to "pry" into their lives. This disposition to outsiders was evident in three situations, namely: when newspapermen and photographers visited the area, when a joint meeting for representative agencies and residents were called by the Neighborhood Association in Garnett Patterson Junior High School and when the Board of Inspectors were evaluating the homes. In the first situation the writer heard two alley dwellers conversing about the paper being "nosey"; in the second situation, there were several comments that all the talking will amount to nothing; and in the third situation, the belligerent reactions of some tenants by not opening their homes to the Board Inspectors are indicative of hostile attitudes.[54]

Yet Pablo also notes that "the tenants got along very well with each other."[55]

Not only did the alley residents conduct visual surveillance of the alleys, but they also utilized a very ingenious psychology as their first line of defense against outsiders. They were extremely successful in letting observers, such as Swinney and Pablo, know that they were not wanted, that they had entered an "alien community." The alley dwellers' activities completely unnerved their visitors, and by "dropping in for visits" and by displaying knowledge of what these outsiders were doing in the alley they were able to keep the outsiders confused and on edge. This fine "early warning system" served as an extremely effective method of (1) discovering the presence and purpose of intruders, (2) scaring off the timid, and (3) creating apprehension in those who were more diligent or fearless.[56]

53. Swinney, "Alley Dwellings and Housing Reform," pp. 136–37.
54. Pablo, "Housing Needs and Social Problems," p. 42.
55. *Ibid.*
56. Nor was this "communications" system a new phenomenon. Lieutenant Hannibal Johnson provided excellent examples of its effectiveness during his escape from a Confederate prison during the Civil War, while J. Winston Coleman, Jr., noted that "It was known for many years before the Negroes were emancipated that, not-

Part of this mechanism had to do with the way in which residents converted the alley as path into a commons area. While this is not unusual for a working-class neighborhood, it is a use of space strikingly different from the experience of most middle-class observers of alley life. It is not surprising that Weller, Swinney, Pablo, and others expressed initial anxiety about entering the alleys and further concern about the apparent "pandemonium" they found there.

Nor were these the only forms of "turf" maintenance. The *Star* reported, in reference to drinking and gambling in Huntoon Alley, that "A sentinel posted at the entrance can give warning of the coming of a policeman in plenty of time."[57] Finally, of course, there remained the ultimate weapon: attack. On a number of occasions police who attempted to arrest alley residents found themselves confronted by mobs of neighbors. In 1881 the *Star* reported that Policemen Branson and Howell were assaulted when they "attempted to arrest a notorious colored woman . . . for being disorderly and blowing a tin horn. . . . A large crowd of colored men and women attacked the officers with sticks and stones, and the fight lasted half an hour."[58] The same paper reported thirty years later that Willow

---

withstanding the patrol system kept up in Kentucky, slaves would secretly travel over a large scope of country at night and manage to be back in their quarters before morning. They had a grapevine telegraph or secret system of communication never known or comprehended by their masters" (Johnson, *The Sword of Honor* [Providence, 1903], pp. 25–35; Coleman, *Slavery Times in Kentucky* [Chapel Hill, 1940], pp. 98–99). Moreover, Young, in her recent study of a southern community, reported that "communication of news in this community is rapid and thorough despite the fact that it is physically scattered and has no central organization of any kind" ("Family and Children in a Southern Community," p. 286).

57. Washington *Star*, June 4, 1930. Ethel Waters, who "acted as a semi-official lookout girl for sporting houses" on Clifton Street in Philadelphia, provided a fine description of a warning system and some insight into the communications systems in general. "Any of us slum children could smell out a cop even though he was a John, a plain clothes man. These brilliant sleuths never suspicioned that we were tipsters for the whole whoring industry. Usually we'd be playing some singing game on the street when we spotted a cop, a game like Here Come Two Dudes A-Riding or the one that begins:

King William was King James's son,
Upon his breast he wore a star,
And that was called . . .

On smelling out the common enemy, we boys and girls in the know would start to shout the songs, accenting certain phrases. If we happened to be playing a singing game we'd whistle the agreed on tune. The other kids, even those who weren't lookouts, would innocently imitate us, and in no time at all the whole neighborhood would be alerted. The street women would disappear, the lights would go out, and the doors would be locked in the sporting houses" (*His Eye Is on the Sparrow*, p. 16).

58. Washington *Star*, Dec. 27, 1881.

Tree Alley was patrolled by two officers at night, because several years before "a policeman while rushing to the scene of a brawl was set upon by a crowd of men and women; had it not been for the aid of a citizen passing outside and the arrival of fellow officers he would have been fatally injured."[59]

Perhaps the most striking and interesting aspect of the alley dwellers' methods of defending their "turf" can be seen in their effective manipulation of white fear. Certainly some police and non-residents were attacked in alleys; yet these instances were clearly and vastly exaggerated. Nevertheless, there was widespread fear of "the alleys," as indicated by the drawing of "The Blind Alley" in Chapter I.[60] In his description of his first night in Blagden Alley, Weller mentioned that the two policemen were greeted with notable civility, but nevertheless kept their clubs at hand. In fact, virtually every source played on the dangers of the alleys. The historian Edward Ingle, writing in 1890, noted that "there are sections in Washington where a policeman carries his life in his hands."[61] Sixty years later, the historian Daniel O'Connell remarked that "it is a significant fact that the police would not go into the alleys except in pairs and always with their hands on their billies," while Jones noted the "testimony of the policemen on the beat who are always complaining of the difficulty of giving effective attention to the blind alley and who in the Southwest always go in pairs after nightfall."[62] Similarly, Dixon's Court had "always been patrolled by what we call a double beat," according to Police Officer Maghan in 1954; "Police have worked it in pairs for their own safety."[63]

These remarks not only were picked up by the press, but appear in travel guides and exposés as well. Smiley's *Glimpse at the Night Side of Washington: A Guide to Night Amusements by One Who Has Been There* (1894) suggested that "if you are a responsible person and wish a guide to the very hells of this city, engage a policeman or detective who is off duty." Yet it warned, "Never go alone into the low negro alleys at midnight . . . as you value your life, for there are dens of vice in this beautiful city where murder lurks and where thieves are

59. *Ibid.*, July 30, 1911. For other examples, see Washington *Daily Morning Chronicle*, Sept. 23, 1872; Washington *Star*, Oct. 18, 1880; Georgetown *Daily Times*, June 12, 1865.

60. Of course, the housing reformers sought to use this fear to rid the city of alley communities.

61. Ingle, *Negro in the District of Columbia*, p. 53.

62. O'Connell, "Inhabited Alleys of Washington," p. 57; Jones, *Housing of Negroes*, p. 68.

63. Officer Maghan, quoted in Washington *Daily News*, Apr. 15, 1954.

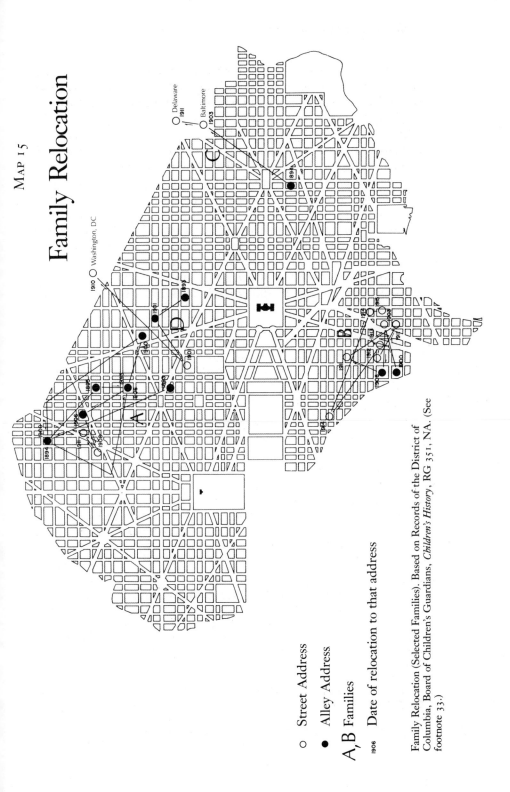

MAP 15

Family Relocation

○ Street Address

● Alley Address

A, B Families

1906 Date of relocation to that address

Family Relocation (Selected Families). Based on Records of the District of
Columbia, Board of Children's Guardians, *Children's History*, RG 351, NA. (See
footnote 33.)

always on the watch for victims. Parties of five or six may be safe from such attacks, but if possible obtain the services of a private detective, for he can not only act as a protector but also as a guide."[64] Jack Lait and Lee Mortimer's *Washington Confidential* of 1951 similarly reported that Goat Alley "is terribly tough, with reefer peddlers, two-dollar wenches, a mugging a minute and murders common."[65]

While such publicity undoubtedly attracted some visitors to the alleys, its total effect must have been to discourage unnecessary entries.[66] Of course, a number of alleys housed businesses, principally stables, blacksmiths, tinsmiths, and carpenter shops, as well as small stores; these establishments drew nonresident owners, as well as customers, into the alleys. Trouble appears to have been rare; certainly no students of alley life were ever attacked while on their visits, and Weller, for one, resided for a month in Blagden Alley with little trouble, despite "evil possibilities and latent danger."[67]

64. Robert Wagner Smiley, *A Glimpse at the Night Side of Washington* (Washington, 1894), pp. 6, 39.

65. Jack Lait and Lee Mortimer, *Washington Confidential* (New York, 1951), p. 51. While some might interpret this violence as arbitrary and indicative of disorder, Michael Feldberg has pointed out, in his study of violence in Philadelphia, that "Sociologists have labeled this form of violence 'instrumental,' that is, well-defined, clearly limited, goal-oriented behavior. Especially for the 'lower orders' whose economic and political power was relatively weak, violence was an effective means for obtaining desired ends" ("Urbanization as a Cause of Violence: Philadelphia as a Test Case," in *Peoples of Philadelphia*, ed. Davis and Haller, p. 56). It also reflects a traditional American response. As Pauline Maier has suggested, the "role of the mob as extralegal arm of the community's interest" is a common pattern ("Popular Uprisings and Civil Authority in Eighteenth Century America," *William and Mary Quarterly*, 27 [Jan., 1970]: 5).

66. O'Connell interviewed a priest born in 1892 who grew up just outside Fenton Place, and who continued to work in the neighborhood. The priest recalled that "he was never in Fenton Place in his life; that as a boy, he would play with the colored children on Defrees Street and in Jackson Alley, but never dared to go into Fenton Place; that he and his friends 'would never take a short-cut' through it no matter how great their hurry might be nor how precious their time." While another resident of the Fenton Place neighborhood told O'Connell that "as a child she and her brothers and sisters were explicitly told to stay away from Fenton Place," a third former resident stated that he had never been "afraid to go into Fenton Place —even late at night. He used to play with the children in the alley; he used to go through the alley on his way to school" ("Inhabited Alleys of Washington," pp. 109, 110). Some of the differences in attitude can be explained by the fact that the third respondent was the son of a tavernkeeper who served and extended credit to Fenton Place alley residents, and who thus had some connection with those residents and was known by them.

67. Swinney notes that Fenton Place had "five private garages and one blacksmith shop which is operated by two white men. The location of the grocery store and the blacksmith shop apparently has had a significant effect upon the inhabitants of the alley. Negroes and a few white persons from outside the alley patronize

While alley residents used various techniques to maintain their "turf" against the more powerful and dangerous outside world, they frequently and cleverly used psychology to manipulate outsiders' fears. Of course, in a city where racism ruled(s) and class hatred was common, and where the white middle and upper classes held all the power, such manipulation could never be totally effective. Certainly police brutality was common, as were arrests for petty and absurd crimes; many were undoubtedly complete fabrications. (See Chapters 4 and 5.) Nevertheless, alley dwellers were able, through guile and manipulation, to trick "outsiders" about the imminent dangers of the alley, thus maintaining their own community, family, and "turf" intact.[68]

This technique should not come as a surprise, for it certainly had played an important part in the slave's efforts to manipulate the overseer and/or owner. Rather, alley dwellers were moving away from the more covert forms of resistance and manipulation used in slavery and toward more overt forms of protest. The alley community was a place for transition, from the slave trickster to the "bad man" of the twentieth-century ghetto. While alley dwellers no longer experienced the slaveowner's constant surveillance and could choose their own employers and homes, they still could not present a substantial threat to the larger community, or lay more than a foundation for the development of large-scale cultural institutions. Because the alleys were sprinkled through the entire city, there was no "defensible space" for the entire black community, and no concentrated critical mass (until the twentieth century) to foster development of the whole range of institutions that serve and unite a community.[69]

To maintain such an effective network of surveillance and control requires a hierarchy, as well as a clear, shared sense of order.[70] We

---

the grocery store, while many white men patronize the blacksmith shop during the day. Thus, the alley inhabitants are used to seeing strangers in the alley. This fact was noticeable in the reception which the writer received in Fenton Place as contrasted with that received in Snow's Court. Although at first the inhabitants of Fenton Place were aloof, they did not question the writer's presence in the alley" ("Alley Dwellings and Housing Reform," p. 112).

68. It is also possible that these descriptions were used to "color" and control other people's images of the new urbanites.

69. This, of course, largely ignores the rest of Washington's black community. Certainly there were a number of very early and important cultural institutions—churches, Howard University, several key schools, and a newspaper, among others. But most of these clearly served the black middle class.

70. In universal terms, this latter may not be a literal requirement; but, given the real dangers alley dwellers had to face, such a hierarchy is not surprising.

can grasp a sense of that order, somewhat perversely, through the eyes of participant-observer Aubry. She found that

> a primitive sort of life exists, a set of rules that are as lawless and non-moral as any primitive tribe. City laws and ordinances are broken with no qualms of conscience, and should one get caught and have to serve time, he returns only to break the same law over again. There is cooperation with neighbors to carry on vice and crime, cooperation to evade the law. Loyalty, yet, as an out-law has for his gang, and the same contempt and hatred for the "stool pigeon." This code of living exists not only among the adults but among the children as well, it can be seen in their play.[71]

That there was a sense of right and wrong, as well as boundaries beyond which an alley dweller should or could not go without punishment or banishment, is clear from Sellew's description of two different children in Center Court. "Martha has very definite ideas of fair play and of 'generosity' as opposed to 'meanness,' and does not hesitate to correct me when she feels that I have violated standards." Sellew finds that "of all the girls, Martha is the most delinquent but her delinquency is well within the standard set by her parents and of her own concept of right."[72] In contrast, "Stanton's delinquency, from the point of view of the Court, differs from Martha's conduct in two ways. With one exception Martha has not stolen and the theft be known to those outside the Court. Her antisocial behavior is a copy of her parents and furthers theirs." On the other hand, Stanton's delinquent conduct "is opposed to the interests of his aunt's family. He stole from them, and he stole from outsiders *for himself*."[73] Stanton, it will be remembered, was taken in by his aunt when his mother died and his father became ill. His short stay in the alley had perhaps been insufficient to socialize him into the ways of Center Court, which clearly did not permit stealing from one's family or neighbors. Moreover, if one stole from outsiders, it was to be shared by the entire family. Stanton paid severely for his transgressions against the alley's moral standards.

71. Aubry, "Ambitions of Youth," p. 3.
72. Sellew, *Deviant Social Situation*, pp. 82–83.
73. *Ibid.*, p. 84. Nor was this necessarily a "new morality." Levine quotes former slave Lewis Clarke, who observed that slaves "think it wrong to take from a neighbor, but not from their master, the only question with them is, Can we keep it from master? But a slave that will steal from a slave, is called *mean as master*. This is the lowest comparison slaves know how to use!" (*Black Culture and Black Consciousness*, p. 125). See also Gutman, *Black Family in Slavery and Freedom*, p. 281.

Another case likewise demonstrates the boundaries of the alley's social order, as well as one of the techniques that the alley community could use against transgressors. Swinney reported being told by a Snow's Court resident that

> the "heavy drinking" started in the alley after the Eighteenth Amendment was passed and that three of the inhabitants now living in the alley were quite prosperous during that period. They made their money by selling "corn whiskey" in mason jars. Their downfall soon came about for they set up a "jim-crow" entrance to their speak-easies. The colored patrons who had been their main standbys, and whom they had known all their lives, were not allowed in the front door. This barrier resulted in dissension that frequently resulted in tips to the police who made constant raids. Later these men were without funds and were forced to ask the same persons they had "jim-crowed" for sandwiches and cigarettes. In the words of the informant, "They belong to the class of use to was and at the present time they ain't from nothing."[74]

Even being a "stool pigeon" could be acceptable to the alley social order, if the offense was clearly an affront to the community—as it certainly was in this case. Calling in the law, however, must have been a last resort—or perhaps, in this case, poetic justice. Swinney also noted the attitude of the same alley's black residents toward outsiders who were black. In order to obtain more accurate and complete information, Swinney had employed Mr. Steen, a black graduate student at Howard University. Steen found that "the people of the court possess a strong feeling of kinship for one another and that they would quickly go to each other's rescue. He states that their attitude in days past towards the strange negro was one of hostility and that they are particularly suspicious of all negroes from the outside for fear they are either stool pigeons for the police or pimps."[75] There was a concern not only about the police coming into the alleys, but also that certain kinds of crime might enter as well. While Snow's Court residents could tolerate speakeasies, they wanted nothing to do with prostitution and maintained vigilance to keep it out of their community.

74. Swinney, "Alley Dwellings and Housing Reform," p. 143.
75. *Ibid.* Similarly, Lucy Belle, in Ernest Culbertson's *Goat Alley*, remarks, "Ain't Nuffin' yo' can do. I oughter put de *po*-lice on 'em—but, yo' knows, dat gwine ter make all kin' -a trouble fo' me" (*Goat Alley*, p. 105).

Alley communities often had a hierarchy that was responsible for maintaining this shared sense of appropriate behavior and the alley's social order. The chief role was often taken by an older, long-term resident. Such leaders seem to have been chosen informally because of their activity on behalf of their neighbors, their leadership ability, and the respect other residents had for them. In Center Court, as we have seen, it was Aunt Jane to whom "everyone turns . . . when they are in trouble." Her daughter, Gladys, was well on her way to inheriting that leadership role; she was a power in the court and had given considerable help and guidance to others, both on internal alley affairs and in dealing with the world outside. In contrast, the "unofficial mayor" of Fenton Place "is a retired government employee who receives a pension that enables him to occupy a position of respect and relative wealth in the 'community.'" He had served as a messenger for the Navy Department when Franklin D. Roosevelt was assistant secretary; this fact, as well as his thirty-three years of continuous residence in Fenton Place, helped account for his position.[76] Similarly, a Washington *Times* article indicated that four women and one man were "the most celebrated of the rulers of [Willow Tree] alley."[77]

These leaders were responsible for a number of activities, including organizing help for needy members of the alley community. Students of alley life all observed that "the strong community spirit in the alleys is their most notable attribute. They feed their own hungry, house their own homeless, lend to their own penniless, and shelter their own refugees from the law."[78] This aid sometimes took

76. Swinney, "Alley Dwellings and Housing Reform," 114.

77. Washington *Times*, Sept. 11, 1904. Smiley, author of the 1894 guide to Washington (a less than reliable source), wrote of Freeman's Alley: "This queer place has a ruler but who it is and where he lives only his people know, and they never ever refer to his existence. But that he does exist and rules with an iron hand is shown by every action of his slaves. One of the best demonstrations of this prince of crime's wonderful power is the manner in which his retainers act when summoned to court to testify against one of their fellow bond servants. A man may be arrested for having assaulted another and beat him in a most inhuman manner; the whole affair may have been seen by the wounded man's family and yet if they are all put on the witness stand to testify, the man who was assaulted will swear that he does not recognize his assailant, the others will know nothing whatever of the affair, and if there is any chance of getting the prisoner released several more will be on hand to swear that at the time the assault was committed the accused was in South Washington or some other place equally remote from the scene of the crime at the time the assault was committed" (*Glimpse at the Night Side of Washington*, p. 40).

78. Forestall, "Trends in Housing," p. 32. See also Bicknell, *Inhabited Alleys of Washington*, p. 31; Weller, *Neglected Neighbors*, p. 47; Aubry, "Ambitions of Youth," p. 3; Sellew, *Deviant Social Situation*, p. 46.

the form of individual help, as when a mother in Snow's Court took "her boy over to a neighbor's and then went away—no one knew where. The neighbor took care of the child for two years until the mother returned." In other cases more concerted aid was given, as in the case of a "woman and her children" who "eat with first one neighbor and another."[79] Activities could range from the community removing and storing wood (as in the case of Aunt Jane and Center Court), to the taking in of children "because they had more room" in neighboring houses.[80] Moreover, as the *National Republican* noted in 1862 of the black population in general, "There has never been a colored person buried in Washington at the public expense. The people of color in the District have charitable societies among themselves—numbering some thirty in all—which take care of the sick and bury the dead. Neither the public nor the government has ever been called on for a farthing for these objects."[81] Forty years later the Washington *Times* came to the same conclusion about alley dwellers:

> Not only do they bury their dead without assistance from the District of Columbia, and provide medical attention for the ill, but if one of them is arrested and taken to the police station the money to secure bail is immediately forthcoming. They go beyond that. Lawyers are retained to defend the serious cases, and witnesses can be produced to swear along any line of defense that is set up.
>
> A friend in trouble is the sole object of their attention for the time being. If one of them is sought for by the police everyone is active in the attempt to hide him. If the officer is not known by them as determined, and a successful fighter, the arrest of a member of the fraternity is the signal for a general attack by the entire alley. If the rescue fails their next move is to take up a swift collection to bail him out. Their

79. Bicknell, *Inhabited Alleys of Washington*, p. 31. See also Sellew, *Deviant Social Situation*, p. 54; Somerville, "Study of a Group of Negro Children," p. 24; Ratigan, *Sociological Survey of Disease*, p. 59; Washington *Daily News*, Aug. 29, 1941; Swinney, "Alley Dwellings and Housing Reform," p. 73; Pablo, "Housing Needs and Social Problems," p. 56; and Board of Children's Guardians, *Children's History*, I-VII. A typical case record reports that the "mother is a young woman about 22 years of age; without friends or shelter in the city. She was taken in by a Mrs. _____, 211 Reeves Court until she could obtain work and make provision for the baby." Another notes that "Having no mother this child has been passed from one to another in O Street Alley" (II, 657; I, 233–34; see also II, 667, 801).

80. Ratigan, *Sociological Survey of Disease*, p. 119.

81. Washington *National Republican*, Mar. 24, 1862. This article was actually a reprint of an article by the New York *Evening Post*'s Washington correspondent.

ability to raise money for such purposes is a constant source
of amazement to the police who are familiar with the lives
they lead.[82]

While most efforts were neither as extensive or as concerted as this
article tries to suggest, it does seem clear that most alley communities did, in fact, attempt to handle the problems that confronted
them.

Alley dwellers sought to establish a community to provide a second safety net, in case the financial resources of the extended-augmented family proved inadequate in a crisis. Yet the community
was considerably more; it also provided a worldview and social
order that supported its residents. Drawing on a culture developed
from the slave experience, alley dwellers were able to take advantage of their environment, creating physical and psychological barriers to isolate and protect their community as well as developing a
strategy for survival in a hostile world. Moreover, the alley community provided a place where residents could relax, interact with
their neighbors, and watch their children play away from dangerous traffic.

There was considerable variation between alley communities,
however, just as between alley families. Ratigan reported that, of
the four alleys she studied, one closely resembled Blagden as described by Weller; in a second, because there were numerous residents from South Carolina as well as from Washington, and because
physical barriers segmented this population even further, several
groups formed. The third alley had a high turnover; as a result,
only the older, more stable residents had formed any meaningful
connections. Finally,

> The fourth alley has ten houses and ten families. There is
> not the din of the first, the seclusion of the second, nor the
> mystery of the third alley. The tenants sit decorously on the
> steps or in front of their own or a neighbor's door. All have
> lived there for several years; one woman had lived there sev-
> enty years! They were friendly with their neighbors and
> three families kept children from neighboring houses "be-
> cause they had more room."[83]

There are a number of further qualifications on the extent and
nature of the alley community. Because of the large numbers of inhabited alleys, the considerable variations in alley size, and the 120-

82. Washington *Times*, Sept. 11, 1904. Willow Tree Alley.
83. Ratigan, *Sociological Survey of Disease*, p. 118–19.

year time period considered here, we should expect examples of virtually every conceivable form of behavior. Perhaps a reasonable comparison would be with the "covenanted communities" that existed throughout New England and the Midwest.[84] Like those religious towns, alley communities had their own life cycles, which could range from a tightly interwoven network of relatives and friends at one point, to a loosely connected group of neighbors at another. Certainly not all alley residents were highly involved in the ongoing alley community, as Ratigan's third alley suggests. Furthermore, some residents lived in the alley only because they could not find or afford street housing. These families resented or even feared the alley environment-community, and openly resisted it. Like the "covenanted town," the alley community, while providing a sense of belonging and meaning for its residents, also imposed constraints. It required a sharing of resources, making it difficult for residents to accumulate the financial base upon which upward mobility was necessarily founded. Moreover, not all forms of behavior were supported. Rather than fostering anarchy, as alleged by housing reformers and others, the alley community supported and permitted a limited range of thought, action, and behavior. Deviants were warned and punished.

In spite of these considerable differences, most alleys had viable communities. Part of the motivation for community came from the very precarious economic state most alley residents found themselves in, as well as from the ever-present danger of the racist white society just outside. Although these negative factors alone were enough to create a community, common experience, background, and culture laid a positive basis for that community, while the alley's physical layout made personal interaction very easy. Judging from the actions of alley dwellers as seen through photographs of the alley commons, and through their residential persistence and their own testimonies of residential satisfaction, the alley community was an important institution. By utilizing the alley as "defensible space," and by manipulating "outsiders'" fears of it, residents were able to control their neighborhood, thus establishing a sense of sovereignty and power as well as security. Alley dwellers were able to delineate the social and moral boundaries of their community, and to maintain its values and worldview. Often a hierarchy existed within the alley world, with those at the top deciding on and overseeing the actions of others, whether to aid a needy family or to punish a deviant. Moreover, the community was based on attitudes

84. See Smith, *As a City Upon a Hill.*

and values that can be traced back to folk roots, and that reflected communal concern through mutual aid when needed. As one alley resident said, "I knows where I'm at here in the alley. . . . Most of us is poor and live in bad houses but we has a good time."

Not only did the alley community provide protection, support, and friendship for its occupants; it also nurtured its young. Through child-rearing practices, both alley community and alley family insured that their worldview would continue.

Chapter 4
Childhood

In the alley it's mostly dark, even if the sun is out. But if
you look around, you can find things. I know how to get
into every building, except it's like night once you're inside
them, because they don't have lights. So, I stay here.
You're better off. It's no good on the street. You can get
hurt all the time, one way or the other. And in buildings,
like I told you, it's bad in them, too. But here it's O.K.
You can find your own corner, and if someone tries to move
in you fight him off. We meet here all the time, and fig-
ure out what we'll do next. It might be a game, or over
for some pool, or a coke or something. You need to have a
place to start out from, and that's like it is in the alley; you
can always know your buddy will be there, provided it's
the right time. So you go there, and you're on your way,
man.—*Peter, a nine-year-old Boston Alley resident,*
quoted in Robert Coles, "Like It Is in the Alley"

One of the surest ways to test the continuing
strengths of family and community is to assess the ability of each to
transmit its values and ways of life from one generation to another.
The literature on alley dwellers reports amazingly similar findings
regardless of historical era. Moreover, a consideration of the nature
of childhood in the alleys helps explain how family and community
deviate from the mainstream. If both institutions had broken down
in the city, it should have been most apparent in the children.

Again, the sources present some difficulty, but we can still determine the role children played within the family. Second, we must
consider the impact of mainstream institutions on the attitudes and
values of alley children. Since schools and popular media allegedly
encouraged children to break from their parents' values, consideration of these two areas is crucial. Within the alley community itself,
children found activities and entertainments that provided key integrating experiences. In contrast, the extent and nature of juvenile

delinquency will be considered as another test of the breakdown of family and community, while the attitudes of children toward both family and community will supplement this information.

Childhood in the alleys was largely training for adulthood. This is not to say that there was no play, no merriment, no fun. Rather, all activities, whether chores, jobs, or play, were oriented toward the alley way of life. Unlike the middle-class ideal of childhood, every activity of an alley child, save perhaps his formal education, prepared him for the life he was later to lead.

Like everything else in alley life, childhood was, first and foremost, functional for family and community. "In these homes a child is valued for his usefulness as well as his other characteristics. The boys 'junk' and run errands, the girls wash the dishes and, in general, help mother . . . there is a great temptation to show partiality to the child who is an asset in any of these."[1] Charles Merrill, a nine-year-old Center Court resident, "gets up while the adults in the home are still in bed and with an axe (man's size) succeeds in breaking off enough kindling wood from the large boards taken from wrecked houses or from boxes found in the streets, to start the fire in the kitchen stove."[2] He also "cuts school whenever possible and borrows a little wagon with which he collects junk and wood for his mother," as well as helping around the house.[3] Johnny Brown, a nine-year-old living in the same court, "'junks,' both working with his family and by himself, bringing in glass, paper and rags."[4] Johnny's sister, Elizabeth (age 14), cooks her stepfather's breakfast, and "for a few hours on Saturdays she works for relatives, scrubbing and cleaning and helping with the babies."[5]

Not only did these children work around the home and "junk," but many of them also had jobs to help support the family and to pay for their own clothes. Besides his other tasks, Johnny Brown "was serving beer at fifty cents an hour" on Saturdays, while sixteen-year-old Harry Hutchins of Center Court "was the most ambitious of all the boys. He was successful in getting a job in a shoeshine parlor a few weeks ago and he is very pleased with it. 'I jist make $4 a week but I also git a plenty of tips.'"[6] Center Court boys and girls parked cars for baseball games at nearby Griffith Stadium, and many of the girls, like Elizabeth Brown, also "helped with housework in the homes on 10th Street."[7]

1. Sellew, *Deviant Social Situation*, p. 26.
2. *Ibid.*, p. 99.   4. *Ibid.*, p. 94.
3. *Ibid.*, p. 101.   5. *Ibid.*, pp. 74, 72.
6. *Ibid.*, p. 93; and Somerville, "Study of a Group of Negro Children," p. 34.
7. Somerville, "Study of a Group of Negro Children," p. 32; Sellew, *Deviant*

Table 19.
*Education and Employment of Alley Children, 1880**

| | | | School age children only | |
Activity (Age)	N	%	N	%
At home (0– 5)	1,812	43	—	—
At school (6–15)	1,194	28	1,194	50
At home (6–15)	315	7	315	13
Employed females (6–15)	77	2	77	3
Employed males (6–15)	75	2	75	3
At school and work (6–15)	8	—	8	—
Not ascertainable	739	18	739	31
TOTAL	4,220	100	2,408	100

	N
Adult males at school (16+)	21
Adult females at school (16+)	33
TOTAL	54

*Based on Federal Population Census Schedules, 1880, Washington, D.C., RG 29 NA.

Other sources confirm that child labor was quite common, despite being underreported in the 1880 census. (See Table 19.[8]) Lewis Hine's 1912 survey of child labor in Washington revealed that alley children as young as seven were employed as "newsies," with most not much older than ten. Dan Mercurio of 150 Schottes Court, who began selling newspapers at seven, was "a chronic tru-

Social Situation, p. 72. Nor was this a new experience for black children. As Genovese notes, slave children's "work in the garden plots, for example, reduced the burden on their overworked parents. The older boys learned to trap squirrels and other small animals to augment and vary the family's diet. Slave parents did not ruthlessly exploit their children in these ways, the children willingly contributed to the household" (*Roll, Jordan, Roll*, p. 503).

8. It is not surprising that child labor was underreported in the census; enumerators were not very diligent about asking all the required questions or filling the form out completely. The situation for unemployment is even more striking, and, as noted earlier, alley residents were not always eager to share personal information about family members with strangers. Moreover, since the forms of work available to children were often temporary, part-time, or involved self-employment (as in the case of newsboys), underreporting is to be expected. Many, if not most alley children worked sometime during their childhood.

ant" even though he had made only eight cents the day Hine interviewed him. Peter Pope of Wonders Court, who was ten, did little better: he averaged only "20 cents a day," although he "begins selling at 5 a.m." Alley children also worked at Washington's markets. Hine noted that eleven-year-old celery vendor Gus Strateges of Jackson Hall Alley, whose family had only been in the country for two-and-a-half years, worked "until 11 p.m. and was out again Sunday morning selling papers and gum."[9]

Photograph 26 provides some interesting indications of another important role of children in the alley family. Not only did alley children tend to stick together, but older children were expected to look out for and often to raise their younger brothers and sisters. As Aubry noted of Center Court, older children often had to "remain at home in order to take care of the younger ones" while parents worked.[10] For example, Charles Merrill, who chopped up kindling in the early morning, was also expected "to take responsibility of his little sisters during all the hours of the day in which he is not at school."[11]

Given the need for children to work both inside and outside the home, it is not surprising that formal education was often expendable. Undoubtedly the 1880 Census figure that 50 percent of school-age alley children were in school (see Table 19) is both overstated and misleading. In 1870 the *Special Report of the Commissioner of Education* indicated that less than a third of school-age black children were attending any school, while Constance Green has pointed out that "in the late nineteenth century relatively few Negro children stayed in school beyond the fourth grade, and of those who finished the eighth grade, still fewer, especially of the boys went on."[12] A survey taken in Blagden Alley in 1905, the year before a compul-

9. National Child Labor Commission Collection, Library of Congress, nos. 2899, 2900, 2904, 2905, 2907, 2908, 2915, 2917, 2925, 2928.

10. Aubry, "Ambitions of Youth," pp. 26–27.

11. Sellew, *Deviant Social Situation*, p. 99. Again, this practice has been observed by students of slavery, by alley residents in other cities, and is visible in current social patterns of rural blacks. See Genovese, *Roll, Jordan, Roll*, p. 508; Young, "Family and Children in a Southern Town," pp. 282–85; Waters, *His Eye Is on the Sparrow*, pp. 3, 7.

12. M. B. Goodwin, "History of Schools for the Colored Population in the District of Columbia," in Department of Education, *Special Report of the Commissioner of Education* (Washington, 1871), p. 255; Green, *Secret City*, p. 138. The extent of illiteracy in the adult alley population in 1880 also lends some support to this statement. While underreporting is quite likely, 52 percent were unable to read and write, and another 8 percent could not write. Not surprisingly, household heads reported even greater illiteracy: 66 percent could not read or write.

PHOTOGRAPH 26.
"Alley Newsboys on Capitol Hill." "In comparison with governmental affairs, newsies are small matters. This photo taken in the shadow of the National Capitol where the laws are made. . . . This group of young newsboys sells on the Capitol grounds every day, ages 8 years, 9 years, 10 years, 11 years, 12 years. The only boy with a badge was the 8 year old, and it didn't belong to him. Names are Tony Passaro, 8 years old, 124 Schottes Alley, NE; Joseph Passaro, 11 years old, (has made application for badge); Joseph Mase (9 years old), 122 Schottes Alley; Joseph Tucci, (10 years old) 411 1/2 5th Street NE; Jack Giovanazzi, 228 Schottes Alley— 12 years old. Is in ungraded school for incorrigibility in school." April, 1912. Photograph by Lewis Wickes Hine. National Child Labor Committee Collection, Library of Congress.

sory attendance law was passed, found twenty-two children between eight and fourteen years of age who were in school and nineteen who were not. Seven children between twelve and sixteen had attended so little school that they were still in the first three grades, while of the children from five to eight years old, only two were in school, with fourteen absent.[13] In his 1938 study, however, Swin-

13. Weller, *Neglected Neighbors*, p. 34.

Photograph 27.
"Family in front of their alley dwelling. The oldest woman is a charwoman in a U.S. Government office building." July, 1941. Photograph by Ed Rosskam. Farm Security Administration Collection, Library of Congress.

ney found that "many of the young people between the ages of sixteen and twenty-one have completed all twelve grades."[14]

For those who did find the school experience enjoyable, there were innumerable obstacles to regular attendance. Older children might be expected to stay home to care for younger ones, and when they reached sixteen (after passage of compulsory attendance) they were often expected to quit school and go to work to help with family finances.[15] Children often missed school "due to sickness, lack of proper winter clothes, dislike of teachers, neglect of parents in insisting on school attendance."[16] Participation in extra-curricular activities by Center Court children was nonexistent, "due to the lack of money to buy the necessary materials. They learn all the songs taught at school, but none of them has ever participated in any of the folk dances, or group songs, concerts, etc., where appearance before a group of people is necessary."[17] Many children were, at best, ambivalent about school. "Harry's record at school shows an absence of 30 days in one stretch . . . he did not like school," while Martha's "records show a considerable amount of absences. The reason may be due to one thing, her teacher." Truancy in Center Court was allegedly "confined to the boys" and caused by "lack of interest in school."[18] A poem written by one Center Court child conveys some typical attitudes:

SCHOOL

is, such, a, Funny, Place,
I, Don't, See, Why, We, Go,
But, Yet, and, Still, We, Have,
to, Go, Each, and, Every, Day.

II

But, yet, And, Still, We, Have,
To, Go, It, Really, Don't Make,
Sence, For, I, Just, Hate, To,
Go, To, School, And, I, Know,
That, You, Will, Agree.

III

For, School, is, Just, A,
Place, For, Fools, and, Fools,

14. Swinney, "Alley Dwellings and Housing Reform," p. 137.

15. Aubry, "Ambitions of Youth," p. 27.

16. Ratigan, *Sociological Survey of Disease*, p. 119; Aubry, "Ambitions of Youth," p. 25.

17. Aubry, "Ambitions of Youth," p. 27.

18. *Ibid.*, pp. 25–26.

> Don't Only, Go, I Go,
> And I, Am, not, A, Fool.[19]

The children of Center Court "do very little reading," and there was little or no "literature" in their homes.[20] Moreover,

> Girls of eleven and fourteen, in their normal school grades, will read books suitable for children six years old with as much interest as books which are suitable for their age and mental development. Their whole attention is centered on the act of reading, quite dissociated from the content. They wish to read aloud to each other, apparently regarding it as an accomplishment or stunt. They do not have books which are favorites and to which they return time and time again.[21]

It is clear from the above that alley children (and, by implication, other alley residents) were more comfortable with oral than with written or literary culture. Other evidence of this oral black culture can be found in Somerville's description of how children played the "dozens."[22] While Washington's segregated schools may have been somewhat more sympathetic toward oral tradition and culture, the school's primary role was to socialize black children into the value structure of the dominant group.[23] Undoubtedly some children were attracted to the more mainstream approach of the school, and were supported in this by their parents. For many, however, the need to work, coupled with an often unsympathetic school environment, led to early abandonment of formal education. Home conditions tended to impose restrictions even for those who might have liked to read: "I can't finish those long stories in one day and we have no lights."[24] This was not an insurmountable problem for other kinds of literature, however—"Often the children may be found gathered around a table with a candle on it reading 'funny books'."[25]

Alley children were also attracted to the movies, which were "regarded as fun by the younger children and the basis for dramatic

19. Quoted in Somerville, "A Study of a Group of Negro Children," p. 47.
20. *Ibid.*, p. 41; Aubry, "Ambitions of Youth," p. 42.
21. Sellew, *Deviant Social Situation*, pp. 34–35.
22. Somerville, "Study of a Group of Negro Children," p. 38: "To say anything against one's family is a source of much contempt and hatred. And, to comment on one's mother calls for physical violence. Fighting and argument are due mostly to defense of one's mother."
23. See Appendix A.
24. Aubry, "Ambitions of Youth," p. 42.
25. Somerville, "Study of a Group of Negro Children," p. 20.

play and vicarious participation in a thrilling life, by the older boys and girls." While they attended movies "made for adults," they "seem only interested in telling over again what they have seen. A half dozen may all help with the details; there is no discussion or interest in the story as such. It is an account of what they saw, a series of discrete acts as opposed to a continuous working out of a story."[26] Gladys Sellew, seeking to offer "more appropriate film experiences" for the children, took the girls to *Heidi* and the boys to *Dead End*. She felt that they could not understand the plots of these films, either; moreover, "Their response was that it was not true and not as exciting as 'Dick Tracy.' They were not interested in the story and in relatively few of the events. The effort to follow through any story, however simple or however thrilling, bores them, while a series of intensely dramatic events satisfies them." Her effort to offer "finer cultural experiences," as conveyed through *Snow White and the Seven Dwarfs*, resulted in a similar reaction—"great interest in certain details, for example, the angry faces of the trees, the caricatures of nose, mouth, and eyes in the different dwarfs, but no interest in the story as such or appreciation of the beauty of this extraordinary film."[27]

It is not surprising that the alley children's response was different from that of the adult white middle-class participant-observer. Certainly, *Dick Tracy* was closer to the alley experience than *Snow White*, not to mention that the latter film had possible racial implications. If emphasis was "laid on physical violence and sex," and if "acts of physical violence are illustrated wherever the recounting of the movie takes place," it was undoubtedly because such elements related to the physical, tactile, expressive alley culture. The fact that alley children were attracted to specific scenes, rather than to the plot, suggests that the culture of the alley (and black experience generally) strongly influenced what they saw, liked, and remembered. By constantly retelling the scenes, they were not only reinforcing that perception for themselves, but also introducing it to others who may have missed the movie, as well as expanding the oral tradition.[28]

Sellew thought alley children liked movies which stressed sex

26. Sellew, *Deviant Social Situation*, p. 44.

27. *Ibid.*, p. 45

28. Drawing on the work of Bruce Jackson, Levine has noted that the "structural units in Negro folksongs are typically the metaphor and line rather than the plot; Negro songs don't tend to weave narrative elements together to create a story but instead accumulate images to create a feeling" (*Black Culture and Black Consciousness*, p. 240).

and violence. That assessment tells us a great deal about her perceptions, but little about those of the children. It suggests an important
fact that has been verified by other investigators: in spite of claims
that the mass media are making a mass audience, not everyone sees
the same thing. Selective perception is a proven fact; suburban
dwellers drive through the ghetto every day yet cannot describe it,
while ghetto residents bus to suburbia every day and have only a
slightly better perception of that community. As Herbert Gans
found in his study of Italian West Enders in Boston, "media can be
used to justify both the peer group society and its rejection of the
outside world."[29] If alley residents were being increasingly bom-
barded by the mass media, the media could have reinforced alley
culture, rather than breaking it down.

The media's influence can be seen in a change of forms, although
not necessarily of meaning or function. Somerville reported that "at
the time the first study [Sellew, 1938] was made it was found that
the children's favorite songs were spirituals or hymns. At the present time [1941], either through radio or records, their favorite songs
are the popular songs of the day," although "for their own amuse-
ment they sing familiar tunes of which they have changed the
words."[30] For example:

> (to the tune of America)
> My country t'is of thee
> I live in Germany
> My name is France
> Hot dogs and sauer Kraut
> Joe Louis knocked Schmelling out
> So what is there to cry about
> Let Freedom ring.[31]

29. Herbert Gans, *The Urban Villagers* (New York, 1962), p. 188. See also
Levine, *Black Culture and Black Consciousness*, p. 228.

30. Somerville, "Study of a Group of Negro Children," p. 47. Too much should
not be made of this "marked change," however. Levine found that songs and language may vary by age among black children (*Black Culture and Black Consciousness*,
p. 154).

31. Somerville, "Study of a Group of Negro Children," p. 47. This song is undoubtedly traditional, rather than a product of alley children. Nevertheless, it
would have been interesting if the observer had followed up on the reference to the
Louis-Schmelling fight. A study of children's singing games reported that, while
white children tend to maintain songs as they learned them, black children make
up their own versions; Leah Rachel Clara Yoffie, "Three Generations of Children's
Singing Games in St. Louis," *Journal of American Folklore*, 60 (Jan.–Mar., 1947):
39–41.

Another song, which might also be traditional, reflects a common alley experience:

> Onward Christian Chinches
> Marching up the sheet
> Twenty-four thousand chinches
> Tickling Grandpa's feet
> Grandpa got excited
> And went to get his gun
> O, my Lawd you ought to see
> Them bowleg chinches run-un.

"When the writer asked them how they came to write such a poem they said, 'One of us jist thought of the chinches on the bed and the rest of us jist put the words and from there we went along.'"[32] Center Court children made up a number of songs; one, reported by Sellew in 1938, was said by Somerville in 1941 to still be "one of the favorite[s] and the one most frequently heard in the court. Many times the children sing it to entertain others but often it is heard in their own homes in the evening when the children are gathered around the fire before bedtime."[33] The song was reported to be the result of a "silly symphony" two girls had seen at a movie theater; it involved a frog who was "sitting on a lily pad, while a bee and a butterfly circled about him. In trying to catch the butterfly the frog caught and swallowed the bee instead."[34]

> A LITTLE BUTTERFLY
> (Sung to a modification of "Water Boy")
>
> It was a little butterfly, hank
> A sailing on the river, hank
> A sailing on the river, hank
> Oh, yes, it was, hank
> A sailing on the river, hank
> Oh, yes it was, hank
> Now listen here brother, hank
> I want a drink, hank
> I want a drink, hank
> It was a forty pound hammer, hank
> That killed John Henry, hank

32. Somerville, "Study of a Group of Negro Children," p. 48.
33. *Ibid.*
34. *Ibid.*

> That killed John Henry, hank
> But it won't kill me, hank.[35]

It is, of course, impossible to know exactly what this song might have meant to the alley children. Certainly this lyric draws on John Henry, the legendary black folk hero. Moreover, the text seems to state that these children knew how the system works, and at the same time chose to reject that system. Trying to get the butterfly—or, in John Henry's case, trying to beat the machine—brought only disaster or death. It could be asserting that the materialistic values of the surrounding society could destroy those who take too seriously the acquisitive spirit of that society.[36] This interpretation is supported by a song written by another Center Court child:

> If I had a Million Dollars
> I know just whut I'll do
> I'd buy myself jist two wings
> Fly high up on the sky.
> Nobody hear me whisper
> Nobody hear me sing
> Me and my two wings
> Fly high up in the sky.
> I may hear the wind blow
> I may see the trees grow
> But me and my two wings
> Fly high up in the sky.
> Some people have their money
> They don't know what to do
> But me and my two wings
> Fly high in the deep blue sky.[37]

Yvonne, the author, rejected material goods ("Some people have their money / They don't know what to do") for a sense and feeling of freedom. On the other hand, Yvonne's song and her following poem do not fully endorse alley life, either:

> When I was a little girl about six or three
> My father took a stick and beated me

35. *Ibid.*
36. Levine has provided another explanation: "black workers saw in the death of John Henry not a defeat but a challenge" (*Black Culture and Black Consciousness*, p. 438).
37. Somerville, "Study of a Group of Negro Children," p. 46. This song was later sold.

I went to my mother but what's the use
When I git a whipping there is no excuse.[38]

Singing played an important part in the children's lives. According to Sellew, "On summer evenings the children spread a 'big, old blanket' on the cobble stones (especially on moonlight nights), and sing late into the evening. In winter, singing and playing accompanies both pleasure and delinquency among the children or pleasure and vice among the adults. Sometimes of an evening a fire will be made upstairs in one of the homes and the children sing around the stove."[39] Much of children's play took place "in a circle," with "all singing the words," or in word games played with two lines of facing children.[40] The peer group was very important for alley children, because through it they learned to act as a community. They "wrote" songs together, participated in retelling scenes from favorite movies, and sang popular songs as well as spiritual hymns to which they often made up their own words, thus imposing their own sense of order and reality through community expression.[41]

Perhaps the distance between the folk-alley experience and the school can best be seen through the communal creation of story and

38. *Ibid.*

39. Sellew, *Deviant Social Situation*, p. 32. Years before, Frederick Law Olmsted had recorded a similar scene: "During the evening all the cabins were illuminated by great fires and looking into one of them, I saw a very picturesque family grouping; a man sat on the ground making a basket, a woman lounged on a chest in the chimney corner smoking a pipe, and a boy and two girls sat in a bed which had been drawn up opposite to her, completing the fireside circle. They were talking and laughing cheerfully" (*A Journey to the Back Country, 1853–1854* [New York, 1970], p. 142).

40. Sellew, *Deviant Social Situation*, pp. 29–30.

41. Again, these are a continuation of earlier slave practices. As Levine concluded, "In both the temple and the field, black song was for the most part communal song. Negroes sang in groups surrounded by and responding to other singers, melting their individual consciousness into the group consciousness." Nevertheless, he notes that "After World War I the images surrounding black music began to change. The work-prayer context seemed to give way to the leisure setting. The communal context faded into the background to be replaced by the image of an isolated individual with a guitar" (*Black Culture and Black Consciousness*, p. 217). While evidence presented here supports the shift to a leisure setting, there is little indication of a shift to individual performers, as opposed to the communal. Ethel Waters remembered both: "My family and the other families who lived in those alley homes harmonized without any instruments to accompany them. There were musicians in the neighborhood, fellows who played the banjo, mandolin, guitar, and the bells (sometimes one man would play all of them). But they played at parties and sometimes on street corners. And we never had the money for a party. There were always people in the house, but that wasn't for any party" (*His Eye Is on the Sparrow*, p. 13).

song. Alley education was communal, corporate, and cooperative; it required a joint effort to create a single story or song. Repetition of the item by everyone, creator or not, is central to the oral folk tradition. In contrast, the school sought to work with each individual. Corporate activities and corporate products were openly repressed (and punished, in cases of "cheating" or plagiarism), except in peripheral activities such as sports and music.

Dancing was also a popular and common activity, among children as well as adults. In 1941 Somerville reported that "'Jitterbugging' is a dance the children enjoy most. This dance requires much exercise and exertion. The entire evening was spent jitterbugging. At recreation they just 'jitter' hours at a time. The familiar dances are the 'Big Apple,' and 'Trucking.'" Buck dancing, however, "is done only in their homes. Sometimes a child might demonstrate how it is done when she is at the house. Hortense and Yvonne are the only children who can perform this dance very well. The others will try in vain to imitate them. It is a very difficult dance which consists of rhythmic movements of the shoulders in a jerking fashion in opposite movement to the feet sliding along the floor."[42]

Dancing was not the only activity that required exertion. "The children of the alley engage in games which require much physical energy. . . . Racing around the alley to the street and back is often enjoyed," as was "wrestling with one another."[43] The children played "very rough, often bruising each other in play."[44] This rough, physical play, of course, is functional to the adult lives they will lead, the demanding physical work of the day laborer and the equally demanding work of the washerwoman or domestic.

As the photographic analysis revealed, few toys or games were available to alley children. No children are shown holding dolls or stuffed animals, nor are any playing "packaged" games, although Sellew reported that dolls and toy soldiers were common in Center Court.[45] Nevertheless, many children played baseball, marbles, and "soldier."[46] These games were not without order and rules, for

42. Somerville, "Study of a Group of Negro Children," p. 45.

43. *Ibid.*, p. 40; Aubry, "Ambitions of Youth," p. 41.

44. Aubry, "Ambitions of Youth," p. 41. This stands in contrast to Young's recent findings. However, the subjective evaluation of "rough" and "gentle" by different observers may be part of the explanation. Young, "Family and Childhood in a Southern Negro Community," p. 283.

45. Sellew, *Deviant Social Situation*, p. 34.

46. See Appendix B. Genovese reports that similar games were common among slave children (*Roll, Jordan, Roll*, p. 505). Young's recent study of a rural black community in Georgia found little use of toys or any material objects in play at all.

when one plays "soldier" "the first to call, 'I've got the drop on you' 'kills.' It is against the rules of the games not to drop dead."[47]

Many of the larger toys were homemade. Center Court had "old wagons and handmade scooters," while Photograph 28 shows a homemade "racer." Later sources suggest that manufactured toys like bicycles and wagons were more common. (See photograph 32.)

Older boys in Center Court enjoyed "games involving gambling. 'Pitty-Pat,' 'Konk,' 'Black Jack,' and 'Poker' are the best liked gambling games. The boys often gather in a secluded corner by the Johnson's house to avoid the police who are always on the watch for them."[48] Swinney observed young men in their "twenties and late 'teens' with many young boys 'hanging around.'" A card game was usually in progress on "a small porch on one of the dwellings. . . . Nearly always there was money 'in the pot' and 'a jar of corn whiskey' slightly hidden under the steps."[49] Nor was gambling solely a male activity: thirteen-year-old Yvonne "often collects a sum of dimes in playing 'Pitty-Pat.'"[50]

Gambling and keeping corn whiskey were illegal activities, of course, and there is evidence that the police were always on the watch for youthful alley lawbreakers. Somerville pointed out that the police "are always suspicious of the children in the alley. They are picked up on the very least suspicion. One of the boys was put in jail because it was suspected that he had stolen a bicycle which was actually given to him."[51] She added, "Police brutality is not entirely rebelled against, but the children recognize that it is not exactly fair."[52] Despite the fact that alley children were probably more frequently arrested than other young people, regardless of their guilt or innocence, observers of alley life often felt that there was much juvenile delinquency there. Nevertheless, a study of the

---

Virtually all the games involved extensive social interaction and oral communication, not unlike those described by Sellew. Young, "Family and Childhood in a Southern Negro Community," p. 283; Sellew, *Deviant Social Situation*, pp. 29–30.

47. Sellew, *Deviant Social Situation*, p. 92.

48. Somerville, "Study of a Group of Negro Children," p. 41.

49. Swinney, "Alley Dwellings and Housing Reform," p. 142. Similarly, Genovese reported that "The bolder spirits among the boys sometimes took to shooting craps and playing cards" (*Roll, Jordan, Roll*, p. 505).

50. Somerville, "Study of a Group of Negro Children," p. 32.

51. *Ibid.*, p. 56.

52. *Ibid.*, p. 61. Some years earlier, the Washington *Bee* found it "a fact that policemen take a great delight in arresting every little colored boy they see on the street, who may be doing something not at all offensive, and allow the white boys to do what they please" (Aug. 6, 1887).

PHOTOGRAPH 28.
"Homemade Racer: Bell's Court." Photograph by John Ihlder. John Ihlder Collection, Franklin D. Roosevelt Library.

case records of the Board of Children's Guardians for the period from 1893 to 1913 suggests that, despite the aggressive activities of the police, very little evidence substantiates the observers' claims.[53] As Tables 20 and 21 indicate, only two alley children per thousand had contact with the Board in a year; moreover, as these tables suggest, many such contacts were due to death, illness, or unemployment. These circumstances brought parents to commit their children until they could once again support them. One two-month-old baby was brought to the Board by her mother, a domestic; because of a crippled hand, the woman was unable to support her child.[54] Often, however, children were committed to a relative or even a neighbor, rather than to an "institution" or family chosen by the Board but unknown to the parents.[55]

Cases of incorrigibility were most often brought by parents against their children. Some of these cases demonstrate real "disorder," since a breakdown had clearly occurred between the generations. One case record reported, "This girl has been staying with her grandmother . . . at No. 5½ Fenton Street, NE. The mother, a widow, goes out to service and this girl is beyond the control of all her people."[56] Another case involved a thirteen-year-old boy whose father was dead. His mother complained that he stayed away from home for days and "sleeps about alleys"; he was "entirely beyond her control."[57] Yet the split between child and parents often seems related to different aspirations. Through the case records one can

53. The Board of Children's Guardians was organized on February 28, 1893, by a special act of Congress. It was "charged with the duty of investigating thoroughly the care of each dependent child. If a child is found to be a proper subject for public care, it will be placed in an institution, or otherwise provided for by the Board, and each institution will then be entitled to public money in proportion to the number of such children that it cared for" (69th Congress, 2nd session, Senate, Committee on the District of Columbia, Document no. 207, *Charitable and Reformatory Institutions in the District of Columbia*, comp. George M. Kober [Washington, D.C., 1927], p. 221). A wide variety of cases were referred to the Board, from parents reporting an inability to support a child and wishing to commit it to the Board, to parents reporting incorrigible children, to children brought in by the police for crimes, and cases where the children's home was thought to be a bad influence on the child's moral and physical development.

54. Board of Children's Guardians, *Children's History*, I, 95.

55. Of course, reliance on any "external" group or organization, as in these cases, suggests the influences of both urbanization and modernization, as well as the weakening of family, kinship, neighborhood, and community bonds. While such factors had an impact on some alley folk migrants, such people seem to have been in the minority, based on Tables 20 and 21.

56. Board of Children's Guardians, *Children's History*, II, 571.

57. *Ibid.*, p. 614.

TABLE 20.
Juvenile Delinquency, 1893–1903*

Parents unable to care for children due to:	N	%
Poverty, illness, death, etc.	39	24
Incorrigibility	40	24
Crime	58	35
Parental neglect, mistreatment, unfit home, etc.	28	17
TOTAL	165	100

Number of annual contacts per 1,000 alley children (age 0–16) with Board of Children's Guardians: 2.19.
Based on estimate of population age 0–16 taken from 1880 alley census (39.75%). 1897 census used as base for the ten-year period. Total alley population: 18,978.
*Based on Board of Children's Guardians, *Children's History*, 1–3 (July 4, 1893 – Dec. 19, 1903), RG 351 NA.

TABLE 21.
Juvenile Delinquency, 1903–13*

Parents unable to care for children due to:	N	%
Poverty, illness, death, etc.	29	16
Incorrigible (may include crime)	57	33
Crime	45	26
Parental neglect, mistreatment, unfit home, etc.	26	15
Parents unable to care for and unfit home	17	10
TOTAL	174	100

Number of annual contacts per 1,000 alley children (age 0–16) with the Board of Children's Guardians: 2.30.
Based on estimate of population age 0–16 taken from 1880 alley census (39.75%). 1897 census used as base for the ten-year period. Total alley population: 18,978.
*Based on Board of Children's Guardians, *Children's History*, 4–7 (Dec. 20, 1903 – May 5, 1913), RG 351 NA.

begin to see the results of conflict between parents with mainstream tendencies and their children who have chosen lifestyles more like those of the "street families" described by Hannerz. The parents were often described as "hard-working," "religious," and "good parents"; calling in the authorities must have been a last resort, although some probably hoped that such an experience would straighten their children out. Since these children were not necessarily out of tune with the alley community, they had another form of support. Some cases were designated as incorrigible by outsiders, rather than by the parents, so not all of these reflect familial breakdown.

Nor can the case records on crime be taken at face value. We have already seen that the police arrested an alley child for theft of a bicycle that belonged to him. In another incident, a thirteen-year-old boy was charged with larceny of $.08 in 1902; the case record notes, four years later, he is a "good boy" and drives a cart.[58] One nine-year-old was convicted of larceny of $.75, despite the fact that he was half-starved and had, in fact, taken the money from an employer who owed him even more. The boy spent the "stolen" money on food.[59] Other children found themselves before the courts for such horrendous crimes as using profane language, "pitching pennies," begging, and shooting off fireworks on the Fourth of July.[60] This is not to suggest that some alley children were not serious criminals, at least from mainstream society's viewpoint. One eleven-year-old "was before the Court with 2 other boys for breaking into a store and stealing tobacco, hams, and other things." He belonged to a gang of "boy thieves."[61] Another "was arrested for stealing. He was also charged with breaking and entering. ———, and ———, aged 11 and 14, were associated with him and were arrested, but during the examination it was ascertained that ——— stole the goods alone; the others helped to carry and conceal the plunder. He has now entered more than a dozen houses."[62] Many of those who were arrested for stealing seem to have been doing so to obtain food or clothing that would be used by alley residents, rather than to gain direct financial reward.[63]

58. *Ibid.*, III, 1272.
59. *Ibid.*, I, 156.
60. *Ibid.*, p. 175; III, 1310; I, 445; III, 1060.
61. *Ibid.*, II, 751.
62. *Ibid.*, p. 924.
63. Ethel Waters "stole because I was always hungry. . . . We never felt there was anything wrong in stealing. We never thought anything about it at all. We were hungry" (*His Eye Is on the Sparrow*, p. 23). John K. Alexander found in his study of the poor in late eighteenth-century Philadelphia that adult crime reflected need more than anything else. "Further, the type of items taken were often not the type that could be pawned. Richard Butcher stole a salmon; Oliver O'Harra took one pair of boots; Joseph, a black man, took two loaves of sugar. In at least half the cases, such items suggested that hunger or need for clothing was the force that pushed these people into crime" ("Poverty, Fear, and Continuity; An Analysis of the Poor in Late Eighteenth-Century Philadelphia," in *Peoples of Philadelphia*, ed. Davis and Haller, p. 20).

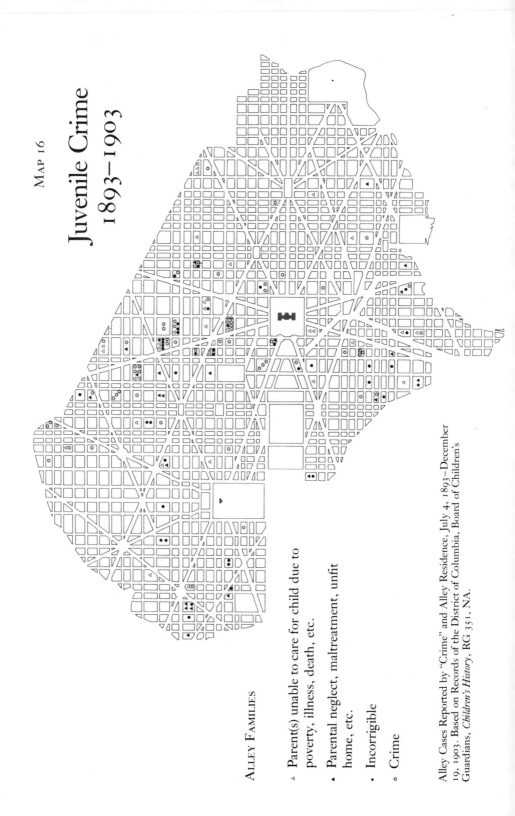

MAP 16

Juvenile Crime
1893–1903

ALLEY FAMILIES

△ Parent(s) unable to care for child due to poverty, illness, death, etc.

▲ Parental neglect, maltreatment, unfit home, etc.

• Incorrigible

◇ Crime

Alley Cases Reported by "Crime" and Alley Residence, July 4, 1893–December 19, 1903. Based on Records of the District of Columbia, Board of Children's Guardians, *Children's History*, RG 351, NA.

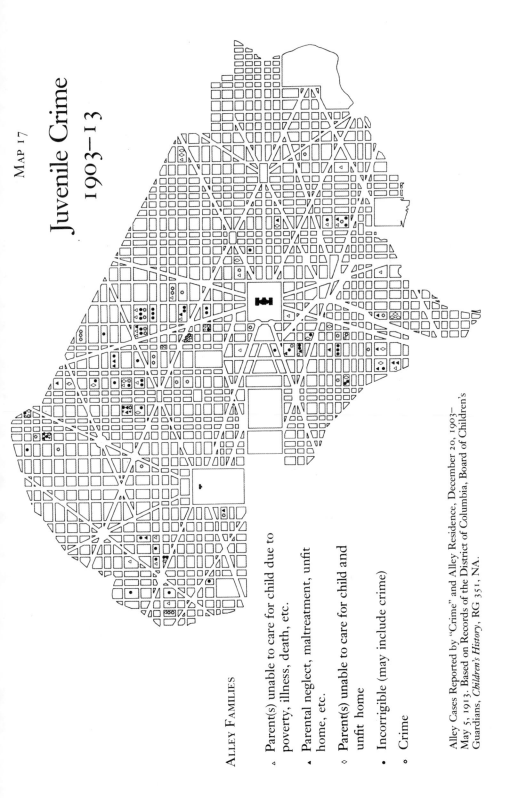

MAP 17

Juvenile Crime
1903–13

ALLEY FAMILIES

△ Parent(s) unable to care for child due to
poverty, illness, death, etc.

▲ Parental neglect, maltreatment, unfit
home, etc.

◇ Parent(s) unable to care for child and
unfit home

● Incorrigible (may include crime)

✿ Crime

Alley Cases Reported by "Crime" and Alley Residence, December 20, 1903–
May 5, 1913. Based on Records of the District of Columbia, Board of Children's
Guardians, *Children's History*, RG 351, NA.

Juvenile delinquency, judged by these records, was not rampant in the alleys. The total number of reported cases for the twenty-year period seems small, given the large numbers of alley dwellers during those years.

If a number of parents had difficulty with their children, there was little evidence of this problem in Center Court: "The children of the alley regard their families with highest esteem. On the whole the children are very polite and courteous to their elders."[64] For example, Martha "loves her mother and idolizes her own father," while "she gets along well with the man with whom her mother is living."[65] In occupational choice, the children "tend toward the unskilled laboring class," suggesting that there is no generation gap in aspirations.

"Like their parents, Center Court children expressed satisfaction with their community. Martha "did not mind letting the people know that she was from the court"; nor did she want to leave the alley for good, because "dem old people on the street thinks they is too good—they thinks they so cute, me I don't like them."[66] Similarly, "friendships in the alley are confined principally to the children within the alley itself. The trend of influence is from the alley into the street. Those few [street] children who have established friendships in the alley have adopted the patterns of the alley."[67] Like their parents, the children have a strong sense of generosity, concern, and community. Martha "is always willing to share with whatever she has. She does not want anyone to refuse something she offers . . . very industrious child . . . her whole attitude is that of protection and bossing."[68] Nor was Martha unique. Somerville found it "remarkable to note the attitude of charity toward the poor in these children when they are so poor themselves. Yet, they are willing to help others who may be worse off than themselves."[69]

Childhood in the alleys clearly provided training for adulthood. Unlike the children of the upper classes, who were encouraged to enjoy "frivolous" play, among alley children "a playful attitude towards certain forms of physical exertion is substituted for play. For example, getting ice and coal, running errands (the handling of money apparently always brings pleasure), washing and cooking, dusting and sweeping." Rather than enjoying handicraft work,

64. Somerville, "Study of a Group of Negro Children," p. 38.
65. Sellew, *Deviant Social Situation*, p. 82.
66. Somerville, "Study of a Group of Negro Children," pp. 29, 39.
67. *Ibid.*, p. 60.
68. *Ibid.*, p. 29.
69. *Ibid.*, p. 41.

washing, ironing, or cooking attracted children. "The girls eleven and fourteen years old will spend two or three hours ironing their school dresses, their father's shirts, or their boyfriends' shirts, and seem happy in the activity itself, as well as in the concrete results."[70] One sees little of the "generation gap" that has been universally reported by observers of urban migrants. What strikes one, rather, is the continuity, as well as a profound ability to find pleasure and fulfillment in what was supposed to be menial and unpleasant labor. The children's attitudes also provide some insight into their parents' attitudes toward work.

Alley children displayed few signs of disorder and delinquency —on the contrary, they appear to be well integrated into the alley community. Rather than succumbing to mainstream values as propagated by the schools and media, they largely rejected the former and used only those elements of the latter that supported their own worldview. Through music and other forms of entertainment alley children created their own amusements; and, more important, by working through traditional forms they maintained key integrating experiences. Not only did the children "create" and pass on traditional songs to each other communally, but they were also participating in an important adult experience, certainly one that bridged the generations. If many of the alley children's activities clashed with mainstream attitudes and values, they were at one with the alley community, as the next chapter will suggest. While the authorities sought to arrest and prosecute them, alley children felt no separation or isolation from their home community and culture.

70. Sellew, *Deviant Social Situation*, pp. 44, 35.

Chapter 5
Work and the Fruits of Labor

The lodging-houses for proletarians are rather numerous (over four hundred), chiefly in courts in the heart of the town. They are nearly all disgustingly filthy and ill-smelling, the refuge of beggars, thieves, tramps, and prostitutes, who eat, drink, smoke and sleep here without the slightest regard to comfort or decency in an atmosphere endurable to these degraded beings only.—The Artisan *(Birmingham, England) October, 1843*

Here, too, are lanes and alleys, paved with mud knee-deep. . . . hideous tenements which take their name from robbery and murder; all that is loathsome, drooping, and decayed is here.—Charles Dickens, AMERICAN NOTES *(describing New York)*

Another way of examining the order and organization of the alley community involves looking at the conditions that were held to be destructive of primary folk groups. Foremost among these were the kinds of employment available to migrants. The financial reward from this demanding work was so meager that social workers often expressed surprise that families were able to survive. The alley store added to these financial difficulties, while the specter of disease and early death provided another significant complication. Moreover, reformers, scholars, and police alike pointed to the presence of crime and violence as *prima facie* evidence of the social pathology in the alleys. A closer look, however, suggests that the "disorder" was, in fact, a continuation and positive adaptation of folk ways of life to a harsh urban setting.

In their 1930 study of *The Employment of Negroes in the District of Columbia*, Lorenzo Greene and Myra Callis found that

> A well-developed color line prevails in the District of Co-
> lumbia. Certain jobs are open to Negroes, while others are
> reserved for whites. Negroes are found chiefly in the "blind
> alley jobs." With comparatively few exceptions they are de-
> nied skilled or responsible positions, either on account of the
> attitude of the employer, the refusal of whites to work with
> them, the opposition of the trade unions or their own lack of
> skill or industrial training.[1]

This description certainly fits the alley experience. Of the 2,774 males sixteen or older in the alley population in 1880, only 8 percent were skilled workers, and the vast majority of those were carpenters, barbers, shoemakers, blacksmiths, plasterers, and brickmasons.[2] (See Table 22.) Less than 7 percent of the adult males had white-collar, proprietorial, or professional occupations;[3] 17 percent of these were variously described as "rag picker," "rag gatherer,"

1. Lorenzo J. Greene and Myra Colson Callis, *The Employment of Negroes in the District of Columbia* (Washington, 1930), p. 65.

2. In the white community a number of these "skilled" occupations, such as barbering and shoemaking, were no longer skilled by 1880. As John R. Commons pointed out, shoemaking had become an occupation of semi- and unskilled workers well before the Civil War, as a result of changes in the market structure ("American Shoemakers, 1648–1895: A Sketch of Industrial Evolution," *Quarterly Journal of Economics*, 24 [Nov., 1909]: 39–84). Similarly, when I sent a copy of my occupational codes, which included barbering and shoemaking as skilled work, to scholars who have worked on occupational classifications, they (Michael Katz of York University, Laurence Glasco of the University of Pittsburgh, and Theodore Hershberg of the University of Pennsylvania) expressed disagreement. While in general terms they are quite correct, within the black community a somewhat different structure and hierarchy exists. It results largely from the restrictive nature of the mainstream society and reflects those areas where blacks were able to gain some entry. Barbering, catering, and transportation, for example, became important in the black community. Since this study deals largely with black alley dwellers, it seemed reasonable to adopt a classification system that would reflect greater variety, as well as more accurately indicating the community's own determination of status. See Appendix C.

3. Some people probably do not belong in this category. For example, the census recorded six males with the occupational listing "works in store"; this could imply either a white-collar job or an unskilled one. Of these six, three were able to read and write. Of course, literacy may not have been a necessity for some clerks; however, it seems safe to assume that most clerks were literate. Moreover, since census enumerators were not always as diligent in asking or recording answers on the latter part of the census form, especially those dealing with unemployment, disability, disease, and literacy, it is entirely possible that *none* of those six were literate. This situation held true for other white-collar positions as well.

"rag man," "rag dealer," or "junk dealer," while one-third were employed as "pedlar," "jobber," "huckster," and "horse-trader." It may seem strange to classify rag pickers and hucksters as proprietors, yet, unlike the vast majority of their alley neighbors, these workers were self-employed. This condition gave them somewhat more control over their own lives, even if the financial reward was no greater.[4] Similarly, the vast majority of professionals were "musicians," although there was one "herb doctor" as well.

The 59 percent figure for those who were unskilled workers is, in fact, the *minimum* for those in such occupations. (Indeed, 56 percent of the adult males were listed simply as "laborers.") When menial service and semi-skilled occupations are added to the unskilled, the proportion of adult males who were so employed swells to 80 percent. Moreover, some men who were listed as semi-skilled or skilled workers had great difficulty finding such work; one hod carrier in O Street Alley was "said to be a sober and honest fellow," but he had been out of work for four months in 1894.[5] (See Appendix C.)

As was pointed out in the first chapter (see Table 6), the vast majority of household heads listed in the 1858 and 1871 city directories were unskilled, semi-skilled, and menial service workers. These concentrations continued in later years as well. Jones reported that the "majority of the male alley dwellers are common laborers or seasonal workers," while Swinney noted of Snow's Court that "all of the adult males are reported as having worked sporadically as laborers, porters, handy-men, with an occasional truck driver, or junk man working on his own account."[6]

There was considerably less occupational variety among employed women. Almost half of the women sixteen or older in 1880 were not employed outside the home and were either "keeping house" (37 percent) or "at home" (10 percent). Those who were employed fell largely into two categories: "laundress," "washerwoman," "washing," or "washing and ironing," and "domestic servant,"

4. This helps confirm the existence of "junking" as a vocation, as well as just an avocation.

5. Board of Children's Guardians, *Children's History*, I, 233–34. Unemployment was clearly underreported in the 1880 census, but the figures are suggestive: 23 percent of heads of households experienced at least one month of unemployment during the preceding year, while the average for this group was six months. Unemployment for all employed adults was about 20 percent, with the average period of unemployment also six months. Federal Population Census Schedules, 1880, RG 29 NA.

6. Jones, *Housing of Negroes in Washington*, p. 49; Swinney, "Alley Dwellings and Housing Reform," p. 89.

TABLE 22.
Occupations, 1880*

Adult Males (16 or older)

Occupation	N	%
Unskilled	1,641	59
Service	251	9
Semi-skilled	318	12
Skilled	233	8
White-Collar	50	2
Proprietor (and self-employed)	112	4
Professional	28	1
Agriculture/Fishing	17	1
None	124	4
TOTAL	2,774	100

Adult Females (16 or older)

Occupation	N	%
Unskilled	4	—
Service	1,742	49
Semi-skilled	70	2
Skilled	6	—
White-Collar	10	—
Proprietor	8	—
None (includes "at home," "keeping house," and "at school")	1,780	49
TOTAL	3,620	100

*SOURCE: Federal Population Census Schedules, 1880, Washington, D.C., RG 29 NA. See Appendix C for a discussion of the categories in this table.

"servant," "in service," or "out in service." The former accounted for 42 percent of employed women; the latter, 51 percent.

Some sources, however, reported that *all* women were employed, although their jobs may have been temporary or part-time, so they could also care for their children. Swinney observed that "without exception, every woman or girl sixteen years of age or over reported that she had at some time or other worked as a domestic either in private homes, or in industry, or in both. Indications are that the majority of them now work sporadically, some working one, two, or three days a week; others working a week or two, with regular periods of unemployment; a few, perhaps ten or fifteen percent, have steady positions."[7] Jones reported that most employed women were involved in laundry work and domestic service, with the latter "the most common to alley women."[8] Ten years later Swinney noted that "apparently none of the inhabitants does outside laundry work in their homes"—a development which undoubtedly reflected the impact of the washing machine, the Depression, and white migration to the suburbs.[9]

These statistics tell little about the nature, meaning, and importance of work to alley residents. Unfortunately, students of alley life were concerned more with housing than with such questions. The one occupation that was touched on most often, and for which numerous pictures exist, is that of washerwoman. (See Photographs 29–31.) Certainly laundry was a task every alley woman had to confront, if only for her own family. Moreover, while washing machines may have robbed alley women of a means of livelihood, few alley families could afford the luxury of such a machine for themselves—and, if they could, the lack of electricity and indoor plumbing would render it useless.

The first step in the arduous task of laundering was to bring cold water from the backyard hydrant (see Photograph 29) into the kitchen, where it would be heated in large wash-buckets on the coal or wood stove. In alleys where there was only one common hydrant, the water had to be carried a considerable distance; in the early years an occasional alley had no water hydrant at all, which made it necessary for women to go several blocks to obtain water. On hot summer days the laundry might be done in the court (as in Photograph 31), but this appears to have been very uncommon. The clothes had to be scrubbed against a washboard in a large washtub. (See Photograph 30.) Drying was most often done in the backyard, although Weller does include a Lewis Hine photograph of a main alley vista shrouded in drying laundry.[10] After they were dry, the clothes had to be ironed. This meant starting another fire in the stove to heat the multiple irons, which were heavy and required

7. Swinney, "Alley Dwellings and Housing Reform," pp. 88–89.
8. Jones, *Housing of Negroes in Washington*, p. 48.
9. Swinney, "Alley Dwellings and Housing Reform," p. 89.
10. Weller, *Neglected Neighbors*, p. 119. The Hine photograph is captioned, "'Washings' Form an Unappreciated Bond between Alleys and Avenues. Indifferent Senators were Closely Related to Alley Problems through their Barber-shop Towels which were Washed in an Alley."

PHOTOGRAPH 29.
"Outside water supply. Only source of water supply winter and summer for many houses in slum area. In some places drainage is so poor that surplus backs up in huge puddles." July, 1935. Photograph by Carl Mydans. Farm Security Administration Collection, Library of Congress.

PHOTOGRAPH 30.
*"Negro Woman Washing Clothes in Her Kitchen." Washington, D.C.
(Southwest Section), November, 1942. Photograph by Gordon Parks. Farm
Security Administration Collection, Library of Congress.*

PHOTOGRAPH 31.
"Washday in Washington's Slums, Northwest." March 29, 1949. National Capital Housing Authority Collection.

considerable pressure. Several photographs of kitchens (Photographs 11 and 12) show such irons heating on the stove, while in the photograph of the one-room apartment in Navy Place (Photograph 9) a wash-bucket is sitting on a table. After they were ironed, the clothes were folded, placed in large fruit baskets, and returned to the owner.

The amount of stamina and strength required for this work is obvious. The Washington *Star* reported the story of "an old grandmother" who was raising her eight grandchildren "by doing laundry work often ironing at night by the light of a sooty old oil lamp."[11] Similarly, Weller described how he first encountered his Blagden Alley landlady "ironing beside a smoking lamp without a chimney." She was "finishing an ironing and laying the white, cleansmelling garments into covered baskets for delivery."[12] Not only was washing an arduous and hot task, but it was also a process which continued from morning until late in the evening.

11. Washington *Star*, July 30, 1911.
12. Weller, *Neglected Neighbors*, p. 17.

Less is known about the jobs of those who were "in service," or "domestics." Some of these women were required to "live in," and were only able to be home on certain days. In such cases other members of the family or neighbors would watch after their children. The working hours for domestics appear to have been as long as for those who did washing at home.[13] Weller reports that Mrs. Archer, a domestic, started at 6:00 A.M. and went until 7:30 or 8:00 P.M.[14] Swinney noted that an average day for a domestic in 1938 was 10–12 hours, for which she would receive "approximately one dollar, in addition to transportation expenses."[15] In 1948 Ben Bradlee described the working hours of Mrs. Fanny Lloyd, a Dingman Place resident who was buying her alley home and at the same time supporting a household of eight persons, six of whom were children. "She works from 8 A.M. to 4 P.M. at the Bellevue Hotel which she can see from the rear of her house, and she works from 5 P.M. to 2 A.M. in the Colorado Building. In her lunch and supper hours she comes home to cook for her children and care for those who are sick."[16]

It should be noted that a geographical analysis of residence relative to workplace, made from the case records of the Board of Children's Guardians when such information was available, indicated that most alley dwellers did *not* work at the street house that abutted theirs. While many alley residents worked in their home areas during the years covered by the case records (1893–1913), that circumstance reflected the transportation system of the day, rather than implying any close relationship between alley and street families. In later years, as the middle class left the city, many domestics had the same long hours and also had to travel considerable distances for employment.

Alley women, especially those who worked as domestics, had considerably more contact with "mainstream society" than did their husbands, who often worked as day laborers and frequently had different bosses every day. Moreover, the primary contacts of these workmen tended to be with workers similar to themselves, rather than with employers or supervisors.

Virtually no sources touch on male occupations.[17] For informa-

13. Ethel Waters's grandmother, who took responsibility for raising Ethel, "was forced to take jobs where she had to sleep in." As a result, "much the responsibility of taking care of us fell on" Ethel's aunts (*His Eye Is on the Sparrow*, pp. 3, 7).

14. Weller, *Neglected Neighbors*, p. 35.

15. Swinney, "Alley Dwellings and Housing Reform," p. 89.

16. Washington *Post*, Dec. 19, 1948.

17. O'Connell does report that "many of the men" from Fenton Place "worked

tion we must resort to unobtrusive measures, such as the fact that 24 percent of heads of household in the 1880 alley population were widowed; most of these were women. Evidence can also be found in photographs like that of the disabled man on his doorstep (Photograph 5), or through the case record of a family whose father "was suffering with asthma and his feet and ankles were very badly swollen. He will go to the hospital." A later notation indicated that he had died.[18] Jones likewise mentioned one man who "was in ill health, and was only able to work at light jobs. But these were so scarce that he had made almost no money within the period of a year."[19] Of course, we cannot positively identify the causes of these men's deaths, illnesses, and handicaps; even death certificates probably would not reveal the actual causes. But extremely difficult work was expected of day laborers, and a wide variety of possible injuries were related to such work, not to mention the health hazards caused by the elements. Although few diseases or injuries were recorded by census enumerators in 1880, two heads of household had lost arms, while others had suffered work-related injuries as follows: "ruptured," "one hand," "loss of both legs at knee from being frozen," "broken foot," "broken leg," "broken hip," "broken back," and "sunstroke." The compounding effects of injury or disease could result in loss of work and income which was already marginal at best; poverty and the ensuing possibility of malnutrition made recovery longer or even questionable, and injuries could be aggravated if the disabled man went back to work too soon. When such factors are considered, the marginality of alley life becomes more apparent, and the need for a family and community to fall back on becomes more obvious.

---

in the coal yards at First Street and M Street, Northwest, for nine to eleven dollars a week," while "some men worked at other jobs, hard work with pick and shovel" ("Inhabited Alleys of Washington," p. 109).

18. Board of Children's Guardians, *Children's History*, II, 804–7. This case record suggests the result of illness or disease for a family on a marginal income. The "family was living in a miserable shanty" in Catons Alley in Georgetown. "Two windows at the rear end of the room were covered with boards and rags to keep out the cold. A window in front was covered over except the top row of panes, and those were so dirty no light came in. When the door was shut, not one object could be distinguished. The family of six lived here. Two wrecks of beds, rags galore, one chair, one stool, a stove, pieces of old iron and a quantity of bones with a packing box which served as a table, one fork, two knives, two plates, an old coffee pot, a tin pan, and a broken iron pot costited [*sic*] their personal property. . . . His wife looked as though all her energy had left her; still she will go into service, and try to save enough to make a home for her children by and bye."

19. Jones, *Housing of Negroes in Washington*, p. 49.

Given these conditions, it is not surprising that so many alley dwellers worked. While reformers noted that, for example, "Henry . . . was found to be loafing every day and it developed that he had been unemployed throughout July," whereas his son-in-law "had been late at work four or five days in the previous week . . . and had been discharged on Saturday," it is evident that alley dwellers did more than their share of the work and received far less than their share of the rewards.[20] In the sample area in 1880, 45 percent of the alley dwellers were employed, while only 35 percent of their more affluent street neighbors were so occupied. When it is considered that the alley families were considerably younger and had many more young children (over 17 percent of the city's total alley population in 1880 was under six years old), these figures take on even more significance. Reformers' claims that alley residents were indolent do not hold up against this evidence.

Most alley dwellers were engaged in strenuous, difficult physical employment for considerable lengths of time each day, and this physical labor must have taken a severe toll. However, nowhere is this reflected in the return they received. Sellew noted that all Center Court families "have incomes far below the minimum of subsistence budget . . . *it is evident that by no careful planning could these families secure the necessities of life without adjustment techniques and methods of their own, not considered by the makers of the minimum of subsistence budget.*"[21] Eight years later, Ratigan found that "The income of the people studied barely reaches the minimal or dividing line between deficit and surplus of more than a quarter of a century ago. Even with the greatest frugality and thrift, a family cannot provide for current needs; to provide for future emergencies exceeds reasonable expectations."[22] The $1,155 annual income that was found to be the dividing line between budget deficit and surplus nearly thirty years before was undoubtedly out of date in the late 1940s.[23] In the even more inflationary year of 1953, Pablo reported the "projected"

20. Weller, *Neglected Neighbors*, p. 20. Johnson pointed out that when black laborers struck for higher wages in 1871, their wage was only $1.25 per day; white workers received $1.50 for the same work ("City on the Hill," pp. 201–2). Similarly, Williston H. Lofton found the pay differential between black and white teachers in 1875 to be an average of $118.79 per teacher per year—black: $570.12; white: $688.91 ("The Development of Public Education for Negroes in Washington, D.C.: A Study of the Separate but Equal Accommodations" [Ph.D. dissertation, American University, 1944], pp. 177–80).

21. Sellew, *Deviant Social Situation*, pp. 18–19. Sellew's emphasis.

22. Ratigan, *Sociological Survey of Disease*, p. 73.

23. *Ibid.*, p. 64.

TABLE 23.
Distribution of Families by Annual Income:
Temperance Court, 1953*

	N	%
$ 250–$ 520	1	4
520– 1,040	1	4
1,040– 1,560	2	8
1,560– 2,080	5	19
2,080– 2,600	6	23
2,600– 3,120	3	11
3,120– 3,640	3	11
3,640– 4,160	2	8
4,160– 4,680	1	4
4,680– 5,200	2	8
	26	100

*SOURCE: Pablo, "Housing Needs and Social Problems,"
p. 52.

incomes of Temperance Court families (see Table 23). However, these incomes were based on full employment, rather than on the real experience of considerable under- or unemployment. These conditions led Ratigan to conclude that "it is impossible to cover the family needs with such an income without doing irreparable damage to health and general well being." If the long, difficult hours did not destroy the worker, the poor wages and long layoffs certainly would.[24]

These conditions led to considerable suffering, especially in times of unemployment or sickness, and certainly were largely responsible for substantially shorter life expectancies. Alley dwellers were, nevertheless, quite skillful in developing strategies to circumvent or forestall imminent disasters. One such strategy involved expanding the family to increase the number of people who could be called on to help in time of need. The alley community also helped protect against an unsure present and future by aiding those in immediate need and gathering wood for residents' later use. Nor were these substantial societal forms the alley dwellers' only ingenious adaptations. Unemployed alley men also seemed "to be quite skillful in

24. *Ibid*. The broad spread of incomes suggests diversity in alley life.

Photograph 32.
"Cartman." March, 1951. National Capital Housing Authority Collection.

catching large carp in the river, and have a considerable amount of success in selling the largest for twenty-five or fifty cents to the more prosperous negroes who are fond of this particular species of fish."[25]

Alley dwellers also used other elements of their environment for survival. The active involvement of many families in "junking" (Photograph 32), as well as in acquiring firewood, has already been mentioned. And as Ratigan reported, "the people studied are admirably resourceful in their use of edible wild plants for food." While that potential food source was "curtailed by their present environment," they were still "able to get a few of these plants from vacant lots and along the river bank."[26]

25. Swinney, "Alley Dwellers and Housing Reform," p. 89. Nor was this an entirely new experience; as Genovese notes, "The slaves would have suffered much more than many in fact did from malnutrition and the hidden hungers of nutritional deficiencies if the men had not taken the initiative to hunt and trap animals" (*Roll, Jordan, Roll*, p. 486).

26. Ratigan, *Sociological Survey of Disease*, p. 102. The *National Intelligencer* provided an excellent description of these activities in the very early years of alley dwelling (1865) when they sought to describe "How such a multitude live and obtain clothing." Alley children "and the old and infirm delve in gutters, among piles of rubbish

Diets represented pragmatic compromises. Women who had ovens baked their own bread, while those who did not purchased "second day, or day-old bread at half the cost of fresh bread." Lard with salt replaced oleomargarine.[27] Meat was seldom eaten; fish was more common due to its availability in the river, and some "thrifty housewives" were known to wait "until closing time to buy the left-over fish, at a substantial reduction, in the neighborhood markets and grocery stores."[28]

Most often clothing was "bought at second-hand stores, permanent rummage or white elephant sales conducted by charitable organizations or at one- or two-day rummage sales."[29] There is also some evidence that clothes were passed around, in the manner that Caroline Stack later found so prevalent in "The Flats of Jackson Harbor."[30] Stack found that residents used this exchange to maintain and enhance links between kin and non-kin so that the interlocking networks were maintained.

Like clothing, "furniture is bought second-hand from the stores."[31] Homemade furniture, multiple-use furniture, and furniture meant for another purpose but adapted to alley house needs often appears in photographs.

Finally, some alley dwellers relied on larceny and fraud to help make ends meet. Alley women "out in service" brought home food and clothing from their employers' homes. Sometimes these items were given by the employer, but often they were covertly re-

---

and cinders on the wharves, end in the trail of wood and coal carts for bits of fuel, which they carry home in old grain sacks that they have picked up about the camps. Their clothing is also gathered to a great extent in the same manner. Boys of twelve to eighteen may be seen in uniforms of grown men" (July 25, 1865, p. 3).

27. Ratigan, *Sociological Survey of Disease*, pp. 98, 99.

28. *Ibid.*, p. 100.

29. Sellew, *Deviant Social Situation*, p. 24.

30. Stack, *All Our Kin*, pp. 32–44. While it is impossible to determine from the fragmented accounts whether these exchanges carry the same societal meaning that Stack and others have suggested, other factors presented in this study suggest that they may. She noted that "Gift exchange is a style of interpersonal relationship by which local coalitions of cooperating kinsmen distinguished themselves from other Blacks—those low-income or working-class Blacks who have access to steady employment. In contrast to the middle-class ethic of individualism and competition, the poor living in the Flats do not turn anyone down when they need help. The cooperative life style and the bonds created by the vast mass of moment-to-moment exchanges constitute an underlying element of black identity in The Flats. This powerful obligation to exchange is a profoundly creative adaptation to poverty" (*ibid.*, p. 43).

31. Sellew, *Deviant Social Situation*, p. 27.

moved.[32] Stealing from local stores and businesses also provided necessities.[33]

If these techniques are rational forms of adaptation to a difficult life, alley residents were clearly aware of the system that locked them in. Weller reported:

> In one of the two shacks an industrious colored woman was found, in August, 1908, who pays $5.00 a month for two rooms only. It was a very hot day. The perspiring woman was too busy at her wash-tub to waste any time in conversation. She was indignant, "Yes," she said, "you folks makes us pay so much rent that we have to scrub our fingers off doing your washing and your scrubbing to earn the money; and we're glad if we can get enough extra to have ash cake and smoked herring for our little ones to eat."[34]

32. Ethel Waters provides an excellent description of this process: "Early in her life Mom figured out a way to outwit her white bosses. She sewed little pockets in an apron and filled the pockets with neatly done up parcels of food—sandwiches, pieces of pie or cake, sugar, and eggs. Then when she was ready to take her day off on Thursday she'd put on the heavily laden apron under her petticoat. Mom could sneak any kind of food out of her boss's house except soup" (*His Eye Is on the Sparrow*, p. 21). This practice, well developed in slavery, was often expected by the slave-owner and employer, and was a necessity for survival for the slave and freedman. The limited provisions given slaves, as well as the small wages of black employees, made it necessary to steal. The punishment for being caught for such "necessary" theft, however, was often severe. See Genovese, *Roll, Jordan, Roll*, pp. 599–612; Liebow, *Tally's Corner*, pp. 35–42.

33. Again Ethel Waters provides excellent examples of this "process," which was most often practiced by children. Often her aunts would send her shopping with a quarter: "Once I had the quarter, I was ready to go shopping and stealing. First I'd buy wood for three cents and charcoal for a nickel. Walking into the bakery, I'd order a loaf of yesterday's bread, which also cost three cents. When the man turned to get the bread from the shelf, I'd slip a half dozen cinnamon buns into my big shopping bag. In the butcher shop I'd ask for three cents' worth of cat or dog meat. The butchers on Clifton Street only had to look at my big hungry eyes to know that I didn't want the meat for any pet animal. They'd give me plenty of good scraps fit for human consumption. Swiping plenty of fresh vegetables was the easiest job of all. If the owner was inside the store I'd just take my choice of the potatoes, onions, carrots, and peas lying on the stands outside of his shop. If he was outside I'd order three cents' worth of salt or something else I knew he kept in the rear of his store. By the time he'd come out with it I'd have my bag full of vegetables covered up by the packages of meat. My ability to go out with a quarter and come back with a whole dinner—and some change—delighted my aunts. They never tired of praising my prowess." However, she points out, "I stole because I always was hungry" (*His Eye Is on the Sparrow*, pp. 24, 23, 25–26).

34. Weller, *Neglected Neighbors*, pp. 82–83.

Not only did alley dwellers pay high rents, but if they needed help in later years, when public assistance was available, they also discovered that "Negroes everywhere seem to fare less well than the white recipients of categorical assistance. Proportionally more white people . . . receive benefits."[35]

If these factors were not frustrating enough for the alley dweller, another institution, the alley store, was perhaps even more of a bane. Weller noted that "one or more white families are usually to be found in every alley, serving as storekeepers or in some other commercial capacity."[36] Other sources suggest that this is an overstatement, since the 1880 census reported only five white families living over their alley stores. The 1897 police census reports many alleys that were totally black, similarly negating the possibility of such a widespread phenomenon. Nevertheless, white merchants did exist in some alleys, while neighborhood grocery stores served in much the same fashion. In Snow's Court in 1912 "all the inhabitants are colored with the exception of the family which keeps a little store," while in Willow Tree Alley "the community is supplied by a store conducted by white people in one of the semi-dilapidated buildings."[37] Swinney noted that there was no store in Snow's Court in 1938, but that one was kept in Fenton Place by a white family. Photographs also reveal alley stores in Navy Place, and a "small neighborhood grocery store" next to the entrance to O'Brien's Court. Whether the store was located in the alley or on the street, it played much the same role. Of the alley store in Fenton Place and the two located near Snow's Court, Swinney noted that "all three stores do a credit business, that is, many of the alley residents have charge accounts. The stores are conveniently located, they cater to alley trade and they extend credit." Not surprisingly, "the alley inhabitants are paying excessively for the convenience and for the privilege of receiving credit."[38] One convenience was that "the grocery stores sell in addition to groceries, ladies' lingerie, hardware, coal, kindling wood, and practically any commodity that the average alley dweller would wish to purchase."[39] The alley merchants could not compete with the larger stores in terms of

35. Ratigan, *Sociological Survey of Disease*, p. 72.

36. Weller, *Neglected Neighbors*, pp. 38–39.

37. Mallalieu, "Washington Alley," p. 70; Washington *Daily News*, n.d. Since Willow Tree Alley was removed in 1913, this article probably appeared around 1912, during the campaign to have that alley converted into a playground.

38. Swinney, "Alley Dwellings and Housing Reform," pp. 138–39. See note 87.

39. *Ibid.*, p. 139.

price, since they could not afford to make quantity purchases, so they sought to compensate in other ways. These included not only extending credit and stocking a wider range of items directed at alley needs, but also maintaining longer hours and being located near the alley homes—both important factors for parents who worked long hours at physically demanding jobs. Yet the alley dweller paid dearly for these conveniences. For example, in 1938 the small store near Center Court sold "Carnation brand of evaporated milk, three cans for twenty-five cents while the chain store sells three for twenty-three cents. Rice at the small store is eight cents a pound box . . . while loose rice is four or five cents a pound at the chain store."[40] The small store owner took advantage of selling in bulk or breaking up the quantities whenever it meant the greatest margin of profit. If rice was sold only in pound boxes, other items were often sold in smaller quantities. Matches "by the package could not be purchased unless they were with a package of cigarettes. The grocer preferred to open a five-cent box and portion out a penny's worth."[41] Because food spoilage was a real problem and because money was in such short supply, residents intentionally bought in small quantities, i.e., "three cents worth of sugar, two eggs, six slices of bread, five slices of bacon, four cents worth of kerosene, two cigarettes, two cents worth of matches, etc. One of the inhabitants states that she checked the weight of some sugar that she bought and that it had cost at the rate of seventy cents a pound."[42] Opportunities for considerable markups were available to the small store owner, who admittedly was only a cog in a much larger system of exploitation. One other "extra" provided by the small store was the selling of "numbers," the cost of which could be added "to the charge accounts."[43]

Besides charging high prices, alley store owners often held their neighbors in contempt. Weller reports that a German woman who kept a store in Blagden Alley "has a stern contempt for most of them and tries to hold her children away from the alley influences, as an anxious hen would hide her chickens beneath ineffective feathers . . . although her business interests require" that she "treat her neighbors somewhat cordially."[44]

The result of long, hard work for low wages, coupled with comparatively high rents and more expensive food and supplies, was a

40. Sellew, *Deviant Social Situation*, p. 20.
41. Swinney, "Alley Dwellings and Housing Reform," p. 139.
42. *Ibid.*
43. *Ibid.*
44. Weller, *Neglected Neighbors*, p. 30.

shorter life expectancy and a higher death rate for alley residents than for those, white or black, who lived on the street. In 1910, the death rate was 17.56 per 1,000 for street dwellers, versus 30.09 for alley residents. Small children accounted for most of this disparity, with the death rate for those under one year of age being 373.49 for alley dwellers versis 158.66 for street dwellers.[45] This high death rate helps account for the large numbers of children in the alley population: because so many youngsters died, women had to give birth more often. For example, of the Blagden Alley mothers, Mollie Jarvis lost 7 of her 8 children; Mrs. Harris, 8 of 10; Mrs. Hilton, 6 of 8; Mrs. Green, 5 of 8; and Mrs. Lawrence, 4 of 6. Two mothers in Guethler Alley reported having lost 13 of 17 and 13 of 14 children respectively.[46] These were extreme cases, however, for some alleys did not have such abnormally high death rates.[47] Rather than reflecting disorder, the disease and death rates were "more closely associated with socio-economic conditions." The most common diseases reflect this fact: they were tuberculosis, pneumonia, diarrhea, and whooping cough.[48]

Extra hazards to alley residents could be laid on the doorstep of landlords who failed to make repairs. Some ignored leaky roofs, and others failed to make immediate repairs on broken or improperly functioning outhouses. Since few landlords equipped doors or windows with screens (Ratigan found "less than one-third have screens in all the windows and doors. A few have screens in some of the windows and more than one-half have no screens in the windows or doors"), alley residents were exposed to greater contagion via insects.[49] The city, then as now, was equally negligent about removing trash and garbage from the alleys, so it was not uncommon to have "rats, mice, flies and mosquitoes abound in the court."[50] Swinney noted that "practically every one of the inhabitants complained to the writer that they were continuously bothered within their houses by large rats, chinch bugs, and other vermin. In one dwelling the writer asked a child about the sore on her arm. She replied that a rat had bitten her one night."[51]

45. Jones, *Housing of Negroes in Washington*, p. 45.
46. Weller, *Neglected Neighbors*, pp. 30, 81.
47. Jones, *Housing of Negroes in Washington*, p. 44; Sellew, *Deviant Social Situation*, p. 54; Wood, "Four Washington Alleys," p. 251.
48. Ratigan, *Sociological Survey of Disease*, p. 61.
49. *Ibid.*, p. 86. Photoanalysis revealed even fewer houses having screens on either doors or windows; see Appendix B.
50. Washington Housing Association, "Report on Temperance Court," p. 3.
51. Swinney, "Alley Dwellings and Housing Reform," p. 146. Almost all sources confirm the existence of such insects as roaches and flies; however, only later photo-

A number of interesting factors must be considered when dealing with disease and death in the alleys. First, while census enumerators were not very diligent in recording (or asking about) disability and disease, the fact that so few were recorded is significant. Only 1 percent of alley residents in 1880 reported some disability, while just under 2 percent reported a disease. The largest number (42 residents) suffered from rheumatism. As has already been demonstrated by their attitude toward relief, alley dwellers were a hardy group not inclined to complain. Given the number who must have been suffering from some illness (Ratigan reported nearly half of the 539 alley dwellers she surveyed "had three or more colds within the last year"), the few illnesses reported in the census are surprising.[52]

Second, it is quite clear that alley residents, especially those who were black, faced considerable discrimination when they sought medical assistance. "Only very grave conditions" would bring about hospitalization, because "they cannot afford to stop working . . . they cannot afford the expense of hospitalization . . . they do not like the hospital." Long waits at clinics for doctors who "were 'gruff' and 'mean,'" and exposure to nurses who were "'harsh' and 'indifferent,'" only reinforced their attitudes toward professional health care. Ratigan reported having heard "an intern angrily shout to a Negro woman 'I'll knock you cold' and a nurse threaten to 'slap a woman's face.'" In another case, a "woman was taken to a private hospital in an ambulance and left in a draughty hall until they could find another hospital, to which to send her." The first hospital, "which is conducted under Christian auspices, had no 'colored' beds at the time." In still another case, the mother, "advised by the surgeon in the clinic, took her child to the hospital three times to be surgically treated for a strangulated inguinal hernia; there was never room until one night she brought him back in a critical condition— the child died on the operating table."[53]

While alley dwellers did turn to clinics as a last resort, they did not lack home remedies for less severe ailments. Nor should these remedies be considered entirely foolhardy and useless, for medical "science" has often found much of value in these time-proven

---

graphs and surveys indicate the prevalence of rodents. It is difficult to say whether such conditions were of more recent origin. Moreover, it should also be pointed out that the presence of roaches and/or rodents does not necessarily reflect on the housekeeping of the tenant; this writer has experienced both kinds of pests in Washington's "middle-class" housing.

52. Ratigan, *Sociological Survey of Disease*, p. 57.
53. *Ibid.*, pp. 168, 165, 169.

"cures." Ratigan concluded that "the use of diet therapy in the treatment of disease is praiseworthy; the use of edible plants for pot-herbs, while less practical in their present environs, displays a worthy botanical cognizance not shared by all underprivileged people."[54]

The occupations discussed above, and the resulting "rewards" of alley life, were almost universally shared. Nevertheless, evidence suggests that these were not the only occupations available to alley dwellers, and that these patterns of life were not the only possible ones. Virtually all observers report that crime and violence were important aspects of alley life, and certainly such conditions suggest disorder and social pathology. Not surprisingly, however, no census of occupations included those that might clearly be illegal.

In later years, especially during and since Prohibition, virtually every study has reported at least one house in a given alley where illegal liquor was made or sold. These home distilleries were probably common in the earlier years as well, but not until Prohibition did strict regulation begin.[55] Swinney reported that there were two houses in Snow's Court "where 'corn whiskey' can be bought which is made by the vendor. Several of the residents stated that 'repeal liquor' is no good and not worth buying." Similarly he found three houses in Fenton Place "which make and sell liquor."[56] In Center Court the Brown family, in whose home the alley's residents often met to socialize, was also involved in the illicit liquor trade. Like much in alley life, however, that trade was functional. It provided another source of income for the family, as well as making available to the alley community, at a reasonable price, a product that could be consumed. Thus, the Brown family was supported by Mr. Brown's earnings as a laborer, and "by the meager earnings of the mother who sells liquor, and holds 'open house' for the Court."[57] Jones also found the practice to be widespread, as did other sources.[58] The manufacture and sale of alcohol did not normally

54. *Ibid.*, p. 107.
55. It is interesting to note that government regulation has greatly benefited the large producer and virtually destroyed the small one. At the same time, the government has maintained an ideology that supports competition and "capitalism," as opposed to an oligopolistic structure.
56. Swinney, "Alley Dwellings and Housing Reform," pp. 142, 144.
57. Aubry, "Ambitions of Youth," p. 13.
58. Jones, *Housing of Negroes in Washington*, pp. 47, 48, 49, 50; Somerville, "Study of a Group of Negro Children," p. 21; Washington *Daily News*, May 5, 1941, Apr. 15, 1954; Washington *Star*, June 4, 1930. Hannerz also found several houses on Winston Street where liquor was made largely for neighborhood consumption.

bother alley residents, as was clear from the example in Chapter 3, except in rare cases where the owners sought to restrict their "speakeasy" clientele.

But if this trade was seen as acceptable and functional to the alley community, it was not viewed in that light by law enforcement agents. The *Daily News* recalled that "in prohibition days the Vice Squad could almost always make a 'half-pint' case if it cared to pay a surprise visit to Naylor Court," while several years prior to the studies of Center Court, Mrs. Brown had been "put in jail for 'boot-legging.'"[59]

Another illegal activity (and another victimless crime) involved policy or numbers.[60] While few students of alley life made serious studies of this enterprise, they were aware of its existence. Only a few sources mentioned the hierarchy of the numbers bank; in each case the bank was controlled and operated out of an alley, although it was earlier noted that white store owners acted as agents for the banks. During the reform effort to remove Willow Tree Alley, the *Star* claimed that one of the most frequent crimes was

> policy writing. One colored woman known as the "queen of policy" was arrested a number of times for this offense. The wheel, somewhat similar to that used in faro, was located across the river in a small Virginia town. Men would bring her their money, ranging from a nickel to several dollars, and this policy queen would write out their plays as directed, carry the paper to Virginia and there make the play on the wheel. The outcome of the gamble and any money that might happen to be forthcoming were then carried back by hand and delivered in Willow Tree Alley.[61]

It is impossible to say how widespread was the control of local numbers operations by alley people, but it was "a daily practice of the people of the court as well as others to 'play the numbers.'"[62] Most players ventured one, two, five, or ten cents a day.[63]

59. Washington *Daily News*, May 5, 1941; Somerville, "Study of a Group of Negro Children," p. 21.

60. Hoggart has noted that the English "Working-class people . . . are fond of a gamble" (*Uses of Literacy*, p. 114).

61. Washington *Star*, July 30, 1911. Smiley reported that "policy, unlike crap, has not been suppressed, and although the police are waging a vigorous warfare against the game it still flourishes under the auspices of the Connellys, in the upper rooms of the small tenement houses which line the sides of the alley" in Freeman's Alley (*Glimpse at the Night Side of Washington*, p. 42).

62. Somerville, "Study of a Group of Negro Children," p. 51.

63. Swinney, "Alley Dwellers and Housing Reform," p. 139.

Equally common was the playing of craps. Like numbers, craps offered a chance to "hit it big," although it was more of a recreational and community activity for alley dwellers than a way to win money. Swinney reported that Mr. Steen, who assisted him in his survey, participated "in one of the card games" in Snow's Court. "Although he soon lost all of his money, he learned several interesting things about the group. During the card game he observed one of his 'colleagues' using a modified sign language to inform his opponent as to the cards he had been dealt."[64] In constrast, the *Star* reported in 1906 that "Residents of Goat Alley entered a vigorous denial of the statement that a game of craps had caused a row in their neighborhood yesterday." One resident observed that "we don't mind taking a drink of good liquor on Sunday, but we stopped the crap business long ago. There was a time when we didn't mind a quiet game, but the police got wise and caused too much trouble. Now we have preaching in the alley instead of crap games and a little liquor on the side."[65] Through this story we can again see the police enforcing laws against alley dwellers who saw little wrong with the alleged offenses; with the possible exceptions of Mr. Steen and other "outsiders," there were probably no victims, save neighbors who could always "win" on another day. Certainly alley children were harassed for playing craps, as were their parents.

Several other activities did involve victims, however. Weller had reported that one man belonged to a gang involved in bootlegging and robbery. Similarly, Jones noted that "along with the liquor trading goes that of so-called 'hot goods.' The majority of these people have very beautiful and expensive clothes. And when seen on the main streets, one would never think that their trail led to such homes as those from which they come."[66] O'Connell interviewed a lawyer who was born in 1896 and who grew up just outside Fenton Place; the man's father had run a bar in the same location since 1867. "He didn't think they were especially prone to stealing except sometimes 'when they had to.' They did engage in dealing with illegal liquor, but outside of that," he remembered, "they weren't so lawless."[67] Yet, except for these and the crimes reported in the case records of the Board of Children's Guardians, it is almost impossible to know how widespread this criminal activity was. Some of it may have been tied to organized crime, as the above suggests, but some, as O'Connell states, was random, "necessary" theft. Given

64. *Ibid.*, p. 142.
65. Washington *Star*, Oct. 29, 1906.
66. Jones, *Housing of Negroes in Washington*, p. 47.
67. O'Connell, "Inhabited Alleys of Washington," p. 109.

the nature of the alley community, it seems reasonable to assume that much of the robbery was of outsiders.[68] And since the alley operated as a community, looking out for its own needy, success in these areas of endeavor eventually benefitted all alley residents. As a result, there would be little reason for them to report their neighbors' "illegal activities," especially since everyone's resources were so perilously low.[69]

Prostitution was connected with the alleys almost from the beginning. Clare de Graffenreid found "three openly disreputable houses," while others were "tainted with the suspicion of being 'fast,' and men in them are supported by women who have no visible income."[70] Weller found in O Street Alley "several 'houses of ill repute.' One was discovered in which there was a piano and some finery in a parlor where a number of young colored fellows, flashily dressed, were found one afternoon lounging or in a drunken slumber."[71] In 1913 the Senate subcommittee on the District of Columbia held extensive hearings on "The Abatement of Houses of Ill-Fame." The testimony, however, produced more heat than light, and provides more insights into policemen's attitudes toward black alley dwellers than into prostitution itself. In his testimony Richard Sylvester, a thirty-year veteran of the metropolitan police who had been chief for the last fifteen years, pointed out that not only were there

> houses of prostitution and assignation, but many of the alleys were the resorts of gamblers, thieves, and I may say, murderers. . . . Or, rather, it is more like an alleyway than it is a street down in there. Those houses are made up of the lowest character of negroes. If one has ever visited the South and seen them in their animal state, he will find in some of these alleys that same condition. The police, if charged with going into an alley of that kind to get evidence against prostitution under the technical terms, would find a job which they could never carry into effect. . . . The lowest moral tone in the past prevailed, and exists to-day, among the negro inhabitants of a few of the alleys in the southwestern section, where cheap tenements and lodgings can be obtained.
>
> This class of people live not only in degradation, but hud-

68. Washington Housing Association, "Report on Temperance Court," p. 4.

69. Genovese notes that slaves often had to share their "loot" with fellow slaves, if only to get rid of the evidence quickly (*Roll, Jordan, Roll*, p. 606).

70. de Graffenried, "Typical Alley Houses in Washington," p. 12. See also Lait and Mortimer, *Washington Confidential*, p. 51.

71. Weller, *Neglected Neighbors*, p. 107.

dled together in a manner which places them beyond the classification of maintaining "suspicious houses" in the ordinary acceptation [*sic*] of the term. . . .[72]

One of the striking features of Chief Sylvester's testimony (or that of the other witnesses, for that matter) was its vagueness in approaching the problem. Since police could not "get evidence . . . under the technical terms," the chief seemed to be admitting that commercial prostitution did not exist in those areas. Nevertheless, some commercial prostitution did exist around the Mall, aimed largely at the white-collar workers and visitors who frequented this area. A map presented by Chief Sylvester to the subcommittee confirms that the vast majority of known "houses," and those that were "suspicious," were located just north and south of the Mall. Others were scattered throughout the city. In no case was prostitution confined to the alleys or to the larger black community. As Swinney concluded, "Evidence of commercialized prostitution was not found in either alley"; in fact, he reported that Snow's Court residents sought to keep it out of their alley. Rather, "hearsay from some of the younger men revealed that there are usually a few girls lounging around the houses in which liquor is sold and that there are many 'parties' in the rooms upstairs. If the men have money, the girls usually get it; if they don't, no issue is made of the fact. Most of the patrons of the houses are inhabitants of the alleys or their friends." Swinney went on to say that "strangers are not wanted and most strangers are afraid of the results of such a visit."[73] Certainly these relationships are far different from those found in commercial prostitution. When the whole form and structure of the alley are considered, alley "prostitution" seems to fit more closely with kinship networks and community than it does with prostitution.

Violent crime has also been long associated with the alleys, and several alleys were especially notorious for such activities. Until its demise in 1913, Willow Tree Alley was considered one of the worst, while in later years this dubious distinction went to Temperance Court. "We've had everything there—dope peddling, murder, whiskey raids, Saturday night cuttings, crap shootings, thievery," claimed Police Lieutenant Philip Abel of the 13th Precinct.[74]

72. Testimony of Richard Sylvester, 63rd Congress, 3rd session, Senate, Subcommittee of the Committee of the District of Columbia, *Abatement of Houses of Ill Fame* (Washington, D.C., 1913), pp. 23, 24.
73. Swinney, "Alley Dwellings and Housing Reform," pp. 144–45.
74. Washington *Post*, Sept. 27, 1952.

Others reported that Temperance Court was "a center of drug traffic, prostitution and other types of crimes. Home owners in the adjacent areas report many petty thefts which they attribute to the court inhabitants."[75]

Other alleys were not far behind, at least in the public's mind. Mallalieu reported finding in the police blotter from March 1, 1911, to March 1, 1912, "114 arrests among the 204 men, women and children living in Snow's Court. These charges were drunkenness, disorderly conduct, assault, unlawful assembly, larceny, cruelty to animals, and accusations relating to sexual crimes." Moreover, this figure does not "represent all the evil, because it does not take into account residents of Snow's Court arrested in other precincts, nor does it include the mischief done in Snow's Court by inhabitants of the neighboring alleys and residents of other parts of the city."[76] Edith Wood sought to determine the number of arrests of residents of the four alleys she studied by going "through blotters of the precincts in which the alleys are located and that nearest adjoining." For 1912 she found that arrests in the city were equal to 10 percent of the city's population, but that black arrests equaled nearly 19 percent of the black population. The arrest rate of the four alleys was greater than one-third of the alley population, or almost twice the rate for all blacks in the city.[77] Another study of arrests in five alleys from October 1, 1934, to April 2, 1935, also reported a substantial number of arrests. (See Table 24.) The Council of Social Agencies also studied arrest records for Snow's Court and Fenton Place from January 1 through June 30, 1936. (See Table 25.)

While the number of arrests is impressive, and certainly supports the claims of police and reformers, arrests themselves do not indicate guilt or innocence. Moreover, black and poor citizens were always arrested more often than their white and well-to-do counter-

75. Washington Housing Association, "Report on Temperance Court," p. 4.

76. Mallalieu, "Washington Alley," pp. 70–71. I attempted to analyze arrest records to determine the extent and nature of alley residents' crimes. Unfortunately, the records do not include the home address of the person arrested, necessitating a search in the city directories to determine every person's address. This arduous process involved the very same kinds of problems encountered in attempting to trace people in city directories over a period of time. As a result, I decided to rely on these fragmented reports, as well as on the far more valuable and complete case records of the Board of Children's Guardians. The latter not only provided much more insight into juvenile delinquency and possible family breakdown (see Chapter 2), but also gave considerably more information on spatial movement, extended families and kinship networks. Of course, "arrest" does not in any way imply guilt, or even necessarily the commission of a crime.

77. Wood, "Four Washington Alleys," p. 252.

TABLE 24.
Arrests in Five Alleys, October 1, 1934—April 2, 1935*

Crime	Logan's Court	Fenton Court	Pierce Street Court	Congress Court	Naylor's Court	
Drunk	6	7	2	3	2	
Disorderly conduct	4	12	12	3	—	
Possessing untaxed liquor	—	1	—	—	—	
Sale of liquor without license	3	—	—	10	—	
Vagrancy	—	—	—	2	1	
Investigation	1	10	—	4	—	
Truant	—	1	—	—	—	
Indecent exposure	—	—	1	—	—	
Attachment	1	—	—	—	—	
Threat	—	2	1	—	—	
Destroying private property	2	1	—	—	—	
Carrying a concealed weapon	1	1	—	—	—	
Petit larceny	1	—	—	—	—	
Assault	4	3	1	—	2	
Assault with a dangerous weapon	1	—	—	—	—	
TOTAL	24	38	17	22	5	106

*SOURCE: Sister Mary Redempta Forestall, "Trends in Housing, Delinquency and Health in the Central Northwest Area in Washington, D.C." (M. A. thesis, Catholic University of America, 1938), p. 114.

parts.[78] Since alley dwellers were almost always poor and usually black, they had to face an even more difficult burden when it came to the police, who considered them the "lowest character of negroes . . . in their animal state." Not only were these largely victimless crimes, but they were also ill defined, requiring considerable exer-

78. Provine, "Free Negro in the District of Columbia," pp. 125–27; Green, *Washington*, I, 389; Green, *Secret City*, p. 128; Ingle, *Negro in the District of Columbia*, p. 53; *Washington Bee*, July 28, 1883, p. 2; Johnson, "City on the Hill," p. 95. Rabinowitz has found a similar circumstance in other cities (*Race Relations in the Urban South*, pp. 43–44).

TABLE 25.
Arrests in Snow's Court and Fenton Court, January 1—June 30, 1936[*]

Crime	Snow's Court	Fenton Court	
Disorderly conduct and drunkenness	14	10	
Possession of an unlicensed dog	—	1	
Mental observation	1	—	
Unlicensed sale of whiskey	—	4	
Investigation	5	6	
Petit larceny	1	—	
Destroying private property	—	3	
Housebreaking	1	1	
Assault	5	1	
Assault with a dangerous weapon	—	1	
Grand larceny	1	—	
TOTAL	28	27	55

[*]SOURCE: Swinney, "Alley Dwellings and Housing Reform," p. 140.

cise of judgment on the part of the arresting officer. Thus these "offenses" could be conveniently used by police to harass or intimidate. The police were by no means reluctant to use force against alley dwellers, and when residents went to obstruct their neighbor's arrest they risked death, as an article in the *Daily Chronicle* warned: "The Perils of Resisting the Law—A Colored Man Shot and Killed by a Police Officer."[79] When alley dwellers confronted the police, officers nearly always emptied their revolvers into the crowd.[80]

This is not to deny that there was crime and violence in the alleys. For "Samuel Bray, colored . . . a sober man" who lived on H Street, the depiction of Blagden Alley in Drawing 1 was a real one. On the night of October 13, 1878, he was found "in Blagden's alley, lying unconscious with two wounds on his head, made by a blunt instrument, and a finger showing marks of having had a ring torn from it."[81] Johnson reports that several rapes took place in alleys in the same decade.[82] Nevertheless, most crime was far less severe, and was often limited and controlled by the alley's social structure and worldview. The *Star* reported that police visited Huntoon Al-

79. *Daily Chronicle*, Sept. 23, 1872, p. 4.
80. *Ibid.*; Washington *Star*, Dec. 27, 1881; Oct. 18, 1880, p. 4.
81. Washington *Star*, Oct. 14, 1878, p. 4.
82. Johnson, "City on the Hill," pp. 336, 342.

ley "frequently and during the week the population is fairly well-behaved. Saturday afternoons and Sundays the idle men get restless and there is much gambling and drinking. It is hidden from the street. A sentinel posted at the entrance can give warning of the coming of a policeman in plenty of time." Moreover, "Bootlegging is reported frequently, and there are many fights."[83] Yet, as one outside observer noted, "they fought among themselves quite a lot, especially on Saturday nights after they had had some liquor; then there would be quarreling, fighting, and maybe, a stabbing; but they did not fight with whites unless the latter started the trouble."[84] Since alley dwellers were, for the most part, hard-working, hard-living people, it is not surprising that they sought to enjoy their short periods of "leisure" in the same spirit. These forms of expression and entertainment reflect, in many respects, the tough yet proud life they lived. Alley dwellers could not afford the more subtle violence found in the "refined pleasures" of the upper classes. Drinking alley liquor, gambling with neighbors, and perhaps even fighting all provided entertainment and helped relieve frustrations, as well as keeping within the community what little resources there were. To survive, it was better to fight with one's neighbor than to attack outside oppressors, especially when those oppressors had all the power.[85] Attack was reserved for the protection and defense of friends, neighbors, and neighborhood.

Even the most notorious alleys seemed less awesome when the alleged crimes are considered. Pablo reported that, based on arrest records, Temperance Court crimes ranged from "petty larceny to disorderly conduct, selling liquor without a license, assault with a dangerous weapon, assault without a weapon, investigation, non-support, disorderly 'craps,' drunkenness, destroying private property, incorrigible and larceny."[86] While some of these are serious charges, others concern essentially petty and victimless crimes,

83. Washington *Star*, June 4, 1930.

84. Statement by a lawyer who grew up outside Fenton Place, in O'Connell, "Inhabited Alleys of Washington," p. 109.

85. Hoggart has observed that "Working-class sports-lovers admire the qualities of the hunter and fighter and daredevil—the exhibition of strength and muscle, of speed and daring, of skill and cunning. The great boxers and footballers and speedway riders naturally become heroes—very modified modern counterparts of the heroes of saga" (*Uses of Literacy*, p. 91). Even more interesting is Michael Feldberg's finding that "Violence was central to the city's artisan culture. While little evidence about artisan life has survived to sit on archive shelves, what evidence we do have about artisan life tells us that their culture was a vibrant and belligerent one" ("Urbanization as a Cause of Violence," p. 56).

86. Pablo, "Housing Needs and Social Problems," p. 54.

ones that can most easily be used by an arresting officer to justify his action.

If the alley communities had been all that dangerous, it would have been foolhardy for so many residents to have slept outside their homes during the summer, as Weller and others discovered that they did. Nearly all outside observers were surprised by the noisy but seemingly friendly atmosphere of the alley. Even though residents spoke courteously to police officers, the police continued to patrol in pairs for their own "protection," and the observers detected a latent danger.

Many activities viewed as criminal by the larger community were not so considered by the alley residents. Certainly more than one urban immigrant group has had to pay a severe price because its values and ways of life differed from those of the people in power. Many of these "crimes" were in fact forms of recreation and enjoyment: numbers, craps, drinking, and even fighting. Seldom was anyone injured, except while fighting, and in very few cases did these activities involve "outsiders" who were not known to the alley community. The fact that the law was enforced so strenuously against alley dwellers can only be seen as an effort on the part of the power structure to restrict and control them.

It is the role of the police to maintain order and control as defined by the dominant culture and class. We have already seen that an alley child was arrested for having stolen a bicycle that was, in fact, his; a number of cases before the Board of Children's Guardians also suggest that less than full justice was administered in these decisions. Several other cases offer insights into the issue of police brutality. One alley woman had decorated her living room with "Two gigantic framed advertisements, showing luxurious accommodations on a former trans-Atlantic liner." The police warned her "that the name of the liner must be removed or she, the owner, would be arrested. This she had not done, but she constantly feared arrest. This is but one instance of a fear of 'the law' which they, the poorer Negroes, feel is not for protection but for persecution."[87] In another case, the grandmother of a dying child became despondent and got drunk. For this she was arrested and sent to the work-

87. Ratigan, *Sociological Survey of Disease*, p. 92. Similarly, a Washington *Daily News* reporter wrote that while he was in Temperance Court interviewing the residents, they "were interrupted by an exciting chase of about 20 young men by a policeman who said they had been shooting craps. None of them was caught," however, for "They melted away in the several approaches to the place." Washington *Daily News*, n.d.; clipping in the Washingtoniana Room, Martin Luther King Memorial Library, Washington, D.C.

house.[88] There are undoubtedly worse instances of brutality and failures in the justice system; certainly the types of crimes for which alley residents were most often arrested suggest this.

Perhaps even more impressive than the efforts of the mainstream society to control, regulate, and "re-educate" the alley dwellers was the strength of the alley community and culture. Despite the establishment's constant efforts at intimidation and persecution, most alley dwellers were able to preserve, adapt, and draw upon a wide variety of cultural experiences and institutions for strength and support. By relying on folk ways of life and by developing some new strategies, alley dwellers were able to establish a viable series of lifestyles, patterns of behavior and social organization that made survival possible in the hostile and difficult urban environment. They responded with a variety of activities that enabled them to live on far less than even social workers and planners thought feasible. These strategies represent important positive adaptations, rather than disorganized or pathological responses. Even with these strategies, however, alley residents found it difficult to avoid the exploitation of the alley store and the ever-present dangers of disease and death. Finally, crime and violence, which have often been used to indicate the pathological nature of the alley population, appear on closer examination to be, as St. Clair Drake and Horace R. Cayton called it, "business under a cloud."[89] While these businesses may have been anathema to the mainstream culture, they represented acceptable and positive institutions within the alley. Similarly, much of the violence reported by middle-class observers reflects cultural perspectives different from those found in the alley. Further aspects of this "different" alley culture can be seen only dimly through the surviving records, but suggestive information exists on religious practices and folklife.

88. Weller, *Neglected Neighbors*, pp. 203–5.
89. The title for the chapter on illegal businesses in St. Clair Drake and Horace R. Clayton, *Black Metropolis: A Study of Negro Life in a Northern City* (New York, 1962), II, 470–94.

Chapter 6
Religion and Folklife in the City

For all its drawbacks, the court does convey a picturesque and cloistered feeling which the external, bye-law reform of the streets would abruptly end. And there is a hint of eighteenth-century grace still lingering in the architecture. One can imagine that newly arrived rural groups might even welcome its sense of temporary shelter and security from the huge and impersonal city.—Walter Creese, THE SEARCH FOR ENVIRONMENT

While much of the modern Western world seemed to become increasingly marked by distinct part-worlds, with time broken down into discrete units, alley life remained relatively free of this segmentation. Extended kinship networks and the incorporation of friends and neighbors into the family unit made it difficult to determine where family ended and neighborhood or community began. The distinction between work and recreation was also unclear in the alleys, if only because there was little time for activities that did not add to the family's limited resources. Children's work was also play, "Some women regard housework as a form of recreation," and men fished for both sustenance and pleasure.[1]

Not surprisingly, then, alley dwellers drew no sharp lines between the sacred and the secular. Like everything else in alley life, religion and folklife were intertwined almost completely. Unfortunately, information on the religious practices and beliefs, as well as on folk practices of alley residents, are the most fragmented and dif-

1. Ratigan, *Sociological Survey of Disease*, p. 115.

ficult to reconstruct. Much of the data must be pieced together from various outside accounts of alley life, although newspaper stories, visual sources, and even census data provide important supporting evidence. It is disappointing that so little qualitative information exists on the role of religion in the alleys, for this was allegedly one of the primary institutions that broke down in the urban environment. This lack of data is especially frustrating because religion provides a key organizing and focal point for both African and slave cultures. Nevertheless, enough fragmented evidence exists to suggest the continuing importance of religion and folklife in the lives of alley residents. A few sources suggest (though by no means confirm) how the interaction of rural migrants with the city environment resulted in the rise of more formal institutions and activities, albeit ones which reflected traditional roles and functions.

Considerable evidence indicates that there was religious activity in the alleys. When he entered Blagden Alley for the first time, Weller heard "a wail of primitive, weird chanting" coming "from the little mission in an alley parlour." He concluded later that this alley mission was "a saddening travesty upon Christ's religion. It impresses one chiefly by the absence of sincerity, the self-conscious posing in formal prayers and exhortations, and the lack of any counsel as to daily living."[2] He also reported the existence of an "alley mission" in a Snow's Court house in 1905; it displayed a "home-made sign, 'Where Will You Spend Eternity?'"[3] Seven years later Mallalieu found, "on the front of one shack" in Snow's Court, "a crude sign reading, 'Charitable Baptist Church,' and announcing services. Report declared that the man in charge was not capable of doing any body any good."[4] The negative tone of these descriptions reflects the same mentality that has been found among antebellum observers of slave religious practices. Genovese noted that "whites, northern and southern, had been misled because the Christian expression of the slaves burst forth as something so different from anything they knew. For such critics the slaves had to become, in effect, either white Christians or no Christians at all."[5]

Two other sources report religious activity in Goat Alley and

2. Weller, *Neglected Neighbors*, pp. 17, 22.
3. *Ibid.*, p. 97.
4. Mallalieu, "Washington Alley," p. 71.
5. Genovese, *Roll, Jordan, Roll*, p. 218. In later years the Wellers became joint founders of a group that sought to bridge the gap between a wide variety of world religions. Since Weller is no longer alive, and the organization he founded has failed to respond to numerous letters and phone calls, it is impossible to say whether he changed his attitude toward the alley church.

Fenton Place, and display the interconnection of the sacred and secular worlds. In response to police gambling raids, residents of the
former alley pointed out that, instead of crap games, they had
preaching with a "little liquor on the side." O'Connell's informant,
who had grown up outside the latter alley, remembered that most of
his neighbors "were Baptist, but they don't go to church at all.
There was one 'fellow' in the alley itself who used to 'get religion'
now and then after he had some liquor, and then preach to the others."[6] In 1948, on the other hand, Ben Bradlee found St. Matthew's
Overcoming Church in "a decrepit tenement on the littered corner
of King's Court," while the 1901 *Union League Directory* had reported
a Mt. Ararat Baptist Church in Snow's Court.[7]

Some alley residents attended established churches on the street.
Aunt Jane's mother was "the only one" in Center Court "who takes
the children to Church. Louise goes to the Baptist Sunday
School."[8] Ratigan found that "some men and women are interested
in church and church work. The men are deacons, ushers, or choir
members and the women belong to 'aid' and auxiliary groups."[9]
One family in Temperance Court also attended a Salvation Army
church.[10] Nevertheless, most sources suggest that alley residents
did not go out of the alleys to attend the city's prestigious churches;
certainly the staid formats of those churches did not fit the exuber-
ant religious practices of most alley residents. Like everything else
in alley life, religion was a physical and emotional experience, as
opposed to the more "intellectual," reserved religious services found
in established white and black churches.

Although little evidence ties alley dwellers directly to the camp
meetings of the nineteenth century or the in-city revivals of the
twentieth, the styles of services and the compositions of congregations suggest that many alley residents were probably drawn to
these meetings. Mrs. E. N. Chapin attended a camp meeting in
Anacostia after the Civil War, and reported finding "An improvised
pulpit made of a huge dry goods box, covered with a rag carpet, and
a rickety, old stand" holding "a Bible and a greasy hymn book,
while around this altar stood black boys holding torches filled with

6. Washington *Star*, Oct. 29, 1906; O'Connell, "Inhabited Alleys of Washington," p. 110.

7. Washington *Post*, Dec. 26, 1948; Andrew F. Hilyer, ed., *The Twentieth Century
Union League Directory* (Washington, 1901), p. 142. Several "alley missions" were
also maintained by established black and white churches; one was kept in Willow
Tree Alley by the Zion Baptist Church of F Street Southwest (p. 137).

8. Somerville, "Study of a Group of Negro Children," p. 25.

9. Ratigan, *Sociological Survey of Disease*, p. 114.

10. Pablo, "Housing Needs and Social Problems," p. 62.

kerosene oil, which had been used in some political procession." A black minister exhorted the five-hundred-member all-black (save for Mrs. Chapin's party) gathering, and was urged on in return by shouts of "'Amen' and 'that's so'," until "Nearly every black woman was in a state of frenzy. Clouds of dust rose from their stamping the ground, and obscured the light of the smoking lamps. Many fell flat on their backs and were stiffened into a catalepsy."[11] In later years at least some alley dwellers must have attended (as did Aunt Jane) the services of Elder Lightfoot Michaux at his "Church of God," or at one of his Griffith Stadium revivals. Some may have listened to his daily radio program, "Happy Am I."[12]

Information on the leaders of the alley congregations is almost as limited. Only four alley residents identified themselves as clergy in the 1880 census, and only one of these indicated his denomination (Methodist). Swinney found two ministers living in Fenton Place. One was "a free-lance evangelist who has worked with Father Divine, Elder Michaux, and other evangelists. He is a former carpenter by trade, possesses a third grade education, and was originally from South Carolina."[13] The second minister, perhaps not unlike the itinerant alley preacher in Photograph 33, was "one of the most picturesque individuals in the City of Washington. He has snow white hair, wears a frock coat, and is a Bishop by his own nomination." Unaffiliated with any denomination, he preaches "in homes and on street corners." He is "opposed to the preaching of 'Hellfire and damnation,'" but "believes in helping people uplift themselves in their daily lives and to better living conditions." This preacher lived "by securing handouts and shelter from strangers. He has been living in Fenton Place since last February when he knocked at the door and asked if he could spend the night." He pointed out that "'although the people ain't religious they've been letting me stay here ever since and I ain't paid 'em a cent. For my meals, I jist go door to door until somebody takes care of me. God is good; he has always taken care of me and I know he will in the future.'"[14]

While both of these ministers were part of the alley experience, they tended to be itinerants. More common, and perhaps more important because of their residential stability, were those who established churches in their own homes. Elder Lucy Wilcox was pastor of St. Matthew's Overcoming Church in Kings Court; another

11. Mrs. E. N. Chapin, *American Court Gossip or Life at the National Capitol* (Marshalltown, Iowa, 1887), pp. 36–37.

12. Green, *Secret City*, pp. 222, 238.

13. Swinney, "Alley Dwellings and Housing Reform," p. 120.

14. *Ibid.*, pp. 120–21.

PHOTOGRAPH 33.
"Traveling Evangelist and His Equipment." July, 1941. Photograph by Ed Rosskam. Farm Security Administration Collection, Library of Congress.

woman, a widow, founded the "First Church of Christ of Galatians 23:13" in her Fenton Place home. Like many such alley-house churches (the alley equivalent to the street's storefront church), this latter woman "rents her house for Jesus," and kept it going with money collected at services and from "doing occasional laundry work." The chapel, in her living room, contained "ten chairs, a pulpit, and an improvised altar."[15]

It is impossible to determine how important these churches were for the alley community, or how they functioned within it.[16] None of the various observers got involved enough with the alleys to determine the importance of such institutions. Nevertheless, the alley church clearly represented another level of organization beyond the extended-augmented family and the alley neigborhood itself, and it probably acted as an integrative force and bond. Because only alley residents were likely to know of its existence, it seems certain that the church was directed at its immediate neighbors. When we consider the form and function of its services, the potential integrating force of the alley church is impressive. Providing the opportunity for a common emotional release as well as for collective involvement in a ritual experience, the alley church brought neighbors together in ways that even the extended family and the alley community could not. Again, the overlapping memberships of family, community, and congregation tended to blur any distinction between the sacred and secular worlds.

Of course, the kinds of primary relations that bring people into such close and prolonged contact can also lead to dissension. The close proximity and high rates of neighborly interaction could easily lead to factions and fighting. Similarly, those who were out of favor with the alley preacher, or who found the preacher's theology questionable, could easily spark disagreements that would split the alley community. But despite the potential for such conflict, the bonds within the alley community tended to hold it together. One can only regret that in their desire to demonstrate a pathological community, Weller and others so easily dismissed the "wail of primitive, weird chanting."

The role of religion in alley life can be seen in a number of unobtrusive but significant ways. The importance of singing, especially

15. *Ibid.*, p. 121. One 1930s photograph not presented here does indicate that some of these alley churches had their own separate buildings, apart from living facilities. This one was a converted one-story alley house.

16. An extensive and determined oral history project could provide some insights into these questions, as well as a number of others for which the visual and written sources are sketchy.

spirituals and hymns, among the children has already been discussed. Whole families would also sing these songs together at night. As Ratigan noted, "Singing was traditionally the most reiterative form of recreation among adults and children. They often have very good voices and join in spontaneously when someone begins to sing."[17] As Levine found to be the case with slave music, religious and secular songs were often interspersed with one another, again reflecting the blurred line between sacred and secular.[18]

One of the most important possessions of alley families was the family Bible. Edward Ambush was born into slavery and was able to purchase his freedom, as well as his own alley house, on his earnings as a whitewasher. At his death in 1864 he left personal property valued at $67.50, "The most valuable single item being a large family Bible worth twenty dollars."[19] The importance of religion can also be seen in the interior decoration of alley houses. Weller described the interior of the Keefe home in Blagden Alley: "Religious pictures ornament the front room walls, for whose patchy, soiled appearance the landlord rather than the Keefe family is presumably to blame. Mrs. Keefe, pointing to a forbidding chromo of a bleeding Christ with His crown of thorns, declares that this is her 'favo-rite' picture and she 'jes' likes to set an' look at it,—coz it's so natchral!'"[20] In the Sammons family's house in the same alley (which was described as "filthy dirty; smells bad") Weller found "rather tasteful colored pictures hanging upon the grimy walls. 'That's Christ before Pilate,' said the sick woman as her eyes followed those of the visitor. Another favorite picture was da Vinci's 'Last Supper.'"[21] In another alley, Weller was led by a "wholesome looking tenant . . . past an original and very interesting picture of 'The Last Supper.'"[22] Ratigan, who made the most complete survey of interior decoration (finding 2.9 pictures per household), reported that numerous reproductions with religious significance included da Vinci's *Last Supper*, as well as "a vast array of calendars, with religious and animal motifs."[23] Photograph 33, of the itinerant alley preacher, contains several examples of pictures that might be found on alley walls. Ben Bradlee found a number of wall plaques

17. Ratigan, *Sociological Survey of Disease*, p. 115.
18. Levine, *Black Culture and Black Consciousness*, pp. 30–31.
19. Provine, "Free Negro in the District of Columbia," p. 108.
20. Weller, *Neglected Neighbors*, p. 19.
21. *Ibid.*, p. 22.
22. *Ibid.*, p. 78.
23. Ratigan, *Sociological Survey of Disease*, p. 92.

in a house in Dingman Court, with statements that included "Teach Me Thy Way, O Lord," "A Little Child Shall Lead Them," and "God Bless Our Home."[24] Of course, such decorative material does not demonstrate the binding power of religion; nor do the "evening concerts" by alley children and adults. Nevertheless, people's choice of these over other formats is at least suggestive of the church's role.

In the alley funeral, the interrelationships of all elements of alley life, both sacred and secular, can be seen in a reaffirmation of family, neighborhood, community, and life itself. When a death occurred, "someone starts a collection promptly. The women coming home from a day out at washing or other work are approached and cheerfully contribute a large part of their day's earnings." The men "give up whatever they have picked up around town that day." For one funeral in Willow Tree Alley in 1904, forty or fifty dollars was collected in an hour. "Out of this amount the undertaker is paid on the spot. If there is not enough money to satisfy him, a second collection will be made. If there is a surplus, it goes for beer, which is dispensed at the house of mourning." In some cases these funds supplemented an insurance policy.[25]

The alley funeral was a communal affair. As Laura Hopkins, a Willow Tree Alley resident, explained to a reporter, "I jes tell you one thing, when eny of us gets sick an' dies, we doan ask nobody outside de alley to help us pay de expenses."[26] When Elijah Chapman was hung on May 22, 1902, for killing Ida Burch, his funeral was not left to the state, but taken over by his alley neighbors, who raised fifty-three dollars and filled "'nine kerrages sides de hearse an' one hack full ob flowers.'"[27]

The death of a relative who had lived in the country resulted in a reunion for the Brown family of Center Court. Somerville, who accompanied the family to the country home of the deceased, was disturbed by what she saw: "To be joyful when going to a funeral was something a bit difficult to understand." If she found the occasion lacking in solemnity, she was nevertheless impressed by the "black-draped relatives of the dead man," who stood about while "His eldest daughter seemed to want to stay beside the casket. The beautiful casket, and neatly pressed suit of the dead man were the cleanest and best looking things in the house." Somerville continues by observing, "at the house the day was ended with much gaiety. A pot

24. Washington *Post*, Dec. 26, 1948.
25. Washington *Times*, Sept. 11, 1904. See Table 28.
26. *Ibid.*
27. *Ibid.*

of cooked water cress was put on the table and everyone ate. Bottles of wine and whiskey could be found in every room in the house, and the women and men gambled on the ground in back of the house. In all, the whole funeral amounted to a 'good time,' to the people present."[28]

Nor was the funeral's role in alley life a new one. For the slave, the "funeral has figured prominently as a religious ritual, a social event, and an expression of community."[29] The form and expense of the funeral remained disturbing to white middle-class observers, whether they were antebellum slave owners, northern travelers, twentieth-century housing reformers, or "objective" social scientists. Genovese has noted that "the sometimes boisterous dinners" held following the slave funeral "provided the occasions for many whites to consider these funerals 'pagan festivals' and to interpret them in one or another self-serving racist way."[30] While he noted that "bourgeois opinion in the Western world generally has manifested outrage at the apparently irrational compulsion of the lower classes to insist on funerals beyond their means," these rituals represented for both slaves and alley dwellers an awareness that "respect for the dead signifies respect for the living—respect for the continuity of the human community and recognition of each man's place within it. The slaves understood their responsibilities."[31]

That awareness of continuity with the past can be seen in other ways as well. Weller's description of one backyard in Phillips Alley invokes a rural setting, closely matching Janet Abu-Lughod's description of a Cairo alley. The woman of this house was asked if there were any animals on the premises. She replied that they owned a horse, but Weller also noted that "in picking my way through the filthy back yard, I saw coach dogs and puppies, cats, geese, chickens, and eight or more goats, besides three horses in the stable." Alley residents also continued rural and folk practices in

28. Somerville, "Study of a Group of Negro Children," pp. 52–55. Weller reports similar "wakes" among the residents in "White Alley." In one case "the dutiful nephew sold off the few sticks of furniture that the house afforded and gathered in all the men and boys and, 'tis said, even the women that he could entice there, for a protracted revel," while in another "the body of Jake Selton went to its last resting place" with a "Bacchanalian escort" (*Neglected Neighbors*, pp. 49, 48). Similarly, Genovese noted that "When they could, the slaves held wakes, which struck white observers as rivaling those famous Irish wakes in their raucousness. Here too we find an echo of Africa in the implicit idea of death, but it must also be considered a comment on the relationship of life to death under conditions of sorrow and oppression" (*Roll, Jordan, Roll*, p. 198).

29. *Ibid.*, p. 201.

30. *Ibid.*, p. 200.

31. *Ibid.*, pp. 201, 202.

their medical treatment, using warm breast milk to relieve the pain of an earache, sweet oil for sores, and fat meat on a boil to draw out the puss.[32] Nevertheless, as with many other folk groups in the city, there was a growing tendency to replace folk remedies whose ingredients were not easily obtainable with patent medicines of similar composition, or to develop new remedies whose ingredients were accessible.[33] Those who relied heavily on such remedies tended to be "the older people because of the conservativeness of the aged"; younger alley dwellers were less aware of such folk practices.[34]

There is little evidence that "Hoodoo" was practiced in the alleys, although Smiley does report that the oldest man in Freeman's Alley was "a 'voodoo doctor,'" who lived "by himself in a style almost princely when compared with that of his neighbors."[35] The 1880 census reports an "Herb Doctor" and four midwives living in the alleys. Ratigan notes, however, that of her sample of 215 births by alley women in the 1940s, only 3 were delivered by midwives or a "granny-lady." Just over a third of the births occurred in home deliveries supervised by professionals; the remaining 65 percent of births took place in hospitals.[36]

Superstition was by no means lacking in the alley. One could experience bad luck by breaking a mirror, having a black cat cross his

32. Somerville, "Study of a Group of Negro Children," p. 52. For a more complete discussion of these folk remedies, see Ratigan, *Sociological Survey of Disease*, pp. 121–61.

33. Ratigan, *Sociological Survey of Disease*, pp. 129–30.

34. *Ibid.*, p. 138. Nevertheless, in cases where grandparents were largely responsible for childrearing, as in the case of Ethel Waters, a wide range of folk remedies continued to be practiced. Waters recalled that her grandmother, "Besides scrubbing me every time she came home," "took other measures to safeguard my health. Each fall, when I put on my red flannel underwear, she'd pin a rag with sticky white pine tar on it to the part covering my chest. It smelled terrible. She pinned another rag, smeared with the same tar, on my nightgown, which meant I had to sleep with it. She also hung a little bag of asafetida around my neck. The combination of the two dreadful odors was almost unbearable, but I had to carry it with me from late September until Spring. The asafetida was to cure child complaints, and the sticky white pine tar was supposed to ward off lung ailments. In the spring she made me take sulphur and cream of tartar and drink sassafras tea, believing they thinned one's blood" (*His Eye Is on the Sparrow*, p. 25).

35. Smiley, *Glimpse at the Night Side of Washington*, p. 43. There is very little evidence to suggest the systematic use of hoodoo, or of any actual practitioners save Smiley. Since few students of alley life had any understanding of hoodoo, it is not surprising that there is little mention of it. However, since Zora Neale Hurston found the practice of hoodoo so common in the South, it was likely tied in to folk beliefs and practices. See Hurston's *Mules and Men* (Philadelphia, 1935).

36. Ratigan, *Sociological Survey of Disease*, p. 138.

or her path, walking under a ladder or around the left side of a post. Some people also believed that "Dreams will foretell events. One child dreamed of a number and said she was going to tell her mother to play it and win money."[37]

While dietary habits had to be adjusted in the new urban environment, they still reflected older patterns. "The diet is largely carbohydrate, little fresh meat is used but bacon ends, 'fat back' or other form of fat is used in cooking. Even the cheaper vegetables are used sparingly."[38] "Boiled water cress with fat meat is a familiar dish in the . . . [Brown] family. Fresh collard greens cooked the same way is a favorite dish of the children."[39]

Virtually no folktales were recorded by the outside observers of alley life. Undoubtedly a number of place names owe their origins to alley dwellers, and although the children jumped rope, none of their rhymes were recorded. Much of the folk music, whether spiritual or secular (as in the case of "John Henry"), did survive in the records, though it is fairly clear that virtually all folk music was altered to fit the new environment. Popular songs also served as a basis for new songs for the oral tradition. Given the high levels of illiteracy in the alleys and the nature of the alley dwellers' songs and dances, it is quite evident that these were part of an active oral tradition.

One folktale concerning an alley resident was widely known in Washington's black community. Sam McKeever, "a rag dealer who pushed a hand cart all over the city collecting and buying old cloth for resale to junk yards," allegedly spent his nights as a body-snatcher and grave-robber. According to some of the versions collected and analyzed by Gladys-Marie Fry, McKeever "lived with his wife and three daughters at Hughes Court." One of Fry's informants "described herself as a former neighbor of McKeever" in that alley.[40]

37. Somerville, "Study of a Group of Negro Children," p. 51. She also reports a story that suggests several alternatives at death: "Yvonne stated that a friend of her aunt died and that her aunt was crying because his spirit was coming back. The rest of the children listened very much excited while Yvonne continued directing her question to the writer, 'His spirit *will* come back; won't it?' Another child interrupted saying, 'No, his spirit won't come back 'cause when you die God will cut your heart out and take it to heaven if you are good—so how kin you come back with no heart in you.'" Waters also records encounters with ghosts and spirits, as well as the reading of cards (*His Eye Is on the Sparrow*, p. 25).

38. Sellew, *Deviant Social Situation*, p. 20.

39. Somerville, "Study of a Group of Negro Children," p. 21.

40. Gladys-Marie Fry, *Night Riders in Black Folk History* (Knoxville, 1975), pp. 202–3.

One night (as the most commonly accepted version of the tale goes) Sam McKeever, a "night doctor" who provided bodies for medical schools, came upon a woman sitting in a park. He failed to realize that the woman was his wife, resting while on her journey to deliver clean laundry. "He stole up there and throwed that mask on her. A big footed fellow like that. And then, he got home and asked his children where their mama at. They said, 'I don't know.' Then it come to him what he had done, you see. He run to the doctors. She was breathing her last breath."[41]

Fry, seeking to determine whether there was a real Sam McKeever, discovered the earliest mention of a Samuel McKeever in the 1883 city directory. Though this man had an address in Clark Alley, his longest period of residence was in Hughes Court (7 years). His name last appeared in the city directory in 1918, after a ten-year absence. All other members of his family, except his wife, also reappeared in the directory at that time. Finally, his various occupations had included "laborer, rags, junk, buyer, and elevator operator, while his wife's occupations included washer, midwife, and nurse."[42]

Fry is not directly concerned with explicating alley life or the impact of urbanization, but she does provide excellent insight on how night-doctor tales changed as their tellers moved from the country to the city:

> Relocation, however, significantly affected these beliefs in that the supernatural element was dropped. The emphasis was completely shifted to science by the Blacks, who structured a detailed system of beliefs concerning every aspect of the body-snatching business. They described in detail such things as the types of dress employed; the kinds of victims body-snatchers sought; techniques of capturing people; methods of abduction . . . and the manner of death people were supposed to have suffered. In other words, from the moment of a person's capture to his slow, torturous death at the hands of body-snatchers, they described every step—often with numerous variations.[43]

If tales like those about Sam McKeever and other "night doctors" became more realistic and less supernatural as a result of urban migration, they continued to serve an important didactic purpose.

41. Quoted *ibid.*, p. 204.
42. *Ibid.*, pp. 206–7.
43. *Ibid.*, pp. 187–88.

Older rural blacks told these tales (often set in the city) to discourage their children from migrating. In the urban environment, the same kinds of stories also served to warn children about the city's dangers. In almost all the versions (save the one about Sam McKeever's wife) the people snatched are weak and helpless, almost always children. Moreover, the stories appear to be told to and by children. As one informant told Fry, "'There was quite a bit of talk about it even up until I got to be, oh, some 15 or 16 years old.'"[44] These stories, rich and full of description, suspense, and danger, were developed by migrants—both alley and street dwellers—to alert their children to the dangers of strangers, strange places, and night in the city. Rather than merely telling their children not to do something, migrants constructed stories that conveyed instructions on how to survive in the city.

Folklore, then, like spirituals and folksongs, changed as a result of migration, but continued to play an important role in socialization and social control. One can see both persistence and change in other areas of the migrants' lives as well, although it is very difficult to document these changes for alley dwellers. One such area concerned street parades and celebrations. For black residents of postbellum Washington, the major celebration was of Emancipation Day, every April; activities included a parade, political rallies, and general merry-making. The *Bee* described the twenty-first anniversary of freedom in the District of Columbia as "the grandest event in the history of the colored race—the street parade, mile and a half long—150 carriages in line."[45] The "civil organizations" participating in that parade provides a glimpse into the extensive organizational life of the Washington black community: Hod-carriers Union (500 men), Sons and Daughters of Liberty (50), Fourth Ward Ethiopian Minstrels (26), West Washington Union Labor Association (40), Young Men's Social Club, Washington Star Pioneers (20), Washington Brick Machine Union Association (16), Gay Heart Social Club, Cosmetic Social Club, The Invincible Social Club, Knights of Labor, East Washington Social Club, Knights of Jerusalem, Chaldeans, Knights of Moses, Galilean Fisherman, Sons and Daughters of Samaria, Osceolas, Solid Yantics, Monitor, Celestial Golden Links, Lively Eights, Imperials, Independent Fern Leaf Social Club, The Six Good Brothers, Twilight Social Club, and the Paper Hanger's Union.[46]

44. Quoted *ibid.*, p. 184. See pp. 179–200 for different versions, and the contexts in which the stories were told.
45. Washington *Bee*, Apr. 21, 1883, p. 1.
46. *Ibid.*

It is, of course, impossible to know how many alley residents took part in these parades and festivities, but several years later, when black leaders were concerned that the celebrations were getting out of hand, they placed the blame on the alleys. As Frederick Douglass warned in 1886:

> The thought is already gaining ground that we have not heretofore received the best influences, which this anniversary is capable of exerting; that tinsel show, gaudy display and straggling processions, which empty the alleys and dark places of our city into the broad day-light of our thronged streets and avenues, thus thrusting upon public view a vastly undue proportion of the most unfortunate, unimproved, and unprogressive class of the colored people, and thereby inviting public disgust and contempt, and repelling the more thrifty and self-respecting among us, is a positive hurt to the whole colored population of this city.[47]

The *Bee*, reprinting his speech in 1888, called "attention . . . to the speech of Mr. Douglass in which he states that these parades 'which empty the alleys and dark places of our city into the broad day light and etc.'"[48] Unlike the procession it described five years before, the *Bee* found the 1888 parade filled "with all kinds of disgraceful carts, wagons and other things that would have been disgusting to the courtesans of murders bay. . . . It was void of dignity, uniformity and respectibility and will be an everlasting injury. . . . The parade . . . showed . . . that class of colored people who live in poverty and spend all their money for one day's festivity."[49]

47. Speech of Frederick Douglass, Apr. 17, 1886, reprinted in Washington *Bee*, Mar. 24, 1888, p. 2. See *National Republican*, Apr. 17, 1886, for the original reporting. Johnson notes that while the annual celebrations had been integrated in the early years, "By the early 1880s it was regarded as a black community institution" ("City on the Hill," p. 288). Increasing racism, combined with the "embarrassing" activities of working-class blacks, apparently led middle- and upper-class blacks to change the nature of the celebration by banning the street parade and holding the entire proceedings in a church; Washington *Bee*, Mar. 31, 1888, p. 2; Mar. 24, 1888, p. 2. This seems strikingly similar to what happened to the "John Kuners festival" in North Carolina. Levine explains, "By 1900 it seems to have disappeared because of the growing opposition of the Negro clergy who felt it was an undignified exhibition, and of a growing number of Negro residents, especially among the middle-class, who were convinced that the event lowered their status in the eyes of the whites" (*Black Culture and Black Consciousness*, p. 150).

48. Washington *Bee*, Mar. 24, 1888, p. 2.

49. *Ibid.*, Apr. 21, 1888, p. 2. To many middle- and upper-class black Washingtonians, the word "alley" had very bad connotations.

These descriptions seem to imply that alley residents were actively involved in a number of celebrations, and that they were, perhaps, also involved in a wide variety of voluntary organizations.[50]
Again, the evidence is only suggestive, as in the case of an extensive
and widely reprinted article on "Washington Colored People" by
the Washington correspondent for the New York *Sun*. The author
noted that the "social instincts" of working-class blacks "are grati-
fied by the organization and maintenance of societies of all sorts,
benevolent, patriotic, social and economic. There are nearly one
hundred of these organizations, supported almost entirely by the laboring colored people."[51] Similarly, Mrs. E. N. Chapin reported:

> Although many are poor, and to a certain extent, illiterate,
> yet, they have more churches, church societies, temperance
> and benevolent associations, than can be found among any
> other people. To belong to a "sessity" is a badge of honor
> among the colored folks. They are very earnest in securing
> money enough to pay their dues, and whether as Free Ma-
> sons, Odd Fellow, Knight of Labor, or the orders of "free
> burial," they will do anything rather than lose their position
> as members: and to their credit be it spoken, they have a de-
> cent burial by their societies, and while living, take their
> places in a street procession with uniforms and feathers
> bright and shining.[52]

Just how many alley dwellers fell into these categories is difficult
to say. Certainly no twentieth-century observer of alley life seemed
aware of alley residents' involvement in voluntary and benevolent
associations. On the other hand, the public display of black associa-

50. This was not the only city celebration that black Washingtonians (probably
including alley dwellers) took part in. Johnson notes that blacks "entered enthusi-
astically into the white institution of the torchlight serenading of successful candi-
dates" ("City on the Hill," p. 282). At least one scholar has argued that the inaugu-
ral parade originated in African practices and was picked up by whites after New
England slaves continued their practice in the New World (Hubert Aimes, "African Institutions in America," *Journal of American Folklore*, 18 [1905]: 15–16). Finally, Levine points out that boxing victories by Joe Louis "were occasions for
street celebrations, with tens of thousands of black residents of northern cities pa-
rading, singing, dancing" (*Black Culture and Black Consciousness*, p. 434).

51. Reprinted in Washington *Star*, Dec. 19, 1883, p. 2.

52. Chapin, *American Court Gossip*, p. 35. Some alley residents were probably
involved in Isaac Cohen's Brotherhood of Labor, which included black laborers in
the government brickyards. In 1878 Cohen "went upon the streets and congregated together a few of the lowest class of colored people and made speeches and excited them to riot" in order to secure higher wages (Washington *Star*, Feb. 11,
1879, p. 4; see also Sept. 25, 1879, p. 1; Oct. 14, 1879, p. 4).

tional life was probably greatly reduced by the 1900s. Furthermore, most students of the alleys were not looking for organizational activity. But observers of the late nineteenth century may not be entirely accurate in their depictions either; many white writers had only a tenuous connection with the black community, and the black press and leaders had "no more social relations with" the working class "than a white family would."[53]

A study of secret and nonsecret beneficial organizations in Washington's turn-of-the-century black community reported substantial numbers of organizations and members. Noting that their count was far from complete, the editors of the Union League Directory gained information on forty-five different organizations with a total membership of 19,842, exclusive of "juvenile societies under the patronage and protection of the Chief Organizations." Many of these groups had been prominent in the Emancipation Day parade. As Tables 26 and 27 suggest, the entrance fees for these organizations were quite high, given alley incomes, but dues (normally about $.25 a month) were not unreasonable. Moreover, membership guaranteed sick benefits of about $4 per week (usually limited to a maximum of eight weeks in a year), and death benefits of $50 to $100 to the survivor.[54]

Just how many alley residents belonged to these organizations is not known. Weller noted that alley dwellers "depend for funeral expenses" on "industrial insurance policies." Nevertheless, George Weber's 1908 survey of a sample of low-income alley and street residents revealed that nearly half of them had insurance policies "carried in either industrial insurance companies or in fraternal or other mutual benefit associations, and the premium payments were usually made in weekly installments."[55] (See Table 28.) Since alley dwellers constituted 64 percent of the black sample, at least some of them probably had insurance policies and belonged to a fraternal or benevolent organization. The older, more financially secure working-class black families that resided on the streets, and middle-class street residents, undoubtedly had the greatest involvement in these associations.[56] Certainly sickness and death benefits were sorely needed by alley residents; thus a membership in one of these orga-

53. Washington *Star*, Dec. 19, 1883, p. 2.

54. Hilyer, ed., *Union League Directory*, pp. 116–36.

55. Weller, *Neglected Neighbors*, p. 23; G. H. Weber, "Sociological Study of 1,251 Families," in George Kober, *Report of the Committee on Social Betterment* (President's Homes Commission) (Washington, 1908), p. 232.

56. None of the officers listed in the directory had alley addresses. Hilyer, ed., *Union League Directory*, pp. 116–36.

TABLE 26.
Nonsecret Beneficial Organizations, 1900*

Organization	Date founded	No. branch
Banneker Relief Association	1889	1
Coachmen's Union and Aid Association	1882	1
Elder Men's Immediate Relief	1898	1
Elder Ladies' Immediate Relief	1900	1
Frederick Douglass Relief Association	1897	1
Friends of Zion	—	1
Immediate Aid Society	—	12
Ladies' Mutual Relief	1890	1
Soldiers' and Sailors' National Benefit Union	1894	1
Ladies' Relief Union Auxiliary	1897	1
United Aid Association #1	1866	1
Young Men's Immediate Relief Association	1888	1
Young Men's Protective League	—	1
Ladies' United Reapers Society	1873	1
Hod Carriers' Society No. 1	—	1
Plumbers' Laborers' Union	1883	1
Knights of St. Augustine Commandery No. 2	1872	1
Knights of St. Cyprian No. 7	1893	1
TOTAL	—	29

*SOURCE: Andrew F. Hilyer, ed., *The Twentieth Century Union League Directory* (Washington, 1901), pp. 116–36.

nizations represented another survival strategy for those who could afford it.

It is especially unfortunate that we lack more complete information on the nature and extent of alley residents' participation in these beneficial organizations or their reliance on industrial insurance, because there changes in social patterns and organizations resulting from urbanization could be tested.[57] Nevertheless, it seems reasonable to conclude that many recent urban immigrants relied more heavily on the immediate primary groups of kinship and

57. As with the role and function of the alley church, a concerted study of these voluntary associations and their membership through written records and oral history might provide important insights on the process of adjustment to the urban environment.

Table 26—*continued*

No. members	Entrance fee	Monthly dues	Benefits expended, 1900	Property and cash
190	$ 5.00	—	—	—
108	5.00	—	$ 350.00	$ 3,300.00
373	4.00	$ .25	957.50	—
310	—	.25	—	1,000.00
151	5.00	.25	364.25	—
125	—	—	—	6,000.00
1,200	—	.35	—	—
61	5.00	.25	175.00	—
40	—	.085	96.00	200.00
100	—	.25	110.00	550.00
83	5.00	.25	399.00	1,096.39
160	10.00	.25	—	2,000.00
90	—	.25	—	1,000.00
140	10.00	.30	300.00	—
450	—	.25	—	—
75	—	.25	—	—
75	5.00	.25	575.00	1,800.00
78	2.00	.25	9.00	700.00
3,809	—	—	$3,335.75	$17,646.39

neighborhood, as was the case for many alley residents. Others, who through longer urban residence and greater relative affluence had an opportunity to join in the associational life, probably took advantage of that membership to acquire sickness and death insurance. Finally, still others probably took out life insurance policies. Undoubtedly, one could find all three types of people living in alleys, on streets, and in all classes. However, it seems reasonable to suspect that alley dwellers tended to fall into the first two groups, while street residents and middle-class blacks tended to fall into the latter two. Thus membership in a benevolent association or ownership of a life insurance policy may reflect length of urban residence, or class.

These findings seem to support the conclusions of other scholars

TABLE 27.
Secret Beneficial and Benevolent Societies, 1900

Organization	Date founded
Grand United Order of Chaldeans	—
Galilean Fisherman	—
J. R. Giddings and Jollifee Union	—
International Order of Good Samaritans and Daughters of Samaria	186
Hosts of Israel	186
Knights of Jerusalem	1886
Knights of Pythias	
Love and Charity	—
Masons	—
Daughters of Eastern Star, Auxiliary	—
Odd Fellows	184
Household of Ruth Auxiliary	185
Sons and Daughters of Moses	—
Sons and Daughters of Liberty	186
True Reformers	188
United Brotherhood	1898
TOTAL	—

Data furnished by authorized sources or found in the latest published reports. The entrance fee vari from $2 to $10; the monthly dues from 15¢ to 50¢; the benefits from $3.00 to $5.00 per week; funerals from $40.00 up. Usually the subordinate lodge may regulate these matters to suit itself.
*SOURCE: Same as for Table 26.

who, like Walter Weare, have concluded that "in the city, where the job replaced the land as the economic base, no vestige of security remained after the death of the breadwinner; thus urbanization and occupational changes sponsored the rise of Negro life insurance on a more businesslike pattern, in place of the folk-oriented burial society."[58] While there is much truth in this statement, it also obscures

58. Walter B. Weare, *Black Business in the New South: A Social History of the North Carolina Mutual Life Insurance Company* (Urbana, 1973), p. 184. While Weare is quite correct in noting that the insurance company became increasingly important in the urban environment (as well as in the rural one), the expansion of this formal institution does not preclude the continuing existence and importance of other forms of social organization. In their efforts to demonstrate the sharp changes that have resulted from "modernization," industrialization, and urbanization, social scientists have often presumed more than their evidence conveys.

Table 27—*continued*

No. lodges*	No. members	Entrance fee	Monthly dues	Benefits expended, 1900	Property and cash
20	1,256	$2.00	$ .25	—	—
10	600	—	—	—	$10,000.00
14	700	—	—	—	—
66	4,700	—	—	7,461.40	15,562.20
6	400	—	—	—	—
12	900	—	—	2,368.17	1,743.00
5	—	—	—	—	—
23	800	—	—	—	—
12	700	—	.50	1,499.25	18,223.25
3	—	—	—	—	—
27	2,378	—	—	4,322.38	23,175.15
14	1,300	—	—	—	—
—	—	—	—	—	—
4	252	—	.25	640.00	540.00
39	2,000	4.60	.35	6,807.00	10,000.00
1	47	—	—	—	—
256	16,033	—	—	$23,098.20	$79,243.60

a number of critical factors. The rise of these more formal institutions does not necessarily imply the disappearance of primary group life; rather, for many alley dwellers they represented just another safety net to supplement the work of those primary groups. Moreover, the origins, forms, and functions of these newer institutions owed much to traditional patterns. Beneficial associations and insurance companies originated in and continued to work out of the black church and a religious milieu.[59] If the beneficial associa-

59. Charles Clinton Spaulding, who was general manager of the North Carolina Mutual Life Insurance Company, noted that "practically all Negro fraternal societies and Negro businesses were organized in Negro churches" (quoted *ibid.*, p. 184). Similarly, Weare found that the "mutual benefit society can best be described as a rudimentary instrument of social welfare that was both secular and sectarian in origin. Education and religious training usually coincided in these organizations;

TABLE 28.
Insurance Policies Held by Individuals with Annual Family Incomes Below $1,000 in 1908**

	No. families in sample	Total sample population (excludes boarders)	No. life insurance policies	% individuals holding	No. sickness insurance policies	% individuals holding
White[a]	594	2,593	1,195	46	90	3
Black[b]	657	2,296	1,007	44	765	33
TOTAL[c]	1,251	4,889	2,202	45	855	17

[a]White alley dwellers = 17% of white sample.
[b]Black alley dwellers = 64% of black sample.
[c]Alley dwellers = 40% of entire sample.
*SOURCE: G. H. Weber, "Sociological Study of 1,251 Families," in George Kober, *Report of the Committee on Social Betterment* (Washington, 1908), pp. 232, 220.

tion was not made up entirely of relatives, friends, and neighbors (as in the case of the primary alley groups), its local affiliate was likely to be an outgrowth of a neighborhood church whose congregation consisted largely of those very people. Furthermore, new associations often occasioned the formation of new primary groups, while the focal point of these groups remained the church.[60] Finally, the traditional blur of sacred and secular continued strong, regardless of the institutional form. If the beneficial association and insurance company reflected some characteristics of "urban" organizations in their bureaucracy and hierarchy, they also reflected folk influences.[61]

---

more often than not, ministers had a hand in the organizing and imposed moral and religious restrictions on the members. And just as the church and the benefit society blended into one another, so there was a hazy distinction between the secret fraternal lodge and the benefit society" (pp. 6–7; see also pp. 6–18). There was much overlap between church and insurance company: "the church and the Mutual formed the matrix of community organization in Durham. The Company's leadership and history gave it a close kinship with the church; indeed, the institutional demarcation between the Negro church and insurance society was never so clear that the two could not share an identity under the aegis of uplift" (p. 87; see also pp. 134, 185–95).

60. Alan P. Bates and Nicholas Babchuk, "The Primary Group: A Reappraisal," *Sociological Quarterly*, 2 (July, 1961): 183–84.

61. Because social scientists often cast city and country as opposites, it is often forgotten that many activities performed by bureaucratic and institutional "agencies" in urban areas are nearly the same as those carried on in the country or in

Religion and folklife, then, remained important in the alley community. Services in the alley church provided another level of interaction for alley neighbors, one through which they could participate in a common ritual experience. Church services, communal singing, and communal re-creation of songs enabled people to remember and pass on their heritage, as well as providing for adjustment to a harsh and difficult urban experience.

Contrary to scholars' and reformers' descriptions of disorder and pathology, alley residents were able to maintain their old cultural patterns in the new environment, adapting and adjusting them when necessary. These patterns provided an integrated philosophy and worldview that resisted the segmentation of the city. Moreover, alley dwellers demonstrated considerable flexibility and ingenuity in accommodating to the new environment. If their world was no longer rural, it was not the one projected by urban sociologists and anthropologists, either. Instead, alley residents built a vital and adaptive culture that enabled them to survive and also provided occasional enjoyment and pleasure in spite of conditions.

---

many folk societies by friends, relatives, and neighbors, and that these "institutions" are historically related. Letitia Brown's fine description of the Metropolitan A. M. E. Church's role provides an excellent example of an institution incorporating many (if not all) of the "services" once provided through extended kinship networks, neighborhood, and community ("The Metropolitan A. M. E. Church," paper delivered at the Conference on Washington, D.C., Historical Studies, Jan. 11, 1974). See also Jack Newfield and Paul DuBrul, *The Abuse of Power* (New York, 1978), p. 99, for the evolution of savings banks out of burial societies. Finally, the development of beneficial associations, insurance, and institutional churches in the countryside prior to or at the same time as their introduction in the city further complicates this issue.

Conclusion

In the 1860s and 1870s some tenements were constructed in the alleys, and they were generally notorious for vice and misery. Close's Alley . . . known for its filth and its immoral denizens, scandalized and terrorized much of the surrounding population in the 1870s and 1880s. By the late nineteenth and early twentieth centuries, alleys were less known for their vice but had become more notorious for their misery.—David Katzman, BEFORE THE GHETTO: BLACK DETROIT IN THE NINETEENTH CENTURY

They had established all sorts of ties in their neighborhoods which meant a great deal to them and around which they had strong feelings.—Charles Levi Sanders, "A Study of the Relocation of Rear and Alley Tenants in Atlanta"

Having considered alley life from various angles, we can now consider a series of questions about the relevance and meaning of the analysis. Before doing so, however, we should briefly sum up the findings. The discussion will then turn to consider the extent to which the Washington alley experience typifies, or varies from, that of other urban folk migrants. To the extent that similarities in residential form, patterns of social organization, and strategies for survival can be demonstrated elsewhere, the findings here have at least a tentative relevance for the experience of other folk migrants. Finally, two important conclusions can be drawn from these findings; the first concerns the transition from plantation to ghetto. While this study is largely concerned with examining the patterns of order developed by folk migrants in Washington over a hundred-and-twenty-year period, the rise and zenith of alley housing took place between the 1860s and the development of massive northern ghettoes in the twentieth century. The alley experience represents part of that plantation-ghetto transition, both in scale and in chronology. Second, this study provides insights into the much studied and discussed "impact of the city" on folk migrants. While the nature of my sources makes it very difficult to trace changes over time, or to delineate patterns of accommodation and adjustment to the urban environment, we can assess the impact of modernization on urbanized folk.

In broad terms, alley housing was a product of the physical and spatial constraints of the walking city and the individual decisions of many private capitalists. Construction began before the Civil War, but the later rapid increase in the city's population, especially its black population, led to corresponding growth in the number of alley houses. While it is not clear who the early builders were, from 1877 to the end of such construction in 1892 "large developers" (professionals, executives, or entrepreneurs) constructed most alley houses. By 1913, alley property ownership had slipped down the economic ladder.

Regardless of the owners' identities or social statuses, there was very little proximity between their own residences and their alley properties at least from the 1870s on. This distance meant that, despite their sizable profits, owners were not able to exert strong control over alley tenants, thus permitting the latter considerable control over their own living arrangements and daily lives.

The alley population grew, as did the proportion of blacks, until about 1897; in that year the reported number of alley dwellers was nearly 19,000, of whom over 90 percent were black. However, the prohibition against alley house construction, as well as concerted attacks by housing reformers and competition for land by businesses and automobile garages, slowly decreased the number of inhabited alleys during the first half of the twentieth century. Since then, restoration efforts radically changed the demographic makeup of nearly half of the few remaining alleys.

Despite the declining numbers of alley dwellers in the twentieth century, alley institutions demonstrated amazing continuity over the entire period. Foremost among these institutions was the family. While its forms varied considerably, the alley family facilitated individuals' survival in difficult conditions. Many alley families which appeared to be nuclear, based on census records, were in fact extended, with relatives either sharing the house or living in the same alley. Considerable evidence suggests the continuing strength of the extended family and kinship network; members performed functions ranging from child-rearing, socialization, and socializing to extending considerable support in times of trouble. Rather than representing a divisive element in the family, boarders were, instead, incorporated to expand the family's network for support in difficult times. These extended-augmented family networks represent adjustments to a new environment, displaying continuity with the slave and post–Civil War rural experience as well as with the larger ghetto experience of more recent years. The more equitable sex roles, overcrowding, and sharing of common facilities also represent continuities with the past. Moreover, the records of social service agencies suggest little reliance on public sources for support on the part of alley dwellers. The interior arrangement and decor of houses demonstrate order and ingenuity in spite of limited space and resources. The backyard clutter reported by most observers turned out to be protection against economic disaster; junk was collected for supplemental income, and often served as insurance for hard times.

Other factors within the alley world fostered the establishment of community. Isolation from the streets, the face-to-face contact resulting from the proximity of the houses, and the extremely homogeneous nature of the population all promoted neighborly interaction. Taking advantage of these factors, alley residents created a behavioral landscape that supported their informal social world. They turned the alley into a commons where children could play safely, adults could lounge and talk, and people could even sleep on hot summer nights. They also utilized the open alley vista and their isolation from the street to defend their neighborhood from unwanted intruders. Outsiders were made to feel uncomfortable, and the threat of violence certainly remained ever-present in the minds of many. Moreover, alley residents expressed satisfaction with their residential location, if not with the specific conditions of their houses. This feeling was especially strong among the children, who clearly perceived "street people" as different from "alley people" and strongly identified with the latter. Not only did alley residents find satisfaction in their communities, but they also tended to stay in a given community or neighborhood for a surprisingly long time, given the fact that only a few owned their own homes. The extent of community can be seen in other ways as well. Not only did residents exercise control over their alley "turf," but they also provided support for those in need. The extent of community involvement was especially evident when a death occurred; virtually the entire community was involved in raising money for the funeral, and the extensive preparations reflected the importance of this ritual within the community. Similarly, there were clear lines of social order in the alley, and any resident who overstepped these could expect chastisement. It is also apparent that alleys had established hierarchies responsible for "administering" these activities.

An examination of childhood in the alleys also reveals considerable social order and continuity. Children were deeply involved in the daily survival strategies, and as a result their activities were closely integrated with those of their elders. Cooking, washing, running errands, cleaning, junking, babysitting and other jobs also served as forms of recreation for alley children. Formal education, while representing a potentially divisive element between the generations, in fact proved to be a reinforcing factor in alley life, since so few children could relate to the school experience. While the popular media represented another potential force for cleavage within the community, alley children merely borrowed materials from those external sources and used them in traditional ways to support the alley worldview. While some delinquency reflected clear generational breaks, these were numerically insignificant and may well have reflected the internal division of alley opinion on lifestyles. Certainly the alley community was clearly able to socialize many of its young into its own worldview and values, providing continuity and order for the future.

When looking directly at alley conditions which more recent scholars have viewed as the causes of social disorganization and pathology, we can also discern considerable order and continuity. Certainly alley dwellers were hired for only the most physically demanding and arduous tasks—which also were those that paid the least wages and had the least job security. As a result, more alley family members worked for considerably less collective return than was true for street families. Hard work, insanitary housing conditions, and low incomes that resulted in inadequate diets led to disability and disease, further reducing the limited family resources. Nevertheless, alley dwellers developed ingenious adaptations to help circumvent disaster. Drawing on their urban environment, they found ways to supplement both incomes and diets. Acquiring secondhand furniture and clothes or taking in friends as boarders also permitted alley residents to survive on incomes far below the subsistence level. Moreover, through illegal businesses such as bootlegging, numbers, and speakeasies, alley residents supplemented their incomes while they provided needed services and entertainment to the alley community. Patronage of such businesses helped keep within the community money that might later be used to help a needy individual or family. Analysis of arrest records reveals few serious crimes, compared to the numerous minor, victimless offenses. There is clear evidence of police harassment of both juvenile and adult "offenders." Nevertheless, much of the reported "violence" seems to result from middle-class misunderstanding of working-class lifestyles.

Finally, alley dwellers made no sharp distinctions between the sacred and secular worlds. For generations religion continued to play an important role in alley dwellers' lives, not only through formal worship but also through a number of rituals, as well as through the pervasive influence of music. Interwoven with these were folk beliefs and practices; modified to fit the urban environment, they continued to be important in alley life.

None of the statements presented here should be taken to suggest that alley life was idyllic. Whether family form, childhood "play," or work itself, virtually every aspect was focused on survival. Alley dwellers had to confront more serious and pervasive problems than any other residents of the city; these included dangerous work, low wages, under- and unemployment, inadequate diet, overcrowding, and unsanitary and unsafe housing, deadly diseases, and a much higher death rate, especially for infants. Finally, black alley dwellers continuously confronted not only the racist attitudes and actions of the police, but the general hostility of the city's white residents as well.[1] Because of class differences between white alley residents and street dwellers, hostility was also directed at alley whites—although with considerably less consistency and intensity.

Not all alley residents escaped the disordered and pathological lives on which the earlier studies concentrated. Husbands did sometimes desert their wives, and parents abandoned their children; wife- and child-beating took place, as did assaults, rapes, and murders. But these were the exception, rather than the rule. Furthermore, there was considerable variety among alleys, and diversity within alley life. Not every alley had a "community" during its entire existence; sometimes more than one evolved within a given alley, and in some cases any sense of community disappeared for a period of time. Because alleys had their own life cycles, neighboring and community involvement could vary from time to time. Intense conflict between residents occasionally tore the community apart. Perhaps the most likely points of controversy concerned questions of lifestyle, where very real differences existed within the alley community.

Nevertheless, most conflicts and differences were moderated and controlled by the tight network of primary relations and social organization, the common alley worldview, the need to cooperate in order to survive, and the constant danger of the world outside the alley. Washington's alley dwellers did not demonstrate the social

1. While this study has largely ignored the question of race relations, save those with the police, this depressing and sad story has been well told in a number of studies, e.g., Green, *Secret City*, and Johnson, "City on the Hill."

disintegration and pathology that had been predicted by social theorists or described by students of alley life. Rather, their families remained strong and functional, with the community providing a buffer against the hostile white world as well as offering viable lifestyles and a common focus for the residents. Children were well socialized into the alley world, despite the mainstream society's efforts to disrupt that process. Intolerable conditions do not necessarily lead to dehumanization: as Herbert Gutman has noted for the slave family, "Evidence that slaves lived in families and were enmeshed in affective enlarged kin groups is not evidence that slaves were either 'badly' or 'well' treated. It instead redefines the context which shaped slave belief and behavior."[2]

Despite intolerable conditions, then, alley residents were able to shape and control their own lives within the economic, social, and political limits imposed by the dominant white society. It is less important to determine the numbers of people who were "disorganized," or the percentage of those who were not, than to assess the extent to which culturally defined patterns of rural behavior continued to be practiced in the city and remained relevant for the urban experience. Changes clearly did take place in those behavior and thought patterns, but they resulted in adjustments and adaptations, not abandonment or rejection. Because their cultural heritage was rich and complex, migrants could choose from among several appropriate or acceptable courses of action. While this choice permitted flexibility within the cultural framework that could easily appear as no pattern at all to "outsiders," there is little question that certain patterns of appropriate (and inappropriate) behavior were largely agreed upon by the folk migrants to Washington's alleys. If these patterns did not work equally well for every person or circumstance, they did help alley dwellers mitigate, circumvent, and occasionally avoid the disasters that confronted them daily, as well as providing meaning, form, substance, and pleasure for their lives.

If the folk migrants who lived in Washington's alleys were able to structure their own world by adapting traditional ways of life, rural migrants who lived in similar conditions in other cities may also have avoided the disorder and pathology described and predicted by reformers and scholars. Chapter I suggested that alley housing was not unique to Washington, but could be found in many other cities throughout the United States and the world. The epigraphs at the beginning of each chapter also establish the similarities in origin, form, and organization between alleys in Washington and else-

2. Gutman, *Black Family in Slavery and Freedom*, p. 324.

where. A number of footnotes have drawn on Ethel Waters's alley childhood in Philadelphia to suggest similarities in alley life there and in the District of Columbia, as well as to expand on or highlight Washington alley practices. These sources are, of course, only suggestive. While much in the Washington alley experience reflects a specific time, place, and people, the general conditions that led to construction of alley housing for working-class residents were widely shared by pre- and early industrial cities.

Such housing forms resulted from the lack of an efficient transportation system that could disperse the population. Well-located land became more scarce, more costly, and more densely settled. The generally dispersed nature of many urban employment centers also meant that clusters of working-class, middle-class, and upper-class residents would be jumbled together, at least by twentieth-century standards. Alley housing, then, became one response to the problem of locating everyone close to his or her workplace. This was not just a response of the "modern" pre- and early industrial era, however; as Robert Adams reported in his study of Mesopotamian towns of the Early Dynastic Period (3000–2500 B.C.), "Along the streets lay the residences of the well-to-do citizenry, usually arranged around spacious courts and sometimes provided with latrines draining into sewage conduits below the streets. The houses of the city's poorer inhabitants were located behind or between the large multi-roomed dwellings. They were approached by tortuous, narrow alleys, were more haphazard in plan, were less well built, and very much smaller."[3]

Because alley housing existed in so many historical periods and in so many parts of the world, we must here limit our consideration to the modern period.[4] Concentration on two countries, Great Britain and the United States, also enables a more careful analysis, since substantial sources exist for each.

Inhabited alleys and courts were found in virtually every British industrial city. Engels noted in 1845 that in "every great city . . . poverty often dwells in hidden alleys close to the palaces of the rich."[5] In London alone "hundreds and thousands of alleys and courts lined with houses" were "close to the splendid houses of the

3. Robert M. Adams, "The Origins of Cities," in *Metropolis in Crisis*, ed. Jeffrey K. Hadden, Louis H. Masotti, and Calvin J. Larson (Itasca, Ill., 1967), p. 41.

4. For an example of alleys in Third World countries, see Janet Abu-Lughod, "Migrant Adjustment to City Life: The Egyptian Case," *American Journal of Sociology*, 67 (July, 1961): 22–32.

5. Friedrich Engels, *The Condition of the Working-Class in England* (Moscow, 1973), p. 66.

rich," but these alleys could only be "entered by covered passages between the houses" on the street.[6] Like observers of Washington alley life, Engels concluded that "Here live the poorest of the poor, the worst paid workers with thieves and the victims of prostitution indiscriminately huddled together, the majority Irish, or of Irish extraction, and those who have not yet sunk in the whirlpool of moral ruin which surrounds them, sinking daily deeper, losing daily more and more of their power to resist the demoralizing influence of want, filth, and evil surroundings."[7]

Engels was by no means the only British observer to report the extensive and "dangerous" alley conditions. In 1835 Jelinger Symons investigated the condition of handloom weavers in southern Scotland, and found in the "low districts of Glasgow, consisting chiefly of the alleys leading out of . . . High Street . . . a motley population, consisting in almost all the lower branches of occupation; but chiefly of a community whose sole means of subsistence consists in plunder and prostitution."[8] The alleys or courts in Birmingham also "are extremely numerous; they exist in every part of the town, and a very large portion of the poorer classes of the inhabitants reside in them." J. R. Martin reported in 1845 that "nowhere else shall we find so large a mass of inhabitants crowded into courts, alleys, as in Nottingham," and in the same year James Smith observed that "by far the most unhealthy localities of Leeds are close squares of houses, or yards, as they are called, which have been erected for the accommodation of working people. . . . The feelings of the people are blunted to all seeming decency . . . the com-

---

6. *Ibid.*, pp. 68, 67.

7. *Ibid.*, pp. 67–68. Expressing condescension not unlike that of white housing reformers toward Washington's black alley residents, Engels notes that "the Irish character, which under some circumstances, is comfortable only in the dirt, has some share in this" (*ibid.*, p. 73). His comments are even worse further on (pp. 129–33). Engels also noted alley conditions in other British cities: London (pp. 67–72), Dublin (p. 73), Edinburgh (pp. 74–75), Liverpool (pp. 75–76), Birmingham (p. 76), Glasgow (pp. 77–78), Leeds (pp. 78–80), and Manchester (pp. 81–107). Of alleys in the latter city, he notes, "Here are long, narrow lanes between which run contracted, crooked courts and passages, the entrances to which are so irregular that the explorer is caught in a blind alley at every few steps, or comes out where he least expects to, unless he knows every court and every alley exactly and separately. According to Dr. Kay, the most demoralized class of all Manchester lived in these ruinous and filthy districts, people whose occupations are thieving and prostitution; and, to all appearance, his assertion is still true at the present moment" (p. 101).

8. J. C. Symons, "My Visit to the Wynds of Glasgow," in Reports from Assistant Hand-loom Weavers' Commission (1839), reprinted in *Human Documents of the Industrial Revolution in Britain*, ed. E. Royston Pike (London, 1966), p. 316.

PHOTOGRAPH 34.
"Close, No. 46 Saltmarket," Glasgow. 1868. Photograph by Thomas Annan. Thomas Annan Collection, George Eastman House, Rochester, N.Y.

bined influence of the whole condition causing much loss of time, increasing poverty, and terminating the existence of many in premature death."[9]

In spite of the accusations of disorder and social pathology that Engels and countless other observers leveled at Irish folk migrants, at least one recent study has demonstrated considerable order. In a study of Irish migrants to London, Lynn Lees concluded, "Although the strains produced upon families by the transition from a preindustrial to an industrial society have been amply demonstrated by various historians and sociologists, it is not necessary for migrant families to disintegrate." Rather, "A variety of responses, including the reconstruction of kin groups and the retention of allegiances to clans or tribes, permit a stable integrated life to continue. . . . Such adaptations, by reproducing in the city relationships characteristic of preindustrial societies, allow migrants to escape extremes of personal anonymity and disorientation."[10]

Alley and court dwelling existed on a much greater scale in these cities than in Washington or elsewhere in the United States. Iain Taylor, who studied court and cellar dwelling in Liverpool, estimated that nearly "half of the town's working-class population for much of the nineteenth century" lived in either cellars or courts.[11] When courts were finally banned in 1864, 3,073 of them lined with 17,825 houses accommodated an estimated population of 110,000. By 1900 over 1,000 courts remained, and, as in Washington, some remained until the slum clearance programs of the 1960s.[12]

9. *Report on the State of the Public Health in Birmingham by a Committee of Physicians and Surgeons* (1843), reprinted *ibid.*, p. 320; J. R. Martin, *Report* (1845), *ibid.*, p. 324; James Smith, *Report* (1845), *ibid.*, p. 323.

10. Lynn H. Lees, "Patterns of Lower-Class Life: Irish Slum Communities in Nineteenth Century London," in *Nineteenth Century Cities*, ed. Stephan Thernstrom and Richard Sennett (New Haven, 1969), p. 374. W. G. Rimmer provides some insights on how the conditions described by Engels and others could be so "bad." Surveyors "sought to report the worst urban conditions they could find. Evidence to the contrary they did not welcome. . . . The worst bits were often used to represent the whole." While conditions were admittedly bad, perhaps worse, Rimmer questioned in what sense they were so. "The occupants were not deprived of amenities to which they had become accustomed. Nor did these amenities ordinarily become scarcer on a *per capita* basis. . . . Middle-class citizens may have been persuaded that the situation got worse in so far as *their* health was endangered, but this is not a relevant nor a reliable indicator of deterioration. Only working class inhabitants themselves could really judge" ("Working Men's Cottages in Leeds, 1770–1840," *Thoresby Society Publications*, 44 [1961]: 167–68*n*183).

11. Taylor, "Court and Cellar Dwelling," p. 69.

12. *Ibid*. For other cities see note 4 of Ch. 1, and Appendix D. Maps and photographs in these sources further substantiate the similarities between the alley experience of Washington and of English industrial cities.

<small>PHOTOGRAPH 35.</small>
"Providence Place, Stepney," London. 1909. Photograph Library, Greater London Council.

If alley housing in the United States never existed on the British scale, it was still found in virtually every kind of American city. New York, Boston, Philadelphia, Baltimore, Pittsburgh, Detroit, Chicago, St. Louis, Milwaukee, Kansas City, New Orleans, San Francisco, and Los Angeles had alley dwellings, as did a host of smaller cities from Columbus and Evansville to Atlanta and Birmingham. Moreover, while the precise forms or layouts varied somewhat, from the minor streets (as well as alleys) of Philadelphia and Baltimore to the "back streets" and alleys of New Orleans, or the back houses of Chicago and Milwaukee, all of these cities had extensive alley populations.[13]

It is difficult to determine how many alley dwellings a given city had, or what proportion of the housing they represented.[14] Emily Dinwiddie, who surveyed the *Housing Conditions in Philadelphia* in 1904, noted, "It is difficult to obtain statistics as to the exact number of these buildings throughout the city, but it is very large, and the alleys are widely distributed."[15] Edith Abbott, who studied the *Tenements of Chicago*, reported that "approximately one-fifth of all the houses visited in our canvass" of 4,965 buildings "were rear or alley houses."[16] In contrast, a 1930 study of the black population of Birmingham suggested "that two-thirds of the city's Negro families lived on alleys," while a 1954 survey of Atlanta revealed 1,181 "back-alley dwellings" still in use.[17]

13. The back houses of Chicago and Milwaukee were special cases, however; many were the original buildings on the lots. In order to pay the mortgage, working-class property owners lived there with their families, while they built and rented out one or two other houses on the front of the lot. In some cases these houses faced toward the streets; in others, "rear houses are entered . . . only through the alley." The owner who lived in the back house retained considerable status as a landowner, but a resident of the back house who was a renter was perceived to be of a lower class than other occupants of that property. See Thomas Lee Philpott, *The Slum and Ghetto* (New York, 1978), p. 25; Edith Abbott, *The Tenements of Chicago: 1908–1935* (New York, 1970), p. 191.

14. This results partly from the dominance of New York housing reformers, who seem to have imposed on reformers elsewhere the idea that tenements were the most evil and dangerous form of housing in existence. As a result, local housing reformers expended much effort on finding and publicizing the evils of local tenements.

15. Emily W. Dinwiddie, *Housing Conditions in Philadelphia* (Philadelphia, 1904), p. 4.

16. Abbott, *Tenements of Chicago*, pp. 191–92.

17. J. Stevens Stock, "Some General Principles of Sampling," in Hadley Cantril et al., *Gauging Public Opinion* (Princeton, 1944), p. 136; Charles Levi Sanders, "A Study of the Relocation of Rear and Alley Tenants in Atlanta" (M.S.W. thesis, Atlanta University, 1956), p. 2.

PHOTOGRAPH 36.
"Baxter Street Alley in Mulberry Bend," New York. 1838. Jacob Riis Collection, Museum of the City of New York.

PHOTOGRAPH 37.
"Court having nine small houses in rear of a tenement house. One hydrant supplies the court." Copied from Emily W. Dinwiddie, Housing Conditions in Philadelphia *(Philadelphia, 1904), facing p. 15.*

Not only was alley dwelling widespread throughout American cities, but we can also find examples of residents who responded positively to conditions as harsh as those in Washington. Margaret Byington, who studied the courts of Homestead for the Pittsburgh Survey of 1909, provided a description not unlike Weller's of Blagden Alley:

> From the cinder path beside a railroad that crosses the level part of Homestead, you enter an alley, bordered on one side by stables and on the other by shabby two-story frame houses. The doors of the houses are closed, but dishpans and old clothes decorating their exterior, mark them as inhabited. You turn from the alley through a narrow passageway, and find yourself in a small court, on three sides of which are smoke-grimed houses, on the fourth, low stables. The open space teems with life and movement. Children, dogs and hens make it lively under foot; overhead long lines of flapping clothes are to be dodged. A group of women stand gossiping in one corner waiting their turn at the pump,—this pump being one of the two sources of water supply for the twenty families who live here. Another woman is dumping the contents of her washtubs upon the paved ground. . . . In the center of the court, a circular wooden building with ten compartments opening into one vault, flushed only by this waste water, constitutes the toilet facilities for over a hundred people. For the sixty-three rooms in the houses about the court shelter a group of twenty families, Polish, Slavic, and Hungarian, Jewish and even Negro: and twenty-seven little children find in this crowded brick-paved space their only playground. . . . In some instances these houses are built in haphazard fashion on the lots; more often they surround a court, such as I have described. . . . Between these rows is a small court connected with the street by a narrow passageway. . . . In summer, to give some through ventilation to the stifling rooms, doors leading to the stairway between the front and rear rooms are left open. As the families are often friends and fellow countrymen, this opportunity for friendly intercourse is not unwelcome. Indeed, the cheerful gossip that enlivens wash day, like the card-playing in the court on a summer evening, suggests the friendliness of village days. . . . On pay Saturdays, the household usually clubs together to buy a case of beer and drink it at home. These ordinarily jovial gatherings are sometimes interrupted by fights,

and the police have to be called in. One officer, who said that while in general these men were a good-natured, easygoing crowd, and in all his experience he had never arrested a sober "Hunkie," when they were drunk there was trouble.[18]

Most alleys in other cities were isolated from street-front populations, as in Washington. St. Louis had "a sea of frame shacks and brick houses. . . of one and one-half to three stories poorly lighted, without plumbing, all served by yard vaults (many unsewered), and many of them crowded around the four sides of a court entered only by covered passageways from the street or alley."[19]

Like the observers of alley life in Washington and Britain, students of alley life elsewhere in America quickly concluded that residents of such housing were disorganized and pathological. W. E. B. Du Bois asserted that the inhabitants of Philadelphia alleys were "at the mercy of its worst tenants; here policy shops abound, prostitutes ply their trade, and criminals hide." Moreover, "there are many evidences of degradation, although the signs of idleness, shiftlessness, dissoluteness and crime are more conspicuous than those of poverty. The alleys . . . are haunts of noted criminals, male and female, of gamblers and prostitutes, and at the same time many poverty-striken people; decent but not energetic."[20] Pittsburgh's alley neighborhoods also sheltered "much immorality . . . speak-easies, cocaine joints and disorderly houses abound. I think I never saw such wretched conditions as in three shanties on Popular alley." As for Detroit, its alleys "were generally notorious for vice and misery."[21]

18. Margaret F. Byington, "The Mill Town Courts and Their Lodgers," *Charities and Commons*, 21 (Feb. 6, 1909): 913, 914, 919–20. This article and her longer study, *Homestead: The Households of a Mill Town* (Pittsburgh, 1974), contain the fine photographic work of Lewis W. Hine. Many of these photographs help document the similarities of alley life.

19. Roger N. Baldwin, "New Tenants and Old Shacks," *Survey*, 25 (Feb. 18, 1911): 825.

20. W. E. B. Du Bois, *The Philadelphia Negro* (New York, 1967), pp. 59–60.

21. Helen A. Tucker, "The Negroes of Pittsburgh," *Charities and Commons*, 21 (Jan. 2, 1909): 600; Katzman, *Before the Ghetto*, p. 74. Another observer of alley life, Janet E. Kemp, made surveys of housing conditions in Washington, Baltimore, and Louisville; she echoed Engels's comment on Irish court dwellers when referring to black alley residents of Baltimore: "it is impossible to observe these gregarious, light-hearted, shiftless, irresponsible alley dwellers without wondering to what extent their failings are the result of their surroundings, and to what extent the inhabitants, in turn, react for evil upon their environment. There is also abundant evidence of failings more serious than improvidence and irresponsibility" (*Housing Conditions in Baltimore* [Baltimore, 1907], p. 16).

In spite of these descriptions, most studies presented ample information to contradict their own conclusions. Extended family and kinship networks continued to be important in the Atlanta alleys, where "friends and relatives . . . lived within calling distance and could easily be reached in times of sickness and trouble."[22] And most studies found interiors clean and orderly despite overcrowding. The description of disorder in Pittsburgh alleys was followed by this note: "Only in Spruce alley and Parke row did I find disorder and a general indifference to dirt and there were some exceptions even there."[23] In her studies of Baltimore and Louisville alleys, Janet Kemp observed "a higher percentage of clean rooms and yards and toilets than [in] any other" district.[24] Moreover, much of the outdoor clutter represented both traditional patterns and survival strategies. Edith Abbott noted of Chicago alleys that there were "many instances of a few goats, and an occasional pig kept in the small and cluttered areas. . . . A great many junk dealers live in the region, and many of the shacks and yards are used for the heaps of old iron, old glass, old bottles, old papers, rags, and similar 'castoffs' of many kinds." In Milwaukee, Carl Thompson found "dogs, pigeons and goats" sharing alley land, as in the Homestead courts.[25]

"Community" developed in these alleys, as it did in Washington. Dinwiddie noted that occupants of those "little alley houses live together on much the same terms as those of a large tenement house," sharing "the use of courts and passageways." Kemp referred to alleys as "'horizontal tenements,'" because "alley dwellers are necessarily constantly in close touch with each other. When nothing but a narrow passage separates one small, crowded house from another, privacy is not easily obtainable, and the old saying that 'no man liveth unto himself' is very literally . . . true in alley as in tenement life."[26] Moreover, alley dwellers utilized the court as the focal point

22. Sanders, "Study of the Relocation," p. 32.

23. Tucker, "Negroes of Pittsburgh," p. 601.

24. Janet E. Kemp, *Report of the Tenement House Commission of Louisville* (Louisville, 1909), p. 10; Kemp, *Housing Conditions in Baltimore*, pp. 18, 75.

25. Abbott, *Tenements of Chicago*, p. 123; Carl D. Thompson, "Socialists and Slums-Milwaukee," *Survey*, 25 (Dec. 3, 1910): 370. Jacob Riis visually documents this phenomenon for a number of New York City alleys; *How the Other Half Lives* (New York, 1971), photographs on pp. 3, 39, 55, 128.

26. Dinwiddie, *Housing Conditions in Philadelphia*, p. 4; Kemp, *Report of the Tenement House Commission*, p. 12. These comparisons of alley and tenement communities are instructive. Certainly Riis was equally disturbed by the lack of privacy and the high levels of social interaction, whether in Washington alleys or in New York tenements. While here we can only suggest similarities, it does not seem un-

236 Alley Life in Washington

of their community and were actively engaged in social interaction, as the description of the Homestead court indicates. Kemp also reported high levels of neighborhood interaction in the Baltimore alleys: "From morning until midnight the beer can circulates with a regularity that is almost monotonous. It forms the attractive center of every neighborly group."[27] Finally, it is clear from a study of their relocation that Atlanta alley residents expressed considerable residential satisfaction. While "some of the tenants expressed a desire to move and said that the houses ought to be torn down," others "had strong reactions against that proposed displacement; and many were reluctant to move." Like residents of Washington's Temperance Court, some Atlanta alley dwellers "had lived in dwellings for more than forty years. . . . They had established all sorts of ties in their neighborhoods which meant a great deal to them and around which they had strong feelings. . . . While others thought of these dwellings as slums, it was home to most of them. It was the place where they had grown up, married, borne children and reared families."[28]

Religion also remained important to alley residents. Kemp reported that Baltimore's beer-drinking alley residents were "found the next day joining with all the fervor of intense religious earnestness in the hymns and prayers of the revival services of the alley church," while Jacob Riis photographed the "Feast of Saint Rocco" in Bandits' Roost, Mulberry Street, New York.[29] Atlanta's alley residents likewise "had strong attachments to their churches."[30]

While this review of the extent and nature of alley dwelling in Great Britain and the United States is far from comprehensive, it is, perhaps, suggestive in light of our more complete picture of alley life in Washington. While we could not reasonably expect life in the Irish alleys of Leeds or London to be an exact replica of black alley life in Washington, there remain striking similarities in the responses of these folk migrants to their urban milieus. What stands out most is the fact that folk migrants were able to effectively control and direct their own lives. Rather than succumbing to the new urban environment, alley folk constructed a lifestyle based on tradition while reflecting adjustment to the new experience. If this is

---

reasonable to assume that many tenements developed "communities" like the alley community, only based on either a single floor or on the entire building.

27. Kemp, *Housing Conditions in Baltimore*, p. 16.

28. Sanders, "Study of the Relocation," p. 31.

29. Kemp, *Housing Conditions in Baltimore*, p. 16; Riis, *How the Other Half Lives*, p. 42.

30. Sanders, "Study of the Relocation," p. 32.

true, at least to some extent, for the broader population considered here, several theories or interpretations must be revised.

Much of the historical literature on the development of the American ghetto, and especially the black ghetto, has concentrated on the massive ghettoes of the twentieth century. Because these settlements were so large and because so few members of the group were permitted to "escape," not to mention the fact that so few "outsiders" shared the same area of residence, the ghetto experience was one of nearly complete segregation. The ghetto arose largely because of the larger, dominant society's reaction to the "new group." This "rejection" usually led ghetto residents to develop their own institutional life. The general tendency was to turn away from the larger society, instead seeking support from within the group.

However, this description closely fits the experience of black alley dwellers, and correlates with that of other ethnic groups as well. But the nineteenth-century walking city had different constraints, as well as different traditions. A single, massive ghetto did not develop to handle the Great Migration; instead, mini-alley ghettoes effectively removed a necessary but unwanted population from sight and social interaction, while it kept them close enough to do the "dirty work" traditionally left for newcomers. The alleys were more highly segregated than virtually any large ghetto today; and if the typical alley ghetto had its white-owned store, and if most alley dwellers worked for white employers, this has remained the case in the massive twentieth-century ghetto as well. Finally, if the mini-ghettoes were too small to develop internal institutions, the development of a community that provided for itself, built on folk precedents, and set the form which larger institutions would follow should suggest that these were proto-ghettoes. The plethora of services provided by the ghetto's institutional church, social service agencies, and beneficial and insurance organizations all reflected activities that had earlier been handled by the extended family–kinship network and the alley community. The massive ghettoes and their self-support institutions did not spring forth full-blown during and after the decade 1910–20; rather, they can be traced back to the slave community through the alley experience.

Many black Americans found the alley experience to be a transitional point in the journey from the plantation to the massive ghetto. That fact is important because it provides valuable insights on the transition from a rural to a modern, urban society, and a way to test the impact of urbanization on folk migrants. This transition from rural to urban was limited in many ways. Numerous footnotes throughout this study suggest the strong continuities not only between slave and alley culture, but also between alley culture and both rural and urban black cultures of the third quarter of the twentieth century.

Certainly alley residents constructed family and kinship patterns, and organized a community and a religious and folk life based on the slave and folk experience. Nevertheless, there were real differences between the slave community or the rural folk society and the alley community. While both slave and folk experiences generally included considerable geographical stability and physical isolation, the alley community was much more mobile, with old members leaving and new residents replacing them. Moreover, despite their isolation, alley residents had considerably more contact with "outsiders" than did either slaves or rural folk. Alley dwellers were usually employed by at least one outsider, and they often had numerous employers over time. They also paid rent to an outsider and shopped at the stores of outsiders, or at white-owned alley shops. If the schools were unable to "re-socialize" alley youth into the "mainstream" worldview and values, children did have a much greater knowledge of the outside world, and were increasingly able to read and write. No one in the alley was fully isolated from the city. If the alley still dominated and controlled one's thought and behavior, if family and community came first, it was also impossible to deny the existence and significance of the world lurking just outside. Folk remedies with unobtainable ingredients were replaced by patent medicines, and younger generations grew to rely on these patent medicines, and even on medical doctors and prescription medicine.

But to overemphasize these changes would be to make the mistake of scholars who confuse their predictions with their findings. Religion continued to play an important role, both through services in the alley-house church and through revivals. Sacred and secular worlds continued to be blurred, while communal re-creation was practiced by both adults and children in spirituals and secular songs. Undoubtedly most alley residents continued to rely on family and community for help in times of trouble, sickness, and death. Kin and neighbors continued to serve many of the same functions they had in the countryside—perhaps more so, if only because of the greater need and proximity.

The city's institutional life usually had no strong connection with the alley community. The extended kinship network, alley community, and alley church oversaw the administration of most services that might otherwise have been handled by institutions.[31] We must not, however, confuse the very real similarities between the functions of primary groups and those of institutional forms—similarities which have often been ignored by those who sought instead to demonstrate sharp discontinuities. Clearly many of those who sought to "correct" the disorders and pathologies in urban life that resulted from the "decline" of primary groups modeled their programs and institutional structures to serve as a surrogate for those groups.[31] Moreover, many organizations and associations grew out of primary groups. Beneficial associations which provided sickness and death benefits are perhaps the best example of the formalization of a folk activity, and grew out of an immediate context of neighborhood and church. Similarly, the institutional church, in supplying every conceivable service to its members, merely replicated many of the "services" provided by the primary group (i.e., extended kinship network, alley community, and alley church). Finally, while the Howard Theater was an important institution in Washington's black community and represented the formalization of entertainment, most alley dwellers continued to entertain each other with communal music in alley speakeasies and kitchens. As Ethel Waters recalled, paid musicians were available for "rent parties," but older entertainment forms persisted in her Philadelphia alley.

Although urbanization has clearly affected folk migrants, the change is more of degree than of kind. What is most impressive is not the extent of change, but the continuity, the persistence of traditional functions, forms, and outlooks. If alley residents were no longer rural folk by the 1940s, they also were not the disorganized, pathological migrants predicted by some of the sociological literature, or the highly urbanized city dwellers projected by others.[32] What seems to have evolved over the years is neither pathology nor the "detached, cosmopolitan" urbanite, nor an unreconstructed folk, but a combination of folk and urban elements. While primary groups remained strong and central, secondary institutions became more important. Sophistication and calculation were combined with more traditional values and outlooks. Although the evidence is far from conclusive, it seems as if urban values have been fused onto folk values, leaving the individual to decide what is appropriate in any circumstance. Nor should we presume that folk and urban values were necessarily in conflict: as a number of studies have pointed out, the secondary institutions of the city did not preclude, and

31. Moreover, Floyd Dotson has pointed out that non-involvement in traditional voluntary associations, as is true of alley dwellers who rely on less formal primary groups, does not necessarily imply social disorganization. "Patterns of Voluntary Association among Urban Working-Class Families," *American Sociological Review*, 16 (1951): 687–93.

32. Borchert, "Social Scientists and the City."

often permitted, the development of primary groups. Those institutions, often outgrowths of more primary associations, became the occasion for such reformulation of primary, face-to-face contacts.

Perhaps my most important observation is that urbanization does not necessarily void the importance of primary groups. While the city may limit the role and impact of such forms of social organization through the myriad distractions an urban place offers, it is also possible that (as with ethnic identity) the city makes primary groups necessary.[33] In an effort to cope with the new environment, migrants rely more heavily on primary groups for support than they would in the countryside. Moreover, since each migrant comes with a cultural complex and a series of perceptual blinders or filters, he or she does not necessarily perceive all of the vast number of attractions and distractions the city offers. The urban experience does not impose itself on the migrant; rather, it provides a set of choices, the perception of which is determined by the extent to which one can recognize them, and influenced by the weighting given by culture and an individual's own experience.

Finally, to the extent that these findings on alley life in Washington and elsewhere are valid, we must reconsider and test interpretations concerning the impact of urbanization on folk migrants, as well as the whole concept of modernization. Central to these theories or interpretations has been the notion that primary groups were severely disrupted and weakened in the process of urbanization or modernization, and that a wide range of institutions, both public and semi-public, have arisen to fill the gap. Supposedly the rise of these institutions further weakened the primary groups' impact and role, eventually resulting in atrophy. The school became the major institution responsible for socialization, while mass media exerted a powerful influence over both children and adults. The end result of this well-known scenario is a homogenized mass culture made up of other-directed, one-dimensional people who live in an affluent society free from conflict—and from ideology.

For some urban migrants this process seems not to have taken place, at least to the extent that the theory predicted.[34] The theory's failure to explain behavior in such cases should make one question its applicability to others as well. If those who faced the most dehumanizing experiences of urbanization and modernization were

33. Others have come to similar conclusions. See Claude S. Fischer, *The Urban Experience* (New York, 1976).

34. E.g., Emilio Willems, "Peasantry and City: Cultural Persistence and Change in Historical Perspective, a European Case," *American Anthropologist*, 72 (June, 1970): 528–44.

able to maintain stability through their primary groups of family, kinship, neighborhood, community, and religion, and if these groups provided their members with a sense of identity and belonging different from that of the larger society, then it is entirely possible that other people also escaped the full impact of these forces, managing to create meaningful worlds that permitted both survival and a sense of identity and belonging. So the depiction of modern man having a "universal outlook" seems, at best, premature. More realistic—and, perhaps ironically, more encouraging and refreshing —is the concept of a modern society made up of many very specific worlds, each the product of a distinct and unique experience, and each with its own worldview and values. While this description is not as tidy as those provided by modernization theory, it does seem closer to reality.

| Appendices |

History is a magical mirror. Who peers into it sees his own image in the shape of events and developments. It is never stilled. It is ever in the movement, like the generation observing it. Its totality cannot be embraced: History bares itself only in facets, which fluctuate with the vantage point of the observer.—Siegfried Giedion,
MECHANIZATION TAKES COMMAND

Historical studies of working-class peoples who left few or no written records are difficult to conduct, at best. The researcher must search through partial and fragmented records, many (if not most) of which are tangential to the lives of the people being studied. Information on one aspect of life at one time often differs quite dramatically from data for another period, making continuity and coherence all the more problematic. Nor do the available records convey the focus or the meaning of their subjects' lives. Furthermore, the people who observed and recorded the information that does exist often, if not always, came from a class, race, and culture different from that of their subjects. Finally, if one needs any further obstacles, those observers and recorders of data nearly always had a "special" relationship to the people they studied vis-à-vis the larger society and culture.[1] This relationship, as well as the substantial cultural differences, colored the recorders' perceptions.

1. A number of methods permit a partial circumvention of these obstacles by going to the "source." Oral history is an important and valuable technique for breaking through to the experiences of working-class people. Initially I planned an oral history–folklore collection as a central part of my research; in the effort to determine the right questions to ask, that project got sidetracked by stacks of computer printouts and photographs. There are, however, some very real limitations involved with the application of such techniques. For a diminished and widely dispersed population such as alley dwellers, the obvious problems include selecting a representative sample for the wide range of experiences and the long time period. Moreover, the usual problems of memory and conventional response lessen the reliability of such studies. Finally, oral histories often tend to focus on the individual, rather than on the family or community—a condition that has only occasionally been successfully avoided, as in William Montell's *Saga of Coe Ridge* (New York, 1972).

A second approach was to involve a participant-observer study which was to be conducted while I lived in an "unreconstructed" alley dwelling during my Smithso-

In addition to these substantial questions about the nature, quality, reliability, and coverage of the sources, a number of methodological issues concern the way in which the various analyses of different sources were compiled, as well as the specific nature and form of the analysis itself. Appendix A is largely concerned with these issues. A descriptive narrative explains the chronology of the sources, their interrelationships, and their collective coverage of the time period under consideration. Historians have seldom used sources like those that constitute the core of this analysis of alley life; nor have historians used them as they have been used here. As a result, some very real methodological issues need substantial explanations. On one level, the analysis here is meant to give the reader a sense of the field experience. Since many major sources on alley life were social surveys and participant-observer studies, works that are often as impressionistic as they are "scientific," it is important to provide a sense of that experience, even if only at second hand. Since there are too many studies to do this individually, and because the studies are used here as sources, with little effort to fit the observations back into precise contexts from which they came, it is more reasonable and useful to attempt a "collective field study experience." Students of alley life had much in common, so such an attempt does not greatly distort those experiences. My approach traces these students through a series of historical steps, beginning with their general background and the factors that shaped their first impressions of alley life, leading to their initial involvement with alley dwellers. It also considers the studies themselves, their motivations and purposes, the nature and extent of the authors' contacts with alley dwellers, the findings, and the proposed "solutions."

On a second level, I make a serious effort to assess the validity and reliability of these studies. Part of my analysis involves a fairly straightforward test of the representativeness of the observers' samples of alley population to determine to what extent and in what ways are these studies biased by their samples. The second part of my analysis, interwoven with the narrative field experience discussion, uses the narrative as an analytical tool to assess the students' possible biases. The group may have possessed or developed attitudes and motivations that led them to bias their studies; this is, of

---

nian Fellowship year. Unfortunately, I was unable to find a vacant alley house or a landlord who would rent to me.

A third possible way to avoid the problem of biased sources is through historical archaeology, an approach that was not practical for this study.

course, an important consideration in its own right. However, given the rather sharp difference in findings between their studies and my analysis, it is critical to explain how this situation could have come about. Finally, the discussion considers the methods used here to control for bias of the sources, as well as the methods used to structure a study based on diverse and discontinuous sources.

Appendix B (the complete photoanalysis) discusses the nature and reliability of the photographs, as well as analyzing their content. Since historians have seldom applied a systematic behavioral analysis to historical photographs, I have attempted to explain both my assumptions and my procedures.

Appendix C provides supplemental data from the 1880 manuscript census and attempts to assess the reliability of the census as a source. Finally, Appendix D presents a compilation of sources on alley dwellings in other cities, especially in the United States and Great Britain.

| Appendix A |

Sources and Methodology

In the study of social disorganization; therefore, as in the study of human social life generally, while it is desirable to concentrate on overt action—of which, of course language itself is one form—it is not so irrelevant as some have thought to take account of what people say. For despite the deflections, distortion, and concealment of their verbal utterances, men do betray, even if they do not always accurately and completely reveal in them, their motive and their values, and if we do not have an understanding of these motives and values, we do not know men as social beings.—Louis Wirth, "Ideological Aspects of Social Disorganization"

This book's major sources on alley life and culture are extremely diverse.[1] The only ones that cover the entire period and are relatively useful are the newspapers; however, newspaper reports of alley life were never consistent. Coverage was sketchy, at best, in both the black and white press, and when there was substantial coverage, it usually came in response to, and was based on the work of, reformers and public officials who provided much more complete and systematic information about alley life. Thus the following observations about the other alley literature hold true, in varying degrees, for newspapers as well. Newspapers were important sources for photographs, although most of those for which negatives or prints are available appeared during or after the 1940s.[2]

Sources for information on nineteenth-century alley life are quite limited, save in the last decade, when this situation improves some-

1. Not included in this discussion are such sources as building and repair records, fire insurance maps, and records that provide information on alley house ownership.

2. While this is true for the Washington *Star* photo files, it is not the case for the Washington Daily *News* files in the Washingtoniana Collection of the Martin Luther King Memorial Library.

what. The major sources are city directories, the manuscript census (of which only the one for 1880 is useful), and census enumerations carried out by local agencies such as the police department.[3] Except for the census, information in these sources is very limited: name, address, occupation, and race (to 1880) are available for those household heads who were reached by a directory agent. One can eke out of these sources, however, some useful information beyond that which is presented; careful analysis can reveal some insights into residential and occupational mobility. But the census contains considerably more information, further analysis of which can shed light on such factors as family form and date of urban migration.

Starting with 1893—the year which also marks the origins of the housing reform movement—records on alley life begin to improve in both quantity and quality. The case records of the Board of Children's Guardians cover the years from 1893 to 1913. The first social survey (of 50 families in 13 alleys) was conducted in 1896, and until 1914 a veritable outpouring of studies ranged from enumerations of alley dwellers and dwellings to social surveys, statistical analyses of data, "observational" studies, and participant-observer studies. Some are methodologically and analytically sound (like those of de Graffenried and Wood); other, more impressionistic accounts are based on little data and only slightly more observation. Many of these studies were extensively illustrated with photographs, some of which were taken by the notable documentary photographer Lewis W. Hine (for Weller's *Neglected Neighbors*). Since housing reformers often used photographs and lantern slides to illustrate their lectures, other photos also exist for this period, like those of Willow Tree Alley by Roy E. Haynes, or in Hine's 1912 study of child labor in the city.

Very few studies of alley life are available for the years from 1914 to 1929, but the revival of interest in alley house reform also fostered a renewed interest in alley life. The quality of these later studies is markedly better, in terms of research design and analysis. There are fewer simple enumerations and general observation reports and many more participant-observation studies and social surveys. Moreover, the quality and depth of information is much better, although the focus is less global. With one exception, these studies concentrated on descriptions of life (or even a specific aspect

3. Earlier censuses did not include addresses; the 1890 census for most parts of Washington was destroyed by fire. The 1900 manuscript census has just been opened to researchers.

of life, such as childhood) in one, two, or four alleys. Documentary photographers working for the Farm Security Administration were sent into the alleys to depict the squalid conditions that the studies reported; in addition, the Alley Dwelling Authority (later renamed the National Capital Housing Authority) photographers, including A.D.A. Director John Ihlder, recorded the interiors and exteriors of numerous alley houses, as well as the immediate alley neighborhood.

The largest number of studies were completed in the late 1930s, although a social survey and enumeration was published in 1929, and individual studies were also completed in 1941, 1944, and 1952. A substantial gap exists between that later date and the final sources from 1970 (a city directory, and my visual survey of existing alley housing). The fact that relatively few alley dwellings were still being used by low-income residents at that time makes the limitations less critical.

While the sources vary considerably in quantity and quality, coverage is fairly good for the entire period under consideration (1850–1970). Gaps from 1914 to 1928 and 1954 to 1969 are not long enough to have resulted in neglect of any substantial changes. Similarly, while the sources for the early years are far from complete, they do provide enough data for feasible analysis. As Table 29 suggests, a sufficiently wide and continuous set of sources enables us to conclude that the entire period is relatively well covered, while the depth and quality of the information during the three periods (1880, 1893–1913, and 1929–44) establishes a scaffolding on which to build the analysis.

If the sources are temporally distributed so as to provide reasonable coverage, the question of representative spatial distribution and alley size is more problematic. The most useful studies provided substantial qualitative information about alley life; of necessity, these were limited to only a few alleys, or sometimes to only one. Moreover, most observers tended to concentrate on alleys located in the Northwest section—although, given the preponderance of alleys in this part of the city, theirs was not necessarily an unreasonable choice. Some clearly took geographic distribution into account when selecting their sample alleys; Ratigan, for example, chose one in each of the city's four sections, while Swinney selected his two in different kinds of neighborhoods. Geographical representation was not always proportional to the inhabited alleys in a given section of the city, and some kinds of areas were even overrepresented in the cumulative sample used here. Fortunately, the fairly large number of general surveys, when used in connection with the censuses and city directories, helps compensate for this imbalance.

Perhaps more important than geographical distribution of alleys is the representativeness of the sample in terms of alley population size. Many of the studies tended to concentrate on the largest alleys. Weller's Blagden Alley had more than 300 residents, while Malla-lieu's Snow's Court had over 200. Wood's four alleys averaged 135; Swinney's two, almost 200 each; Ratigan's four, nearly 110 each; Pablo's Temperance Court, 134. Only the three studies of Center Court dealt in any depth with a smaller alley (9 families), although Ratigan also sought to provide a numerical balance. While the general surveys, directories, and the censuses help offset this bias, larger alleys and those in the Northwest clearly remain overrepresented. (See Table 30.)

The most critical bias has to do with the kinds of alleys selected, rather than merely with size or location—although these are interrelated issues, since larger alleys were often considered to be the most dangerous and disordered. Newspaper accounts and some of the more popular studies tended to concentrate on those alleys which were thought to be the most "deviant" or dangerous. These also tended to be among the largest alleys Northwest and Southwest, the two sections of the city that had the greatest number of inhabited alleys. Certainly some photographers sought to document the worst conditions they could find, although physical deterioration and social pathology were not always as closely related as the observers thought. But a number of studies, including the bulk of the most important ones used here, sought to avoid this tendency. Blagden Alley was "located in one of the most wholesome, prosperous sections," and it was "not so immoral or disorderly as many others." It was, in fact, an "average alley," according to Weller.[4] Similarly, the "Center Court" of Sellew et al. reflected a relatively normal alley experience, rather than the extreme. Finally, Ratigan's carefully selected samples (and, to a lesser extent, those of Swinney) clearly reflected an effort to obtain a cross section of alley life. Although most students did note that the alleys were very diverse, the overall results of their research (with the possible exception of Ratigan's) ignore those alleys that were the most stable, "orderly," and affluent. That such alleys existed is clear from several sources. Census data verify the existence of several alleys where substantial numbers of skilled workers, proprietors, and professionals lived, while Jones mentioned in passing that "several years ago it was not

4. Weller, *Neglected Neighbors*, p. 14.

TABLE 29.
Alley Studies

Date	Source	Sample size	Spatial distribution
1858	City Directory	All heads of household	Complete
1871	City Directory	All heads of household	Complete
1880	U.S. Census	Total population	Complete
1880–95	Census–City Directories	211	6 alleys, NW
1893–1913	Board of Children's Guardians Case Records	239	Random
1896	de Graffenried	248 (50 families)	13 selected alleys
1897	Police Census	Total population	Complete
1901	Union League Directory	46 black shopkeepers and artisans	Random
1907–08[a]	Kober[b] (2)	1,058	18 selected alleys
1897/1904/1908[a]	Sternberg[b] (3)	1,058	18 selected alleys
1906/1909[a]	Weller	248 alleys, 318 population (66 families)	Random t/o 1 selected alley, NW
1907	Reynolds	—	—
1905–15[a]	Photographs	—	—
1912[a]	Jones, T. J.	—	—
1912[a]	Mallalieu	204	1 selected alley, NW
1913[a]	Wood	540	4 selected alleys, NW
1913	Sherman's Directory	All heads of household in black population	Black population t/o
1928–29	Jones, W. H.	9,000	Total, NW and SW
1932–70[a]	Photographs	—	—

Table 29—*continued*

		Methods Used		
General observation	*Social survey*	*Participant-observer*	*Analysis of records*	*Directory*
				X
				X
	X			X
			X	X
	X		X	
	X			
				X
				X
X	X			
X	X			
X	X	X	X	
X				
X	X			
X			X	
X			X	
	X		X	
				X
X	X		X	X
X	X			

Table 29—*continued*

Date	Source	Sample size	Spatial distribution
1936–38	Sellew[c]	9 families	One selected alley, NW
1938	Aubry[c]	9 families	One selected alley, NW
1938[a]	Swinney	396	2 selected alleys, NW
1940	Somerville[c]	—	2 selected alleys, NW
1944	Ratigan	539	4 selected sample alleys, 1 in each section
1952[a]	Pablo (two other briefer studies conducted in conjunction with this one as well)	134	1 selected alley, NW
1970	City Directory	All heads of household	Complete
1970[a]	Photographs	Total	Complete

[a] Study includes photographs.
[b] Kober and Sternberg report different parts of the same study.
[c] Sellew, Aubry, and Somerville conducted studies of the same alley in conjunction with the settlement house established by Sellew outside "Center Court."

considered dishonorable to live in an alley. Some of Washington's leading Negroes were born in a 'court.'"[5]

Writers on alley life, then, tended to select larger alleys that ranged from "disorderly" (in the popular accounts), to "average" (in the more scholarly works). The culture and behavior in the smaller, more stable and economically secure alleys were virtually ignored. Since the selection processes for sources considered here were biased, that bias affected their findings.[6]

Beyond the questions of bias in representation lie the more

5. Jones, *Housing of Negroes*, p. 51.
6. In one sense, this tendency might be partly counterbalanced by data from censuses and city directories, to the extent that enumerators avoided "dangerous" alleys and collected data on the less threatening ones.

Table 29—*continued*

General observation	Social survey	Participant-observer	Analysis of records	Directory
		Methods Used		
		X		
		X	X	
X	X		X	
		X	X	
X	X		X	
	X		X	
				X
X	X			

thorny problems of bias in observation, organization, and presentation. While it is relatively easy to determine whether samples are numerically and geographically representative, it is quite another thing to decide, on the basis of the observations, data, and conclusions in these studies, whether they have been fair in their assessments and characterizations. One must follow a tortuous path through a series of analyses that reveal the general orientations, concerns, motivations, and ideologies of students of alley life. We might begin by discussing the backgrounds of those students, and then consider in turn their connection to the housing reform movement, the extent and depth of their contacts with alley residents whom they studied, and their definitions of and solutions for the "alley problem."

TABLE 30.
Alley Size, 1897*

Population	No. alleys	Total population	%
1–49	143	3,230	17
50–99	52	3,693	20
100–149	26	3,116	17
150–199	18	3,088	16
200–249	9	2,075	11
250–299	7	1,951	10
300–349	3	980	5
350–399	1	376	2
400–449	—	—	—
450–499	1	469	2
TOTAL	260	18,978	100

Average population per alley: 73. Slightly more than half (54%) of alley residents lived in alleys with fewer than 150 residents. Clearly, most studies of alley life in the Progressive period focused on larger alleys; while later studies tended to study somewhat smaller alleys, the diminished alley population again made many of these unrepresentative.

*SOURCE: Commissioners of the District of Columbia, *Annual Report – 1897* (Washington, 1897), pp. 195–202.

Unfortunately, like their subjects, some students of alley life are nearly anonymous, although we can make some relatively accurate observations about their lives. Perhaps the most striking fact about those who produced social surveys and participant-observer studies is their apparent financial stability, as reflected in their quite impressive educational achievements. Of the eight who produced studies during the Progressive period, seven had at least one college or professional degree.[7] Indeed, the average person had two degrees—an extraordinary number, given the time period.[8] All had

7. Background information was not available for Mallalieu.

8. This included two physicians (Kober and Sternberg); two who eventually held doctorates in sociology (Thomas Jesse Jones and Wood); two B.D. degrees (Reynolds and Jones); and one degree each in social work (Wood) and law (Reynolds). Weller and de Graffenried held college degrees as well. Wood had not earned advanced degrees before her alley study, but at that point she was already the author of a number of novels and a contributor to numerous magazines and to the New York *Times*.

apparently obtained middle-class standing by acquiring academic degrees and practicing their professions.[9] All four for whom family background is available were clearly of middle-class origins.[10] Finally, almost all were born and raised in small towns, had strong Protestant backgrounds, and (save Mallalieu) were successful enough to have been included in *Who's Who in America* by at least 1920.[11]

Considerably less is known about those who wrote between 1929 and 1953, although they had even more impressive educational achievements (including many degrees earned during the Depression) than their Progressive predecessors. All seven held at least two university degrees; two had Ph.D.'s in sociology, and a third, who had completed all but his dissertation, possessed an M.A. and a B.D. Two others had M.S.W. degrees, while the remaining two had M.A.'s in social science. However, these New Deal students of alley life differed from their predecessors in several ways. Most were women, many were Catholic, and all had attended urban universities.[12] If this later group did not achieve the prominence that earlier students of alley life did later in their careers, nevertheless, Sellew was named to *American Men of Science* and Jones was included in *Who's Who in America*.

Clearly, then, all students of alley life considered here either had obtained or were in the process of obtaining middle-class and professional positions, and many had come from similar origins. Moreover, all had spent considerable years in institutions of higher edu-

9. Kober was a professor of medicine at Georgetown University; Sternberg, surgeon-general of the army; de Graffenried, an author and a government statistician; Weller, the secretary of Associated Charities; Reynolds, a lawyer; Jones, a government statistician; and Wood, an author.

10. Kober's father owned a spinning mill in Germany; Weller's was a prominent physician; Sternberg's father and grandfather had each been head of a Lutheran seminary; and Wood's father was a naval commander.

11. This description exactly fits those that have been developed for prominent sociologists of the time, especially the particular school concerned with "social pathology." Students of alley life and these scholars also shared the view that urbanization caused the destruction of the primary groups of folk migrants, leading to social disorder and pathology. See Roscoe C. and Gisela J. Hinkle, *The Development of Modern Sociology* (New York, 1954), p. 3; Robert E. L. Faris, *Chicago Sociology 1920–32* (Chicago, 1970); C. Wright Mills, "The Professional Ideology of Social Pathologists," in Mills, *Power, Politics, and People* (New York, 1963), pp. 527–30.

12. Five of the seven were students in sociology or social work at Catholic University, and their studies of alley life were part of their degree requirements. A number of these studies were written under the direction of the Reverend Paul Furfey. The remaining two (and the only two males in this group) were graduate students in sociology (Jones) and social administration (Swinney) at the University of Chicago.

cation, the institution most central to middle-class and professional America.[13]

Nearly all students of alley life came to their study through Washington's middle-class housing reform movement. Kober and Sternberg, two of the first to write on alley life, were, in fact, instrumental in founding the movement, while Weller also became a key leader. De Graffenried, Thomas Jesse Jones, and Mallalieu were also active, while Wood went so far as to mention in her biographical sketch for *Who's Who in America* (1920–21) that she had been "actively engaged in [the] movement to eliminate inhabited alleys in Washington." All studies by these Progressive era reformers were commissioned, either directly or indirectly, by that movement.

By the time of the New Deal the role of the scholar had become more specialized; as a result, no authors in this period were central figures in the housing reform movement.[14] Nevertheless, W. H. Jones's study was initiated directly by that movement, and those by Pablo and Swinney were carried out under its auspices. The remaining authors were also involved in housing reform and settlement house work.[15]

Their involvement in housing reform helped determine the questions asked by students of alley life, as well as the evidence they looked for. Whether consciously or unconsciously, they adopted the conventional wisdom of the reform movement, although these views varied over time. Progressive reformers demanded the elimination of alley housing not only because it was detrimental to the occupants, but also because such housing represented a danger to the entire city's health and safety. They did not seek to prove, or even test, the assumption that alley housing per se adversely affected its occupants; rather, they simply sought to collect as many

13. Burton J. Bledstein has noted, "The time has come to view the American university in a different light, as a vital part of the culture of professionalism in which it first emerged and matured in the years 1870 to 1900. The middle class cultivated and generously supported the American university and its distinctive character and structure" (*The Culture of Professionalism* [New York, 1976], p. 288).

14. Again, all but one of these studies were part of a degree requirement; even that exception may have been intended to be a dissertation, since Jones was A.B.D. at the time of his study.

15. It is no coincidence that the dates for rising and declining interest in the housing reform movement in the Progressive and New Deal periods almost exactly overlap the dates of the alley studies. For a more complete discussion of the reform movement, see Borchert, "It's a Nice Place to Visit"; Fant, "Alley Dwelling Authority"; Preston, "Desegregating and Resegregating Publc Housing"; and William R. Barnes, "A National Controversy in Miniature: The District of Columbia Struggle over Public Housing and Redevelopment: 1943–46," *Prologue*, 9 (Summer, 1977): 91–104.

data as they could to verify that alley life resulted in social disorder and pathology. The fact that much contemporary thought, and especially social science theory, tended to support their deterministic view on the destructiveness of alley life makes their studies more understandable—if no more scientific.[16]

Later researchers were aware that most of the earlier "studies have consisted either of case histories, with an emotional appeal, or general descriptive analyses of the inhabited alleys and the problems that they were presenting to the community."[17] While New Deal studies did broaden the causational factors to include the urban environment's impact on folk migrants, as well as the specific alley influences, they still set out to "analyze the type of housing in which the residents live and relate it to subsequent social problems."[18]

These reformers, then, commenced their alley studies with fairly clear ideas of what they "were going to find." Moreover, since many had already been exposed to alley life either directly (as in the case of Weller and others who had worked with alley residents as professionals or volunteers) or indirectly (through the writings and lectures of other reformers or social service workers), they had already sensed what alley life was like. Much of their earlier contact with alley dwellers had been with those who were most "deviant," so that experience biased their view and reinforced any preconceptions they might have had about alley life. It was easy to assume that all alley residents were disordered, or soon would be through moral contagion.

I do not mean to suggest that middle-class reformers and students of alley life were either ill intentioned or poor social science observers. Rather, existing social thought and structures limited their efforts. The structures through which they had to work had traditionally been responsible for preserving and maintaining the social

16. For a discussion of the background of these ideas, see Borchert, "Social Scientists and the City."

17. Swinney, "Alley Dwelling and Housing Reform," p. 5.

18. Pablo, "Housing Needs and Social Problems," p. 1. Louis Wirth has observed of related efforts that "to set up ideal-typical polar concepts such as I have done, and many others before me have done, does not prove that city and country are fundamentally and necessarily different. It does not justify mistaking the hypothetical characteristics attributed to the urban and rural modes of life for established facts, as has so often been done. Rather it suggests certain hypotheses to be tested in the light of empirical evidence which we must assiduously gather. Unfortunately this evidence has not been accumulated in such a fashion as to test critically any major hypothesis that has been proposed" (*Community Life and Social Policy*, ed. E. W. Marvick and A. J. Reiss, Jr. (Chicago, 1956), pp. 173–74.

order (i.e., education, church, social services), and, in spite of their best efforts, few were able to avoid performing the traditional functions of mainstream society.[19]

Because students of alley life were conditioned to assume disorder, they set out either to count it, as in the case of the social surveys, or to describe its extent and impact as participant-observers. While these conditions alone would lead to biased studies, analysis of the "conventional categories" of the social surveys, and the relationship of researchers with alley dwellers in both the social survey and the participant-observer studies, raises even more questions about their objectivity. Because the social surveys assumed middle-class culture and patterns of behavior, when they discovered overcrowding (a culturally defined condition) or family forms that varied from the middle-class ideal type, researchers attributed such phenomena to disorder. Those who did secondary analyses of arrest records merely tallied the numbers of arrests without considering the context, the severity of the alleged offense, or whether the accused was ever prosecuted and convicted. Working from allegedly universal patterns of social order and organization—patterns which were instead specific to middle-class culture (and ideal types, at that)—it is not surprising that observers found so much disorder.[20]

It is equally clear that few students of alley life got very close to the alley experience. Those who conducted social surveys complained that even after the alley residents "became familiar with the writer the majority of the inhabitants would not reveal the whereabouts of any of their neighbors or any general information about them. In two instances the sought-after neighbor later revealed that the person who had disclaimed knowing them was a close relative."[21] "Racial barriers" also served to restrict information-gathering by white surveyors.[22] Perhaps the most revealing case is that of Sellew, who had the most continuous and substantive relationship with alley dwellers. For more than two years she lived just outside "Center Court," but for the first seventeen months she had "rela-

19. Members of the middle class, and especially those who were involved in social service activities, did in fact have far greater contact with members of other classes and cultures than many Americans of either the upper or working classes. However, those contacts were often mediated through a culturally and socially defined role that determined the relationship and the information gained, as well as the perceptions of the viewer. Thus, although those involved in social services were concerned with providing help, they also wanted to maintain order and preserve specific cultural patterns.

20. Perhaps what is striking is that they found so much order.

21. Swinney, "Alley Dwellings and Housing Reform," p. 136.

22. *Ibid.*, p. 8.

tively little immediate and close contact" with its residents, because it was "difficult for a white woman to move into a segregated district, and friendly intercourse grows slowly." The last eleven months, however, were marked by "daily intimate contact with four families."[23] By establishing a settlement, "Il Poverello House," Sellew, as well as Aubry and Somerville, were able to become acquainted with many children of the court who came "to the house for two meals a day, as well as for religious instruction, girls' and boys' clubs, and supervised recreation."[24] Sellew's apparent close relationship to Aunt Jane was central to her study, because through Aunt Jane she had at least partial access to the alley community. Sellew placed considerable trust in her: "I would turn to her for help and protection at any time, sure that she, not only is fond of me and willing to help me but that she knows how to meet all the dangers of life in Center Court."[25] Similarly, "Gladys' protecting kindness to me is genuine."[26] In spite of this protection, and the fact that Aunt Jane not only held the power in the court, but also was effective in dealing with the world outside, Sellew felt that her "attitude toward white people is that they are a superior group."[27] Whether or not this was really the case, Sellew's knowledge of Aunt Jane's family was not intimate. She had seldom seen and knew nothing about one of Aunt Jane's grown daughters, although the woman lived in the court, and "I have only once seen open" the windows of the house—"next to Auntie Jane, and said to be the house of her mother."[28] Even more striking is Sellew's admission that, while she knew families in four of the nine houses, "I do not know who lives in the other houses in the Court."[29]

Sellew was closer to alley residents for a longer period of time than any other researcher, so this statement provides a real context in which to analyze their work. Given their preconceived notions about what they would find in alley life, their ethnocentric categories for evaluating what they found, and their tendency to select more "disorderly" alleys, it is not surprising to find that researchers' conclusions matched their expectations. Since few students of alley life got close enough to see that another form of order and set of cultural rules were operating, no other result was likely.[30]

23. Sellew, *Deviant Social Situation*, p. ix.
24. Somerville, "Study of a Group of Negro Children," p. 3.
25. Sellew, *Deviant Social Situation*, p. 64.
26. *Ibid.*, p. 63.   28. *Ibid.*, pp. 58, 118.
27. *Ibid.*, p. 59.   29. *Ibid.*, p. 118.
30. Of course, some students must have been confused by those alley dwellers whose behavior and values appeared to be middle class. The proximity of two "dif-

Virtually all studies focused on explicating the "alley problem." Just what the problem was or how it was defined varied somewhat among observers. Weller and other Progressive reformers emphasized isolation from the street: "Alleys are communities distinct from the life around them." "The basic evil is the alley's ground plan, the particular arrangement whereby a little community is walled about and shut off from the common influences of the city's general life."[31] In addition to isolation, Weller noted that "alley houses lack privacy, lack provisions for making family life distinct and sacred. Instead there is a discord, disorder and a constant seething 'mixup' of the population."[32] For those "quiet, orderly people" who resided in the alleys, "there is an aggressive, evil influence in alley life, which makes it hard even for those better people to maintain the higher standards they have known and which must drag down and corrupt the weaker spirits that come beneath its influence."[33] Thus, "the social and moral characteristics of alley life became as distinctive as the arrangement of their hidden roadways."[34] For Weller, then, as for many other Progressive reformers and scholars, the central problem involved isolation and a lack of privacy. Implicit in such an assessment, however, is the notion that alley culture was "in a state of arrested development."[35]

Other students of alley life, especially during the New Deal period, picked up on this notion of arrested development, although they did not discard the isolation interpretation. Their scenario began with a "culturally backward people" who, as "simple folk from the country," suffered severely from "culture conflict" when they moved to the city.[36] The alleys became the "nuclei of a certain retrograde kind of Negro culture" which had "low standards."[37] Because this "backward, simple" culture was not strong or complex enough to work effectively in the urban environment, alley "neighborhoods . . . experienced serious breakdowns in their customary modes of

ferent" groups, one that approximated middle-class behavior and one that did not, could easily have led them to assume that one was ordered (but threatened), and the other disorganized.

31. Weller, *Neglected Neighbors*, pp. 15–16.
32. *Ibid.*, p. 69.
33. *Ibid.*, p. 47.
34. *Ibid.*, p. 15.
35. de Graffenried, "Typical Alley Houses," p. 14.
36. Jones, *Housing of Negroes*, p. 24; Mallalieu, "Washington Alley," p. 71; and Pablo, "Housing Needs and Social Problems," p. 76.
37. Jones, *Housing of Negroes*, p. 40; Somerville, "Study of a Group of Negro Children," p. 1.

control. Their institutions have become weakened and self-centered, and lack the power to deal vigorously with community problems."[38]

It is hardly surprising that observers, having so defined the problem, concluded that alley residents were experiencing clear or incipient disorder.[39] Moreover, the pervasive influence of middle-class culture on the students of alley life strongly colored their perceptions and conclusions. As William Foote Whyte observed, based on his study of an Italian "slum" in Boston in the 1930s, "The middle-class person looks upon the slum district as a formidable mass of confusion, a social chaos. The insider finds a highly organized and integrated social system."[40]

The generally biased view of alley life was exacerbated by the researchers' concern for social order and control based on a narrow, middle-class ideal, and their fear that the different behavior found in the alleys was a threat to the "larger society." As Swinney noted, alley dwellers were isolated, "relatively free from police supervision, and unrestrained by the social standards which exist in the community at large."[41] While this concern for social order and control runs throughout their writings (as quotations here and in the text suggest), it is most apparent in the programs they advanced to "solve" the "alley problem."

Weller and other progressive reformers felt that the first step involved ending the isolation of the alleys so that more "progressive" and wholesome influences could prevail.[42] They also advocated programs that would "re-socialize" the alley dwellers; these were designed to augment or replace the primary groups that had degen-

38. Jones, *Housing of Negroes*, p. 87.

39. The one major exception is Ratigan, who, while partly accepting the idea of social disorganization, nevertheless refrained from applying it to all alley residents. She was the only one who did not "blame the victims," and who refrained from solutions of moral "regeneration." Instead, she noted that "alley dwellers cannot be helped without removing such national blights as income deficiencies, 'racial' discrimination or other inequalities" (*Sociological Survey of Disease*, p. 180). Her study is also much more "objective" in that it presents considerably more data, often in a non-judgmental way.

40. William Foote Whyte, *Street Corner Society* (Chicago, 1955), p. 286.

41. Swinney, "Alley Dwelling and Housing Reform," pp. 164–65. This is extremely close to Riis's earlier warning to Congress, quoted at the end of Ch. 1.

42. A few years later Robert Park came to similar conclusions when he noted that "certain urban neighborhoods suffer from isolation. Efforts have been made at different times to reconstruct and quicken the life of city neighborhoods and to bring them in touch with the larger interests of the community" ("The City," p. 8).

erated to such an extent that they were no longer able to provide order and social control in the alleys.[43]

One of the most important programs involved the use of "friendly visitors," usually middle-class volunteers who went to the alley dweller's home to provide inspiration, guidance, encouragement, and a model of appropriate behavior. Weller advocated this approach during his tenure as secretary of Washington's Associated Charities, and the number of such volunteers increased from 24 to 758. He also helped establish a Conference Class of Colored Volunteers to aid in this effort; at their periodic meetings they considered such topics as "Moral Standards in the Alleys," "Intermittent Husbands and Lax Family Ties," "Unthrift," "Colored Offenders and the Police Court," and "Improper Nourishment: The Root of Intemperance and Other Evils."[44]

Students of alley life also urged that a compulsory school attendance law be enacted and enforced, "especially for the children who lack proper home influences. The public school is the only general instrumentality which the city possesses for systematic upbuilding of all its future citizens. It is the only sure and universal means of impressing upon the growing youth of the city those standards of conduct which the community approves and deems essential to the public weal."[45]

Later students of alley life were no less concerned with this "reordering process." However, since "the older generation are often either unwilling or unable (they are the result of their own limited environment)" to change, alley children often became the major

43. Even a social survey could help support the cause of social control, according to Harriet M. Bartlett. She argued that "The social survey is thus seen to be both a method of investigation and a means of social control" ("The Social Survey and the Charity Organization Movement," *American Journal of Sociology*, 34 [Sept., 1928]: 331).

44. Max West, "A Civic Awakening at the National Capital," *Review of Reviews*, 31 (Mar., 1905): 316; West, "The Negro in the Cities of the North," *Charities*, 15 (Oct. 7, 1905): 4–5. Kenneth Kusmer's excellent study of charity workers in Chicago, where Weller began as a social worker, reports that charity workers "viewed poverty as a cultural problem, not an economic one. Whatever was wrong with the social system, summer outings and vegetable gardens, thrift clubs and a new infusion of 'neighborliness' would solve the problem. When the charity worker confronted a problem that challenged his system of values, he turned to social control not social reform" ("The Functions of Organized Charity in the Progressive Era: Chicago as a Case Study," *Journal of American History*, 60 [Dec., 1973]: 668).

45. Weller, *Neglected Neighbors*, pp. 34–35. When one considers the communal process of creativity and education in the alleys in relation to the individualism fostered in the schools, this emphasis on "those standards of conduct" of the community can only mean resocialization.

focus.[46] Although these later students were more aware of the positive aspects of alley life that should be preserved, and of their own limited abilities to bring about change, they still felt that "alley dwellers need a better culture"; their role, as social workers and settlement house workers, was to provide that "better culture."[47] Those who still hoped to change adult alley residents realized that the "social maladjustment of the families requires individualized treatment," of which "adequate rehousing is only part."[48] Social order and control were to be established by resocializing children in the public school, playground, and settlement house, while social workers sought to "develop personality [of adults] through adjustments consciously effected, individual by individual," adapting the maladjusted alley resident to more mainstream, middle-class values.[49] Rather than seeking structural changes that could make life easier and safer for alley dwellers, observers of alley life proposed instead that alley dwellers be individually adapted to fit the mainstream society.

This concern for social order and control is visible in other ways as well. Philanthropic housers (Kober and Sternberg) sought to provide alternatives to alley dwellings through two housing companies. Their housing plans incorporated as many features and values of the middle-class suburban home as possible, given the limited space and cost factors. The homes were constructed "on broad streets and deep yards," to facilitate surveillance. Their two-story, two-apartment row houses sought to correct the lack of privacy of alley housing by providing "each tenant a separate home, having nothing in common with any other family," with "two independent flats, one on each floor." Planners made sure that each flat had "a separate entrance and exit, separate yard, cellar, and bathroom." The backyard was even to be "divided into two parts by a high

---

46. Sellew, *Deviant Social Situation*, p. 120.

47. Paul Henly Furfey, "Cultural Factors in Delinquency," quoted in Somerville, "Study of a Group of Negro Children," p. 62.

48. Swinney, "Alley Dwelling and Housing Reform," p. 167.

49. Mary E. Richmond, *What Is Social Case Work? An Introductory Description* (New York, 1922), p. 98. William Whyte noted that settlement house workers in "Cornerville" "thought in terms of one-way adaptation. Although in relation to the background of the community, the settlement was an alien institution, nevertheless the community was expected to adapt itself to the standards of the settlement house." Rather than dealing with the social organization within the urban folk community, the settlement house sought to "stimulate social mobility, to hold out middle-class standards and middle-class rewards to lower-class people" (*Street Corner Society*, pp. 99, 104). Philpott came to similar conclusions in his study of settlement house workers in Chicago (*Slum and the Ghetto*, pp. 62–88).

board fence, so that each family has an independent yard."[50] Finally, not satisfied that their physical plan would ensure middle-class behavior, the philanthropic housers would keep agents on the premises to exemplify appropriate behavior and to check up on any backsliders.[51]

In addition to altruism, then, students of alley life were motivated by strong concerns for social control, order, and conformity to middle-class values.[52] These concerns, combined with certain preconceived notions about what alley life was like and about appropriate forms of order, resulted in overemphasis on factors of disorder and pathology.

Despite their tendency to seek and describe disorder, students of alley life were quite aware that it was not universal. They refer to the fact that "many respectable families live in the alleys," or that there were "a few wholesome" homes.[53] While living in Blagden Alley, Weller "asked himself frankly whether he had not been wrong during previous years in believing that Washington's alleys are plague spots which ought to be cleared out entirely," because there seemed to be "many worthy families in the alleys."[54] These

50. George M. Kober, "House Sanitation," in *A Reference Handbook of the Medical Sciences*, ed. Albert Buck, 2nd ed. (New York, 1902), IV, 7 , George Sternberg, "Housing of the Working Classes: A Factor in the Prevention of Tuberculosis," *Journal of Outdoor Life* (Nov., 1910), in Sternberg, *Collected Papers*, II, 8, National Library of Medicine; Kober, *History and Development of the Housing Movement*, p. 20; Sternberg, *Report of the Committee on Building of Model Houses* (Washington, 1908), p. 98. It is interesting to note the strong similarities in design, layout, and motivation among other planners and housers, e.g., Riis, *How the Other Half Lives*, p. 229; Clarence Arthur Perry, "The Neighborhood Unit," in *Neighborhood and Community Planning*, Vol. 7 of the *Regional Survey of New York and Its Environs* (New York, 1929). Finally, others have noted the role and concern of planners for the maintenance of social order and control; see Alan S. Kravitz, "Mandarinism: Planning as Handmaiden to Conservative Politics," in *Planning and Politics*, ed. Thad L. Beyle and George T. Lathrop (New York, 1970), p. 245; and Robert Goodman, *After the Planners* (New York, 1973).

51. George Sternberg, "Small Houses within the City Limits for Unskilled Wage Earners," National Housing Association Publication no. 27 (New York, 1914), p. 3. Almost every apartment had at least one room, either the living room or kitchen, that came much closer to the 16 x 16 foot imperative of Anglo-American folk houses than to the 12 x 12 foot imperative of Afro-American folk houses. Sternberg, *Report of the Committee*, pp. 74–75, 77–78, 80–81.

52. This should not be especially surprising in light of the growing body of revisionist writing on the roles of social workers, settlement house workers, housing reformers, planners, and scholars; see Borchert, "Social Scientists and the City."

53. Swinney, "Alley Dwelling and Housing Reform," p. 2; de Graffenried, "Typical Alley Houses," p. 7.

54. Weller, *Neglected Neighbors*, pp. 19, 20.

descriptions of orderly families provide information about some styles of alley life, while at the same time showing that breakdown was not universal. When we remember that the biased sample consists of larger and more disorderly alleys, it seems likely that these orderly families who came closest to mainstream lifestyles, and those alleys in which they predominated, undoubtedly constituted a more substantial proportion than is reported in these studies.

It is also clear that many families were reported to be "disordered" simply because they deviated in some way from the observers' ethnocentric view of the proper family. When descriptions of family functions and activities are compared with descriptions of black families before emancipation and urban migration, as well as with current descriptions of urban black families, it becomes evident that many families were following patterned behavior and culturally approved activities. As a result, the roles of the extended kinship network and the alley church congregation in the larger alley community were passed over. If the observers provide too little data on these social organizations, and if they failed to supply sociograms to indicate the patterns of neighboring and interaction, they still supplied enough information to suggest, with the aid of other sources, the dim outlines of the structure and an occasional example of its function.

Many readers may find this shaky ground on which to build the present study of alley life.[55] Nevertheless, there does seem to be some justification for doing so when the full nature and scope of the analysis are considered. Certainly, these studies of alley life are not our only sources of information; while the other sources are often more tenuous and tangential, they are somewhat less likely to be biased, at least in quite the same way.

It may also seem questionable to mix such widely differing sources as case records, city directories, censuses, newspaper accounts, photographs, social surveys, and participant-observation studies. It undoubtedly seems even more dubious to compare information from one source with that from a very different kind of source, and for a different time period. But such sources are, for the most part, all one has to work with, and they do work together very well. For instance, census data report on family structure, and, by

55. One might even consider agreeing with Gustav Le Bon's comment: "Works of history must be considered as works of pure imagination. They are fanciful accounts of ill-observed facts, accompanied by explanations that are the result of reflection. To write such books is the most absolute waste of time" (*The Crowd* [New York, 1960], xxvii).

carefully noting people with similar names in the same alley, one can infer extended kinship networks for 1880. Substantial evidence for the presence of such networks can also be gleaned from the case records of the Board of Children's Guardians (1893–1913), from Weller's 1906 and 1909 studies and from the more complete descriptions of "Center Court" in the 1930s and Temperance Court in 1950. Census data confirm the existence of homogeneity, while insurance maps demonstrate the extent of proximity and face-to-face contact. Photoanalysis presents visual evidence that the alley served as a community center and meeting place, while newspaper accounts and the remarks of participant-observers and reformers also describe the alley functioning as commons. Finally, residential persistence rates help substantiate the presence of neighboring and community as detailed in the participant-observation and social survey studies.

The tangential nature of the sources, and the fact that they were not generated with the intention of demonstrating what is being contended here, often makes them more valuable. While one could, of course, wish for more complete descriptions from these sources, they do provide important pieces of information that are confirmed in other very different kinds of sources. In making comparisons across time and between different sources, I generally felt that, in order to make a major conclusion or statement about some form of social organization, I must have evidence for that observation in all three time periods for which substantial sources exist. Moreover, the confirmation also entailed locating that evidence in as many different kinds of sources as possible. Of course, this procedure was used as a guide, not as a hard and fast rule, for in some cases the full contextual setting of the evidence made confirmation less critical, whereas in others the evidence was so thin that only tentative conclusions could be advanced. Finally, a number of studies of black life in other places and times were used either to "flesh out" the description or to suggest that Washington alleys might evidence the same kinds of social patterns or behaviors found elsewhere. While much of this evidence seems to be tenuous when examined on a piece-by-piece basis, the results are quite strong and substantial when it is put together. Only in comparison to more traditional historical studies do these sources appear fragmentary and limited. This may also be because these sources or methods have not traditionally been used by historians, and thus seem more suspect, rather than because they are inherently weaker.

Chronological Bibliography of Social Survey and Participant-Observation Studies of Washington Alleys

de Graffenried, Mary Clare. "Typical Alley Houses in Washington, D.C." Woman's Anthropological Society *Bulletin*, 7 (Washington, 1897).

Sternberg, George M. "Report of the Subcommittee on Permanent Relief and Sanitary Dwellings for the Poor, Central Relief Committee to the Commissioners of the District of Columbia." January 27, 1897. Extensively reprinted in Martha Sternberg, *George Miller Sternberg: A Biography* (Chicago, 1920), 251–53.

———. "Housing Conditions in the National Capital." *Charities*, 12 (July 30, 1904): 762–64.

Weller, Charles F. "Neglected Neighbors in the Alleys, Shacks and Tenements of the National Capital." *Charities*, 15 (Mar. 3, 1906): 761–94.

Kober, George M. *The History and Development of the Housing Movement in the City of Washington, D.C.* Washington, 1907, 1927.

Reynolds, James B. *Preliminary Report of the President's Homes Commission.* 1907.

Kober, George M. *Industrial and Personal Hygiene: A Report of the Committee on Social Betterment* (President's Homes Commission). Washington, 1908.

Sternberg, George M. *Report of the Commission on Building Model Houses (President's Homes Commission). Washington,* 1908.

Weller, Charles F. *Neglected Neighbors.* Philadelphia, 1909.

Jones, Thomas Jesse, comp. Monday Evening Club, *Directory of Inhabited Alleys of Washington, D.C.* Washington, 1912.

———. "The Alley Houses of Washington." *Survey*, 28 (Oct. 19, 1912): 67–69.

Mallalièu, Wilber V. "A Washington Alley." *Survey*, 28 (Oct. 19, 1912): 69–71.

Wood, Edith Elmer. "Four Washington Alleys." *Survey*, 31 (Dec. 6, 1913): 250–52.

Jones, William Henry. *The Housing of Negroes in Washington, D.C.* Washington, 1929.

Sellew, Gladys. *A Deviant Social Situation: A Court.* Washington, 1938.

Aubry, Leonise Ruth. "Ambitions of Youth in a Poor Economic

Status." M.A. thesis, Catholic University of America, 1938.

Swinney, Daniel D. "Alley Dwellings and Housing Reform in the District of Columbia." M.A. thesis, University of Chicago, 1938.

Somerville, Dora Bessie. "A Study of a Group of Negro Children Living in an Alley Culture." M.A. thesis, Catholic University of America, June, 1941.

Ratigan, Marion M. *A Sociological Survey of Disease in Four Alleys in the National Capital.* Washington, 1946.

Pablo, Leonor Enriquez. "The Housing Needs and Social Problems of Residents in a Deteriorated Area." M.S.W. thesis, Catholic University of America, June, 1953.

| Appendix B |

Photographs and the
Study of the Past

It is impossible that the immense worth and use of systematic and comprehensive photographic records of our country and our time can much longer fail to be recognized. —George Francis, "Photography as an Aid to Local History" (1888).

Documentary photography has vast and as yet unrealized potentialities for recording as well as for presenting data that should be of vital interest to social scientists and historians. . . . Documentary photography is a new means with which the historian can capture important but fugitive items in the social scene. —Roy Stryker and Paul Johnstone, "Documentary Photographs" (1940)

The use of photographs and film has begun to play a more important part in social science research and analysis. Ethnographers utilize film analysis in order to understand the behavior and culture of "primitive" peoples, while psychologists and psychiatrists employ microanalysis to such sources to determine personal and group behavior of members of more "advanced" societies. Furthermore, anthropologists have expressed an interest in preserving and researching visual sources made by earlier scholars and filmmakers.[1] As two scholars have pointed out:

Investigators in many disciplines, faced with the fact of nonrecurrence, or their inability to recreate phenomena in which

1. E.g., E. Richard Sorenson, "Toward a National Anthropological Research Film Center—A Progress Report," Program in Ethnographic Film *Newsletter*, 3 (Fall, 1971): 1–2; Sorenson, "A Research Film Program in the Study of Changing Man," *Current Anthropology*, 8 (Dec., 1967): 443–69; Emilie de Brigard, "The History of Ethnographic Film," in *Principles of Visual Anthropology*, ed. Paul Hockings (Chicago, 1975), pp. 13–43.

they are interested, are confronted with the problem of recording, preserving, and retrieving data on non-reproducible
events for future study. The astronomer studying unique
celestial events . . . and the biologist happening on anoma-
lous or passing speciation are no less concerned with the data
of such events than . . . the anthropologist investigating dis-
appearing cultures, and the historian trying to reconstruct the
past.[2]

While this basic concern can be addressed by the use of visual
records, a brief review of the ways in which historians have used
photographic sources, and the methods developed for such study,
reveals the need to turn to other disciplines. Following this historiography, a case study of alley life utilizing social science techniques of photo-interpretation is presented to demonstrate the value
of this approach for historical study, as well as to show which methods are the most effective for this kind of analysis.

It is important to define what is meant here by using photographs
as a "primary source." Such use involves the study of the content
and meaning of a visual image to locate information on a particular
subject. One must "read" and analyze the photograph much as one
reads a manuscript or document: with a concern for authenticity and
accuracy.[3] A given photograph contains information that can be
cited or "quoted," either through a written paraphrase or through
reproduction. However, since photographs, unlike quotes, carry
myriad other information, they can present unique problems.[4]

Documentary photographers were the first to see the value of
their work for historians. The work of Roger Fenton on the Cri-
mean War, or that of Mathew Brady and Alexander Gardner on the
American Civil War, reflected not only a concern for financial gain,
but also an interest in preserving "non-recurring" events. As Gardner noted in the preface to his book of Civil War photographs, "Ver-

2. E. Richard Sorenson and D. C. Gajdusek, "Investigation of Non-recurring
Phenomena," *Nature*, 200 (Oct. 12, 1963), p. 112.

3. The reading process begins by developing a general sense of what is going on in
a given photograph—what the elements are and how they are related, as well as the
mood and tenor of the image. More precise determinations of data and evidence on
such things as material culture and behavior are made later. For an excellent description of this process, see Howard Becker, "Photography and Sociology," *Studies in the
Anthropology of Visual Communication*, 1 (Fall, 1974): 6.

4. This approach contrasts sharply with most of the historical studies considered
here. Many studies merely use photographs as illustration, while others are organized
around the photographs, attempting to explain each image individually, rather than
to use visual data as evidence for other factors or events.

bal representations of such places, or scenes, may or may not have the merit of accuracy; but photographic presentments of them will be accepted by posterity with an undoubting faith."[5]

Others were quick to see the value of photographic records for the study of history. In 1888 George Francis addressed the American Antiquarian Society on the issue of "Photography as an Aid to Local History," and urged "the prompt collection in a systematic way" of photographs as "the best possible picturing of our lands, buildings, and our ways of living."[6] Not only did Francis demonstrate an awareness of both the range of uses of photographic sources and their "systematic" collection, but he also had a sophisticated knowledge of the possible "error caused by the bias or prejudice of the operator."[7] Nearly thirty years later an English publication viewed *The Camera as Historian*, going so far as to argue that photographic sources have "a value greatly outweighing" other historical records. Like Francis's work, however, this study sought mainly to provide guidelines for local historical societies wishing to carry out planned, orderly visual surveys of material culture and landscape for current and future historical work. Their interest was more in recording and preserving than in the actual use and interpretation of such documents.[8] This study and others had a strong influence on the efforts of amateur and professional photographers who sought to record the visual landscape, while at the same time a new breed of documentary photographers, often motivated less by historical concerns than by aesthetic and social ones, focused on social problems. Unfortunately, while the "New History" of the Progressive era viewed history as "every trace and vestige of everything man has done or thought," establishing the intellectual basis for the use of photographic records as primary sources, few if any historians used photos as evidence.[9] During the 1920s, however, a number of historians became interested in using illustrations to convey information. The works of Arthur Schlesinger, Sr., and Dixon Fox as editors of the "History of American Life" series, Ralph Henry Gabriel's work as editor of the *Pageant of America*, and Roy Stryker's illustrations for such studies as *American Economic Life* laid the foun-

5. Alexander Gardner, *Gardner's Photographic Sketch Book of the Civil War* (New York, 1959).

6. George E. Francis, "Photography as an Aid to Local History," *American Antiquarian Society Proceedings*, ser. 2, vol. 5 (Apr., 1888): 279, 275.

7. *Ibid.*, p. 276.

8. H. D. Gower, L. Stanley Jast, and W. W. Topley, *The Camera as Historian* (London, 1916), p. 1.

9. James Harvey Robinson, *The New History* (New York, 1965), p. 1.

dation for the movement toward use of visual records that was to come to fruition in the 1930s and 40s.[10]

The Depression brought with it a renewed interest in the use of photographs, reflecting changes in the history profession as historians turned to new subjects (the "comman man") and new approaches (the result of Robinson and other New Historians urging their colleagues to view the social sciences as allies). The result of this ferment can be seen in the 1939 American Historical Association convention, which was devoted to the "Cultural Approach to History." Besides hearing papers on demography, folklore, folk music, and linguistics, historians were presented with a clear statement of the possible value of photographs for historical study. Roy Stryker (then director of the Historical Division of the Farm Security Administration) and Paul Johnstone argued that "photography can easily reach the vast number of human beings whose lives ordinarily are unrecorded either in literary sources or in formal graphic sources." It offered, they contended, "a new means with which the historian can capture important but fugitive items in the social scene." They went beyond the *Camera as Historian* by suggesting the areas in which photographs can be utilized in historical research; these ranged from the most obvious—recording physical details of material culture—to "clues to social organization and institutional relationships," and interpretation of the "human, and particularly the inarticulate elements." Stryker and Johnstone contrasted a "Michigan Iron Miner's Home" with that of a black "Sharecropper Family" in Louisiana to suggest social organization and institutional relationships, while a photograph of an "Italian Immigrant Mother and Child at Ellis Island" in 1905 "reflected the order, the security, the sense of status, and the personal relationship which characterized the peasant culture from which this immigrant had come."[11]

While Stryker and Johnstone offered insights into the possible uses of photographs as primary documents for historical research, they did not elucidate methods for analyzing a large body of photo-

10. Arthur M. Schlesinger, Sr., and Dixon Ryan Fox, eds., *A History of American Life* (New York, 1927–48), 13 vols.; Ralph Henry Gabriel, ed., *The Pageant of America* (New Haven, 1926–29), 15 vols.; Rexford G. Tugwell, Thomas Munro, and Roy E. Stryker, *American Economic Life* (New York, 1925). See also F. Jack Hurley, *Portrait of a Decade: Roy Stryker and the Development of Documentary Photography in the Thirties* (Baton Rouge, 1972), pp. 11–16.

11. Roy Stryker and Paul Johnstone, "Documentary Photographs," in *The Cultural Approach to History*, ed. Caroline Ware (New York, 1940), pp. 326–30. The latter photograph was taken by Lewis Hine.

graphs, or suggest how such information could be readily incorporated into a study. Like Francis and a number of later scholars, they left historians to work out their own forms and methods. This may help to explain why historians have remained reluctant to use photographs as primary sources.

Of course, historians have used photographs, or drawings made from them, for illustrations. Moreover, in recent years certain subfields have employed photographs as research documents. Most commonly they are used for discovering remains of earlier societies, as in the case of the Smithsonian Institution's study and projected restoration of Maryland's first capital, St. Mary's City.[12] Historical archaeologists also use photographs to record artifacts recovered from excavation sites. Less common is the analytical use suggested by David Miller, involving "the reconstruction of a landscape as it existed or developed at some time in the past." Photographs here provide the relationships of one part of the landscape to another, thus indicating possible forms of social organization and control.[13] Nevertheless, the photographs used in these studies are taken or generated by the particular study; such research does not involve analysis of historical photographs.

A number of recent studies have sought to use photographs as primary documents directly in their analysis. In their 1969 study of *Chicago: Growth of a Metropolis*, Harold Mayer and Richard Wade claimed that they were breaking historical ground by using "photography as evidence instead of as mere illustration." Although they do include a brief essay on their sources, including a discussion of the limitations and biases, they neither apply nor develop methods for photoanalysis. Their study does, however, provide extensive visual sources that could be subjected to such an analysis.[14]

12. For other examples, see M. D. Knowles, "Air Photography and History," in *The Uses of Air Photography: Nature and Man in New Perspective*, ed. J. K. S. St. Joseph (New York, 1966), pp. 126–37; E. R. Norman and J. K. S. St. Joseph, *The Early Development of Irish Society: The Evidence of Aerial Photography* (Cambridge, 1969).

13. David Miller, review of Norman and St. Joseph's *Early Development*, in *Journal of Interdisciplinary History*, 4 (Fall, 1972): 592–95.

14. Harold Mayer and Richard Wade, *Chicago: Growth of a Metropolis* (Chicago, 1969), p. 1. Many studies, both scholarly and popular, try in varying degrees to use "the photograph as historical technique and source" (Robert F. Harney and Harold Troper, *Immigrants: A Portrait of the Urban Experience, 1890–1930* [Toronto, 1975], p. x). For a more popular account, see John Betjeman, *Victorian and Edwardian London from Old Photographs* (New York, 1969). While these studies are valuable and interesting in their own right, and often apply strict rules of historical evidence to the photographs to insure validity and accuracy, they are designed to "re-create the past" by explaining visual images of it, rather than interpreting or analyzing that past.

Pete Daniel's study of the 1927 Mississippi River flood also uses photographs extensively, although they are used largely as illustrations and are not subjected to analysis. Moreover, there is no discussion of the methods used. Daniel does, however, use a valuable technique developed by anthropologists and others to sharpen and deepen responses in interviewing.[15] This technique of interviewing with photographs elicits much more complete and precise information from respondents.[16]

Without a doubt, the most impressive and provocative uses of photographs by a recent historian are in Michael Lesy's *Wisconsin Death Trip* and *Real Life: Louisville in the Twenties.* In his efforts to reveal the psychological climate of the place and time of these subjects, Lesy has subjected his visual sources to analysis and has organized and arranged them to tell a larger story. While his methods are not without problems, Lesy's approach to photoanalysis stands out as a model for future studies.[17]

While historians have continued to use photographs as illustrations, they have not often used them as sources in any systematic and comprehensive way. This condition exists despite numerous encouragements over the years by scholars to use photographs as primary sources.[18] We must instead turn to the social sciences for possible models and methods applicable to historical records, although that applicability will, of course, be restricted because of the different nature of the sources.

Fortunately, social scientists have not been as timid as historians in developing and explicating their techniques for photo interpretation. This may be because they can make their own visual surveys,

15. For a full discussion of this technique, see John Collier, Jr., *Visual Anthropology: Photography as a Research Method* (New York, 1967), pp. 46–66; Collier, "Photography in Anthropology," *American Anthropologist*, 59 (Oct., 1957): 843–59.

16. Pete Daniel, *Deep'n As It Come: The 1927 Mississippi River Flood* (New York, 1977).

17. Michael Lesy, *Wisconsin Death Trip* (New York, 1973); Lesy, *Real Life: Louisville in the Twenties* (New York, 1976). It is unfortunate that Lesy fails to provide more discussion of his methods and technique. A number of other studies, such as those by art historians, are not considered here because they are largely concerned with different sets of questions; e.g., William Seale, *The Tasteful Interlude: American Interiors through the Camera's Eye, 1860–1917* (New York, 1975).

18. Several of the more recent ones include Arthur M. Schlesinger, Sr., "The Materials of History," in Oscar Handlin et al., *Harvard Guide to American History* (New York, 1967), pp. 64–68; Marsha Peters and Bernard Mergen, "'Doing the Rest': The Uses of Photographs in American Studies," *American Quarterly*, 29, no. 3 (1977): 280–303; Norman McCord, "Photographs as Historical Evidence," *The Local Historian*, 13 (Feb., 1978): 23–25.

and thus can control factors that the historian cannot. Yet, as Sorenson and Gajdusek have pointed out,

> Film, [and photographs] more easily than most other types
> of records, can become the source of information and obser-
> vation unforeseen by the filmer. The camera, even when
> aimed at specifically chosen material, invariably picks up, un-
> apprehended and unanticipated, incidental surrounding in-
> formation which we may neither understand nor recognize at
> the time. Review of such data can be the basis for un-
> categorized, intuitive impressions supplying the clues to fruit-
> ful avenues of inquiry.[19]

Perhaps the most useful approach to the analysis of historical
photographic records has been developed by a number of anthropologists, although some work by sociologists and psychologists
also provides important techniques and insights. The methods employed in photoanalysis are largely the result of trial and error,
drawing from a variety of techniques and approaches. Regardless of
which approach is taken, all students of photoanalysis stress that
certain key steps must be taken before the actual analysis of photographs may be made. These steps include determining where photographs can be located, collection techniques, sample size and randomness of the collection, and information on the context of the
photographs. Such steps are critical for determining the accuracy,
bias, and validity of the visual sources, and are not unlike other
"tests" of historical sources.[20]

19. Sorenson and Gajdusek, "Investigation of Non-recurring Phenomena," p.
113. Not all anthropologists interested in the use and interpretation of visual materials agree with this statement; some take strong issue on methodological and philo-
sophical grounds, e.g., Duncan Holaday's review of Hockings's *Principles of Visual
Anthropology*, in *Studies in the Anthropology of Visual Communication*, 4 (Spring, 1977):
59–62. His critique is aimed largely at the articles by Sorenson and Margaret Mead.
On another level, the exchange between Mead and Gregory Bateson, "Margaret
Mead and Gregory Bateson on the Use of the Camera in Anthropology," *Studies in the
Anthropology of Visual Communication*, 4 (Winter, 1977): 78–80, provides a sense of two
dominant approaches used by anthropologists. In many respects my approach reflects that of the Mead-Sorenson school, while Lesy's more closely approaches Gregory Bateson's.

20. These concerns for source validation are shared almost universally; e.g.,
Joanna Cohan Scherer, "You Can't Believe Your Eyes: Inaccuracies in Photographs of
North American Indians," *Studies in the Anthropology of Visual Communication*, 2 (Fall,
1975): 67–79; Becker, "Photography and Sociology"; Robert A. Weinstein and Larry
Booth, *Collection, Use, and Care of Historical Photographs* (Nashville, 1977), pp. 9–119;
Harold Troper, "Images of the 'Foreigner' in Toronto, 1900–1930: A Report," *Ur-*

Relevant photographs can be found almost anywhere. For this study, the most important ones were in archival collections. Unfortunately, few photographic archives are organized to facilitate searches by subject; most are arranged by the photographer's or collector's name, making it necessary for the researcher to examine a variety of collections that appear to be tenuously connected with the topic. (One of the very few exceptional cases is the Farm Security Administration Collection in the Library of Congress.) For this analysis of alley life, pertinent photographs were located in the Lewis Wickes Hine Collection, George Eastman House; the John Ihlder Collection, Franklin D. Roosevelt Library; the National Child Labor Committee Collection, the Farm Security Administration Collection, and the Washington, D.C., Street Survey Collection, Library of Congress; the photographic collection of the Washingtoniana Room of the Martin Luther King Library in Washington, D.C.; and the photographic collection of the Columbia Historical Society.

Other important sources included the photo files of newspapers. The Washington *Daily News* files are available at the Washingtoniana Room of the King Library; I was also able to gain access to the Washington *Star* photo files. Magazines, newspapers, books, and pamphlets also provided important photographs, including some for which original prints or negatives may no longer be available. Weller's two publications on alley life were also very useful, since most of their original photographs were no longer available. Government agencies—in this case, the Alley Dwelling Authority (or rather its successor, the N.C.H.A.)—had quite extensive and valuable photographic collections. Finally, personal collections are often very rich.[21]

Possible collection techniques range from taking notes on the content and background information for each photograph in an archive, to ordering some or all of the prints in archival sources for subsequent analysis. The first method was rather quickly ruled out for this study because of the large number of photographs and the nature of the subject; only when the complete visual record was assembled would I be able to begin to abstract and analyze these materials. The second approach was ruled out for financial reasons. Because obtaining a large number of photographs from archival

ban History Review, 2 (Oct., 1975): 1–8; Peters and Mergen, "'Doing the Rest,'" pp. 286–300.

21. I had hoped that many of Weller's original photographs, as well as those taken by other photographers for his two studies, would be available in his papers. Unfortunately, as indicated earlier, repeated efforts to gain information on these were never answered.

sources can represent considerable investment, I copied these photographs with my own camera. Fortunately, most archives will permit a researcher to make copies with a hand-held camera. (Occasionally they will even permit use of a copy stand, although lights are seldom, if ever, permitted.) Almost any 35mm single lens reflex camera with a built-in light meter, using fast film (Tri-X, for example), will suffice in archival conditions without unduly burdening the researcher.[22] Copies lack the clarity and contrast of the original, but this can become a serious problem only when the original is very poor, or when precise behavioral analysis is to be made. The major drawbacks that result from using a hand-held camera in light-available situations are occasional blurred negatives, unintentionally cropped photographs, or light spots from reflections on glossy pictures. When prints are to be made later (especially at a considerable distance from an archive), this can present a very real problem. However, since absolute clarity may not be required for study and analysis, this problem may not be so great. Occasionally a negative is so blurred that one must obtain a positive copy from the archive, but the costs and numbers are minimal, when compared to those that would be involved in so ordering every photograph.[23] For publication and illustration purposes it is better to obtain prints directly from archives, although some copy prints may even be sufficient for this purpose.

When copying the prints, one must note as much information as possible about each photograph, including archive number, complete caption, photographer, date, location, and, if at all possible, full information about how the photograph came to be taken. Often such data are partly or completely lacking, but any available information can be of crucial importance.

The size of the sample will depend on the subject, the needs of the researcher, and the number of extant photographs. Under certain conditions only a few photographs might be necessary to facilitate analysis. On the other hand, the approach I have taken, which

22. A camera that will focus down to 13 inches or less is most practical, although the researcher will have to use extension rings for smaller photographs in any case. Another advantage of this kind of camera and the use of extension rings is that one can obtain a close-up of a specific part of a photograph, or enlarge close-up views to "recover data" otherwise too small. (The cropped photograph should be accompanied by the complete photograph during analysis, in order to provide as full a context as possible; cropping, of course, is methodologically dangerous unless handled in this way.) With the development of high-quality photocopy machines, one can even use this process to make copies, although this reduces the information content of some photographs.

23. Some archives do provide small study prints for minimal cost.

is an adaptation of Sorenson's "research film," requires as complete a collection as possible.[24] Because the historian has neither the advantage of selecting his initial sample nor the opportunity to direct his own filming (unlike the anthropologist or other social scientist) he or she must compile as large a collection as possible to help circumvent the obvious limitations. Careful research into other documents may strengthen the claim that the "visual sample" is representative.

In the present study, approximately 700 copy prints and 40 archival prints were collected and processed for analysis. While this collection probably does not include every extant alley photograph, it certainly represents the greater part of them, and provides sufficient basis for analysis. There are some biases in this collection, however. Although the visual sample tends to have better coverage of the smaller alleys than do the participant-observer studies, it still tends to concentrate on larger alleys. Moreover, shadows and other indicators suggest that most of the photographs were taken during normal working hours, and probably on weekdays.[25]

The randomness of the sample is also strongly affected by the roles, interest, attitudes, and values of the photographers. As Sorenson has pointed out, "Although film emulsions record objective visual data, the use of cameras is, nevertheless, dependent on human direction. Thus, whatever is photographed in any field situation depends on the objectives, desires, and personality of the filmer. This intrudes a necessary and important subjective element into the collection of the research filmed data."[26] It is crucial to know as much as possible about the photographer's background, motivation, values, and employer, as well as to understand the general context in which the "recording" took place and to possess a general knowledge of photographic technology and history. Finally, it is very useful to know the relationship between the photographer and the subject.

Unfortunately, the frequent lack of such information means that historical analysis must be very tentative and suggestive. For example, a recent study of historical photographs of North American Indians revealed that nineteenth-century photographers "posed the

24. E. Richard Sorenson, "Research Filming and the Study of Culturally Specific Patterns of Behavior," Program in Ethnographic Film *Newsletter*, 4 (Spring, 1973): 3–4.

25. Since few photographs provide even the date on which they were taken, and often not even the month or year, this latter conclusion is purely speculative.

26. Sorenson, "A Research Film Program," pp. 446–48; Collier, *Visual Anthropology*, pp. 4–6; Becker, "Photography and Sociology," pp. 11–12.

Indians" in costumes not their own, and then retouched the negatives.[27] In spite of this fact, however, the researcher was able to determine "visual errors," as well as to elicit important information from the photographs by comparing them with other sources.

Alley photographers, about whom an entire book could be written, generally fall into three groups. One is made up of amateur photographers who were professional housing reformers. Their work illustrated their own numerous books, articles, and unpublished studies. Moreover, like the students of alley life discussed in Appendix A (of whom a number are also considered here), these photographers sought to capture both the unsanitary and the "evil" social conditions. While the quality of their work varies considerably, they tended to stress the worst conditions, further emphasizing their commitment to the reform mentality in the moral tone of their captions.[28] But the photographs often either conflict with the captions, or enable one to develop a number of alternative explanations. Some photographs were clearly posed, and only a few are at all convincing in terms of their captions.

The second group of photographers is more difficult to characterize or critique, although they were all professionals, and many were among the best documentary photographers in the country. Lewis W. Hine, Carl Mydans, Gordon Parks, Ed Rosskam, Marion Post Wolcott, and Arthur Rothstein visually reported the disorder in the alleys, but their pictures often managed to present a positive view of their human subjects. Not unlike Sellew's written description of Aunt Jane, the photographs by Hine and Parks, in particular, demonstrate considerable strength and order.[29]

Finally, a fairly large number of newspaper photographers, along

27. Scherer, "You Can't Believe Your Eyes," pp. 67–79.

28. E.g., in Weller's *Neglected Neighbors*: "Midday Group of Merry Idlers in 'Hughes' Alley"; "'Rushing the Kettle' for Beer in Phillip's Alley"; "Two *Un*trained Nurses of a Servant Girl's Baby"; "Receptive Children whose Future Citizenship is Molded by the Evil Sights and Sounds of Average Alley"; "Stunted and Misshapen by Alley Life"; "Cigarette Fiends and a Shack in 'Church Alley'"; "A Typical Alley Loafer; a Problem"; or "The Inefficient Life. Loafing, Drunk, at Midday." Similar captions can be found in Swinney's study of Fenton Place and Snow's Court— "Hidden 'Eyesores'"; "A Blind Pocket" (Photograph 24)—or from the Washington Housing Association's 1952 study of Temperance Court—"Hardly a Children's Paradise," or "This is where our children play, no swing, no slide, no grass."

29. A number of studies provide a useful background for the work of Hine and the F.S.A. photographers: Judith Mara Gutman, *Lewis W. Hine and the American Social Conscience* (New York, 1967); Hurley, *Portrait of a Decade*; William Stott, *Documentary Expression and Thirties America* (New York, 1973); Becker, "Photography and Sociology."

with an equally anonymous group of professional photographers who worked for the A.D.A. and N.C.H.A., provided a substantial number of photographs. Like the housing reformers, they tended to dramatize the poor housing conditions, albeit while displaying a slightly better visual sense.

It is very difficult to gain accurate information on photographic techniques, and even harder to discern the relationship between photographer and subject. Some of the alley family portraits are rigid and formal, while others clearly reflect a fairly good rapport between photographer and subject. If subjects' postures and expressions are valid criteria on which to judge, many alley photos appear not to have disturbed the residents. Occasionally there are obvious reactions to the photographer, as in Carl Mydans's photograph of three startled boys (003–004), or an obvious face-covering (028–008).[30] Nevertheless, since much of this information remains beyond the realm of the historian, one must be very careful about drawing inferences from a research collection.[31]

Photoanalysis

Before reporting the results of the photographic analysis, I must first state the broad objectives of my study, as well as the categories that I will consider. The examination was intended to determine the extent to which photographic analysis was a useful and valid technique for historical research. As a sample study dealing with a group of people at the bottom of society, it can only be suggestive for studies which might deal with more affluent groups, for whom other sources and many more photographs (often taken by the subjects themselves) are available. Moreover, my study is largely a macro analysis seeking broad validity, rather than an analysis of specific behavior of individual persons or various residents of a given alley. I organized the study around certain pertinent questions, some drawn from the concerns of historians, and others reflecting the interests of social scientists. In either case, the questions focus directly on alley life and culture.

30. These and subsequent numbers refer to specific photographs in the author's collection, which has been donated to the Columbia Historical Society, Washington, D.C. Photographs from the Washington *Star* and those in the Washingtoniana Collection of the King Library are not included in that collection, however.

31. Scherer, "You Can't Believe Your Eyes."

My general concerns include: (1) the extent to which historical photographs are useful in establishing context, setting, and information on material culture; (2) the value of photographs for determining the "behavioral landscape" of a place; (3) the extent to which photos reveal information on child-rearing practices; (4) their usefulness in revealing information on social life and culture in general; and (5) the extent to which visual records provide insights and suggest hypotheses that may be tested by further research.

Context, Setting, and Material Culture

Aerial Views (Folder A). One of the best sources for context and setting, for either a rural or an urban landscape, is the aerial photograph. While fire insurance maps can provide much more precise information on building size and land use, they leave out much of importance for the historian. The aerial (027–019) and oblique (027–018) views of Southwest Washington, an area of high alley concentration, demonstrate the extensive building on both streets and alleys. While the streets are lined with trees, the alleys stand out stark and clear. The alley forms vary from the more common Form A, to Form B in 027–019, or the less common Form C of King's Court (020–017, 020–018).

| Form A | Form B | Form C |

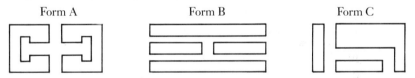

Yet all of these views show the inward orientation of the alley houses, and their physical isolation by the larger and taller wall of street houses that surrounds each block, broken only occasionally by a vacant lot or by the narrow entrance alley that cuts through the block. This apparent physical isolation is further confirmed by the photographs of alley entrances taken from the street (Folder B). The oblique view of Southwest (025–012) shows in more detail the inward-oriented, isolated nature of Dixon's Court, as well as the treeless alley landscape. Two aerial views (018–000, 021–017) and the raised view of Logan Court (Photograph 1; 003–001) more clearly demonstrate this finding, and suggest that alley dwellings were further isolated from street houses by the continuous rows of sheds that lined the backs of street properties and alley houses. Because the alley-house backyards were small and street dwellings were not particularly tall, even the alley backyards were largely out of view of the street dwellers.

From aerial photographs one can estimate the numbers of residences in alleys, although varieties of house forms and the transformation of some houses into garages and warehouses make this figure approximate. Here the variations in alley size become immediately apparent:

ALLEY	NUMBER OF HOUSES
Logan's Court	63+
Dixon's Court	43
Schottes Alley	33
King's Court	15
Wonder Court	13
Temple Court	11

(It might also be noted that social science techniques permit analysis of aerial photographs to determine the approximate number of residents and the extent of crowding.[32]) The number of houses in an alley certainly must have affected the types of social organization and control that existed. Similarly, alley locations must have had an effect on the types of residents attracted, and their places of work. Locations near the hotel district and other parts of the central business district might be more inclined to have such illegal activities as gambling, prostitution, and bootlegging, while those in Southeast and Southwest, near the Navy Yard and waterfronts, were probably linked through employment with these centers and were perhaps less inclined toward organized crime. Again, female alley dwellers near the central business and government districts were probably employed as washerwomen and charwomen for such facilities, while alley dwellers located in strictly residential areas probably served as domestics and washerwomen for middle-class residents on the neighboring streets.

Street Views (Folder B). Like the alley layouts, the alley entrances varied greatly, from a two-foot-wide entrance to Logan Court (AAA), to a walkway to O'Brien's Court (022–017), to the wider alleys of Green's Court (018–016), Bell's Court (A-9), Willow Tree Alley

32. Norman E. Green, "Aerial Photography in the Analysis of Urban Structures, Ecological and Social" (Ph.D. dissertation, University of North Carolina, 1955); Green, "Aerial Photographic Analysis of Residential Neighborhoods: An Evaluation of Data Accuracy," *Social Forces*, 35 (Dec., 1956): 142–47; Green, "Scale Analysis of Urban Structures: A Study of Birmingham, Alabama," *American Sociological Review*, 21 (Feb., 1956): 8–13.

(Photograph 16; both entrances 007–009, 007–010), K Street Alley (020–008), Snow's Court (025–004, 025–003, 025–002), Bland's Court (026–018, 026–017), Temple Court (003–031), and King's Court (021–002, 020–015). Some alley houses in O'Brien's Court, Green's Court, Willow Tree Alley, K Street Alley, Snow's Court, Bland's Court, Temple Court, and King's Court are visible from the street, but the vast majority are hidden from view. While these access alleys generally cut straight through the block, they were seldom used except by alley residents, for both social and logistical reasons. Most alleys were between six and twelve feet wide and were not readily noticeable from the street; these factors could only have furthered the isolation of alley residents.

The Alley (Folder C). Unlike the aerial views, photographs taken within the alley are somewhat disorienting. It is extremely difficult to know where one is in the alley, let alone in the city. The sensation is like that of being in a maze, further enclosed by the three-story brick street buildings. In contrast to the visual experience of the "canyon" streets in American cities, where, despite the height of buildings, one can see several miles in four directions, alley views are severely restricted and disorienting.[33] All visual contact with the rest of the city is lost, while the two-story alley houses create a sense of great concentration. The two long rows of nearly identical houses are only thirty feet apart on the main interior alley and are enclosed at both ends by similar rows of houses. Moreover, no trees or other physical barriers obstruct the open alley, creating a most unusual landscape. (Photographs 18, 20, 21, 22, 24, 25.)

These alley "vistas" offer very little from an aesthetic standpoint. The monotony of brick row houses is broken only by an occasional frame dwelling, garage, warehouse, or vacant lot. And while the alleys themselves were generally clean, corners of clutter were scattered throughout (A–7, 026–001, 025–009, 016–012, 002–006; Photograph 22). Shutters and window boxes occasionally offer the eye a brief respite, but the overall visual impression is one of a monotonous, man-made maze devoid of Nature and beauty. It might be noted, however, that these features, enclosure and monotony, have also been incorporated into some of the most recent urban designs. And, as will be suggested later, the close proximity of residents may not necessarily be a disadvantage.

A problem of definition must be raised here. It has already been

33. See Jean-Paul Sartre, "American Cities," in *The City: American Experience*, ed. Alan Trachtenberg, Peter Neill, and Peter C. Bunnell (New York, 1971), pp. 197–205.

noted that there were various alley forms; to housing reformers and police census-takers, an alley often appears to have been defined by social considerations as much as by physical form. Thus minor streets like Golden Street (018–011, Folder F) and Seaton Place (014–001) were occasionally included in alley surveys and photographs. Although these streets lacked the totally enclosed nature of the alleys, they do provide something of that experience, and as a result represent a sort of "middle ground" between street and alley.[34]

The Alley House (Folders D–H). Like the alleys themselves, alley houses came in various sizes and shapes. These buildings fall into four general categories, each reflecting a stage in the development of alley housing: (1) shacks and sheds, (2) frame row houses, (3) brick row houses, and (4) multi-purpose buildings or buildings converted to serve several functions. While forms and types overlap considerably, these four represent a generally chronological order that can be reconstructed.

Shanties and sheds were common in the earliest years of alley dwelling (1850–1900), but most were removed by the District Health Officer and Condemnation Board. Only a few pictures exist to document these structures. The construction of shanties and shacks (indicated in photographs 000–A and 028–002, Folder D) were poor. These buildings, very likely put up by residents who sought to squat on alley land, offered only the barest protection from the elements and certainly provided little room in which to maneuver. The barrels and buckets evident in both pictures suggest that water for drinking, cooking, and washing was collected in this manner. The other shanties and shacks (000–B, 000–D, 012–000, 020–004), while certainly not sturdy, represent a transition from the initial "squatter's huts" to the more substantial frame and brick structures. These were probably constructed by property owners who sought to take advantage of the freedmen who flocked to the city following the Civil War. Migrants, faced with a severe housing shortage exacerbated by economic and residential restrictions, found housing in the alleys. These dwellings did offer more protection from the elements, as well as considerably more room. All appear to have had fireplaces and chimneys to facilitate both heating and cooking indoors. Water was still available only through the rainbarrel (000–D) in some instances, although an outdoor water hydrant is visible in a 1935 photograph (020–004).

34. See Ch. 1 for a more complete analysis.

The sheds represent another response to the housing shortage for working-class migrants in the postbellum years. Sheds originally constructed for other purposes, such as fuel storage (000–F), were rented out as dwellings. While built better than the first shacks, they provided little more than basic shelter (000–C, 000–F, 000–E, 020–014). The rain barrel is again visible (000–C), indicating that these sheds lacked water, sanitary facilities, and electricity (in later years). While some were of considerable size (000–C), others (000–F, 000–E, 020–014) provided scarcely enough room to sleep in.

Frame row houses represent the first substantial type of dwelling construction in the alleys (Folder E). One of the first such buildings was constructed in Snow's Court before the Civil War, but most went up in the 1870s and 1880s. This was the entrepreneurs' first response to the housing shortage, and they realized significant profits from renting dwellings to members of the working class. While built on the ground, like the shanties and sheds, these frame row houses were substantial dwellings. Most common were the two story, two- to four-room row houses (026–010, 026–013, 023–006, 000–G); variations included one-story row houses (020–006) and a two-story, four-apartment arrangement (A–3), among others. These dwellings contained fireplaces and/or stoves for heating, had gutters, and occasionally were decorated with shutters. The facades were simple (023–011, 023–012), but in some cases the roof line was accentuated with decorative features (026–010). While they were built directly on the alley, most row houses had small steps and occasionally a tiny porch or curb that could accommodate a chair or bench above the alley's drainage line (023–006). They also contained numerous windows, permitting both light and ventilation. Although it is difficult to judge the dimensions of these houses from photographs, it is safe to say that they were tiny, no wider than the length of a 1920s automobile (026–010). (Generally alley houses were about 12 feet wide and 30 feet deep, with a small backyard 10 to 15 feet long.)

Brick two-story row house construction came to predominate during the 1880s and early 1890s. (A prohibition on alley house construction in 1892 virtually terminated dwelling construction.) Brick houses have continued to exist long into the twentieth century, as the collection of photographs indicates. These houses must have been constructed by relatively large contractors, given the extent of building and the continuity of design in some alleys. (Photograph 003–001 in Folder A gives an excellent portrayal of one such continuous row of houses.)

The brick row houses (Folder F) came in various numbers, from the sets of eight or more in Logan Court (003–001 in Folder A), Naylor's Court (013–000), and Golden Street (018–011), to five units in London Court (019–014), four in Valley Street (018–016), three in Bell's Court (A–13), and two each in Oddfellows Court (023–002) and Naylor's Court (022–008). These relatively well-built structures were usually set on the ground or slightly raised, as with other alley houses, although a few did have basements. Like the frame row houses, the brick units were small, with two to four rooms (approximately 12 by 30 feet) and with three windows in front and four in the rear.

Unlike the frame houses, however, the brick facades were considerably more decorative, if somewhat repetitious. While the bricks were laid in common bond, decorative features highlighted the doors, windows, and cornices, and often compared favorably with brick row houses on the street. (See 022–017, 022–016, 018–016, A–9, 007–009, 020–011, in Folder B.)

Although the vast majority of alley houses surviving in the twentieth century fit the two-story brick row house pattern just discussed, there were some variations. One-story brick row houses (007–015) and detached brick block houses (probably occupied by more than one family; 015–000, 004–017, A–2), multi-story alley tenements (000–H, 000–J), tight knit U-shaped courts (Photograph 24; 023–013), and three-story "minor" street houses with English basements (027–015) represent possible variations, although they constitute a small minority of the total.

Virtually any building in an alley could become a dwelling; sometimes stables were even converted into houses. In earlier years some housing was located over stables or warehouses (003–014, 017–008), while in later years the ground floor was converted into garages, with the second floor utilized for dwelling (015–003, 014–016, 018–007, 022–002, 025–010 in Folder G).

Photographs not only provide information on the facades of houses no longer part of the urban landscape, but they can also give information on types of construction, interior arrangement of rooms, and room size. Many of these photographs were taken at the time of demolition, either shortly after 1900 or in the 1930s and 40s.

The frame houses appear to have been constructed on low brick bases, with the first floor about a foot above the ground (008–005 in Folder H) or with two perpendicular rows of beams laid on the ground (026–011, 026–012). The siding was attached to upright beams at the standard interval, with the interior covered by lath and plaster (011–016). No insulation appears to have been used, and units were separated by only plaster, lath, and beams; however, this construction provided sound, well-built structures and sufficient protection from the elements, with at least a partial sound barrier between units. These units contained two rooms per floor, a central chimney, and flue and draft holes for heating and cooking stoves. The houses in Bland's Court appear to have had draft and flue holes for each of the four rooms, although only one side is visible in the photograph (026–012), while in Navy Place the two front rooms had fireplaces as well as flue holes for stoves, and the back room also had such flue holes (007–014). Whether such heating units were actually provided in every room is unknown. The relative size of the people visible in the pictures (026–011, 026–012, 007–005) suggests just how small these houses were.

More complete information is again available on the brick houses. As the trenches on the ground of what once was O'Brien's Court suggest, those houses were built on a brick base laid below the freezing line to provide structural stability (023–001). For the first floor wood beams were laid about a foot above the ground (008–005). In some Navy Place houses, basements were dug out and bricked in (017–015). In either case, the units were separated by plaster-covered brick which provided considerable privacy from neighbors and protection from the elements. Stairways were constructed against one of the side walls, starting at either the back of the house (008–002, 015–013), or the front (024–010). Almost every unit was broken into two rooms per floor, with what appears to be a small closet on the second floor. As with the frame houses, flue and draft holes for heating and/or cooking stoves appear to have been a feature of every room (007–020, 018–020).

Unlike many of the frame houses, the brick dwellings had flat tin roofs with either a single chimney per unit or (as in the case of Rupert's Court) a double set of chimneys, one running across the front, and another for heating stoves set between units in the rear (024–ooA). Again, workmen present in the photos suggest both the size of the rooms and the effect of a person in one of them (007–020).

Despite the claims of many reformers, these houses were well-built—a fact attested to by the persistence of some dwellings today. The before-and-after pictures of Snow's Court (oo–N, ooo–M, 010–016) and the restored Terrace Court (ooo–o) indicate that these Victorian structures were (and are) sound. However, photographs of alley houses suggest considerable variation in the quality of construction; and even among similar houses there were variations in maintenance. The better alley houses probably attracted

people different from those who lived in some of the shabbier structures. At an aggregate level like this, such an observation can only
be suggestive; but future study might test individual variations between alleys, based on quality of physical structure, alley form, and
socioeconomic status. There was considerable variation in lifestyles
among alley dwellers, and through an analysis of such materials a
typology might be developed (perhaps along the lines suggested by
Ulf Hannerz in *Soulside*).

Yards, Interiors, and Material Culture (Folder I). Photographs also provide information on the household arrangement, facilities, decoration, material culture, and patterns of domestic life. While alley
plans are available from fire insurance maps and exterior construction can be deduced partly from existing structures, the interiors
and backyards of alley dwellings fall almost entirely into the realm
of "non-recurrent" events.

One of the nearly universal phenomena of alley dwellings was the
outdoor water hydrant. Of two basic types of hydrants, the first,
which was probably the oldest and most common, was a large cyl-
inder with a lever at the top which was depressed to release the
water (Folder I: 000–BB, 000–AA, A–8, 006–018, 005–002, 005–
003, etc.; also Photograph 29). More recent was the thin pipe extended out of the ground with a turn valve at the top (027–013,
028–014, 027–010, 010–013). In later years drains were installed in
conjunction with the hydrants, but, in many alleys which had no
such conveniences, excess water merely spilled onto the ground in
the yard where the hydrant was located. Some alleys had only one
or two hydrants for the entire population (027–013), thus adding to
the problems of obtaining water.

The outhouse was even more of an alley institution than the
water hydrant, and was usually found near the hydrant. Outhouses
ranged from relatively modern facilities, with water flush mecha-
nisms and china bowls, to the less pretentious board seats with me-
chanical controls for opening and closing. Similarly, exterior structures varied from poorly constructed doorless houses to more
substantial forms. Photo captions indicate that a number of these
outhouses leaked into the backyards, presenting serious health hazards.

The backyard in which the hydrant and outhouse were usually
located varied considerably in size, sometimes even within a single
alley. The tiny yards of Douglas Court (017–012), St. Mary's Court
(025–014), and Navy Place (016–007) contrast sharply with the

more spacious ones in Navy Place (016–015) and Brown's Court (015–017). Generally these yards are quite cluttered; it is difficult to determine when this is organized clutter resulting from the lack of storage space in the tiny houses, and when it is the result of disorganization. Several features do stand out, however. Most notable are the large washbucket and washboard, utilized not only for the family laundry but for washing the clothes of others as well. The wheelbarrows which appear in several pictures were probably used for transporting coal or wood for the stoves, as well as for various day labor jobs.

Interiors of alley houses also contained some of the simple but decorative features that adorned the exteriors. Woodwork, both plain and fancy, lined the windows, doors, floors, and ceilings (023–008, 018–008, 019–019). Coal or wood stoves were used to heat living rooms (005–013, 028–012, 000–FFF), but almost all rooms were illuminated with oil lamps. Interior decoration ranged from wallpaper (005–013), to plaster in varying conditions of repair (028–012, 016–019, 001–032). Furnishings appear to be few and well used, with chairs covered with slipcovers (016–019, 028–012) and beds and straight chairs serving as combination living room/bedroom/kitchen furniture (021–016, 021–014, 016–016). Nevertheless, most of the living room interiors appear clean and functional.

Kitchens could be located at either the front or the rear; in cases where there was only one downstairs room, the kitchen took up a large part of it. In any case, the kitchen appears to have been the center of activity within the household, for a number of reasons. As the tiny houses did not permit the specialization of room functions common in middle-class houses today, the kitchen was not only the place for meal preparation, but often the place where food was consumed as well. A wood-burning stove, oil lamps, a small table, and an icebox were common kitchen furnishings. Occasionally there was a cold water tap (020–000B, 019–009, 024–000B, 022–019). The kitchen was also important because it was where all washing took place. Many kitchens gave evidence of this activity by the preponderance of washboards, large washtubs on or near the stove, and numerous irons that required heating on the stove (see especially 010–014, 001–024, 016–018, 001–027, 001–031).

Bedrooms were normally located upstairs, although almost any room could also fill this function. The wide variety in furnishings, depending on the tenant and the location, suggests a wide variation in alley dwellers' incomes, values, and aspirations. One house in

O'Brien's Court had a small bedroom containing an ornately decorated mirrored dresser, chair, table, wallpaper and wall decoration, besides a bed (022–018; Photograph 13), while a more simply furnished bedroom was found in an alley near Union Station (001–016). At the other extreme was an alley "bedroom" discovered by Jacob Riis, where plaster was almost entirely gone from the walls and the inhabitants slept on the floor.

It would be both interesting and rewarding to apply the analysis of household furnishings and placement set up by Jurgen Ruesch and Weldon Kees in their study of *Nonverbal Communication.* I will not attempt it here on a house-by-house basis because of the limited number of interior photographs, the lack of complete photographic coverage for at least several houses, and the absence of supporting data from other sources. Nevertheless, several overall observations can be made about alley house interiors and decoration. Generally they were simply furnished and organized on the basis of function and utility. Some current social scientists, like the housing reformers and social scientists of an earlier era, might look at these alley interiors and see disorganization in the fact that many rooms had mixed uses, with kitchens serving as dining rooms, bedrooms, and living rooms as well as work areas.[35] The reformers and social scientists who were active during the height of alley housing considered these photographs as exemplary not only of slum conditions, but also of the disorganization that resulted from living in the alley. Certainly these conditions differed from middle-class experience; but, given the limited space alley dwellers were permitted to live in, and the high rents, their adaptation appears to have been positive and realistic, rather than disorderly. (See Chapter 3.)

These houses were, in the final analysis, functional and well used, but there is little evidence of the disorganization that reformers and scholars alike sought, except in several extreme cases. Undoubtedly there was considerable variation in interiors, as in exteriors, and houses shared by two families or one family and several boarders would have more multi-use rooms and would show more

---

35. Edward T. Hall has made just such a claim: "Even the inside of the Western house is organized spatially. Not only are there special rooms for special functions, food preparation, eating, entertaining and socializing, rest, recuperation, and procreation—but for sanitation as well. If, as sometimes happens, either the artifact or the activities associated with one space are transferred to another space," this is the result of people "who fail to classify activities and artifacts according to a uniform, consistent, or predictable spatial plan" (*The Hidden Dimension* [Garden City, N.Y., 1969], p. 103). See also Collier, *Visual Anthropology*, pp. 80–81; Jurgen Ruesch and Weldon Kees, *Nonverbal Communication* (Berkeley, 1956).

wear and deterioration. Yet such circumstances were within the cultural experience of most alley residents, who came to Washington from single-room slave quarters or sharecropper cabins.

Behavioral Landscape (Folder 2)

One of this volume's major issues concerns the extent to which the urban environment adversely affected folk migrants, restricting their ability to maintain order and control. If alley dwellers were able to use and remake their environment to fit their own needs, then clearly there was no such effect, or at least not to the extent predicted by much of the literature. The more the behavioral environment supports a community's social order and organizations, the greater will be the integration and order within that community.

Photographs represent a nearly unique source for establishing the behavioral landscape. While descriptive accounts can be helpful here, visual evidence is virtually alone in its ability to record unobtrusive information on how people use and adapt their environment to their own needs (or fail to do so).

Every chapter in this study has indicated the great need for collective action if alley residents were to survive. Moreover, all forms of social organization (especially extended kinship networks, neighboring, and community) depended on high levels of face-to-face contact. In order to facilitate this contact, alley dwellers literally remade their environment. To begin with, they utilized a number of "natural advantages" offered by the alley landscape.[36] The isolation from street-front neighbors and nonresident traffic aided interaction among residents, as did the single exit alley, the extreme proximity of alley houses and their inward focus. Much that went on, whether in the alley or in alley houses, would be common knowledge unless residents made concerted efforts to maintain their privacy and personal space. Finally, the hot, humid summers of Washington encouraged residents to spend as much time as possible outside their small, crowded homes, while the tiny, cluttered backyards with often malodorous privies discouraged many from moving in that direction.

One key aspect of this transformation of the alley landscape had to do with alley dwellers' use of the alley itself. While builders of

36. Festinger, Schacter, and Back, *Social Pressures in Informal Groups*; Whyte, *The Organization Man*.

alley dwellings (and later middle-class residents of the alleys) conceived of the alley only as a path to permit movement into and out of the block's interior, residents converted the alley into a multipurpose commons and community center.[37] Alley dwellers then turned their homes inside out by projecting part of the house into the alley and opening the rest to the alley. This often involved moving household furniture out into the alley, although virtually anything could be used for sitting or lounging, from chairs and benches to stoops, stairs and boxes. (See Photographs 4, 5, 6, 14, 17, 18, 19, 20, 21, 22, 23, 24, 25, 27, 31, and 32 here; also A–4, 004–004, 020–016, 004–010, 018–014, 021–000, 016–008, 003–017, A–5 in Folder 2.) Their use, as well as the general use of the alley for neighboring, was nearly universal among alley dwellers and seemingly continuous throughout the day, except in the worst weather. (See previous photographs and 004–008, 004–006, 007–012, 004–001, 004–002, 017–011, 000–EEE, 003–036, 000–AAA, 000–FFF, 028–006, 028–007, 028–008, 014–013.) Moreover, while builders had installed small doors and windows in the facades, alley dwellers figuratively "knocked out" these "tentative" openings. It was not unusual to find heads sticking out of doors and windows into the alley, or heads pushed into first-story doors and windows from the alley. While there were occasional screens, the overall impression of the alley was one of open doors and windows, with curtains pulled back and shades raised. Neighbors apparently moved back and forth from house to alley to neighbor's house, unimpeded by either physical or social barriers. In addition, the open alley house served as a symbol of the interdependence of the residents, and made visual surveillance, social control, and maintenance of defensible space much easier.

A small number of houses stand in sharp contrast to this finding. These houses have closed doors, drawn blinds, shades or curtains, and occasionally even the shutters are closed.[38] (See especially Photograph 25.) Many of these residents, undoubtedly those who most

37. While it is easy to presume that everyone would utilize these "natural advantages" in the same way, or that the conversion of alley path into commons is a desirable or simple thing, this is simply not the case. Middle-class residents of today's alleys have turned the alley back into a path, as well as a parking place. In contrast to the earlier practices, these residents are almost never seen. Any interaction between neighbors appears to occur inside the houses, or in backyards. (See Photograph 3.) For a more complete discussion of the different uses made of alley landscapes, see James Borchert, "Alley Landscapes of Washington," *Landscape*, 23, no. 3 (1979): 3–10.

38. Ethel Waters described the same practice in Philadelphia alleys. See note 23, ch. 2.

closely approached mainstream values, perhaps sought to set themselves off from their neighbors by avoiding contact. Their imposition of barriers in the facade not only increased their privacy, but also represented a nonverbal message to neighbors about their concerns.[39] Nevertheless, the vast majority of houses reflect the open pattern described earlier.[40]

Based on this analysis, it seems reasonable to conclude that alley residents transformed the physical environment into a behavioral landscape that facilitated their social organization and ways of life.[41] The fact that the behavior evident in the photographs is consistent with and supportive of the survival strategies developed by alley residents indicates considerable order and integration in their response to the urban environment.

A note of caution should be added to this assessment. Since the historian analyzing historical photographs cannot test conclusions by interviewing residents or constructing a sociogram of alley interactions, findings on the extent of interaction must be tentative. Other sources can strengthen these conclusions, and (as in this case) visual evidence greatly strengthens the theoretical and observational information from other sources.

Childhood in the Alley (Folder 3)

Photographs also provide insight into the child-rearing process and the material culture of alley children, information notably absent from most other sources. "Portraits" suggest the type and quality of clothing, while less formal photographs indicate the nature of informal play, material culture of play, child labor, and family setting.

Alley children appear to have been reasonably well dressed, although not necessarily in fashionable clothes. On apparently warm winter days, boys had jackets and girls sweaters, while heavier coats were worn on colder days (000–AAA, 002–020, 003–032, 005–024, 005–017, 005–016, 005–010, 005–001, 005–000, 026–019). On warmer summer days, clothing was suitably light (010–

39. Residents of restored alley houses have developed this nonverbal message to considerable lengths, by installing porches with sharp railings, projecting small yards out into the alley, and using their parked cars as an added buffer, as well as by closing up every opening on the facade. See Photograph 3 and Borchert, "Alley Landscapes."

40. Sometimes shutters were kept closed to keep out the hot afternoon sun. See Photograph 20.

41. See Chapter 3 for a more complete discussion of these issues.

010, 004–005, 003–025, 003–019). While garments did not always fit—a common problem for growing children, whether their clothes are new, secondhand, or "hand-me-downs"—they do appear to be clean and well cared for (013–009).

Unlike their parents, young children appear to have spent some time in the backyard, often playing near trash or other items that were either stored or discarded there (002–026, 020–012, 010–015, 005–026, 003–004, 003–009, 003–005). Much of this play involved digging or playing with dirt or discarded objects. More common was play in the alley itself (020–003, A–12, 000–BBB, 003–003, 010–004, 003–037, 010–009). In both backyard and alley play, there appears to have been little sex segregation.

Photographs of more formal play are few in number. Nevertheless, a form of baseball (019–010, 019–011, 000–EEEE, 000–CCC), marbles (004–006, 000–DDDD), and an undetermined game involving the use of a forked stick to draw circles on the ground (028–009, and closeup) suggest that such games did exist, and, in the cases of baseball and the "circle game," involved a considerable number of children.

Toys and games appear to have been in short supply in the alleys. No children are pictured holding dolls or stuffed animals, nor are any playing "packaged" games (although these were probably available only in the later years). Pets appear in a number of photographs, but in only three are they in contact with humans (A–30, 000–FFFF, 006–011). The baseball players in 019–010 and 019–011 were equipped with a catcher's glove, bat, and ball, while in 000–EEE the "boy gang" Weller discovered had a catcher's mask (?) and baseball bats, although these might have been used for activities other than baseball, as Weller seems to think. (There is not much other visual evidence of teen or preteen gangs, although this lack does not, of course, rule out their existence.) A homemade cart and a soapbox racer appear in the earlier years (000–FFFF, A–14; Photograph 28), while later photographs (018–009, 014–012) indicate that commercially produced toys of this type became more common. Tricycles and bicycles (021–018, 027–020; Photograph 32) are also present in later years, along with equipment for basketball (017–002), archery (027–009), and roller skating (003–034). Small toys are almost nonexistent in the alley photographs; a miniature car (005–025) is the sole example. More common were makeshift toys (024–011, 004–000) or games (015–009, 015–010).

Photographs of family groups suggest family size, ages, sibling relationships, relations with parents, and occasionally eating habits.

Five photographs show various numbers of children, ranging from ten (000–GGGG) to five (000–JJJJ), four (011–014), three (012–018), and one (000–KKKK). In two (012–018, 011–014) a child is holding onto a parent or older child. In fact, except for the obviously proud mother with her baby (001–033), older siblings in these and later photographs seem to have had considerably more contact with and responsibility for their younger brothers and sisters (000–GGGG, 000–JJJJ, 001–024, 001–036). Feeding of babies, however, remained the mother's prerogative, if the sequence of three photographs (006–011, 002–005, 004–009; Photograph 27) is representative. The feeding process was overseen by a grandmother, suggesting that three generations lived under one roof. Complete family scenes are also extremely rare, undoubtedly because of the time of day when most photographers were working. Only 006–009 (Photograph 4) and several earlier photographs include the father, making intrafamily relations extremely difficult to discern. In contrast, alley scenes of children and adults interacting are far more common (000–MMMM, 024–009, and throughout other folders; Photograph 5), suggesting that the alley "community" hypothesis has further validity and import for child-rearing.

Many children may have been watched, cared for, and socialized by their older siblings, rather than by their parents. Reformers often pointed out that younger children were left in the care of older brothers and sisters (012–016, 012–012; Photograph 26) while their parents went to work. Many mothers who worked outside the home used this child care alternative, or left their children under the watchful eye of a neighbor or grandmother (if the latter did not work outside the home). Nevertheless, the number of young children who appear to be playing unattended suggests that peer group socialization must have been important, as were the overriding influences of the "enclosed alley" where friendly neighbors watched out for the children in a confined situation (000–MMMM, 024–009; Photograph 5).

Interestingly, teenagers seldom appear in photographs (000–0000). Most likely the financial needs of the family required that older children be employed. Certainly census data confirm that some were, while some must also have been at school. Black alley children worked as domestics with their mothers or elsewhere, or as laborers, or helped their mothers who did washing at home (016–014, 103–019). Considerably more is known about white alley boys from the visual record. Lewis Hine's child labor photographs of Washington portray a number of such children, many not yet in their teens and virtually all recent migrants from Italy with their parents. They were employed as newsboys (019–008, 019–006, 019–005, 019–004, 019–003, 019–002, 019–001, 019–000; Photograph 26) and vendors (019–007). Even though much of its proceeds went to support the family, such independent economic activity took children out of the alleys and involved them in peer group relationships for which earlier alley life may have prepared them. They were able to cope in the "street market" without parental guidance; at the same time, they could follow the lead of the older working children, as they had done in the alleys with their older brothers and sisters. Thus the alley could have been a training ground for the "apprenticeship" of child labor, preparing the alley child for survival in a difficult world.

Another hypothesis is that alley housing served families at a particular point in the life cycle, during early parenthood. This is as difficult to demonstrate as the preceding hypothesis, yet it may offer partial explanation for the absence of adolescents from alley photographs.

Other Aspects of Alley Life (Folder 4)

Many aspects of alley life and culture eluded the photographer's camera, although occasional glimpses suggest some of these. Alley houses shared the alley with other land uses, including stables, blacksmith shops, carpenter shops, and occasional stores. In some cases these businesses were owned and operated by residents who lived above their establishments. The grocery stores in Navy Place (016–013 in Folder 4) and Fenton Place (017–020) are two examples of a rather uncommon alley phenomenon that made shopping, and perhaps credit, somewhat easier. Other marginal enterprises included a fish market (018–002) and fish peddling (028–003).

Because coal for heating and cooking stoves had to be purchased, many alley dwellers instead used pieces of wood left at construction sites, or from crates and boxes. Piles of such materials were often found in alley areas (006–014, 006–013, 002–011, 000–ABB, 016–014).

One of the most important aspects of alley life involved religion. A few printed sources mention religious services in homes, but visual sources are almost entirely lacking. Two different approaches to religion are suggested by the tiny Baptist church (002–022) and the "traveling evangelist" (002–016, 022–008; Photograph 33).

While there are few visual sources for adult employment, a substantial number do exist on home laundries. Chapter 5 considers them in detail. (See Photographs 29–31 here, and 000–ABC, 003–023, 003–024, 012–014, 001–015, 001–018, 027–005, 001–008, 017–004, 001–000, 003–026.)

Hypotheses and Other Notes

Several tentative hypotheses can be advanced in addition to those already suggested in the analysis. The first concerns the physical-spatial dimension of the alley. Given the relatively high densities of many alleys and the proximity of the houses, it would seem that, when social order did break down or when conflict between several families broke out, it could lead to considerable disruption.

On the other hand, other sources contain little evidence to indicate that this kind of breakdown actually took place. Perhaps the social structure was able to control and limit these incidents. If so, it may be partly because of long experience in similar environments. Certainly, on a superficial level, the alley form seems similar to the West African residential landscape, where villages are encircled by timber or brush walls, with houses facing one another across a narrow common area.[42] At least some plantations also had housing that approximated that of the alleys. Many slaves lived in rows of small detached cabins, with the area between cabins serving as a commons.[43] City slaves either lived in dwellings at the back of the master's lot next to the alley and congregated in the alley, or lived apart from their owners, often in alleys. In fact, the alleys in southern cities were meeting places for slaves and freedmen—which may help account for the rapid decline of urban slavery after 1820.[44]

If we attempt to apply Edward Hall's "System for the Notation of Proxemic Behavior" to alley dwellers' interaction, only four of eight categories are ascertainable from photographs. Postural-sex

42. Philip D. Curtin, ed., *Africa Remembered: Narratives by West Africans from the Era of the Slave Trade* (Madison, 1968), pp. 52–54.

43. Blassingame, *The Slave Community*; Harvey Wish, ed., *Slavery in the South* (New York, 1964); Ralph Flanders, *Plantation Slavery in Georgia* (Chapel Hill, 1933), pp. 3–16; Flanders, "Two Plantations and a County of Antebellum Georgia," in *Plantation, Town, and County*, ed. Elinor Miller and Eugene D. Genovese (Urbana, Ill., 1974), p. 230; Frances Anne Kemble, *Journal of a Residence on a Georgian Plantation in 1838–1839* (New York, 1961), pp. 57, 198.

44. Wade, *Slavery in the Cities*.

identifiers, sociofugal-sociopetal orientation, kinesthetic factors, and touch code are visible; retinal combinations, thermal code, olfaction code, and voice loudness scale are impossible to discern. This study highlighted the tendency for sex-segregated interactions among adults during working hours. Nevertheless, much necessary information was difficult to determine from photographs, largely because interaction between alley residents was not the alley photographer's primary subject, and as a result it usually occurred far from the camera.[45]

Because so few pictures provide accurate data, a more complete study of these photographs using the first four categories of proxemic behavior notations was not carried out. Such a study should, however, be considered by historians who have numerous photographs that provide clear and precise views of human interaction. A notation system should allow the research to distinguish "in-group" members' interactions with those of another group.

Conclusions

Photographic sources have a great deal to offer the historian, especially the social historian of everyday life and groups at the bottom of complex societies. For developing and providing settings and contexts, photographs are a crucial source. They also represent virtually the only method for determining the material culture and behavior of groups who no longer live in the same circumstances.

Yet historical photographs must be used with great care, taking into account the problems of sample size and photographer bias. The historian cannot rely solely on photographs any more than he can rely solely on printed sources when dealing with subjects for which those are quite limited.

For historical study, the photograph's import is largely suggestive, rather than definitive. Photographic analysis offers a wide range of possible hypotheses and insights; some of these may be tested or confirmed in other sources, while others represent ideas that could not have come from more traditional sources. Despite the level of analysis, photographic sources can stand on equal footing with printed ones.

45. Edward T. Hall, "A System for the Notation of Proxemic Behavior," *American Anthropologist*, 65 (Oct., 1963): 1003–26; Hall, *Handbook for Proxemic Research* (Washington, 1974).

Bibliography of Photoanalysis

Akeret, Robert U. *Photoanalysis.* New York, 1973.

Avery, T. Eugene. *Interpretation of Aerial Photographs.* 2nd ed. Minneapolis, 1969.

Bascom, William R. "Anthropology and the Camera." In *The Complete Photographer*, I, ed. Willard D. Morgan. New York, 1942.

Bateson, Gregory and Mead, Margaret. *Balinese Character: A Photographic Analysis.* New York, 1947.

Becker, Howard S. "Photography and Sociology." *Studies in the Anthropology of Visual Communication*, 1 (Fall, 1974): 3–26.

Birdwhistell, Ray. *Introduction to Kinesics.* Louisville, 1952.

———. "Kinesics and Communication." *Exploration*, 3 (1954): 31–41.

———. *Kinesics and Context.* Philadelphia, 1970.

de Brigard, Emilie. *Anthropological Cinema.* New York, 1978.

Beyers, Paul. "Cameras Don't Take Pictures." Columbia University *Forum*, 9, no. 1 (1966): 27–31.

———. "Still Photographs in the Systematic Recording and Analysis of Behavioral Data." *Human Organization*, 23 (Spring, 1964): 78–84.

Collier, John, Jr. *Visual Anthropology.* New York, 1967.

———. "Documentary Image." In *Encyclopedia of Photography*, ed. Willard Morgan. New York, 1974. VII, 1170–77.

———. "Photography in Anthropology" *American Anthropologist*, 59 (Oct., 1957): 843–59.

Francis, George E. "Photography as an Aid to Local History." *American Antiquarian Society Proceedings*, ser. 2, vol. 5 (Apr., 1888): 274–82.

Frankenberg, Celestine G., ed. *Picture Sources.* New York, 1964.

Gernsheim, Helmut and Alison. *A Concise History of Photography.* New York, 1965.

———. *The History of Photography.* Englewood Cliffs, N.J., 1970.

Gesell, Arnold. *An Atlas of Infant Behavior.* 2 vols. New Haven, Conn., 1934.

Gower, H. D.; Jast, L. Stanley; and Topley, W. W. *The Camera as Historian.* London, 1916.

Green, Norman E. "Aerial Photography in the Analysis of Urban Structures, Ecological and Social." Ph.D. dissertation, University of North Carolina, 1955.

———. "Aerial Photographic Analysis of Residential Neighborhoods: An Evaluation of Data Accuracy." *Social Forces*, 35 (Dec., 1956): 142–47.

———. "Scale Analysis of Urban Structures: A Study of Birmingham, Alabama." *American Sociological Review*, 21 (Feb., 1956): 8–13.

Gutman, Judith Mara. *Lewis W. Hine and the American Social Conscience*. New York, 1967.

Hall, Edward T. *Handbook for Proxemic Research*. Washington, 1974.

———. *The Hidden Dimension*. Garden City, N.Y., 1966.

———. "Proxemics: The Study of Man's Spatial Relations." In *Man's Image in Medicine and Anthropology*, ed. I. Gladstone. New York, 1963. Pp. 422–45.

———. "A System for the Notation of Proxemic Behavior." *American Anthropologist*, 65 (Oct., 1963): 1003–26.

Harney, Robert F., and Troper, Harold. *Immigrant: A Portrait of the Urban Experience, 1890–1930*. Toronto, 1975.

de Heusch, Luc. "The Cinema and Social Science: A Survey of Ethnographic and Sociological Films." *Reports and Papers in the Social Sciences*, 16 (Paris, 1962).

Hockings, Paul, ed. *Principles of Visual Anthropology*. Chicago, 1975.

Honigmann, John. *Culture and Personality*. New York, 1954.

Hurley, Jack F. *Portrait of a Decade: Roy Stryker and the Development of Documentary Photography in the Thirties*. Baton Rouge, 1972.

Ittelson, William H.; Proshansky, Harold M.; and Rivlin, Leanne. *Environmental Psychology*. New York, 1970.

Ivins, William M., Jr. *Prints and Visual Communication*. Cambridge, Mass., 1953.

Kates, Robert W., and Wohlwill, Joachim F., eds. "Men's Response to the Physical Environment." *Journal of Social Issues*, 22, no. 4 (1966).

Katz, Leo. "Photographic Analysis." In *Encyclopedia of Photography*, ed. Willard Morgan. XIV, 2668–79.

Knowles, M. D. "Air Photography and History." In *The Uses of Air Photography: Nature and Man in New Perspective*, ed. J. K. S. St. Joseph. New York, 1966. Pp. 126–37.

Kolodny, Rochelle. "Towards an Anthropology of Photography: Frameworks of Analysis." M.A. thesis, McGill University, 1978.

Laumann, Edward O., and House, James S. "Living Room Styles and Social Attributes: The Patterning of Material Artifacts in a Modern Urban Community." *Sociology and Social Research*, 54 (Apr., 1970): 321–342.

Lesy, Michael. *Real Life: Louisville in the Twenties.* New York, 1976.
———. *Wisconsin Death Trip.* New York, 1973.
Lynch, Kevin. *The Image of the City.* Cambridge, Mass., 1968.
McCord, Norman. "Photographs as Historical Evidence." *The Local Historian*, 13 (Feb., 1978): 23–25.
McLuhan, Marshall. *Understanding Media.* New York, 1964.
Mayer, Harold M., and Wade, Richard C. *Chicago: Growth of a Metropolis.* Chicago, 1969.
Mead, Margaret. "Anthropology and the Camera." In *Encyclopedia of Photography*, ed. Willard Morgan. I, 166–84.
———. "Some Uses of Still Photography in Culture and Personality Studies." In *Personal Character and Cultural Milieu*, ed. Douglas G. Haring. Syracuse, 1956. Pp. 79–105.
———, and Byers, Paul. *The Small Conference: An Innovation in Communication.* The Hague, 1968.
"Margaret Mead and Gregory Bateson on the Use of the Camera in Anthropology." *Studies in the Anthropology of Visual Communication*, 4 (Winter, 1977): 78–80.
Michaelis, Anthony R. *Research Films in Biology, Anthropology, Psychology and Medicine.* New York, 1955.
Newhall, Beaumont. *The History of Photography from 1839 to the Present Day.* New York, 1964.
———. "Historiography of Photography." In *Progress in Photography, 1955–1958*, ed. P. A. Spencer. London, 1959. III, 119–22.
Norman, E. R., and St. Joseph, J. K. S. *The Early Development of Irish Society: The Evidence of Aerial Photography.* Cambridge, 1969.
Peters, Marsha, and Mergen, Bernard. "'Doing the Rest': The Uses of Photographs in American Studies." *American Quarterly*, 29, no. 3 (1977): 280–303.
Row, John Howland. "Technical Aids in Anthropology: A Historical Survey." In *Anthropology Today*, ed. A. L. Kroeber. Chicago, 1953. Pp. 895–940.
Ruesch, Jurgen, and Kees, Weldon. *Nonverbal Communication.* Berkeley, 1956.
Rudisill, Richard. *Mirror Image: The Influence of the Daguerreotype on American Society.* Albuquerque, 1971.
Saarinen, Thomas F. *Environmental Planning: Perception and Behavior.* Boston, 1976.
———. "Perception of Environment." Association of American Geographers' Resource Paper no. 5. Washington, 1969.
Scherer, Joanna Cohen. "Pictures as Documents: Resources for the

Study of North American Ethnohistory." *Studies in the Anthropology of Visual Communication*, 2 (Fall, 1975): 65–66.

———. "You Can't Believe Your Eyes: Inaccuracies in Photographs of North American Indians." *Studies in the Anthropology of Visual Communication*, 2 (Fall, 1975): 67–79.

Schiller, Dan. "Realism, Photography, and Journalistic Objectivity in 19th Century America." *Studies in the Anthropology of Visual Communication*, 4 (Winter, 1977): 86–98.

Sommer, Robert. *Design Awareness*. San Francisco, 1972.

———. *Personal Space*. Englewood Cliffs, N.J., 1969.

———. *Tight Space*. Englewood Cliffs, N.J., 1974.

Sorenson, E. Richard. "Anthropological Film: A Scientific and Humanistic Resource." *Science*, 20 (Dec., 1974): 1079–85.

———, and Gajdusek, D. C. "Investigation of Nonrecurring Phenomena." *Nature*, 200 (Oct. 12, 1963): 112–17.

———. "A Research Film Program in the Study of Changing Man." *Current Anthropology*, 8 (Dec., 1967): 443–69.

———. "Researching Filming and the Study of Culturally Specific Patterns of Behavior." *Program in Ethnographic Film Newsletter*, 4 (Spring, 1973): 3–4.

———. "Toward a National Anthropological Research Film Center—A Progress Report." *Program in Ethnographic Film Newsletter*, 3 (Fall, 1971): 1–2.

Stott, William. *Documentary Expression in Thirties America*. New York, 1973.

Stryker, Roy, and Johnstone, Paul. "Documentary Photographs." In *The Cultural Approach to History*, ed. Caroline F. Ware. New York, 1940. Pp. 316–30.

Taft, Robert. *Photography and the American Scene: A Social History, 1839–1889*. New York, 1942.

Troper, Harold. "Images of the 'Foreigner' in Toronto, 1900–1930: A Report." *Urban History Review*, no. 2 (1975): 1–7.

Vanderbilt, Paul. *Guide to the Special Collection of Prints and Photographs in the Library of Congress*. Washington, 1955.

Watson, O. Michael. *Symbolic and Expressive Uses of Space: An Introduction to Proxemic Behavior*. Reading, Mass., 1972.

Webb, Eugene; Campbell, Donald; Schwartz, Richard; and Sechrest, Lee. *Unobtrusive Measures: Non-Reactive Research in the Social Sciences*. Chicago, 1966.

Weinstein, Robert A., and Booth, Larry. *Collection, Use, and Care of Historical Photographs*. Nashville, 1977.

Werner, Oswald. "Ethnographic Photography: A Survey of Photographic Techniques in Anthropological Field Work Including Motion Pictures." M.A. thesis, Syracuse University, 1961.

Worth, Sol. "Film as a Non-Art: An Approach to the Study of Film." *American Scholar*, 35 (Spring, 1966): 322–34.

———, and Adair, John. *Through Navajo Eyes: An Exploration of Film Communication and Anthropology*. Bloomington, Ind., 1972.

| Appendix C |

The 1880 Manuscript Census:
Reliability, Occupational and
Residential Mobility, and
Additional Data

*The historian who writes history, therefore, consciously
or unconsciously performs an act of faith . . .—Charles
Beard, "Written History as an Act of Faith."*

The manuscript census provides a wealth of infor-
mation that can shed considerable light on the social life of anonymous Americans. Inclusion of addresses and family relationships in
the 1880 census enables historians and others to literally re-create
the residential patterns of urban areas, to discern family forms, and,
when used with other sources, to trace movement over time. Undoubtedly more sophisticated analyses of the census will, in the future, provide even more valuable and revealing information. Like
any historical source, however, the manuscript census is not without its problems. It always misses a substantial number of people,
most often those in the working classes and in racial and ethnic mi-
norities.[1] In addition, enumerators were only human, and they
sometimes made mistakes. Since it is almost impossible (and certainly impractical in any large-scale study) to either catch or correct
those mistakes, historians, like sociologists who work with more recent aggregate census data, must always keep in mind the limita-.
tions and biases of these sources.

One case revealed the kinds of mistakes that might be made by an
enumerator, giving me considerable cause for concern about the ve-
racity of the manuscript census as a source.[2] One enumerator re-

1. John B. Sharpless and Ray M. Shortridge, "Biased Under-enumeration in
Census Manuscripts: Methodological Implications," *Journal of Urban History*, 1
(Aug., 1975): 409–39.
2. As suggested earlier, my own experience as an enumerator for the 1970 census did nothing to reassure me as to its validity and accuracy.

corded the following information about a household in 6th Street Alley, Southeast, on June 8, 1880:

House Number 1: Matthews, Eliza Negro Female Age:
40 Head of Household Marital Status:
Single Occupation: Washer . . .
————, Joseph Negro Male Age:
3 Relation to Head of Household: Son
. . .
————, Harriet Negro Female Age:
62 Relation to Head of Household:
Mother Marital Status:
Widow Occupation: Keeps House . . .

However, on the following day the same enumerator returned and made, on another page, the following entry for the same address:

House Number 1: Mathews, Eliza Negro Female Age:
30 Head of Household Marital Status:
Widow Occupation: Washer . . .
————, Harriet Negro Female Age:
62 Relationship to Head of Household:
Mother Marital Status:
Widow Occupation: Keeps House . . .
————, Joseph Negro Male Age:
4 Relationship to Head of Household:
Grandson . . .
————, Samuel Negro Male Age:
14 Relationship to Head of Household:
Grandson Occupation: At Home . . .
Grass, Savinia Negro Female Age:
24 Relationship to Head of Household:
Blank Marital Status:
Single Occupation: Servant . . .
White, Rebecca Negro Female Age:
20 Relationship to Head of Household:
Blank Marital Status:
Single Occupation: Servant . . .[3]

Apparently, the enumerator forgot that he had already visited the Matthews' house, or else he went back to finish the enumeration. (He also returned to another house in the same alley and recorded a fam-

3. Federal Population Census Schedules, 1880, Washington, D.C., vol. 4, pt. 4, pp. 103B, 107C.

ily completely different from the one detailed on his earlier visit.) Whatever the case, he left both Matthews entries to be counted.

Many of these obvious discrepancies can be resolved and corrected, in light of the two versions and the application of "normal" behavior patterns. Nevertheless, one cannot always determine which version, if either, is correct. It is difficult to know how often enumerators made serious errors, or how different the results might have been if the census had been taken on two different days. If we use this "sample" as a test for accuracy, the results are quite sobering: either the second enumeration reveals a 50 percent undercount on the first day, or it is itself a 100 percent overcount.[4]

The fact that some of the information remains the same offers a small reassurance, in light of our inability to control or assess the possible amount of error. Moreover, there remain the obvious problems of conventional responses to enumerators' questions, and the individual and collective biases of the enumerators. Some enumerators diligently recorded answers in all categories; others seem to have systematically avoided recording responses to some of the questions, most often those relating to unemployment, sickness, disability, and literacy. Census records, like photographic sources, should be used very carefully, and always with supporting evidence.

In addition to these general problems of bias or inaccuracy, another set of difficulties concerns the categories used in recording census data. In many cases, especially for workers in the lower-middle occupational categories, the occupational notations are so vague that they are difficult to group. For example, a "barber" may be a proprietor, a well-paid skilled craftsman, or an itinerant journeyman; he might own a substantial shop and employ other barbers, or he may have set up shop in the front room of his rented house.[5] It is therefore extremely difficult to determine social status from the manuscript census of 1880 without more substantial information.[6] Even with this further data, a fair estimate of social status must ultimately consider other aspects of a worker's life.

4. While most studies consistently underenumerate, they tend to ignore possible cases of overenumeration that can equally bias the results. Of course, overenumeration is likely to occur anywhere and can be assumed to be a random error. The cases of live-in servants who were counted both at the place of employment and the home address involve a less random error.

5. I am indebted to David Katzman for pointing out the difficulties in determining rank from census listings.

6. Eric Lampard, "Historical Contours of Contemporary Urban Society: A Comparative View," *Journal of Contemporary History*, 4, no. 3 (1969): 23–25.

For this study, an extensive occupational analysis was not necessary to provide a general sense of social status, since the mere fact of alley residence tended to put one in a specific category. The fact that most alley residents were black provides further evidence of social standing vis-à-vis the city's white population. Finally, since nearly all alley residents were generally considered to be at the bottom of the economic and occupational structure, further analysis was not necessary. All of these factors help substantiate the notion that the alley population was homogeneous. While this was the case in general terms, and while alley dwellers saw themselves as different from those outside, neither of these facts provides much insight into the variations in alley life that most observers reported. One can attempt to get at this "variation" by developing occupational categories based on considerations of the people themselves, rather than using a generalized set of categories that reflect mainstream values. Table 22 thus reveals considerably more diversity in status and occupation than most scholars would allow. A second approach, which helps account for the organizational scheme used to construct Table 22, involves a general analysis of the nature of different occupations to suggest possible variations in lifestyle.

If nearly all alley dwellers were badly paid and lacked job security, there were, nevertheless, vartiations in both of these areas, as well as in the types of work performed. Certainly the life of the day laborer who regularly had to look for work, who experienced persistent short-term unemployment, and who worked in gangs often made up of neighbors (and spent nonworking days with those same neighbors) contrasted sharply to the experience of those who had long-term employment that involved regular hours, work at the same location (often with people who were not neighbors), and longer periods of unemployment between jobs. Finally, the self-employed junk man, washerwoman, or small entrepreneur had work patterns which were probably the most varied of all. These work experiences could vary with the individual's point in life cycle as well. In addition, the fact that the black community had status categories based on experience different from that of whites suggests that use of a different classification scheme is more likely to reveal diversity in alley life. This difference in work experience may also help account for the difference in lifestyles.

The classification scheme is much more sensitive to occupational changes than one based on the mainstream experience. Nevertheless, occupational mobility was a minimal part of the alley experience, to judge from an examination of the occupations of alley residents who persisted in the city from 1880 to 1895. Willis Peacket, a

plumber in 1880, was one of the few who had any occupational mobility—his was downward. In later years he was listed as a laborer,
although eventually he regained his standing as a plumber, according to city directories. Census and city directory occupational categories are so vague that the study of occupational mobility over time
becomes even more difficult than merely trying to determine social
status from a single census's occupational listings.

Nearly as problematic is the effort to determine residential persistence and mobility from census records and city directories. Directories often fail to provide sufficient information to allow the
researcher to "link" one set of records with another, and thus determine whether both sets are for the same individual. Variations in
spelling (e.g., Meckins, Alex, House Painter vs. Meekins, Alex, Laborer; Peacket, Willis, Plumber vs. Pickett, Willis, Laborer; and
Toland, Louden, Boatman vs. Tolliver, Louden, Cook), coupled
with inadequate information, or the prevalence of common names
and occupations (John Brown, Laborer) or different addresses make
linkage difficult, at best.

It seems more useful here to stress that those linked examples
constitute the *minimum* number of persisting residents, and to base
our analysis on known information, rather than on that for which
there is as yet no evidence. And even here it is imperative to put
these findings in a larger context. As Paul Worthman concluded, "A
full understanding of these workers' actions requires examination
of their cultural, social, economic, and political lives. Quantitative
findings about geographic, social and economic mobility cannot be
isolated from the larger social context."[7]

The following tables provide supplemental information. Table 31
reports the results of the residential persistence and mobility study
for sample area alley dwellers; it includes both the census sample
and a sample of residents in the same alleys drawn from the city
directory. Persistence here, however, is based on continued residence in the city, not in the alley of origin. The remaining tables are
based on the 1880 census.

7. Worthman, "Working Class Mobility," p. 209.

Supplemental Tables:
1880 Census

TABLE 31.
Residential Persistence Rates for Sample Area Alley Dwellers, 1880–95[*]

	1880[a]	1885		1890		1895	
	N	N	%	N	%	N	%
Black	211	128	61	86	41	49	23
White	22	11	50	8	36	7	32
Random[b] from directory	123	43	35	24	20	18	15
TOTAL	356	182	51	118	33	74	21

[a]From the census, names of all heads of household and all employed alley dwellers in sample area were sought in the 1880, 1881, and 1885 city directories. Of the 546 black and 33 white residents, 211 black and 22 white names were traced in at least one of these directories (39% and 67%, respectively). The persistence rates are computed on that basis.

[b]During the initial search in the 1880 directory, a number of names were found with addresses in the sample alleys but without any reference in the manuscript census. I decided to check the persistence of these residents, but I picked up the names (123) only as I "happened upon" them while searching for the census names. Because the city directories had dropped race by 1880, only occupation and address are available for these names.

[*]Based on Federal Population Census Schedules, 1880, Washington, D.C., vol. 2, pt. 2, RG 29 NA; and William Boyd, *Directory for the City of Washington* (Washington, 1879, 1880, 1881, 1884, 1885, 1886, 1889, 1890, 1891, 1894, 1895).

TABLE 32.
Alley Size, 1880

Population	No. alleys	Total population	%
1–49	141	2,883	27
50–99	35	2,448	23
100–149	18	2,013	19
150–199	7	1,136	11
200–249	6	1,324	12
250–299	3	810	8
TOTAL	210	10,614	100

Average alley population: 50. Half of alley residents lived in alleys with fewer than 100 residents.

TABLE 33
Alley Families, 1880

Form	Black		White		Total	
	No.	*%*	*No.*	*%*	*No.*	*%*
Unattached						
Live alone	216	8.3	16	.6	232	8.9
Unrelated	57	2.2	8	.3	65	2.5
TOTAL					297	11.4*
One-generation families						
Husband-wife	272	11.8	36	1.6	308	13.4
Husband-wife-relatives	23	1.0	5	.2	28	1.2
Husband-wife-boarders	53	2.3	1	.0	54	2.3
Other-related	8	.3	0	—	8	.3
TOTAL					398	17.2**
Two-generation families						
2 Parent	733	31.8	150	6.5	883	38.3
2 Parent-extended	16	.7	1	.0	17	.7
2 Parent-augmented	108	4.7	10	.4	118	5.0
2 Parent-extended-augmented	8	.3	0	—	8*	.3
2 Parent-multi-nuclei	37	1.6	4	.2	41	1.8
Other 2 Parent	43	1.9	3	.1	46	2.0
Subtotal 2 Parents					1,113	48.2
1 Parent	311	13.5	43	1.9	354	15.3
1 Parent-extended	9	.4	0	—	9	.4
1 Parent-augmented	70	3.0	6	.3	76	3.3
1 Parent-extended-augmented	5	.2	0	—	5	.2
1 Parent-multi-nuclei	23	1.0	5	.2	28	1.2
Subtotal 1 Parent					472	20.5
TOTAL					1,585	68.7**

Table 33—*continued*

Form	Black No.	Black %	White No.	White %	Total No.	Total %
Two generations representing three generations						
2 Parent	17	.7	1	.0	18	.8
1 Parent	8	.3	1	.0	9	.4
TOTAL					27	1.2**
Three-generation families						
2 Parent	141	6.1	18	.8	159	6.9
2 Parent-augmented	22	1.0	0	—	22	1.0
2 Parent-multi-nuclei	3	.1	0	—	3	.1
Subtotal 2 Parent					184	8.0
1 Parent	74	3.2	6	.3	80	3.5
1 Parent-augmented	16	.7	0	—	16	.7
1 Parent-multi-nuclei	3	.1	0	—	3	.1
Subtotal 1 Parent					99	4.3
TOTAL					283	12.3**
Four-generation families	14	.6	0	—	14	.6
TOTAL					14	.6**
TOTAL ALL HOUSEHOLD UNITS	2,290		314		2,604	
TOTAL FAMILY UNITS	2,017		290		2,307	

* Percent of all household units
** Percent of all family units

| Appendix D |

Bibliography of Alley
Dwellings in Other Cities

Great Britain

GENERAL
*Gauldie, Enid. *Cruel Habitations: A History of Working-Class Housing, 1780–1918*. London, 1974.
Pike, E. Royston, ed. *Human Documents of the Industrial Revolution in Britain*. London, 1966.

BIRMINGHAM
Engels, Friedrich. *The Condition of the Working-Class in England*. Moscow, 1973. P. 76.
*Sutcliffe, Anthony. "A Century of Flats in Birmingham: 1875–1973." In *Multi-Storey Living: The British Working Class Experience*, ed. Anthony Sutcliffe. London, 1974. Pp. 181–206.

DUBLIN
Engels, Friedrich. *The Condition of the Working-Class in England*. P. 73.

EDINBURGH
Engels, Friedrich. *The Condition of the Working-Class in England*. Pp. 74–75.

GLASGOW
*Annan, Thomas. *Old Closes and Streets of Glasgow 1868/1877*. New York, 1977.
Engels, Friedrich. *The Condition of the Working-Class in England*. Pp. 77–78.

LEEDS
*Beresford, Maurice W. "The Back-to-Back House in Leeds, 1787–1937." In *The History of Working Class Housing*, ed. S. D. Chapman. London, 1971. Pp. 93–132.
*———. "The Making of a Townscape: Richard Paley in the East

*Includes photographs or other visual materials on alleys.

End of Leeds, 1771–1803." In *Rural Change and Urban Growth, 1500–1800*, ed. C. W. Chalklin and M. A. Havinden. London, 1974. Pp. 281–320.

*Creese, Walter L. *The Search for Environment: The Garden City: Before and After*. New Haven, 1966. Pp. 61–86.

Engels, Friedrich. *The Condition of the Working-Class in England*. Pp. 78–80.

Rimmer, W. G. "Working Men's Cottages in Leeds, 1770–1840." *Thoresby Society Publications*, 44 (1961): 165–99.

LIVERPOOL

Engels, Friedrich. *The Condition of the Working-Class in England*. Pp. 75–76.

*Taylor, Iain C. "The Court and Cellar Dwelling: The Eighteenth Century Origin of the Liverpool Slum." *Transactions of the Historical Society of Lancashire and Cheshire*, 122 (1969): 67–90.

*———. "The Insanitary Housing Question and Tenement Dwellings in Nineteenth-Century Liverpool." In *Multi-Storey Living*, ed. Sutcliffe. Pp. 41–87.

LONDON

*Betjeman, John. *Victorian and Edwardian London from Old Photographs*. New York, 1969.

Engels, Friedrich. *The Condition of the Working-Class in England*. Pp. 67–72.

George, M. Dorothy. *London Life in the Eighteenth Century*. New York, 1964. Pp. 63–107.

*Olsen, Donald. *Town Planning in London: The Eighteenth and Nineteenth Centuries*. New Haven, 1964.

*Winter, Gordon. *Past Positive: London's Social History Recorded in Photographs*. London, 1971.

MANCHESTER

Engels, Friedrich. *The Condition of the Working-Class in England*. Pp. 81–107.

Germany

COLOGNE

Weyden, Ernst. *Köln am Rhein vor fünfzig Jahren*. Köln, 1862. P. 17.

BERLIN

Ihlder, John. "Slums in Berlin." *Survey*, 25 (Dec. 17, 1910): 474–75.

Egypt

CAIRO
Abu-Lughod, Janet. "Migrant Adjustment to City Life: The
    Egyptian Case." *American Journal of Sociology*, 67 (July, 1961):
    22–32.

United States

ATLANTA
Sanders, Charles Levi. "A Study of the Relocation of Rear and
    Alley Tenants in Atlanta." M.S.W. thesis, Atlanta Univer-
    sity, 1956.
Rabinowitz, Howard N. *Race Relations in the Urban South: 1865–
    1890*. New York, 1978. P. 106.
ATLANTIC CITY
Brett, Margaret L. "Atlantic City: A Study in Black and White."
    Survey, 28 (Sept. 7, 1912): 723–26.
BALTIMORE
*Kemp, Janet E. *Housing Conditions in Baltimore*. Baltimore, 1907.
BIRMINGHAM
McCrae, Lee. "Birmingham's Probation Plan for the Little
    Negro." *Charities and Commons*, 19 (Mar. 14, 1908): 1729.
*McGrath, W. M. "Conservation of Health." *Survey*, 27 (Jan. 6,
    1912): 1508–11.
Stock, J. Stevens. "Some General Principles of Sampling." In
    Hadley Cantril et al., *Gauging Public Opinion*. Princeton, 1944.
    P. 136.
BOSTON
Handlin, Oscar. *Boston's Immigrants: 1790–1865*. New York, 1971.
    Pp. 107–8, 116.
*Warner, Sam Bass, Jr. *Streetcar Suburbs*. New York, 1969. P. 19.
CHICAGO
Abbott, Edith. *The Tenements of Chicago, 1908–1935*. New York,
    1970.
*Mayer, Harold M., and Wade, Richard C. *Chicago: Growth of a
    Metropolis*. Chicago, 1969. Pp. 255, 258–60.
Philpott, Thomas Lee. *The Slum and the Ghetto*. New York, 1978.
    Pp. 24–41.
Wald, Sadie T. "Chicago Housing Conditions." *Charities*, 15 (Jan.
    6, 1906): 455–61.

COLUMBUS
"Poindexter Village Opens Doors." *Public Housing Weekly News*, 1
(May 21, 1940): 1.
*Davis, Otto. "The Discoveries of Columbus." *Survey*, 26 (July 1,
1911): 508–13.
Gerber, David A. *Black Ohio and the Color Line: 1860–1915*. Ur-
bana, Ill., 1976. P. 105.
DAYTON
Woofter, T. J., Jr. *Negro Problems in Cities*. New York, 1928. Pp.
105–6.
DETROIT
*Franklin, Rabbi Leo M. "The Housing Problems in Detroit."
Charities and Commons, 19 (Jan. 4, 1908): 1338–44.
Katzman, David M. *Before the Ghetto: Black Detroit in the Nineteenth
Century*. Urbana, Ill., 1973. Pp. 26–29, 74–75.
EVANSVILLE
*Bacon, Albion Fellows. "Beauty for Ashes." *Survey*, 31 (Dec. 6,
1913): 245–49.
———. "The Housing Problem in Indiana." *Charities and Com-
mons*, 21 (Dec. 5, 1908): 376–83.
GRAND RAPIDS
———. "Good Housing Standards Set in Grand Rapids." *Survey*,
32 (Apr. 4, 1914): 4.
GREENWICH
*Ayres, May. "The Rich Town and the Poor Schools." *Survey*,
28 (Aug. 3, 1912): 603–9.
INDIANAPOLIS
Bacon, Albion Fellows. "The Housing Problem in Indiana."
Charities and Commons, 21 (Dec. 5, 1908): 376–83.
KANSAS CITY
Martin, Asa E. *Our Negro Population: A Sociological Study of the
Negroes of Kansas City, Missouri*. Kansas City, 1913. P. 90.
LOS ANGELES
———. "Housing Commission of Los Angeles Reports." *Charities
and Commons*, 21 (Mar. 13, 1909): 1200.
*Matthews, William H. "The House Courts of Los Angeles." *Sur-
vey*, 30 (July 5, 1913): 461–67.
LOUISVILLE
*Clay, Grady. *Alleys: A Hidden Resource*. Louisville, 1978.
*Gray, Mary Belknap. "Housing in Louisville." *Survey*, 23 (Dec.
18, 1909): 391–94.
*Kemp, Janet E. *Report of the Tenement House Commission of Louisville*.
Louisville, 1909.

MILWAUKEE
Thompson, Carl D. "Socialists and Slums—Milwaukee." *Survey*,
    25 (Dec. 3, 1910): 367–76.
NASHVILLE
Rabinowitz, Howard. *Race Relations in the Urban South*. Pp. 114–15.
NEW ORLEANS
Lewis, Peirce F. *New Orleans: The Making of an Urban Landscape*.
    Cambridge, Mass., 1976. Pp. 44–45.
Walker, Mabel L. et al. *Urban Blight and Slums*. Cambridge, Mass.,
    1938. P. 96.
NEW YORK
*Riis, Jacob A. *How the Other Half Lives*. New York, 1971.
*Rogers, William A. "Tenement Life in New York: Sketches in
    'Bottle Alley.'" *Harper's Weekly*, 23 (Mar. 22, 1879): 224, 226–
    27.
*———. "Tenement Life in New York: Rag-Pickers' Court,
    Mulberry Street." *Harper's Weekly*, 23 (Apr. 5, 1879): 265–67.
PHILADELPHIA
Alexander, John K. "Poverty, Fear, and Continuity: An Analysis
    of the Poor at the Turn of the Century." In *The Peoples of Phila-
    delphia*, ed. Allen F. Davis and Mark H. Haller. Philadel-
    phia, 1973. Pp. 13–35.
*Dinwiddie, Emily W. *Housing Conditions in Philadelphia*. Phila-
    delphia, 1904.
Du Bois, W. E. B. *The Philadelphia Negro*. New York, 1967.
*Goldenweiser, E. A. "Immigrants in Cities." *Survey*, 25 (Jan. 7,
    1911): 596–602.
*Newman, Bernard J. "Block Reconstruction: How A Congested
    City Block Can Be Made Fit for Human Habitation." *The
    American City*, 5 (Sept., 1911): 131–35.
Sutherland, John F. "Housing the Poor in the City of Homes:
    Philadelphia at the Turn of the Century." In *Peoples of Phila-
    delphia*, ed. Davis and Haller. Pp. 175–201.
Turner, Edward R. *The Negro In Pennsylvania: 1639–1861*. New
    York, 1969. Pp. 155, 163, 202–3.
Warner, Sam Bass, Jr. *The Private City*. Philadelphia, 1968. Pp. 16,
    50–57.
PITTSBURGH
Adams, Samuel Hopkins. "Pittsburgh's Foregone Asset, the Pub-
    lic Health." *Charities and Commons*, 19 (Jan. 2, 1909): 945.
*Byington, Margaret F. "The Mill Town Courts and Their
    Lodgers." *Charities and Commons*, 19 (Jan. 2, 1909): 913–22.
*———. *Homestead: The Households of a Mill Town*. Pittsburgh, 1974.

*Crowell, F. Elizabeth. "What Bad Housing Means to Pitts-
    burgh." *Charities and Commons*, 19 (Mar. 7, 1908): 1682–98.
*————. "The Housing Situation in Pittsburgh." *Charities and
    Commons*, 21 (Feb. 6, 1909): 871–81.
Roberts, Peter. "The New Pittsburghers: Slavs and Kindred Im-
    migrants in Pittsburgh." *Charities and Commons*, 19 (Jan. 2,
    1909): 539–45.
Tucker, Helen A. "The Negroes of Pittsburgh." *Charities and Com-
    mons*, 19 (Jan. 2, 1909): 600–601.
PROVIDENCE
Ihlder, John. "The Housing of Providence." *Survey*, 37 (Nov. 11,
    1916): 143–44.
SAN ANTONIO
McLean, Francis H. "Passage to Texas." *Survey*, 25 (Nov. 19,
    1910): 285–94.
ST. LOUIS
*Baldwin, Roger N. "New Tenants and Old Shacks." *Survey*, 25
    (Feb. 18, 1911): 825–28.
SAN FRANCISCO
Working Men's Party of California. *The Chinese Must Go*. San Fran-
    cisco, 1876.
YOUNGSTOWN
Hanson, J. M. "The Youngstown Housing Experiment." *Survey*,
    28 (July 6, 1912): 497–500.

Canada

TORONTO
*Harney, Robert F., and Troper, Harold. *Immigrants: A Portrait
    of the Urban Experience, 1890–1930*. Toronto, 1975. Pp. 24–26,
    30–31, 40–41.

Index